Routledge Revivals

Understanding Interaction in Central Australia

First published in 1985, this book gives an intimate account of the cultural-political conflict between Australian Aboriginal people and Anglo-Australians, presenting the Australian social world from the perspective of the Aboriginal person.

Adopting a rigorous ethnomethodological analysis and the techniques of ethnolinguistics, Liberman looks at the interactional detail of the everyday life of traditionally oriented Australian Aboriginals. He uses tape transcripts of actual interaction to identify chief characteristics of Aboriginal social life. Liberman goes on to show how differences in systems of interaction have influenced relations between Australian Aboriginals and Anglo-Australians.

With its account of the politics of cultural conflict in a multi-cultural environment, this book is an apt extension of ethnomethodological issues to political concerns. It also exposes Aboriginal perceptions of Anglo-Australian/Aboriginal interaction to a degree not previously achieved in any sociological or anthropological study. As such, this book will be a valuable case study to students of social anthropology, race relations, intercultural communication and sociolinguistics.

Understanding Interaction in Central Australia

An Ethnomethodological Study of Australian Aboriginal People

Kenneth Liberman

Routledge
Taylor & Francis Group

First published in 1985
by Routledge & Kegan Paul plc

This edition first published in 2017 by Routledge
2 Park Square, Milton Park, Abingdon, Oxon, OX14 4RN
and by Routledge
711 Third Avenue, New York, NY 10017

Routledge is an imprint of the Taylor & Francis Group, an informa business

© 1985 Kenneth Liberman

Publisher's Note
The publisher has gone to great lengths to ensure the quality of this reprint but
points out that some imperfections in the original copies may be apparent.

Disclaimer
The publisher has made every effort to trace copyright holders and welcomes
correspondence from those they have been unable to contact.

A Library of Congress record exists under LC control number: 85001905

ISBN 13: 978-1-138-71658-2 (hbk)
ISBN 13: 978-1-315-18091-5 (ebk)
ISBN 13: 978-1-138-71665-0 (pbk)

Directions in Ethnomethodology and Conversation Analysis

Series Editors: Andrew Carlin, Manchester Metropolitan University, UK and K. Neil Jenkings, Newcastle University, UK.

Ethnomethodology and Conversation Analysis are cognate approaches to the study of social action that together comprise a major perspective within the contemporary human sciences. Ethnomethodology focuses upon the production of situated and ordered social action of all kinds, whilst Conversation Analysis has a more specific focus on the production and organisation of talk-in-interaction. Of course, given that so much social action is conducted in and through talk, there are substantive as well theoretical continuities between the two approaches. Focusing on social activities as situated human productions, these approaches seek to analyse the intelligibility and accountability of social activities 'from within' those activities themselves, using methods that can be analysed and described. Such methods amount to aptitudes, skills, knowledge and competencies that members of society use, rely upon and take for granted in conducting their affairs across the whole range of social life.

As a result of the methodological rewards consequent upon their unique analytic approach and attention to the detailed orderliness of social life, Ethnomethodology and Conversation Analysis have ramified across a wide range of human science disciplines throughout the world, including anthropology, social psychology, linguistics, communication studies and social studies of science and technology.

This series is dedicated to publishing the latest work in these two fields, including research monographs, edited collections and theoretical treatises. As such, its volumes are essential reading for those concerned with the study of human conduct and aptitudes, the (re)production of social orderliness and the methods and aspirations of the social sciences.

Socialization: Parent–Child Interaction in Everyday Life
Sara Keel

Conversation Analysis and Early Childhood Education
The Co-Production of Knowledge and Relationships
Amanda Bateman

Ethnomethodology at Play
Edited by Peter Tolmie and Mark Rouncefield

Respecifying Lab Ethnography
An Ethnomethodological Study of Experimental Physics
Philippe Sormani

Adjudication in Action
An Ethnomethodology of Law, Morality and Justice
Baudouin Dupret

Ethnomethodology at Work
Edited by Mark Rouncefield and Peter Tolmie

Analysing Practical and Professional Texts
A Naturalistic Approach
Rod Watson

Preference Organisation and Peer Disputes
How Young Children Resolve Conflict
Amelia Church

Talk and Social Interaction in the Playground
Carly W. Butler

Ethnographies of Reason
Eric Livingston

There is No Such Thing as a Social Science
In Defence of Peter Winch
Phil Hutchinson, Rupert Read and Wes Sharrock

Orders of Ordinary Action
Respecifying Sociological Knowledge
Edited by Stephen Hester and David Francis

The Academic Presentation
Situated Talk in Action
Johanna Rendle-Short

Institutional Interaction
Studies of Talk at Work
Ilkka Arminen

Ethnomethodological Studies of Work
Edited by Harold Garfinkel

Understanding Interaction in Central Australia
An Ethnomethodological Study of Australian Aboriginal People
Kenneth Liberman

Understanding interaction in central Australia

An ethnomethodological study of Australian Aboriginal people

Kenneth Liberman

First published in 1985
by Routledge & Kegan Paul plc

9 Park Street, Boston, Mass. O2108, USA

14 Leicester Square, London, WC2H 7PH, England

464 St Kilda Road, Melbourne,
Victoria 3004, Australia and

Broadway House, Newtown Road,
Henley on Thames, Oxon RG9 1EN, England

Set in Times, 10 on 11pt.
by Columns of Reading
and printed in Great Britain
by Thetford Press

Library of Congress Cataloging in Publication Data

Liberman, Kenneth, 1948-

  Understanding interaction in central Australia.
  (Studies in ethnomethodology)
  Bibliography: p.
  Includes index.
  1. Australian aborigines—Australia—Western
Australia—Social life and customs.   2. Social
interaction—Australia—Western Australia.
3. Ethnomethodology.   I. Title.   II. Series.
GN667.W5L53   1985   305.8'9915'0941   85-1905

British Library CIP data also available

ISBN 0-7102-0473-6

Contents

Acknowledgments

I would like to acknowledge the following people and institutions for their assistance. Financial support was provided by Murdoch University and the University of California, San Diego. The latter assistance was made possible by a fellowship generously endowed by Kenneth and Dorothy Hill of Rancho Santa Fé, California, and allowed me to carry out historical research in the Hill Collection on Pacific Discovery of the University of California, San Diego's Central Library.

Human support, without which this study could not have been completed, was given by Professor Ronald M. Berndt of the University of Western Australia, Professor John R. Raser of Murdoch University, the Western Australian Museum, the Office of Graduate Studies and Research (UCSD), and especially the wise old men and women of Docker River, Giles, Warburton, Laverton, Leonora, Wiluna and so many parts in between.

To my wife, Ms Anne Zonne Parker, goes the credit for first recognizing the unique sociability of the Western Desert Aboriginal folk, for some of the best insights of Part III and for her usual acute descriptions of whatever natural physical environment we find our way to. ·

Part I
The collaborative production
of congeniality and consensus in an
Aboriginal society

1 Congenial fellowship and consensus in central Australia

Across the flat central desert of Australia, the *Pitjantjatjara-,* *Ngaanyatjarra-* and *Pintupi-* speaking Aboriginal people are early risers. The coldness of the last hour of darkness, or something more ineffable, awakens them from their outdoor sleep and brings them to stir the fires which have kept them warm through the night and which have waned with inattention during the late hours. Possibly one and a half to two hours before the visible sunrise, Aboriginals begin sitting up cross-legged from their sleep to warm themselves by their fires or walk off into the bush for more wood and to urinate. All the stirring and movement makes enough noise to awaken late sleepers by the neigboring fires, and through the darkness a dozen or more fires gradually begin to grow in strength.

At some point, still an hour or more before sunrise, an Aboriginal person begins to call out to the camps with what is on his mind. The topic of his short discourse may be a problem which has been troubling the community lately, notions about where the best kangaroos or bush turkeys may be found that morning, news from another Aboriginal community which has come with someone who arrived during the night, a major grievance, proposals for shifting the camp to a better location, circumlocutions expressing joy, sorrow or anger, or whatever else occurs to her or, more frequently, him as newsworthy. When he has completed his brief oration, spoken to no one in particular but to the camp as a whole, and possibly after a brief intervening silence, a second Aboriginal will respond to the communication which has been made or offer a separate message for the people of the camps, who listen with varying attentiveness as they warm themselves by their fires.

It is the Aboriginal equivalent of the morning paper. In the intimate space of the pre-dawn darkness, the camps share the news as well as their states of mind about events important to the community. Occasionally two or three people will call out at the same time, but generally these 'announcements' are made by non-sequential 'turns' and the speaking will move about the camps until quite a few of the fires have had their full say. However, it is not always a personal say which is offered; more frequently it is a sort of public statement rendered as the comments of a community person. Topics become developed and clarified over a number of such 'public announcements,' as each contributor builds upon the formulations which have come before, often repeating what has already been said. The themes are formulated and received as publicly available discourse, which continues as the eastern horizon grows brighter with the dawn.

One observer (Wallace 1976: 50) has described the scene in this way:

> In the early morning and evening, the air is still, everyone is in the [camps] by these times and words spoken loudly can be heard over the whole camp area. Someone with something to say (and it must be stressed that the matter will be one of importance, not just gossip or trivia) will say it, and it will be heard by all. Another person will add comment, then another, and another.

By the time the sun is actually visible on the desert's flat horizon, the Morning Discourse has ceased. It is as if with the arrival of the day the public space of the pre-dawn darkness has imploded, and the camps exercise more privacy as the Aboriginal people go about their chores, finishing their breakfasts and quitting their fires. No one calls out anymore, but there are many lingering thoughts about what has been discussed. While for an hour the community has shared a vigorous collective life, with the sunrise the individual participants begin to go their separate ways as they take up the day's activities.

In brief, what has transpired is a capsulized and perhaps more formal version of the ordinary discourse which is common in many areas of everyday Aboriginal social life. In the Morning Discourse as well as in much group discourse during the day, the speakers' comments are addressed to all persons present. They have a public nature which minimizes personal interests – one speaks to the public matter as it stands before the community of speakers. Conversation proceeds not by paired addressors–addressees but in a serial fashion, with each next contributor building upon the public formulations of previous contributors and thus assisting the participants to arrive at a final account which becomes the consensus of the associating parties. Such consensus is a consensus without personal authorship, the unanimous possession of the group as a whole. Frequently, it is also the emblem of the group's fellowship, marking the congenial feelings which are productive of it and which make consensus such a vital part of the social life of Aboriginal people.

Congenial fellowship

One of the traits most identifying of everyday interaction among Aboriginal people is the congeniality which characterizes many of their ordinary conversations and social relations. Despite the recurring conflicts of camp life, there is nothing quite so distinctive about their ordinary lives as the way they are able to enjoy each other's presence without a deluge of dissonant pressures arising from egoistic competition. The practice of 'enjoying each other's presence,' though difficult to describe formally, is one of the essential activities of Aboriginals, as they are found sitting on their red earth in the shade of the trees considering the day.

An anthropologist who has studied the central desert people (Meyers 1976: 97) has commented that 'informality and affection are what characterize Aboriginal communities.' Their affective and congenial disposition, along with the openness and spontaneity which is a property of their relative lack of self-assertiveness, have not failed to impress most of the social scientists who have lived with them. However, because it has been difficult to uncover the specific organization of such a 'subjective' social activity, most sociological studies have ignored the important aspect of Aboriginal social relations which is congenial fellowship, in favor of investigations which lend themselves to more precise descriptions and analyses. As Durkheim and Mauss (1863: 88) have observed, 'emotion is naturally refractory to analysis, or at least lends itself uneasily to it, because it is too complex.'

Durkheim long ago recognized the importance of these 'social sentiments' which are responsible for much of the feelings of well-being and vitality of a community. Durkheim (1915: 242) speaks of a feeling of comfort based upon mutual affection which sustains the members of a community. He turns his attention to the ritual and religious life of central desert Aboriginal people in order to elucidate these social sentiments which are the origins of collective life and to examine the 'communion of minds and a

5

mutual comfort resulting from this communion' (460).

These sentiments are surely to be found in the ritual life of Aboriginal people, and there is no question that the vitality of Aboriginal social relations receives a recharge in the congenial ambience of their ceremonial life. As the Aboriginals sit in subsection groups around their ceremonial fires, singing the stories of the Dreaming which are the spiritual and 'historical' foundations of their lives, the celebrants continue to chant in unison until after many hours – closer towards morning – they seem to be fused into one collective life. R.M. and C. Berndt well describe such ritual activity (1945: 242):

> The singing . . . was . . . vividly expressed, much energy, both emotional and physical being expended; the singers became part of the song, completely merging their individual identities in the rhythm of the wording. The voices were blended, with no lagging behind and no discordant note, giving the impression of one voice only, constantly varying in rhythm and tone.

But religious activity is not the only location where fellowship has its life in Aboriginal communities. While Durkheim addressed an issue of great sociological importance in a setting where it is indeed operative, the social sentiments basic to Aboriginal collective life may be found also in their ordinary secular relations. Simmel has studied congeniality in everyday life, treating the ordinary 'associative process as a value and a satisfaction' (1971: 128). His concern to describe sociability as 'a pure form of mutuality' (177) is exemplary of the concern motivating my present inquiry into the organization of fellowship in Aboriginal society. While the affective basis of this fellowship may be partly invisible to sociological analysis, such congeniality must by necessity find its way into ordinary discourse, and it is there where the sociologist may be able to capture the phenomenon and make it observable.

Heidegger has suggested that the three vital components of being-with-others are mood (or state of mind, which satiates a person in his activities), understanding (as the disclosedness of the world), and discourse (as the articulation of the intelligibility of the world) (1962: 172, 182 and 203ff.). These three components are not separate from each other but are claimed to be equiprimordial in founding the everyday life of human beings. While it may be next to impossible to uncover the work of congenial fellowship as mood, except through oblique references based upon ethnographic material, it is possible to capture it with some precision as it functions as part of – and is articulated in –

ordinary discourse. One of Heidegger's commentators writes: 'Our being-with-others is already essentially manifest in mood and understanding. In discursive logos our being-with-others only becomes explicitly articulated. In our discourse it becomes explicitly shared in an appropriate way' (Kockelmans 1972: 22). It is just *as* the participants are visibly engaged in sharing their fellowship via their discourse that the life of congenial fellowship may be studied in explicit detail; however, if Heidegger's thoughts are to be accepted here, there is also a warning to be taken: the work of congenial fellowship locatable in discourse is only one aspect of this important sentiment identifying of Aboriginal social relations. We must keep in mind that there will be realms of experience which a rigorous sociology, based upon what is observable in discourse, will remain unable to capture.

For the rest we must rely upon characterizations derived from perspicuous ethnographic illustrations; however, the anthropological literature on the Australian Aboriginal provides few considerations of the mundane, massively present phenomena of ordinary Aboriginal social interaction. Most researchers have offered only brief remarks about the congeniality of Aboriginal people and the nature of their sociability; these remarks are more in the character of asides than they are sociological scholarship. Only very recently (Meyers 1979, Tonkinson, 1978: 120-8, Sansom 1980) have the issues of harmony and consensus in everyday Aboriginal social life begun to receive close sociological attention.

It is typical for studies of the desert Aboriginal people to include no more than a single reference to the character of Aboriginal human relationships. Elkin (1938: 113) devotes only a sentence to the fellowship which makes an Aboriginal community more than just an aggregate of individuals. Stanner, in a nationally celebrated series of lectures (1969: 47) makes only a single reference to Aboriginal gentility:

> Their lives together certainly had a full share of conflict, of violent affrays . . . But in some ways they were more skilful than we are in limiting the free play of men's combative propensity . . . The subject is a fascinating one but unhappily the research we have done upon it in Australia has neither been plentiful nor distinguished. I cannot, therefore, take it very far, and I can mention a few points only.

The Berndts (1946: 251) have observed the tolerance which Aboriginals demonstrate towards each other, and they record an incident in which a child destroyed the carving on a highly prized spear-thrower without suffering the slightest remonstrance. The

Berndts remark, 'They do not like to see a child cry and will give it anything to make it stop.' We will see that this is illustrative of Aboriginal relations generally; however, the Berndts explore the matter no further. Apart from a brief reference to the 'courteous' nature of Aboriginal people (1969: 69), Gould's sole remarks about the Aboriginal person's attitudes towards other members of his society are also about their child-rearing (15). He reports that Aboriginal children are indulged to an extreme degree and that physical punishment is almost unheard of.

Mountford's single reference to Aboriginal social feelings in a popular study of desert Aboriginals (1948: 183) deals not even with their relations with their children but with how they relate with their dogs – he discusses how rare it is for Aboriginal people to hit their dogs. In his major study, *Nomads of the Australian Desert* (1976), Mountford pays a little more attention to the human side of the matter but still devotes less than two pages (51-2) to Aboriginal sociability:

> Esteem also is not always a matter of ability in one particular field, but of personality and character. The ideal people, by no means rare among the Aborigines, are those with a quiet and friendly manner, cheerful and generous, who show a readiness to join in group activities and are capable of making firm decisions.

While Mountford has characterized the congeniality of Aboriginals, nowhere did he take up the issue of what making decisions is like in ordinary Aboriginal society; his reference is no more than a mention of the phenomenon.

In the preface to *Desert People*, Meggitt (1962:xi) announces his intention to investigate social organization rather than the totemic rituals and religious phenomena with which previous Australian anthropologists had primarily concerned themselves, but his contributions to the study of ordinary social relations are brief. He discusses the fact that Aboriginal people gather in large groups for the mere pleasure of being together, but he doesn't investigate what that pleasure might consist of or how it may be organized. Meggitt refers to the Aboriginal desire to maximize the consensual basis of collective activity (242), but he never inquires about the production of that consensus. He refers to Aboriginal interpersonal policies which minimize the spread of quarrels (58) but does not locate such phenomena in any descriptive detail.

Maddock (1975: 187) devotes several paragraphs to the positive features of Aboriginal society, among which he counts a certain anarchy, egalitarian mutuality and an emphasis upon the 'all-round development of the person.' Tonkinson's single reference in his 1974 study records the fact that 'visiting and gossiping are favored adult pastimes' (60), yet there is no investigation into what it is about Aboriginal 'visiting' which makes it noteworthy. The congenial sociability of Aboriginals is indeed worth noting, and my aim in this chapter is to elucidate what it is about such mundane social relationships which makes them so essential to any definition of the character of Aboriginal social life. As Sansom writes (1980: 137), 'that which is valued (and is, for countrymen, the source of all realized value) is called "going through somethin along with [longa] somefella(s)".'

Burridge, in his 1973 review and assessment of anthropology's investigation of the Australian Aboriginal people, attributes the inattention to the everyday features of social life to the very mundaneity of the phenomena concerned. Burridge observes the large gap between the character of the Aboriginal people and the intellectual constructs of Aboriginal social life developed by anthropologists (he refers to those of Durkheim, Radcliffe-Brown and Lévi-Strauss):

> Despite the herculean efforts of field ethnographers who, knowing the Aborigines at first hand, have appreciated the skew and sought to find the evidence to put the record straight, what has caught the imagination of the scholarly world and public at large are the force and persuasion of the intellectual construct rather than the lineaments of the people themselves. What Aborigines actually do and think and feel is in a sense as irrelevant and trivial as anything anyone does or thinks or feels in the course of his daily round – until, that is, all the doing and thinking and feeling reverberate with intellectual excitement. Life among nonliterate peoples often tends to be dull and dulling. Just as washing the dishes, ironing shirts or a roadside conversation with a tramp can be quite forgettable experiences without the aid of a gifted dramatist or novelist to make them memorable, so it is with the simpler peoples and their anthropologists. (55)

Both Gould (1969: 54) and Tonkinson (1978: 8-10) title major subsections of their books 'Who Are The Desert Aborigines?' In answering this 'who,' Gould's chapter provides a review of which possible races and groups may have composed the desert Aboriginal people's ancestors, what the physical characteristics of the Aboriginals are and what their language is. Tonkinson answers the 'who' with data referring to their average height, skin and hair color (dark to honey-colored) and to their customary vestiments. Is this the 'who' with which social anthropologists should be most concerned? In what sense are cranial size and blood type identifying of Aboriginal people in any meaningful way? And what alternative kinds of sociological investigation exist which can provide us with a more meaningful response to the question of the 'who'?

Heidegger takes up this question of the 'who' in his study of ordinary human existence (1962: 149):

> We shall approach the phenomenon of being-in-the-world by asking *who* it is that man [*Dasein*] is in his everydayness. All the structures of being, together with the phenomenon which provides the answer to this question of the 'who,' are ways of his being.

What Heidegger is saying here is that we cannot treat the person we are studying as an object, an inert entity with definite properties which exist in the world like roads and geosynclines; rather, we must recognize that a human being is an active potentiality for existing. As one who exists with others, he produces his world: he is not merely *in* the world but *has* a world. That is, the truth of a society is to be found in the praxis which is never static but always emerging and which addresses itself to that yet to be determined future which is their world. An adequate investigation of the 'who' must capture that praxis in its openness and in its activity; it cannot reify it because if it does it conceals the 'who' which is most central to their social being. What is required here are penetrating and non-sentimental investigations of ordinary Aboriginal social praxis and sentiments.

Before I take up a systematic presentation of Aboriginal congeniality and consensus as it is observable in their ordinary discourse, I review some ethnographic material which sheds some light on what the breadth of the issue of congeniality might be. While we seek a rigorous and fully documented description of these issues, we must not forget the warning that what lends itself to rigorous study and documentation may not compose the full scope of the phenomena involved. As sociologists we must simultaneously exploit our analytical strengths and minimize the weaknesses of our perception by periodically stepping back and assessing the field.

During the first period of my fieldwork with Aboriginal people, I lived among partly acculturated Aboriginal people living at the fringes of the small towns at the edge of the desert in the Western Australian outback. These were people who had regular daily interaction with persons of European descent, and they knew the ways of both their own people and the European-Australians.

After some of the most respected Aboriginals in one of these towns had approved of my participation in the Aboriginal life of the region, one middle-aged 'full-blooded' Aboriginal man took some pride in demonstrating to me what separates the *wangkayi* [an Aboriginal person] from the 'whitefella.' He spoke about how Aboriginal people are concerned to look after each other while white people are more inclined to compete against each other. A trip was arranged for me with some of the Aboriginal elders to sacred areas in the region so that I might be able to assist them in securing legal protection for the sites. I spent several days camping with the men, sharing their kangaroos and hearing their stories as they escorted me about the countryside. By the end of the expedition, we had developed much affection for each other, and as we drove back into town on the final evening, quite exhausted but pleased with ourselves, my Aboriginal friend who had remained in town could see at once that we had shared some friendship. Recognizing the quality of our association, he remarked, 'So how'd you get on?,' while offering a smile which seemed to say, 'Yes-our-kind-of-fellowship-is-pretty-good-isn't-it?' I detected a good deal of pride in his expression as well as pleasure in the fact that my own experience had borne out the accuracy of his descriptions. There was something light and spontaneous about the Aboriginal fellowship I had shared which was difficult to describe but pervasive nonetheless.

Another incident throws light on the congenial 'mood' of Aboriginal fellowship so 'refractory' to formal analysis. I am concerned here with locating congenial fellowship in its full phenomenological life. After living with Aboriginal people in the settled outback of Western Australia, I began to assist more traditionally oriented Aboriginal people who lived in the more remote regions of the desert. Eventually I came to accept a position as the community adviser to one of the remote Aboriginal settlements in the central desert region known as Australia's Western Desert, but for many months I assisted these remote Aboriginal people in securing governmental protection for sites of sacred religious importance, just as I had previously assisted Aboriginal people in areas closer to the centers of European settlement. A group of Aboriginal men to whom I was assigned by the community suggested that we visit an important sacred site which they hoped one day would be the center of a reestablished community. They took me to the location where the site's traditional owners were encamped about sixty miles from the site, so that we might be properly escorted to the region.

When we arrived at the camp of the owners, I was surprised to find that it was not at all certain that we would actually make the trip to the site. Despite the fact that I had already driven many hundreds of miles to make the trip, discussion of our plans was introduced only gradually and in a casual manner. Much friendly discussion, a meal and rest period, and more discussion transpired before it was finally decided that all would make the trip to the site. It was not only that it was necessary for a clear consensus to emerge before taking action, but the environment in which such a consensus was achieved had to be a congenial one, predicated upon a friendly solidarity among the participants. It appeared to me that one of the primary functions of the discussions was to establish warm relations between myself, my Aboriginal friends and the traditional owners, without which a decision to visit the site would not be made. The discussions continued until all felt encompassed by an ambience of congeniality; after such fellowship had been established the decision to visit the site was made, and what is more, by such a practice the trip to the site and the visit there was made effortless, an enjoyable exercise for us all.

In this instance, as throughout Aboriginal life, Aboriginal people were reluctant to commit themselves to abstract decisions, which may be scheduled and subsequently followed without regard to intervening events. While this lack of commitment to abstractly constructed plans may be due in part to the modes of temporality operating in traditional Aboriginal life, it probably has more to do with the fact that Aboriginal people are more conscientiously addressed toward sustaining positive mutual feelings than they are concerned with efficient work practices. Whereas persons of European descent are accustomed to committing their energies to abstract social structures, emphasizing productivity and the completion of projected plans, Aboriginal people allow themselves to become easily 'distracted' by other people and the local human requirements of the moment, to the point where many plans are sacrificed for the benefits of social harmony. Where European-Australians are often 'workaholics,' Aboriginal people want to be able to witness the local relevance of a proposed task and work best when they are sustained by a congenial fellowship of co-workers.

Harmonious practices

Apart from genuine feelings of congeniality, Aboriginal people have a number of practices for preserving harmony in everyday social relations. The key to such practices is the strict refusal to force one's own way upon a social ensemble. If an Aboriginal person feels strongly about some matter, he or she will find a discrete way to express his feelings without coming into direct confrontation with anyone. More often than not, if direct confrontation is the price to pay for securing adoption of one's view, then such adoption will usually be sacrificed in order to avoid the confrontation. This is done in order to prevent ill feelings developing among the assembly, feelings which can affect interaction in the succeeding weeks and months. The maintenance of good relations is always the primary concern of Aboriginal social life.

One elderly Australian of European descent who has lived with traditionally oriented desert Aboriginals for most of his life summarized their character aptly when he told me that an Aboriginal person will strive never to embarrass his fellow men. They avoid imposing their own individual ideas upon a group and work to harmonize with others. 'They'll never damage another's personality,' he says. Even when a person fails to fulfill his responsibilities, they remain very tolerant and will avoid making public criticism. If an Aboriginal person fails to do his share of the work, an Aboriginal is likely to explain, 'Oh, that fella doesn't like to work,' and leave it at that.

One young traditional Aboriginal man explained to me, 'I never run a black person down.' Further, he explained that it was improper to selfishly hold onto material possessions: 'What I've got you've got. When they come to me and ask, "Do you have fifty cents?" I don't go, "What you want it for?" I give 'em fifty cents.' Traditionally, any person needing food was given something to eat without any questions being asked. Now that Aboriginals have come into contact with more material goods, such mores are being applied with only a few restrictions to these items also, which include radios, cassette-players and automobiles. Sharing is a dominant aspect of Aboriginal life, at one time well suited to their means of economic livelihood but now, just as importantly, a valued qualitative principle of ordinary social relations.

But more important are the constraints against confrontation and public criticism. Even on critical matters one must respect another's feelings. One anthropologist has remarked, 'To openly refuse or disagree with someone "to his face" [*kuru lingku*: "right to his eyes"] is difficult and very unusual for an Aboriginal person' (Meyers 1976: 391). Such constraints required some modifications in my own personality. Criticism of obvious social inequities and explanation of the political structures surrounding difficulties the Aboriginal were suffering had to be offered without any acrimony; even criticism of offending governmental leaders had to be muted. As a European myself, it was improper for me to be too critical of other Europeans in the region who were opposed to Aboriginal interests and who in many cases were extreme racists. To take one illustration, an Aboriginal elder in one of the outback towns asked me about a European-Australian who had been causing the Aboriginals some problems. While I suggested that the person concerned was a big talker, it would have been improper for me to be too direct in my criticism:

AP *Yuwa, ngananya* big boss*pa?* (Yes, he's a big boss, huh?)

KL *Ngurrpa.* (I don't know.)

While the elder understood my feelings, he was pleased that I responded in a typical Aboriginal manner by feigning ignorance when I felt that some criticism was warranted.

Although Aboriginal people do end up in arguments with each other, they strive to avoid them. They are always invoking for each other the rule that interaction must be kept harmonious. While persons of European descent have similar policies, arguments may be much more easily sustained in European societies without causing serious damage to social relations. Arguments in Aboriginal society (usually over women or alcohol) tend to become more serious quickly, and so they are strenuously avoided. Meggitt (1962: 58) has noted that 'limitations on the spread of quarrels is to some extent connected with the notion of personal "space" and of minding one's own business.' Aboriginal people see *arkamin* [argument] as something which Europeans engage in a good deal of the time, and I have heard them tell each other, 'Not *arkamin*, that's whitefella way.' One member of an Aboriginal community council in a remote desert settlement complained about a European mechanic employed by the council who was always arguing: 'Every talkin' back way, like that, make 'em funny feeling all the council.' While Aboriginal people may argue, such displays are more rare and carried out to extremes, after which it is expected that the participants will return to congenial behavior. What is not permitted is consistently aggressive or argumentative behavior. Such disruptive emotional feelings are not welcome. On another occasion I was advised myself, 'Don't *arkamin*,' and Aboriginals have advised each other, '*Let's keep it nice*' [*wirutjaku;* italics indicate that the original text was spoken in the Aboriginal language], 'we don't like too much *arkamin. Speak softly* always.'

Such sociability structures the participation of Aboriginal

members in ordinary interaction. Harmony and congeniality are not achieved exclusively through the compassion of the Aboriginal soul but largely through a body of consistent structures for producing such harmony. Such structures need to be described in detail if we are to win an accurate description of everyday Aboriginal social relations.

Consensus

In Aboriginal society nothing is done on the authority of just one man. There exist no formal leaders, and their political life is highly egalitarian. The question of sociological importance which presents itself is how they manage to get along without formal headmen. In an environment where not only is there no headman but individuals are proscribed from advocating their own positions too strongly, decision-making is a very skillful affair. One of the answers is that Aboriginal people's points of view are more corporate and less individualized – i.e., they are not always concerned with advocating positions but frequently are oriented toward receiving direction from the group as a whole. They attend the consensus. The corporate state where a unity of feelings and opinion exists is valued for its own sake, and such a condition must be preserved throughout any period of inter-action. Much of the social activity of an Aboriginal encampment is addressed toward the active production of collective solidarity. Meggitt (1962: 244) recounts the testimony of an Aboriginal elder who emphasized the importance of consensual action; on important matters (e.g. ceremonial activities) the members of the community should, he said, 'all think in the same way with the same head, not in different ways.'

A common reply I received when I asked people how they felt about a matter being discussed by a group of Aboriginals was, '*I am listening*' (*Ngayulu kulira*). Such a reply could have meant that they did not consider it proper to voice their personal opinions or that they did not yet have opinions but were waiting for direction from the ensemble. Their word for 'to listen' is '*kulira*,' which also means 'to think' – this may indicate that thinking itself may be more of a passive activity than in European society, an activity more oriented toward others. Aboriginal decision-making is a dynamic interactive process which consti-tutes the corporate life of the group as originary. This is to be contrasted with Western models of decision-making which are based upon individual view-points which are brought into a process of negotiation.

Where points of view do exist, the process of negotiation is tacit rather than formal. The gathering comes to a decision by what is almost a hidden consensus, with the concessions being made without public argument. This process may take a great deal of time, but time is something Aboriginal people have in abundance. When discussion takes a turn for the worse, an Aboriginal person will offer a comment like, *'Let's speak with one voice, harmoniously'* (*wangka kutjungka walykumunu*), and the chief participants are likely to wait for a consensus to emerge by itself. The very process of decision-making and negotiation is referred to by participles of the verb 'to sit down' (*nyinara*), which implies a willingness to attend a solution congenial to everyone present. During deliberations regarding a community response to a governmental policy, I was told, 'You might find out from Darwin [the territorial capital], and by that time, alright we'll sit down.' And when Aboriginal elders wanted to discuss their land rights with the anti-Aboriginal Premier of Western Australia, they kept asking for an opportunity to 'sit down' with him, a prospect which was highly unlikely.

In order to obtain a broad picture of the issue of consensus in ordinary Aboriginal decision-making, here are four ethnographic summaries illustrative of the phenomenon. They demonstrate conclusively the primary role which unanimity and consensus play in Aboriginal community life.

(1) A prospector had been flying into a remote region of the Aboriginal reserve without a permit in order to look for minerals. Under State law, he would be able to commence mining operations for any minerals he discovered and properly recorded with the State. The only protection the Aboriginal community had was to refuse him a prospecting permit in the first place.

In this instance the prospector had paid large sums of money to the traditional Aboriginal owners in one region and received their permission and assistance in building an airstrip adjacent to a sacred site which was renowned in all corners of the Western Desert. The site was connected to tribal ceremonies which were performed from South Australia to the northwest coast. Aboriginals in nearby settlements were angered about the incident, particularly about the airstrip so close to the site, and asked me to drive them to the home of the traditional owners responsible so that they could discuss the matter. We were also to record the location of the site in order to seek State protection under legislation regarding Aboriginal sacred sites.

It was a two-day trip by four-wheel drive vehicle from the settlement to the home of the Aboriginals responsible. Throughout this journey, my three Aboriginal friends spoke with great vehemence about what a terrible thing it was to have allowed a prospector into a sacred area. They were outraged at the sacrilege, and Aboriginal people in a number of homeland camps were upset about the incident and wished the three Aboriginals well in their mission. When we arrived at the home camp of the traditional owners in the early afternoon, discussions did not begin immediately, but an afternoon meal was made and an early camp prepared on the site of the encampment corresponding to the home region of the Aboriginals with whom I had arrived. After the meal was concluded, discussion was further delayed as all engaged in making rounds of greeting and exchanging news and messages. After several hours, the people I brought discussed the matter with the elders of the community. They spoke for a couple of hours, without ever uttering a word of direct criticism. In the end, they concluded their meeting without changing the minds of any of the traditional owners and without ever really expressing the true gravity of the concern of Aboriginal people in other regions of the desert. For their part, the traditional owners spoke about the sincerity of the friendship of the prospector concerned. The meeting finished with an amicable decision to make a visit to the site. In effect, no solution to the matter was found; since it was not possible for any consensus to emerge at this juncture, the call for a decision was suspended. No argument took place. At the most, the traditional owners received a first hint that their actions might not have been sitting right with some people, and surely that was a matter for them to consider in the weeks and months ahead.

(2) In another remote Aboriginal settlement, the members of the community attempted to oust their chairman, who had been chosen according to a synthesis of Aboriginal and European customs. While government legislation requires that there can be an elected chairman and council for each community, Aboriginal custom usually dictates that the person who has the major religious affiliation to a site will have the most to say about the course of life of those living about the site, and that person is usually chosen to be chairman. If there is more than one person with proper affiliation to a region, then the chairman will be selected from among them. While in traditional times the hundred or so residents would have been scattered over more than ten thousand square miles of desert, governmental policies have resulted in the construction of a central mission-type settlement, and the persons belonging to the site of the settlement have come to possess an amount of prestige greater than they would have experienced in previous times.

In this instance most members of the community wanted to replace the chairman, who had been doing a substandard job, with another person native to the region. After several days an argument ensued, and when the community finally became quite adamant that the chairman resign he finally consented; however, just as soon as he acquiesced, the community 'felt sorry for him' and protested that he shouldn't resign after all. Many felt that there was too much bitterness about the resignation, and they did not want to initiate relations which would create disharmony for a long time to come. The chairman was allowed to retain his post. He had gained in stature, because he was not willing to stand against the will of the community, and the community had acted properly by not bringing an offense to a community member to its consummation. (In the end, after another full year had passed, the community succeeded in removing the chairman under more congenial circumstances.)

(3) Much intercommunity communication in the desert takes place today by way of short-wave radio contact. During a meeting to discuss land rights at which many communities attended, it was decided that the next meeting would be held shortly after (in light of a current crisis) at community A. Communities B, C and D decided on their own that they would change the site of the meeting to community B. This upset the people at community A, who decided that they would not allow that to happen and wouldn't attend the meeting if the venue was changed. Community A contacted community C by short-wave radio to discuss the matter, and community C said that it would be best that the meeting be held at B and that most communities agreed with that. The people at A responded by saying, '*Alright, that will be fine*' (*walykumunu paluna*); however, when the radio contact ceased, they expressed their strong displeasure, and no one from A went to attend the meeting at B. Here again, direct confrontation was avoided, despite the actual feelings of the participants.

(4) The secretary of one of the pan-tribal councils in the desert had arranged a meeting with the Western Australian Ministers for Lands and Social Welfare about land rights. While the State Premier was unwilling to meet with any Aboriginal people about their land rights, the ministers would make a report to the Premier about the wishes of the Aboriginal people. It was necessary for the Aboriginal secretary to collect half a dozen of the senior elders for the meeting from communities as far away as a thousand kilometers from Perth, the State capital. When he arrived at the last settlement in the desert before heading on into the European-occupied region of the State, some 800 kilometres

by road from Perth, the people at the community were undecided about attending. Despite the fact that the meeting with the ministers had been set, the secretary had to wait several days at that community in order for them to come to some consensus about the matter. This caused the meeting with the government ministers, which was set up only after much negotiation, to be postponed a few days.

At the subsequent meeting of the pan-tribal council, the secretary reported about the events in connection with the trip to meet with the ministers, including the delay at the community concerned. None of the members of that community was present at the pan-tribal council meeting. The secretary told the meeting, 'When we got to X it was too quick for us.' The use of the first person plural here is noteworthy. It could not have been too quick for the secretary, since it was he who had planned the trip in the first place and had set the schedule of events. It was only 'too quick' for the people at the community mentioned. His comment is indicative of the fact that when he arrived at the community to find that they were not at all certain about the wisdom of making the long journey, he suspended his own opinion regarding the matter in order to attend the consensus of the community. Such a consensus could not be hastened; it was important for it to emerge naturally so that there would be no discontent resulting from the decisions and actions taken. The secretary was willing to abandon his interests to follow the will of the community and identified himself naturally with the process of decision-making the community was undertaking. His report to the meeting was therefore accurate and related truly his participation in the events. In this case, as in the others, a consensus was required before action could be taken.

The organization of consensus

Such behavior is occasionally confusing to Australians of European descent who must deal with Aboriginal communities on behalf of the Australian or State governments. An Australian Senate Select Committee notes the phenomenon (Senate 1976: 31):

> For Aborigines, time is not of the same overriding importance as it is in virtually all non-Aboriginal affairs. Members of an Aboriginal community tend to talk at length around issues and so arrive at a consensus. In exchanges between them and non-Aborigines the contrast in attitudes to time is of crucial

importance. Failure to take due account of this contrast has contributed to poor communication of Aboriginal views.

While the Senate committee's comments are correct, they have done little more than to state the problem, glossing the differences of social interaction under the heading 'time.' What is required here is a rigorous investigation of ordinary Aboriginal interaction and decision-making. Similarly, Western Australia's Laverton Joint Study Group (1975: 102) has commented: 'Traditionally, Aboriginal decision-making processes were based upon consensus arrived at through considerable discussion'; however, nowhere in Australian anthropology has the detailed discursive work productive of consensus been fully described.

Aboriginal people will not take action until all those present are in agreement about the matters proposed. The question is how they proceed to a consensus without formal leadership. One of the chief mechanisms for consensus in Aboriginal gatherings is the practice of verbally formulating and acknowledging – and thereby *making publicly available* – the developing account of the state of affairs which is emerging anonymously as a collaborative production. As general discussion proceeds, participants formulate aloud accounts of what has been discussed so far and what seems to be the general agreement about the events under deliberation. Such formulations will be repeated many times and will be uttered to the group as a corpus rather than to individual participants. As the group moves towards a consensus, the public accounts will be repeated aloud by most of the participants, who by so doing seem to take physical hold of the developing decision of the gathering. Some of the public formulations will pass unaccepted – either they will have been initial attempts superseded by later contributions, or they will have been tacitly rejected by the ensuing course of events. The organizational work identifying of ordinary Aboriginal interaction involves the enterprise of making 'objectively' available, on the surface of the discourse, the summation (formulation, account, gist, crux, point, essence, what-about) of the matter at hand so that the progress and results of a group's deliberations may be observed by all.

However, these public accounts are not the results of detached reflection about the current state of an assembly's sentiments. The accounts are spontaneous, unreflective, 'objective' formulations of the status of the group's deliberations at any given moment. Only rarely are they something first considered and then deliberately offered; in such instances the account could have political motives. In their original and natural life they are uttered without self-consciousness and within the life of the 'We-relationship' of the ensemble. They are the gathering's way of making available their achievements for the collective life of those present.

By 'objective' here I refer to the sense of objective meaning developed by Schutz (1967: 32-7), which refers to what is equally available to all the members of a group. 'Objective' here does not presuppose any *a priori* truth value. The objective meaning of an utterance is what 'anyone' can make of it, without referring to the actual processes of its production – it is what is available on the face of the utterance, the meaning it would have regardless of who spoke (166). As something objective, such an utterance has a corporeality (134) which lends itself to becoming possessed in common; hence, its objectivity is a practical objectivity (Garfinkel 1975: June 16) which consists of its public availability. It facilitates and makes possible the corporate life of the group.

Husserl (1970: 314) distinguishes between objective expressions and essentially subjective and occasional expressions. He writes: 'We shall call an expression *objective* if it pins down (or can pin down) its meaning merely by its manifest, auditory pattern and can be understood without necessarily directing one's attention to the person uttering it, or to the circumstances of the utterance.' What is noteworthy about such a phenomenological definition of what is objective is that it stands in contrast to the subjective life of the speaker not as an *a priori* truth, but as a practical, intersubjective and essentially communicative realm.

Objective utterances have an 'anonymous' nature (Schutz 1961: 34). 'What we would call the world of objective meaning is, therefore, abstracted in the social sphere from the constituting processes of a meaning-endowing consciousness, be this one's or another's. This results in the anonymous character of the meaning-content' (37). But in our investigation anonymity is more than just a formal property; in ordinary Aboriginal discourse the anonymity is the mode of self-presentation of the participating speakers. They want to claim nothing more than their anonymous membership in the assembly. Their accounts are impersonal utterances by which the gathering is able to monitor its own achievements. The consensus emerges gradually until at last the assembly is presented with its solution.

Nevertheless, the consensus is the ongoing accomplishment of the gathering's participants. It is a collaborative production, although the mechanism of authorship remains hidden and the objective solution is hypostatized as existing absolutely. 'Collaboration,' however, may be something accomplished by individuals who come together in a process of negotiation, or it may be a being-with one another which precedes all deliberation, i.e., a 'We-relationship' which mediates the world from the beginning. The collaboration identifying of Aboriginal decision-making is normally of the latter style. Scheler describes this character of association well and calls it a genuine 'community of feeling,' which is to be distinguished from an association based upon people who have merely come together with similar sentiments or amidst some sort of emotional infection (as at a party, pub, or with laughter that is catching, etc.). Scheler writes (1954: 13), taking the case of a sorrow held in common, 'It is not that A feels this sorrow and B feels it also, and moreover that they both know they are feeling it. No, it is a feeling in "common".' A and B do not act externally to each other, somehow adding their sentiments together in a subsequent synthesis; rather, their experience originates in common. Phenomenologically, their sufferings are not two different events.

This sense of collaboration differs from the one employed by many symbolic interactionists and cognitive sociologists, who operate according to an intersubjective model whereby participants are seen as individual monads who engage in processes of negotiation and sense-assembly. A corporate body is thus depicted like this (after Schwartz 1980):

The initiative here rests with the individual participants. Such a model may be identifying of the social life of *Gesellschaft* relationships, but it is not representative of ordinary Aboriginal social relations. For Aboriginal people, the group is originary and mediates the world for the participants. An Aboriginal model of social relations would look more like this:

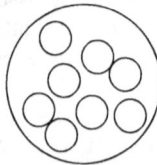

Here it is the 'We-relationship' which is foundational. The problem is not to understand how individual transcendental egos constitute the world of objects but rather how, given a world of objects in which all are immersed together at the outset, the ego participates in the collective life of his society. Ultimately the question is what does constitute collective life.

Schutz describes the 'We-relationship' (1971, vol. II: 32-3):

> But in face-to-face situations, in consequence of the continuous reciprocal modification of experience by the partner in the We-relation, I may 'participate' in the constitution of motives in my partner's life. . . . Since we are jointly engaged in our common experiences, I 'participate' in the projection and realization of his plans. Social interaction, characterized in all its forms by an interlocking of the actors' motives, gains an outstanding feature if it occurs in face-to-face situations. The motivational configurations of the actions of my fellow men, as well as his overt conduct, is integrated into the *common* experience of the We-relation.

The problem with this characterization is that Schutz does not specify what the 'jointly,' 'interlocking' and 'common' refer to. The notion that social activity 'is integrated' implies the mechanistic model of collaboration we have rejected in our analysis of Aboriginal interaction; however, in the idea of 'participation' and in the 'continuous modification of experience' there is reference to the collective life we are seeking.

In his study of the religious life of the central desert Aboriginal people, Durkheim recognized the phenomenon I have identified: 'It is no longer a simple individual who speaks; it is a group incarnate and personified' (1915: 240-1). But this is a mystification of what is objective. While the life of the group is originary, anthropomorphizing society only obscures the real collaborative activities which can be the only adequate grounds for making assertions about the transcendental character of social life. Durkheim provides us with a commonsensical notion of the objectivity of ordinary activities (Garfinkel 1975: June 23) which fails to reach the real-world character of the social activities constitutive of collective life. While accepting Durkheim's vision of collective life as the fundamental topic of sociological analysis, Garfinkel seeks to discover the real activities productive of social order. He asks (1979: Nov. 21):

> Can we be addressed to the world in such a fashion as to discover that topic as an agenda of researchable matters, where the agenda is furnished by the existence of a social order as the *detailed* texture of a collaboration of a cohort of practitioners, an orderliness which their practices make up, in a depth of detail which is indefinitely deep? If so this would furnish

Durkheim with adequate grounds for speaking about collective life.

Thus Garfinkel's program consists of bringing the analysis to address the circumstantial detail which makes up the collective life of social encounters. In the case of consensus in Aboriginal social relations, I am concerned to discover the actual practices which are productive of that consensus. While these practices are specific, we will discover that they are uniform over a large number of occurrences regardless of the particular participants who comprise the ensemble – they are mundane, standard, repeating and repeatable.

Sociologists have made the mistake of confusing the unanimity of Aboriginal social interaction with a massive conformity. There is said to be little individuality in Aboriginal society. Durkheim writes (1915: 5-6):

> Things are quite different in the lower societies. The slighter development of individuality, the small extension of the group, the homogeneity of external circumstances, all contribute to reducing the differences and variations to a minimum. The group has an intellectual and moral conformity of which we find but rare examples in the more advanced societies. Everything is common to all. Movements are stereotyped; everybody performs the same tasks in the same circumstances, and this conformity of conduct only translates the conformity of thought.

Later in the same study, (215) Durkheim writes: 'The dispersed condition in which the society finds itself results in making its life uniform, languishing and dull.' Aboriginal artists are said not to be creative in their work but to paint according to static traditional designs. Most everyone thinks in the same way. Aboriginal life is thus almost a monotony, with most actions being utterly predictable. Such views, while not entirely incorrect, do not capture the phenomenon. Aboriginal people do not have as great an investment in a personal identity as do persons of European descent, who utilize a public identity to mediate relations with the wide variety of people they encounter. Aboriginal people, by contrast, mediate ordinary external relations by way of the group structure. But within that group structure, Aboriginal people are highly creative in maintaining social harmony and the consensus which accompanies the congeniality they value so highly. Aboriginals are incredibly artful in the skills of ordinary interaction – they rarely miss so much as a wink. Free of abundant plans and preconceived notions about what the results of a conference should be, they are open for the slightest direction of movement of the sentiments of an ensemble. What is more, they take great pleasure in engineering convivial social interaction.

Persons of European descent, being members of urbanized, industrial, mass societies, pay more formal attention to questions of personality and identity, which obstruct one's access to the life of the group. This egoism is likely the result of the very fragility of identity in mass society. Simmel has written (1971: 291): 'Life in a wider circle and interaction with it develop, in and of themselves, more consciousness of personality than arises in a narrower circle; . . . the ego is apparently perceived as the one constant in all the alternation of psychological contents, especially when these contents provide a particularly rich opportunity.' The relative lack of eogism in Aboriginal society does not necessarily mean they are conformists, but only that the creativity of Aboriginal social relations has other outlets which are identifying of their Aboriginality.

What is more, along with the emphasis upon individual personality in contemporary Western life, there exists a uniformity of social being which social philosophers have termed one-dimensional (Marcuse 1964) or as inauthentic (Sartre's *on* (1956) and Heidegger's *Das Man* (1962)). Simmel suggests that modern life, 'precisely because of its mass character, its rushing diversity, its unboundable equalization of countless previously conserved idiosyncrasies – has led to unprecedented levels of the personality form of life' (1971: 291). What is interesting about Aboriginal social life is that because Aboriginal people place less emphasis upon the personality form of life, one's eccentricities are not a matter of great note. One cannot even say that they are more 'tolerant' of such eccentricities because there seems to be no burden involved. Aboriginals are not quick to judge others personally, and hanging around the Aboriginal camps are as wide a collection of original characters and eccentrics as are to be found in any society.

While Aboriginal people seek unanimity in social intercourse and are not highly egoistic, they have a certain independent-mindedness nonetheless. They will not speak for others, considering that to be an unwarranted extension of one's own personality; correspondingly, they resent having been spoken for. For example, an Aboriginal friend of mine was asked if a white electrician could enter his house to inspect its interior. He replied that it would be alright. The questioner then mentioned to him that some of his friends were in the house at the moment and asked him a second time if it was still alright to enter. The

Aboriginal replied that it was up to his friends. The same deference which requires that an assembly reach a consensus before any corporate action is taken also requires that decisions not be made for others. A single person in strong opposition to a verdict can cause a decision to be suspended. In speaking of Aboriginals as lacking in individuality, it is important to define just what individuality consists of.

A young fully initiated Aboriginal man whose lifestyle was partly Europeanized explained to me, 'Not like blackfellas in the U.S.; *wangkayis* [Aboriginals] all independent.' Acculturated Aboriginals have the idea that American blacks always act in concert to improve their conditions. Aboriginal people, however, are deeply divided according to family and tribal differences. In pre-contact times the desert Aboriginals lived about home sites in numbers usually ranging from ten to forty, and while they identified with groups in adjacent areas, their political lives were highly decentralized. Even the occasional gatherings of particular people in today's camps or settlements is ephemeral, as new families are always moving in and old ones moving away to circulate to other places. Sansom (1980: 262) has noted that 'mobs in their relative instability are not corporations.' The solidarity of most Aboriginal communities is too short lived to give it any permanent status, despite governmental policies, and the relevant social divisions are familial. This means that in ordinary life the collective social forms must be actively produced and maintained by whatever cohorts are on hand. The collective life of Aboriginal society is not anything like a blind conformity but is the creative product of a collaboration among living persons.

While Durkheim has provided sociology with a seminal formulation of the object of its investigations, his remoteness from the scene where Aboriginal actors comprise the social order upon which he based his observations prevented him from recognizing the real world bases of the collective phenomena he was nevertheless correct to concern himself with. Were he a party to their social life, he would have been able to fill in with detail what he was forced to render as social fantasy:

> In order that [collective consciousness] may appear, a synthesis
> *sui generis* of particular consciousness is required. Now this
> synthesis has the effect of disengaging a whole world of
> sentiments, ideas and images which, once born, obey laws all
> their own. They attract each other, repel each other, unite,
> divide themselves, and multiply, though these combinations
> are not commanded and necessitated by the condition of the

underlying reality. The life thus brought into being even enjoys so great an independence that it sometimes indulges in manifestations with no purpose or utility of any sort, for the mere pleasure of affirming itself. (915:471)

Although Aboriginal collective life surely involves 'combinations,' attractions, divisions and unifications, which operate according to standard interactional structures, and also involves spontaneous lapses into congenial pleasures for their own sake (pleasures which find expression in interactional form as much as content, as we shall discover), the orderliness does not produce itself but is the collaborative production of the Aboriginal participants.

Self-deprecation

Before I turn to the actual practices which are productive of congeniality and consensus and describe in detail the structure of Aboriginal interaction, I will make one more brief detour into ethnographic characterization, in order to familiarize the reader more with the participants whose discourse we will be examining. Such characterization is useful chiefly for heuristic reasons. Although one can use such characterizations to prove formulations about Aboriginal interactional praxis, it is a far weaker analytical pursuit than to show the actual work of that praxis in its circumstantial detail; nevertheless, such reportage is not without value.

The avoidance of emphasizing the self in public is an important aspect of Aboriginal social life. One central desert ethnographer has written, '[Shame] is a major construct of the Aboriginal view of what it means to be a person and how a person should comport himself in public relations' (Meyers 1976: 151). Aboriginals are extremely shy about personal matters and prefer to keep public discussion corporate so that their personal selves are not made conspicuous. As a matter of politeness, Aboriginal people will not draw excessive attention to the personal self of another. There are few formal greetings among those who interact with each other on a daily basis, and entrances as well as departures are unobtrusive, without the declarations of presence common to most European interaction.

But a sense of embarrassment is not only a natural aspect of Aboriginal personality; it is also a way in which one may indicate his or her good character. Shame and embarrassment are institutions which demonstrate to others that one does not have a conceited view of oneself. What is more, shyness is institutionalized in a variety of social settings, including visits to other communities, observance of sacred articles and meeting new people. A certain amount of embarrassment is expected from discrete persons.

During conversation Aboriginals will avoid looking too directly into each other's eyes, especially when the discussion involves a personal matter or is with someone one does not know very well. Many Aboriginal people have developed a remarkable capacity to listen carefully while feigning an intensive interest in some bird or other which is rustling over in some nearby trees. Also, it is discourteous to ask direct questions without first establishing some sort of congenial relationship.

It is as if the entrance of another person, particularly a stranger, causes an Aboriginal to fold upon himself. The embarrassment lies in being exposed to an Other's look, which renders one's private life an object in another's world. As Sartre (1956: 264-5) writes, 'Thus in the shock which seizes me when I apprehend the Other's look, this happens that suddenly I experience a subtle alienation of all my possibilities.' The space which heretofore was mine suddenly becomes grouped around the Other (255), and I am referred to my self (259), i.e., I become an object for the Other. Most are familiar with the natural shyness of small children. The roots of such shyness lie in the fact that the entrance of another reveals one's own freedom as limited and introduces an ontological transformation of one's 'selfness' (285) and world (255). One comes to see one's own self as an object for the first time. Under the feeling of exposure beneath the Other's look, one experiences shame.

On many occasions, when my own comments addressed Aboriginals in a personal way, Aboriginal people would respond in an embarrassed whisper or with very tight-lipped speech. Aboriginals do not like to be made available to an assembly in a personal way. A common method of declaring that one wishes to engage in a conversation is to cough lightly or make sounds as if one is clearing one's throat. The proper response to this is a light, positive nod accompanied by an attentive silence. In one instance, when I desired to dispense with a proposed conversation as quickly as possible, I replied to the slight cough with 'Speak up!' (mawatjala: literally, to speak by 'projecting outward' (ma)). This is precisely what the Aboriginal did not feel he had license to do, and he reverted to an inhalated whisper which was hardly audible. On later occasions, I found that a more successful reply was 'Keep talking' (puru watjanma), which is more of a passive acceptance of an event already in process and therefore a more agreeable and less conspicuous way of beginning.

Above all, an Aboriginal is never heavy-handed in expressing his views. Respect for others implies a civil moderation of one's own activities. Early advice given me by a part-Aboriginal person well acculturated into European sociability was, 'If you go musclin' in, they get self-conscious.' One may attempt to affect the outcome of a deliberation, but it must be done without becoming conspicuous. Correspondingly, among the most effective criticisms one can receive is to be slated for being too egotistical; for example, '*You* council *people act like big shots*' (*Nyuntu pala* 'bin councillors *purlkarilanguru*). A major irony here is that an assertive presentation of one's views, while reducing one's reputation, may have a substantial effect upon the outcome of a group's deliberation, under the rule which demands consensus and not insulting another. Opposition to a strongly presented view would imply a personal rejection which would be disruptive of congenial relations. Just as Aboriginals will do anything to stop a child's crying, they will readily submit to the wishes of one who appears to be aggrieved. While the one speaking up risks losing some of his good reputation (which could be damaging for him in the long run) his damages usually do not include losing his interests in the immediate discussion.

The proper way to speak up is to begin one's remarks with self-deprecatory comments, for example, by referring to one's ultimate ignorance in a matter: '*I don't know*, (*but . . .*)' (*ngayulu ngurrpatjarra . . .*); to one's hesitancy about what one is saying: '*Maybe it's like this . . .*' (*alatji tjinguru . . .*); or by displaying one's equanimity about the ultimate outcome: '*Maybe I speak correctly, or maybe not . . .*' (*Tjinguru ngayulu palya wangkanyi, tjinguru wiya . . .*); and other similar rhetorical devices.

What Aboriginals find the most difficult is to speak up and deliver an extended address. The favored strategy here is to depersonalize one's remarks and tone of voice as much as possible. The effect is something like acting as if someone else is doing the talking. When one must speak before a group other than one's home community, one feels especially awkward, and I have known only very few traditionally oriented Aboriginal people who could deliver extended remarks before a strange audience. Not only does one's 'natural' sense of shame dictate pause, but one really does not have the right just to go ahead and speak directly, without first receiving license from the group for such a personal display.

At an Aboriginal encampment some distance from one Aboriginal person's home region, all the men of the camp gathered together to listen to his proposal regarding some religious ceremonies between that community and his own. After all had been sitting for some time awaiting his remarks, the Aboriginal was still unwilling to launch bluntly into the discussion, which everyone had already anticipated anyway. He offered instead, 'Wonderful, very happy to be here!' (walykumunu, pukurlpa). At that point, and quite in accord with correct Aboriginal etiquette, one of the elders of the local community said, 'No reason to be shy here, brother. You're speaking right,' after which the speaker felt it was appropriate to turn to the topic which brought him to the region.

On another occasion, an Aboriginal elder who was elected to represent a wide region of traditional Aboriginal communities at a newly established national Aboriginal congress came to tell the communities what had transpired at the first meeting of the congress. At one community, all the men and women gathered together to hear his important words, but when it was time for him to begin speaking, he turned to me (as the community adviser) and said, 'Good, not for me [to speak]. Later I'll speak' (Palya, wiyakurna. Marla ngayuku wangkanyi). Another person, speaking at a meeting of a pan-tribal council, prefaced his remarks with, 'Just a little bit I have to say' (Tjuku-tjuku tjuku-tjuku wangkama), despite the fact that he intended to speak for a long while.

During one's turn at speaking, it is unwise to carry on too long without checking with the assembly to renew one's license to speak, and to verify that one is 'speaking correctly,' that is, voicing the sentiments of all. Here are three brief examples of receiving such license:

A	All right?	(Munta?)
B	Yes.	(Yuwa.)
C	Yes.	(Yuwa.)

A	O.K.?	(Palya?)
B	Yes.	(Uwa.)
C	Yes.	(Uwa.)

A	. . . like this, is this O.K.?	(. . . alatji. Palyaku munta?)
B	Yes.	(Uwa.)

If one overlooks this petition for license, he will be considered too self-assertive. In a noteworthy instance, discussed in some detail below (cf. chapter 2, Transcript A), an Aboriginal was selected by the government for a high post on a public committee. The Aboriginal could not accept the position on his own authority, even though he was not meant to be representing the community. He told the State Premier that he had to first secure the approval of his community. When he went to the people to discuss the post, he made conspicuous the propriety of his pursuit of the post, telling the gathering. 'Cause I can't *speak up and go on my own. I have to ask* the community first' (*ngarnmanpa watjarnurna ankurna; tjapilku*). This way of proceeding served to mitigate any opinions that he was beginning to consider himself too important.

Such unassertiveness is the hallmark of Aboriginal public life. The indirectness and displays of embarrassment involved take up a good deal of time. Frequently, one is able to avoid having to advocate one's own views by letting another person speak for oneself, i.e., by using what Sansom (1980: 78) calls 'brokers.' The idea may then circulate and be ratified by the group before one presents his own personal views. Self-aggrandizement is avoided strenuously, at least in its most conspicuous forms.

A final and most illustrative example of Aboriginal self-deprecation is in the local organization of the welcome one community gave the Governor-General of Australia when he paid a formal visit to the remote desert settlement. It had been decided that the elders of the community, affiliated to the local sites of sacred importance, would greet the Governor-General as he and his entourage disembarked from his airplane. But as the large plane circled overhead for the landing, the elders decided that it was time they found some new clothes and went off to the camp's store to outfit themselves properly. This took so much time that when the plane had landed on the settlement's dirt landing-strip, with most of the community looking on from the bushes, the elders still had not arrived. The Governor-General stepped off the plane, and no one moved forward to welcome him. Women were prohibited from doing so by social custom; it was also not the place of young men to do so; middle-aged men who were community leaders were prevented by the general proscription against setting oneself up as being important – they did not wish the negative social comment which would have followed any such self-election; and elders not affiliated with the sacred sites in the immediate region could not come forward because that would be overstepping their authority. Thus the Governor-General and his party stood there alone by their plane with a hundred people looking on, until a couple of middle-aged Aboriginal men shoved me vigorously toward the plane and instructed me to extend a greeting. Such is Aboriginal etiquette.

Let us now turn from general descriptions of the phenomena identifying of Aboriginal social relations and take up the phenomena themselves; however, I would strongly caution against the facile dismissal of the ethnographic descriptions I have been presenting. While one may consider them to be mere 'anecdotes,' we are seeking the most mundane, regular, repeating phenomena of Aboriginal social life. It would be a mistake to overlook the hermeneutic clues which such 'anecdotes' can provide for understanding Aboriginal personality and social interaction, in favor of anthropological data which are gratuitously nominated as being of greater consequence. To ignore what seems to be too mundane, on behalf of anthropological topics whose careers may have won favored status in the profession, is to mistake intellectual blindness for profundity. It is because such incidents are so obvious, and personal, that they are so quickly dismissed, but it is precisely because they are such that they merit special attention as what is most indicative of Aboriginal personal relations.

2 A competent system of organizational items

1.0 Facilitators

1.1 'Yes' (*yuwa*) and its variants.
1.2 'Good' (*palya*) and 'Wonderful' (*wiru*).
1.3 'Like this' (*alatji*) and 'That one' (*paluna*).
1.4 Repetition.
1.5 Vocal gesture.

1.1 'Yes' (yuwa) and its variants

To begin at the most elementary level, 'yes' facilitates conversation in any language and provides in the Western Desert Aboriginal language the chorus for natural discourse. In Aboriginal society nearly everyone is a participant in discussions, and '*yuwa*' or its dialectal variant '*uwa*' provides each person present with a way to demonstrate his accord with the discussion, and by so doing to participate in the unanimity being produced. It is at once a concurrence and an assertion of trust and friendship. In most instances approval is obvious without such concurrence. Besides, one '*yuwa*' is capable of standing for the approval of all because Aboriginal contributions are commonly formulations on behalf of the sentiments of the entire gathering. After several such declarations of approval, one would think that more declarations would be superfluous, but such a cascade of affirmations is important as 'phatic communion,' the function of which is not to convey meaning but to produce fellowship (Malinowski 1923: 315).

The utterance '*yuwa*' and its variants are so ever-present that their absence is noteworthy and an indication that possibly the current comments are not being accepted favorably. Given the Aboriginal reluctance to voice direct criticism, the absence of some concurring remark can halt conversation in its tracks. While the many repetitions of '*yuwa*' may sound like too many echoes of concord, it provides important lubrication for Aboriginal discourse and composes part of the congenial environment. In case (1) an Aboriginal elder (APe) has spoken on behalf of the approval of all; nevertheless, further confirmation is provided:

APx . . .
APe *That seems fine. This seems fine.*
APy *Uwa.*
APz *Uwa.*   (1)

By widening the ratification more persons are able to participate physically in the life of the discussion.

While the semantic content of '*yuwa*' provides confirmation which encourages further discussion, its congenial work lies mostly in the tone of the utterance. '*Yuwa*' has many paralinguistic variations which can inject a convivial mood into the interaction. Frequently, the speaker may not be considering the semantic content of his utterance (he may not even have been listening to the utterance immediately preceding his '*yuwa*'), but the comment provides a ready vocal medium to convey his emotional tenor to the group. This is the case in (2),

Yuwa! Yuwa, yuwanmara, yuwankara.
(yes) (yes) (agreeing) (all agree)   (2)

which had its life as a complex expression of the interior sentiments of its speaker.

Other variants of '*yuwa*' include '*yuwanpa*' ('of course'), '*yuu*' ('sure'), '*yuwaputa*' ('I suppose') and the most lively of all, '*yuwoah!*'. In case (3) this last variant is both a strong confirmation and an expression of the congenial fellowship of the ensemble:

APx *We might get some money for our community.*
APa ⌠*Yuwa.*
APb ⌡*Uwa.*
APx *Like that.*
APc *Uwa.*
APx *Like that.*
APd *Yuwà.*
APe *Good.*
APx *I will tell them about our needs. I'll ask about getting houses for us.*

APn ⎡ *Yuwoah!*
APn ⎨ *Yuwoah!*
APn ⎣ *Yuwoah!* (3)

(NB. Cf. Appendix 1 for original texts and key to transcription.)

1.2 'Good' (palya) and 'Wonderful' (wiru)

'*Palya*' has an affective force even stronger than '*yuwa*,' and the approval of '*wiru*' is greater still. '*Palya*' functions less as a general lubricator than '*yuwa*' and is a more formal expression of universal concurrence.

APx *Uwa, he speaks correctly in this way.*
APy *Palya, that one.* (4)

'*Wiru*' is occasionally used as a more final formulation of general approval, but it may also be used interchangeably with '*palya*':

APe *This!*
APa *Wirunya.* [variant: 'wonderful, of course']
APb *Uwa.*
APc *Wiruku talk.* [var.: 'wonderful' + possessive]
APe *Palya, that one.*
APn ⎡ *Uwa.*
APn ⎨ *Uwa.*
APn ⎣ *Uwa*
APx *Wiru.*
APy *Palya.*
APz *Uwa.* (5)

'*Palya*' is also used to smooth over discussions which are endangered by an argument or unpleasant confrontation. In (6) I was about to speak further about a matter which, unknown to me, would have caused an argument between two of those present. APa 'cooled' my comments, and I followed swiftly in the same tune:

APa *That's right. 'Cause, the, can't talk, argu-
ment, palya.*
KL *All right, then.*
APn Mm.
KL *Uwa.* (6)

In such a fashion these facilitators may function to maintain congeniality.

1.3 'That's it' (alatji) and 'That one' (paluna)

1.31 Alatji 'That's it' is a verbal affirmation which refers more directly to the content of the previous utterance. It may also be used as a prefacing remark ('Like this . . .') calling for close attention to the comment which immediately succeeds it, but as a facilitator it has its life as a positive affirmation which almost always embodies the ratification of the entire group. Continuing illustration (1), we find '*alatji*' as the consummation of the group's approval:

APx . . .
APe *That seems fine. This seems fine.*
APy *Uwa.*
APz *Uwa.*
APa *This ceremony has many songs.*
APb This, *for this region's countryside.*
APc *Alatji.*   (1)

Having an extra syllable, '*Alatji*' provides more scope for tonal expression than the other facilitators and so may play an important role in setting a congenial mood. In company with Europeans, Aboriginal people will frequently employ its English equivalent, 'That's it!'. to set an amicable tone for the interaction. While this next transcription (7) is a docile text, making it difficult to recover such subjective orientations, '*alatji*' functions as both approval and demonstration of congeniality:

APa *But this,* anyway, *when you go for* holidays,
     *you must take the old men. Don't leave them
     sitting in the camp.* Anybody, later *coming
     by, pick them up.* Like this.
APb *Alatji.*
APc *Alatji.*   (7)

1.32 Paluna This demonstrative, and its dialectal cognate '*paluru*,' also function to ratify approval and to perpetuate congenial attitudes. While it has its most common use as a general pronoun, its use as a facilitator is to provide more confidence in the approval already indicated by other means:

APa *Yuwa.*
APb *Paluna.*
APc *This is the way.*
APd *Yuwa, paluna.*   (8)

'*Paluna*' finds its force as an objectified concurrence speaking on behalf of everyone present. This 'of course' character is part of its content, but its tonal variances can perform a great deal of work besides. In (9) the gathering is speaking about getting some kind of housing for the people in the settlement:

APx   *Yuwa.*
APy   All for the Aboriginals.
APz   *Alatji.*
      That's it.

APe   *Nyaapa-nyaapa-nyaapa.*
      (this)   (this)   (this)
      Yes, this is the way.

APa   *Kutju paluna wangkaku.*
      (one) (that one) (will talk)
      We all agree on this.

APb   *Palu-palunangka.*
      (that) (that way+ablative)
      All are agreed.   (9)

APe's '*Nyaapa-nyaapa-nyaapa*' is also approval, but more importantly it has in its repetition a congenial force. The repetition is not only emphasis, it is a celebration of the ensemble's unanimity, and it is appropriate for an elder to be undertaking such authentication. The additional ratification by APb in the final line also celebrates the consensus, not only through its repetitive structure but via its employment of the Aboriginal ablative form '*-ngka*,' which designates proximal physical location ('with,' 'by,' 'at,' 'in,' 'under,' etc.): not only was the matter under discussion confirmed, but the confirmation was so secure that it could 'settle into itself' so. The collaborative result provides a resting-place for the objective social life of the group. This is a consensus which is also fellowship.

1.4 Repetition

The congeniality of Aboriginal fellowship is available not only in a content which becomes shared but in the structure of the utterances. Foremost among these structural provisions for congeniality is repetition, as I have noted in (9). Repetition has a very wide variety of uses. It is a complex phenomenon, and producing congeniality is only one of its many functions. Repetition is able to serve as a conversational item where some brief reply is called for when one has not understood what has been said. It may be reassurance for a speaker, encouraging her to continue. It may also be a polite way of disguising disagreement, or a way of coming to understand the utterance more fully. Here I am concerned with repetition as a celebration of congeniality.

One finds repetition for the mere pleasure of its sound. When several repeat the same utterance or phrase of concurrence many times, they are usually engaged in producing the group's self-affirmation of its positive state of being. Where repetitions of phrases are uttered without there being an accompanying communication of sense (a frequent phenomenon of intercultural discourse), one has a case of what Durkheim described above as indulgence 'in manifestations with no purpose or utility of any sort, for the mere pleasure of affirming itself.' But the production of congenial relations is purpose enough.

As a processual feature of discourse, repetition also guarantees that all present are alerted to the consensus which is developing. In interaction which is highly egalitarian, repetition guarantees that everyone will have access to current topics; thus, it constitutes part of the structure of the egalitarian character of Aboriginal discourse.

Perhaps an illustration of the use of repetition to express congeniality in Western discourse would be useful here. During a national charitable telethon in the United States, the master of ceremonies was informed: 'Over $500,000, and it's still coming in'; he replied with enthusiasm: 'Over half a million, and it's still coming in.' In the repetition pleasure was expressed and made objective for the viewing public. In Aboriginal discourse, repetitions are far more frequent than in European discourse, both a consequence of and productive of the congenial fellowship common to Aboriginal social relations.

Durkheim acknowledged the congeniality and unanimity which repetition is able to produce: 'It is by uttering the same cry, pronouncing the same word, or performing the same gesture in regard to some object that they become and feel themselves to be in unison' (1915:262). Here are three illustrations of this:

APx If you =
APy   = *don't work.*
APx *Don't work.*
APy *Don't work.* Half pay.
APx Half pay, *you'll get*, every time.   (10)

APx *It was a bad idea to take them to* Wolman Rocks.
APy Wolman Rocks.   (11)

APx Money, *they'll give you for* work, *for* work, money *for* work.

APy   *He's speaking of* money *there.*
APz   *He's speaking of* money *there.*   (12)

The import of the comments of APz in (12) does not lie so much in its content but in the congenial tone of the speaker as he makes his repetitive utterance. This is also true of the dialogue in (13), where two elderly women express great pleasure with viewing their home country for the first time in several years:

WPx   *Kayili.*
      North.

WPy   *Ngura kayili palatja.*
      Home [is] north, there.

WPx   *Kayili, Alyintjarra.*
      North, (place-name).

WPy   *Alyintjarra, kayili.*
      (Place-name), north.   (13)

Here the repetition structures the congeniality. An additional structural feature, whereby the positions of the central syntagma are reversed in the repetition, emphasizes the women's pleasure. Such reversals, to be discussed further below, are used within a structure of repetition to add force to the concurrence embodied in the repetition and is an illustration without parallel of 'taking pleasure in affirming oneself.'

In (14) the repetition is extensive, as every person present has to get their word in even though they hardly provide additional information:

APa   *There in* Areyonga [place-name].
APb   Areyonga.
APc   ⌠Areyonga.
APd   ⌡*That place.*
APe   Areyonga *they're bringing them.*
APf   Areyonga *they're bringing them.*
APg   *To* Areyonga.
APh   [inhalated whisper] Areyonga.
APi   *To* Areyonga.
APj   *And they'll give them to* Areyonga.
APk   *That's it, there in* Areyonga.
APl   *Alright, so it's that.*   (14)

In (15) APz has not even heard APx's comment, and so repeats APy without intending any semantic content. His repetition is merely tactile, an expression of his congenial fellowship:

39

APx Oh, it's *you.*
APy Hey?
APz Hey.   (15)

But such repetition is not merely facile, for it helps to maintain the group's positive feelings. In (16) a repetition provides a stronger validation of the consensus than would '*yuwa*' or another facilitator:

APx *And they said to the* whitefella *there*, 'Hey, look
     here. We got no house, and you gonna come up
     here for nothing. *We're living without any houses.'*
     No houses, we got no good house, *Nothing, there*
     isn't a single house. We're just sitting down with all
     the dogs.
APy Mm. *With all the dogs.*   (16)

1.5 Vocal gesture

Vocal gesture is important in the work of all the facilitators we have analyzed, particularly in establishing congenial fellowship. But it is not necessary for formal words to be uttered to be able to accomplish this vocal work – any bleat or whistle will do. Perhaps the most common vocal gesture is the Aboriginal equivalent of 'Mm-hm,' which is a standard form of approval variously registered as 'Mm ↓ Hm ↑ ,' ' ↑ Mmmm ↑ ' or 'Mm ↑ Hmm ↓ ':

APx *We will ask him straight away.*
APy *Mm ↑ Hmm ↓ !*   (17)

An apt vocal gesture will do more to solidify a group than many turns of talk. By line 14 of case (18) all present are in accord and moving at the same pace. AP's ' ↑ Hm Hm ↑ ' is a mark of the group's having achieved congenial fellowship:

APe *I have something else to say about some sacred items.*
APx *Uwa.*
APe *I have only a little bit of the sacred material at my*
     home camp.
APn *Uwa.*
APn ⎡*Uwa.*
APn ⎨*Yuwa.*
APn ⎣*Oh.*
APy *Mm Hm!*
APe *I still have to get those things.*   10
APa ⎡*Uwa.*

APb ⎰ *Yuwa.*
APe *Two of them.*
APb ↑ *Hm Hm* ↓ !
APe *This one.*
APc *That one.* (18)

A recurring feature of Aboriginal discourse is the simultaneous utterance of a facilitator by several speakers, giving the impression of a single voice. The effect in the case of '*yuwa*' is as if the group itself was speaking, and the sound produced is something like 'Wom'pa!':

APe *So I'll stop here for a spell.*
APa ⎧ *Uwa.*
APb ⎨ *Uwa.*
APc ⎩ *Uwa.* (19)

This gestural phenomenon lends terrific vitality to a gathering and is the Aboriginal idea of satisfying discourse. Shouts ('*Ohuuu!*') and a variety of exclamations ('*Nyangkarpa!*,' '*Yakaku!*') are very common and freely punctuate most talk, adding to the congenial ambience. And not to be overlooked is their ever-present laughter, the congenial force of which is known to all societies.

2.0 Congeniality

2.1 Congenial rhythms.
2.2 Displaying-the-obvious.
2.3 Objectification of discourse.
2.4 Contentious interaction.

2.1 Congenial rhythms

As an ordinary gathering approaches a congenial ambience, the discussion becomes less discordant and the contributions of each participant flow together better with the other utterances. In such a way, congenial fellowship may have symphonic properties, rhythms and repetitions which seem to cascade from one speaker to the next, maintaining a constant rhythm across a number of speakers. It is as if the speaking alone has precedence, with the speakers having only adjunctive roles. Aboriginal people revel in such occasions – they are the primary social pleasure of everyday Aboriginal discourse.

Durkheim speaks of a 'collective effervescence' (1915: 405, 441) which buoys a social gathering. Such a corporate emotion has its roots in congenial fellowship and frequently finds its force in the rhythm or tonal features of the talk, although not infrequently it may be occasioned by a precipitate silence. When all are in agreement the congeniality transcends the current topic, and the agreement becomes a medium for fellowship, with all present offering a resounding chorus of '*yuwa*' and vocal gestures which sound like chaos to a novice observer, especially since it seems (and may indeed be the case) that most are not paying attention to the speakers anyway.

There are times when Aboriginal discourse resembles the litany of a black American baptist church:

APe   *Sure, there, this thing here, probably in vain he tried– that fellow. He should just go away and leave it alone.*

APa   *Go away and leave it alone.*

APb   *Go away and leave it alone.*

APe   *Go away and leave it alone.*

    . . .

APx   *Uwa.*

APy   *We are all agreed.*

APz   *Alatji.*   **(20)**

In case (21) the speakers have not yet established any unanimity, but they are engaged in developing it. By the end of the excerpt (lines 20-2) they have begun to gather the assembly into some sort of harmony, which develops gradually over the subsequent talk. We can witness here the beginning of a 'symphonic' rhythm, which replaces the discordant rhythms in lines 1-12.

APa   *We'll get one the proper way.*

APb   *The elders will get a truck to use for going to ceremonies.*

APa   *Ladies and old men.*

APe   *There will be elders at the* Ernabella meeting.

APc   Meeting, meeting, *truly they're having.*

APb   We got to get, *no*, different way *we need to speak.*

APa   Different one.

APb   Different way, *no. This way,* anyway, *we must speak* properly.   10

APa   *For the Aboriginal people. The proper way – we'll sit down and talk with them.*

APb   Mm. *Talk and listen.*

APa   *Whitefella.*
APd   *Uwa.*
APf   *Maybe the old men should ask for the truck to use for going to ceremonies.*
APn   *That way.*
APi   *Uwaoh.*
APf   *So like that we are speaking.*   (21)

As we shall see, such rhythms may carry across long periods of discourse. Once a group finds its form it prefers to reside within it, letting the structure of that form lead their interaction.

2.2 Displaying-the-obvious

Summarizing or repeating what the previous speaker has said, even though what was spoken may be patently obvious to all, is a familiar feature of Aboriginal discourse. An illustration of this may be found on line 10 of case (21). In that instance it is quite possible that APa hadn't really understood the intended meaning of the phrase; however, his purpose was not to explain APb's comments so much as to orient the participants to the utterance.

At the conclusion of a lengthy meeting of the Pitjantjatjara Council, one of the pan-tribal land councils in the central desert region, an elderly Aboriginal person announced, 'So we've had some Pitjantjatjara talk' ['*Pitjantjatjara wangka*'], a fact about which all were fully cognizant. The elder's utterance was purely affective, absolutely unnecessary as far as its propositional content was concerned but vital in giving the elder a sense of participation in the group's activities and important in establishing a congenial atmosphere.

There is no need to present more than one illustration of this phenomenon. Case (22) is prototypical:

APa   *The Papunya mob has arrived at* Areyonga.
APb   *Yes, at Areyonga, he says.*
APa   *At* Areyonga *they've arrived.*   (22)

2.3 Objectification of discourse

In such articulation of what is obvious and in the processes of repetition and providing summary accounts something is achieved besides a congenial accord. The essential elements of discourse are made over into publicly visible events. As publicly visible, these formulations assume an existence which is available as a common possession and which may be ratified generally by the gathering. In such ratification not only are the elements of discourse objectified but so is their content – the gathering finds its way to an objective formulation of events, which provides the participants with an absolute sense of reality. Out of a developing ensemble of multiplicities, Aboriginal interlocutors work to objectify their discourse in order to arrive at a totalization (Sartre 1976: 45-7, 830) of their world.

This organizational procedure is productive of both congeniality and consensus. The ease with which Aboriginal gatherings objectify their experience is an identifying feature of Aboriginal social life and is related to the production of group solidarity. Through their collaborative discursive activity they produce a determination which is unquestioningly accepted as the absolute character of events, and the progression from supposition to reality may occur very quickly if there is no visible dissension. In summarizing the obvious and in repeating summary accounts, the accounts are made publicly available; they may then be taken up in turn by a number of parties to the discussion, and in such serial articulation they win an incontrovertible objective life.

To illustrate, I once took some Aboriginal men from a remote region of the central desert to visit a coastal region of Western Australia. The hills in this district were more extensive than they had seen in their own district, and one of them supposed (on the basis of oral knowledge about the travels of the sacred beings of the Dreaming) that the hills may have been the work of a particular world-creative being. The others took up the idea, more or less to see how it 'played.' After several rounds of repeating the account of the landscape's origin, the account began to develop some force. In the objectification produced by their own discourse, they produced an elemental fact of their social world.

Objectification of discourse occurs in a more proximate way as well. Two features of Aboriginal discourse which serve to objectify formulations and which celebrate developing totalizations are 'reversals' and 'redundancies'. The 'reversal' is a standard form for concluding a ratification of a section of discourse:

. . .
APa *Three children.*
APb *Children three.*   (23)

. . .
APa *Palumpa watjala.*
     That's what he says.

APb *Watjalu paluru.*
     So says he.   (24)

KL   House, *warli*.
        (house)
AP   *Warli*, house.   (25)

Reversals embody a certain finality and discourage dissenting notions.

'Redundancy' is a gloss for a variety of Aboriginal speech events which involve semantic duplication through the use of synonyms. There is an unmistakable self-assurance in such autochthonic confirmation, which is hardly distinguishable from other pleasures associated with congenial relations. Here are some examples:

Boss*pa kutjarrapula nyinanyi.*
(boss) (two + two) (is there)   (26)

Ngayukurna.
(I + me)   (27)

Kutjupa ngura kutjarra nyakukitja.
(another) (camp) (two) (intend to see)   (28)

Frequently redundant ratification will take the form 'not (-x), but x' as in (29):

Watiku wiya, minymaku.
Not the men, the women.   (29)

The emphasis consecrates the objective character of the utterance. The structure is thus indicative of its value as a formal public acquisition.

These insular duplications offer little additional cognitive content but provide an affective force which enhances the certainty of the utterance. Accustomed to such redundancy in their own speech, it was natural for Aboriginals to exploit the introduced language for lexical padding; thus one finds English terms commonly employed alongside cognates of their own language (cf. (25)), and this is even true for Aboriginals who do not speak English.

These rhetorical devices serve to reduce the degree of doubt to which a formulation may be subjected. It is as if they are saying, 'No matter how many ways you look at it, it comes to the same thing.' And one speaker's confidence is contagious for all: this objectifying praxis of Aboriginal people is productive of congenial relations as well as of unanimity.

What is important about the highly specific work of these

practices is that the participants are able to produce concrete objective forms about which their collective experience can cohere. For example, on one occasion it was decided that important ceremonies would be held 'in one moon's time' (*kinara kutju*). The two words expressive of this fact circled among those assembled many times and came to stand as an index for a detailed consensus about the proposed course of activity; the produced objective account carried the consensus through the succeeding month of activity. Men would point to the moon in the sky for each other and thereby reaffirm the corporate decision. Sansom (1980: 222) tells of a similar occasion when an organizer's suitcase came to stand as the objectification of proposed ritual activities. The suitcase harbored the necessary material resources which would enable the camp to carry out the planned ceremonies, and through weeks of preparation it was the concrete embodiment of the collective aspiration.

What I am primarily concerned with here are the processes of verbal objectification – what Sansom (1980: 158) calls 'the making of the word': the production of accounts which, once ratified, embody the will of all and become the basis for a group's collective life. Sansom (40) describes it this way:

> The precondition of the warranted continuity of a mob is that each determination contributed to the mob's holding of words be consensually formulated and 'objectified'. When the word is objectified, it can be recited by all members of the mob who now subscribe to it because each mob member assented to its fabrication. The objectified word, held in possession by all mob members, is made the nexus of a mob.

A graphic illustration of this praxis is displayed in case (43) below, where the summary account, '*And they won't run off doing other things*' (*kirti-kirti makatintja wiya*), becomes 'the word' of the assembly, a consensus which is perpetuated by the objective form of the uttered formulation. This formulation is then repeated, in (43) and beyond the limits of what has been transcribed, as if 'by rote' (Sansom 1980: 85), and so a standard version of the group's deliberation is produced, which continues to be available for later conversations.

Aboriginal life has been characterized as static and conservative, a characterization which originates in their desire to perpetuate the forms of life just as they were established in the Dreaming. In their religious life and mores, they tolerate few modifications – the world is thought to have already achieved its harmony and all that humans need to do is to perpetuate it. Of course there is change, even in their ritual life, but change is never articulated *as* change. Reality is absolute, no matter what developmental components are productive of it. (Such conservatism accounts for the fact that most Aboriginal people vote against proposed constitutional referendums, on the grounds that laws, once made, should not be changed.)

This fundamental passivity of Aboriginal cognitive life is coterminous with their praxis for objectifying discourse. The accounts of ordinary discourse solidify into a practico-inert field (Sartre 1976: 318) whose very inertia provides it with an objective character which is passively accepted by the gathering as total fact. Sartre writes (1976: 169), 'Society in its most concrete movement is shot through with passivity and unceasingly totalizes its inert multiplicities and inscribes its totalization in inertia.' But this totalization, as a developing production, requires interactional work. The local interactional work which in the Aboriginal case is productive of such objective social forms rests upon the highly skilled employment of summary accounts and with other organizational items of ordinary discourse.

Another of these organizational items is the activity of making the previous utterances publicly visible. This interactional work is evident in line 10 of case (21), and in this example:

APa   *No, houses, that's what.*
APb   *Houses for Walpapuka.*
APc   *Houses they're going to build.*
APd   *They're talking about houses.*   (30)

Frequently, there is an affective 'of course' tone to such repetitive formulations, as in line 4 of (31) and line 3 of (32). This increases the authority of the ratification:

APa   *Listen!*
KL   Um, if you want to choose a new council.
APb   *The council, he says.*
APc   *The council.*
KL   So you have to decide who you want to put on the
      council.   (31)

APa   *Yuwa.*
APb   *Palya.*
APc   *Wirunya.*   (32)

The '-*nya*' in the final line is a nominalizer which makes the collective approval something objective.

Each aspect of a topic will be summarized aloud. In the abiding life of the repetitions of a summary account, the group converges upon what is available to them as identical. The first few repetitions may be only tentative attempts at making the account a common possession; some participants may be unclear about what is going on, and there may exist a number of interpretations. Through each repetition the group's acquisition of the account becomes more homogeneous. The repeated utterances are the medium for orienting the mutuality of the participants. Repetition is one of the mechanisms of Aboriginal discourse which is productive of social objectivities while at the same time it preserves the fundamental passivity of Aboriginal deliberation.

The work of repetition here is similar to what has been observed by a sociolinguist working in the field of primary school education (Malcolm 1977: 10). He says: 'It is, of course, common for teachers in receiving children's answers to repeat them . . . but in this case the answer is not simply repeated, it is "standardized", so that it is rendered unambiguous for the rest of the class.' The only difference is that in the case of customary Aboriginal discourse, the author of such standard versions is corporate.

Throughout their daily lives it is common for Aboriginal people to assent to the conditions they believe to be natural and absolute. This aspect of Aboriginal cognition is a feature of their religious and economic lives and also characterizes their ordinary deliberations. In their orientation to achieving congeniality and unanimity in everyday social relations, they readily produce objective forms whose inertia allows a gathering to produce and preserve its solidarity. These conventional forms of Aboriginal social relations are thus compatible with certain cognitive attributes, and they are possibly productive of them.

2.4 Contentious interaction

Despite their emphasis upon congenial fellowship, when Aboriginal people reach a stage of argument, they frequently become quite violent towards each other. I am not in this study attempting to claim that Aboriginal people are more amicable in their relations than people in other societies. While they seek harmony in their social lives, they do not always consummate this aspiration. Their unique attribute lies in the by no means rare phenomenon that when congenial fellowship is achieved, they are quick to recognize it and feel no special compulsion to proceed with other affairs; however, in no way can it be proposed that Aboriginal people are non-violent.

What I am attempting to do here is describe something about the structure of Aboriginal sociability. Aboriginals are concerned to husband the feelings of others and engage in elaborate work to preserve harmonious relations. Equally important for them, however, is the preservation of certain kinship interests. Desert Aboriginal society contains clear family alliances which frequently impede a wise and judicious resolution of controversies. When fellowship does break down, it is usually along the lines of kinship divisions – occasionally over political issues but more frequently emotional ones, including sexual rivalries. Aboriginal people bear grudges a long while, and past conflicts can be perpetuated for many years. Allegations that one's family has been the object of a rival family's sorcery can initiate long-term animosities; here, paranoia leads to a perpetuation of conflict.

Sansom (1978) has said that the relationship between discreteness and 'action-in-violence' 'is one of the keys to all social action within an Aboriginal encampment.' It may be that the speed with which controversies in Aboriginal society become escalated into physical contents, particularly spear-throwing, provides some encouragement for their avoiding disagreements. I believe this is only a minor factor, however, secondary to the positive value of convivial social relations. Nevertheless, it remains to be explained how such extremes of congeniality and personal violence can coexist.

Besides the kinship rivalries, another possible explanation lies in the important role which emotional factors play in all aspects of Aboriginal life. Lacking material wealth and rarely abandoning local considerations on behalf of long-term projects, Aboriginal life is concentrated upon interpersonal relationships. Living in open camps encourages a lively involvement in the affairs of others, which enhances the emotional content of their lives. This may make both congenial fellowship and violent argument more likely. Herbert Marcuse once asked me to describe for him the sort of violence common in Aboriginal societies, and I briefly characterized some of the family quarrels, spearings and drunken fights I had witnessed among both remote and town-dwelling Aboriginals. Marcuse insightfully remarked, 'Oh I see, they limit their violence only to personal matters.' That is to say, conquest, domination and institutionalized (i.e., dehumanized) forms of violence are not practiced.

Such interpretive sociology is essentially speculative, however, while in this chapter I am concerned only to identify and present a few of the actual structures of Aboriginal society, social practices which are enduring, mundane, and observable throughout ordinary Aboriginal life. These investigations are concerned with description rather than explanation.

3.0 Consensus

The organizational detail which is productive of unanimity is a vital component of the competent interactional system of ordinary Aboriginal gatherings I am describing. Because there is almost no centralization of political power (other than among men in general) and because it is seldom the case that there is forthright advocacy by individuals of strongly held personal opinions, the production of consensus in Aboriginal society involves a set of practices which are highly diffuse and dependent upon the collaborative activities of the interacting parties. We have just seen how Aboriginal people are essentially passive in relation to decision-making and are attuned to the objectivities which may be generated by the gathering. Yet the group is made up of individual participants, and if we are not to repeat Durkheim's error of mythologizing collective life we need to identify the actual interactive work individuals perform which leads to the production of unanimously accepted objective determinations.

Moerman and Sacks (1974) have argued for the importance of local organizational work in providing for the practical successes of ordinary communication:

> What forms of social organization secure the recurrence of understanding among parties to conversation, the central institution of language use? What forms of social organization get participants to do the work of understanding the talk of others in the very ways and at the very times which they demonstrably do that work?

I am searching for the specific practices which are identifying of ordinary Aboriginal interaction. Sansom (1980: 195) has called a fringe-dwelling Aboriginal community 'a society of jurisdictions of the word' and recognized that such orientation results in the establishment of 'a common public eye' (102). Sansom (1978) has recognized the overriding importance of unanimity in Aboriginal social relations, and he argues that the social analyst must be able to describe how it is related to the specific events of its production: 'Assent has to be created, sustained, and from time to time the grounds for assent must be shifted.' This implies organizational work. The production of consensus is a competent system of organized activities composed of a number of organizational items. Among these organizational items are these:

3.1 Summary accounts.

3.2 Calling for the consensus.
3.3 The serial order of accounts.
3.4 Traditional models.
3.5 Letting-it-pass.

Consensus is not always achieved easily. Because those with the strongest feelings are the least likely to speak up, it can take a great deal of time to lay out the issue of a matter before a group. I have mentioned the role of the simple repetition of summary accounts in producing accord; however, in situations where serious differences exist it may be some time before these discursive processes are initiated. A group of Aboriginals may spend a very long while 'murmuring' in several separate conversations, waiting for a consensus to develop. This may be agonizing for a European, especially if he well knows what differences exist. As an illustration, a meeting of the community was 'called' to take care of an individual's personal grievance. The discussion began, but the person who requested the meeting refused to speak up, not wanting to appear too bold; instead, he waited for the group to initiate the topic. On his behalf, other participants gently moved the conversation closer to the topic of his concern. Only after the group had spoken about the matter for some time did the individual enter the discussion; and what is more, this entrance was by way of the particular objective formulations developed by the group's previous talk.

When the deliberations involve people from different districts, the initial period of superficial talk will be preceded by several minutes of silent waiting: no one wants to be the first to breach the silence because such forwardness may be considered too manipulative. Speakers avoid appearing conspicuous or intent upon a point of view, and those who have programmatic notions are the most vociferous in declaring their equanimity. Meyers (1976: 550) writes, 'Men oratorically belittle their own contributions to discussion and decision and only in private brag about how they "turned" the discussion in their favor.' A frequent interjection after a more lengthy remark is 'This is only my way of thinking,' which is meant to indicate that the speaker has no special interest in influencing public opinion. This is roughly the English equivalent of 'Ngayulu kulira' (cf. p. 15) which means, 'That's what I have to say, now I'm going to sit back and listen to what the group decides.'

It is at this stage that the summary accounts begin to be taken up and circulate about the group, accompanied by a great deal of repetition. The work of the serial order of summary accounts is the chief organizational phenomenon we will examine. Another

Western Desert researcher has observed this work of ordinary Aboriginal deliberation (Bardon 1970: 9): 'The unhurried nature of discussion is obvious; it is important that all grasp what is going on; men delight in going over the same ground again and again until they become familiar with it; the intention seems to be to reach an informal consensus that is a clear cut and irrevocable decision.'

Differences are highly muted. Disharmony impedes the work of accounting, and in such instances repetitive summarization of the most facile aspects of the discussion occurs and fewer matters of substance are breached. The desert Aboriginal people talk of 'speaking correctly,' which means saying what everyone else agrees with. Participants will try to speak only to what has been validated as part of the existing consensus. If a certain congeniality has been established and the opinions are more public than personal, dissenting comments may be raised without harm. But where the differences are serious, the public talk adheres to what is 'correct.' By so doing, one speaks not for oneself alone but on behalf of everyone.

This was clearly illustrated during a series of negotiations over land rights in South Australia with the Minister for Aboriginal Affairs and the South Australian Premier. After a full day of discussions ('sitting down' in Aboriginal style) the Minister remarked that the only Aboriginals making vocal contributions about the importance of land rights were young men. He had expected that the elders, as the chief custodians of the 'Law' (the customary sacred knowledge of the Dreaming) would be the primary persons to express the Aboriginal case. He wanted to know whether they indeed considered land rights to be important. The young men explained to the Minister that the elders could not speak English very well and in any case were too 'ashamed' to speak up before such a large group of government officials. If the young men, who had learned English at mission schools and were more accustomed to interacting with Europeans didn't speak up, then the Aboriginal interests would not be articulated. They told the Minister that no one is allowed to put forward an opinion on an important matter which is not shared by all, particularly when one speaks forcefully. That was 'the Aboriginal way,' he was told. The Aboriginal way is for participants to speak 'as one.' This is not only a tacit policy; it is official ideology which is invoked frequently in Aboriginal discussions.

3.1 Summary accounts

When an Aboriginal completes a turn of talk, it is likely that his turn will be followed by another Aboriginal who will formulate a summary account of what he has said. This account may employ some of the identical words the speaker has used, or it may translate the concepts into a more concise form. A third, and possibly fourth, speaker may take up the account, reducing it to the briefest capsule of its original form. Alternatively, the summary account may become the basis for additions and expansions, which in turn have their summary accounts. It is by this process that Aboriginal people make observable the essential components of a discussion.

Scheler has argued that mental life is not essentially private (1954: 258). Geertz concludes similarly (1973: 360): 'Human thought is consummately social: social in its origins, social in its functions, social in its forms, social in its applications. At base, thinking is a public activity – its natural habitat is the houseyard, the market place, and the town square.' In Aboriginal communities deliberation proceeds publicly by way of accounting practices. Of course, such summary accounting is a part of discourse in any society. Most particularly, the kind of summarization which European speakers undertake after a discussion has been interrupted briefly and is resumed again closely parallels the phenomenon of summary accounting in Aboriginal discourse. But in Aboriginal discourse the accounts are the chief embodiment of the cognitive life of the assembly. The objective life provided for a gathering by the summary accounts is similar to that provided for an audience by the accounts of an auctioneer. The summary accounts constitute a sort of narrative which seems to 'float above' the group, and which orients the mutuality of the group. In making the progress of the discussion available for all, it provides for the group its objective life.

Not only are the developing achievements of an ensemble made publicly available, allowing the participants to move forward in their thinking together, but when the group has secured any substantial conclusion, it is *already* a conclusion which is unanimous. And the matter is not left only to such agreement – when such accounts are ratified the organizational fact that a consensus has been produced is made observable as well. For example, when a summary account had circulated several times without undergoing any changes, one of the participants announced, 'There, we are all speaking as one' (*Kutju nyarangka wangka*). The remark would seem obvious; however, it is a significant part of the important praxis of announcing and making publicly observable all consequential corporate productions.

It is time to turn to some actual occasions of the employment of summary accounts. (In these illustrations an asterisk (*) will appear beside each summary account.)

[This discussion is about choosing the people who will compose the new community work crews, a process which involved my taking down the names of those chosen. Ten people have been chosen at the time the transcript commences, and I have written their names on a chart.]

```
 . . .
```

APx   Hmm.
APy   *And him, that one.*
APz   *He is writing down all the names, the names of those who will work.*
[. . .   38 turns of talk]
*APa   *The names, he is putting down.*
APb   *Perhaps he will put down more people.*
APc   Good idea, Aboriginals.
APd   *Oh.*
*APe   *A list.*
APf   ⌠*[laugh]*
APg   ⌡*Yes.*
*APh   *A list.* Mm ↓ Hm ↑!   (33)

In (34) an Aboriginal elder (APe) who was a representative at a meeting of a national Aboriginal 'congress' reports on the meeting for an Aboriginal settlement:

APe   *Aboriginal people from every homeland came to the meeting. From every settlement they came to sit down . . . From every side they came to listen.*
APa   Good.
APe   *With the white people there, the Aboriginal people came to deliberate as one.* [*deliberate:* nyinantjaku]
APb   Ohh.
*APc   *Nyina kutju.*
      (sat) (one)
      Deliberated as one.
APd   *Nyinantja* one.
      (sat)
      Deliberated as one.
*APf   *That's it, Aboriginal people as one.*
APg   *That's it.*
APh   ⌠*Yes.*

APi ⌊ *Yah!* (34)

[This next discussion is about voting in the upcoming public elections.]

APa   D.A.A. [Department of Aboriginal Affairs] *will come to talk to us.*
APb   *Yes.* [gestural tone of finality]
APc   *They always have a lot to talk about.*
KL   *Yes, so =*
*APd   *= It's like this . . . whole lot. Me, you, and all.*
KL   So maybe we'll sit down next week, and we'll go through the whole list. We should have a big meeting, let everybody know.
APd ⌈ *Yes.*
KL ⌊ *Telling everybody, so* everybody will find out about it.
*APe   *Telling everybody.* (35)

APx   *We're having a* council meeting, *lots of important talk.*
*APy   Meeting council*nga wangkarringkupayi.*
               (+ nominalizer)(talk + future + continuous) (36)

The summary account of illustration (36) is particularly apt because the Aboriginal formulation (future + continuous) of the current event (the meeting) captures perfectly the exhaustion with the seemingly endless ideas and detailed discussions which council meetings usually generate and which fatigue many Aboriginal participants. As is frequently the case, APy's capsule summary is right on the mark.

APa   *Put* [a pension house] *for* Docker River.
APb   *It will be for the* Docker River *area, like that.*
*APc   Docker River *talk!* (37)

EA   I'll ask the Minister for Aboriginal Affairs.
*APa ⌈ *He'll ask him now.*
APb ⌊ *Yes.* (38)

KL   He's trying to bring a little drilling thing.
APa   *Oh yes.*
KL   He might bring up, he doesn't know yet.
*APb   *That fellow doesn't know.* (39)

It might appear than in (38) and (39) the Aboriginal speaker providing the summary account is merely translating the English into the Aboriginal language so that those present who do not speak English may understand it. But it is almost as common for such 'translation' to take place from the Aboriginal language to English, which would indicate that the repetitive account has an organizational purpose other than mere translation. Case (40) is an illustration of Aboriginal discourse which involves such 'translation' into English (line 9):

KL	*I have a small question.* Alright for the construction bloke to *inspect your house?*
APx	*Yes.*
KL	*Good.*
APy	Yeh.
EA	No, no worries?
KL	And, *this, the other house, is it alright to inspect the two of them?*
*APy	Two.
APz	Oh. 10
EA	Yeh, two. **(40)**

Here are some slightly longer illustrations of summary accounts:

KL	*The tree comes from my home country. I know that one.*
APa	*Yes.*
KL	*When I was a child I used to see that tree all the time.*
*APb	*Yes, when he was a child he saw that one all the time.*
KL	Jojoba, *an* Indian *tree.*
APc	Hm.
KL	And you get the seeds.
APa	*Yes.* 10
KL	You crush the seeds and, ohh, lovely oil. Smells wonderful, and put 'im in the hair and everywhere. Put 'im on the face.
APn	[laughs]
KL	And *white people will pay lots of money for these seeds.*
APc	Hm.
APd	*Yes, that's the one.*
APe	*Yes.*
KL	Now this oil is very similar to the oil that they get 20 from whales.
*APe	*White people's country, where Shorty lives.*
APf	*Where is this country?*
APe	*Over that way.* **(41)**

KL   Well, *a little bit more talk about getting some* houses. We've got ten thousand dollars for sheds and houses, mostly for the outstations.

*APx   *For the outstations.*

APy   { Hm.

APz   { *Listen.*

KL   . . . Wherever people stopping, we can put a shed, a closed shed that you can lock 'im, or we can just put up a shade, just a big top, anything you fellows want, but you've got to decide yourselves what it is   10 you want.

*APa   *He says he's going to get some houses.*

. . .

*APb   *For all the outstations.*

*APc   *Houses for all the camps.*

*APd   *Big houses.*

*APe   *Yes.*

*APf   *Yes, for the outstations.*   **(42)**

Case (42) demonstrates the circulation of summary accounts. Ideally, such serial accounting will be able to distill the most concise summation of the topic possible, thus making the group's consensus available for itself in an iconic fashion.

The Aboriginal preference is for summarizing an entire conversation or experience in three or four words, or even less if possible (as in (43)),

. . .

APa   *Good, truly.*

APb   *That way, truly.*

EA   *Like this, does the camp want it this way?*

APc   *Good.*

EA   Well, *the camp should do it this way. The* secretary *will have his work and the* chairman *will have his work. That way a lot of work will be done for every-one who needs it. The* stores *and the* mail *will be taken care of. Everyone will be satisfied.* Well, *when*   10 *the* secretary *is finished with his* work, *he can sit down, and the* chairman *can then do his* work. *What is the camp thinking? If everyone wants it like that,* well, *the camp and the* council *should* back *it* up, *good?* [Pause: 4.0 seconds.] *And they won't take the car aside and run off doing other things. Good?*

*APn   { *Uwa.*

APn   { *Uwa.*

APn   { *Uwa.*

APd	*Uwuaoh!*	20
*APe	*And they won't run off doing other things.*	
*APf	*And they won't run off doing other things.*	
APg	*Uwa, that way.*	
APh	*That's the proper way.*	
APb	*That way, truly.*	
*APi	*Uwa. This, not running off.*	(43)

The single-worded summary of (44) presents an account which encapsulates the essence of KL's utterance and orients the gathering to the topic:

KL	*These whitefellas look after the children. They assist the children.*	
*AP	*Children.*	(44)

Amidst an atmosphere of general sadness, an elderly Aboriginal once commented, 'Sorrowful compassion' (*nyaru*), and by that made publicly available even the interior emotional life of the group. Once I took an elderly Aboriginal to visit the desert country of his birth he had not seen for many years. He was born in a remote part of the desert but had lived in the region of pastoral settlement since he was a middle-aged man. We visited the places at which he had camped as a boy, caves in which he had slept during severe storms, etc. When we were on our way back to the pastoral district, he gazed out at the passing landscape and uttered matter-of-factly, '*Pukurlpa*,' meaning 'contentment.' Meyers (1975: 1975) has referred to the 'seeming zest for the oblique but descriptive reference' which Aboriginal people have. This inclination serves an important organizational function in the production of consensus in ordinary Aboriginal deliberations.

Alongside these succinct accounts are a variety of vocal gestural capabilities which can serve to emphasize a particular reduction of the collective experience and congeal group opinion. Foremost among these is the inhalated expression (cf. section 1.5 above). A summary account which has been uttered on an inhalation (for example, '*That's very sacred, that's where He was speared*') will likely be the ultimate expression of an account. Inhalated comments are almost always accounts which have already won universal acceptance. Although an expression, when inhalated, may borrow from the association of inhalated expressions with universal confirmation and thus win for itself a speedy acceptance it may not have earned otherwise, it is very rare for the semantic content of an inhalated expression not to have already been corroborated. An inhalated utterance is something like the objective ghost of a social gathering.

Finally, here is a more extensive case where a four-word summary account (line 29) synthesizes the essential aspects of the previous multi-party conversation (lines 6, 15 and 17). Such a summary account, while apparently mundane, involves significant synthetic activity and provides the gathering with a corporate version of its conversational work:

APa *And that fellow Peter he's a liar.* He shouldn't do that, you know. Must be listening all the black-fellas. They gonna say.

APb ⌈He got to listen to the council.

APa ⌊Council. Not, not, not come up here for whole lot of talk, this way. People don't like that way, you know.

APn *Yes.*

KL *What?*

APc *Always causing trouble.*   10

APb Should be listening to the council. To the council.

APa He gotta, yeah, he gotta listen, you know. And he gotta tell 'im, 'Me and what's her name 'bin arguin' from this.' He should tell like that, out, you know, straight out talk. That little bit, you know. People not happy about that. That mechanic little bit too rough for you whitefellas.

APb *This is an Aboriginal place.*

KL He, he =

APa = He's a good bloke, waarkin'. Good.

KL He's a good workin' bloke, but but *maybe he*   20
should stay =

APa   = *Yes he should stay,* well he should!

KL Mechanic shop.

APa *Mechanica, he should stay there, that fellow,*
he gotta, talk silly way, you know. Some of the people might go, 'Ohh, that bloke = fuckin'

APb   = rough

APa rough that bloke.

*APb No good, people, *no.*   **(45)**

3.2 Calling for the consensus

When discussion appears to be getting ambiguous and participants are uncertain about what direction an ensemble is taking, someone may call for the consensus. A call for consensus may serve one of several purposes: it may be a request by just one person to be brought up to the present on the gathering's deliberations; it may be a request to clarify a status quo which has become ambiguous; it may reveal a general frustration with the group's inability to cohere about a solution; persons advocating a certain point of view may call for the consensus (in the voice of an unbiased observer) to force a decision to its consummation; or persons in opposition to a seeming course of action may raise a matter for the group's reaffirmation to be sure that the group's will was accurately determined. Calling for consensus has the force of diminishing the influence of individual notions and directs everyone's attention to the corporate life of the group. It helps to bring the collaborative decision to maturity at the same time as celebrating the paramount role of the general will.

Above all, the effect of a call for consensus is to bring a gathering's state of mind about a matter to public view; thus, this organizational item helps to give the participants a corporate handle on their deliberations. The most simple form of calling for the consensus is '*Munta?*' ('So?,' 'What?,' 'Well?,' etc.). It brings forth a reply which is a summary account. But the call may take the form of any interrogative formulation of a potential account. Calls for consensus are illustrated here and are depicted with an asterisk (*):

*APa	*Alright, don't you think?*	
*APb	*It's alright, I suppose we think?*	
APc	*All the old men say it's agreed.*	
APd	*That's just fine.*	**(46)**

*APa	*Maybe we'll let him come,* or *maybe we'll forget about it.*	
APb	*Let him come.*	
*APc	*Let him come, will we?*	
. . .	*Then it's alright so it seems?*	
APe	*Yes.*	
APf	*It's O.K.*	**(47)**

Case (48) is an instance of a call for consensus by two people who favor the decision proposed. Although it may not appear so from the transcript, APb's advocacy is stronger than that of APa. In fact, APa is not really concerned to conclude anything which is beyond the general will. APa's qualification of his advocacy with a call for consensus is not a strategic move but a genuine openness to the group's feelings, whereas APb's equanimity is a public face:

*APa   *Wonderful, this one, don't you think?*

*APb *Do you think it's O.K.? I am ignorant about what to
do. It's up to you, all the people in the camp.*   (48)

In (49) the consensus seems to shift almost mid-stream:

KL   EA *entered without a* permit *to look for minerals.
Without a* permit. *Should we give him to the* police?
APa   *Yes. Yes. We seem to agree.*
APn ⌈ Hm.
APn ⟨ *Yes.*
APn ⌊ *Yes, there he can explain.*
APb   We don't want him.
APc   No, *listen.*
*APd *Oh, you say we should leave it.*
APe   *Yes.*   (49)

APa's response in line 4 is only tentative, oriented toward the
thoughts of the group. It begins to be affirmed in a typical fashion
until APc presents a new perspective. At once, APd repeats APc,
in order to make the new perspective observable, so that the
group can decide what it intends to do.

Case (50) provides another illustration of a conflict of views:

APe   *This is what I am thinking.*
APx   *This one, it is not.*
APy   *This one, it is not.*   (50)

APe's ['e' denotes 'elder'] advocacy is not personal – he is more
or less thinking out loud, according to the common practice of
making possibilities available for the group's work. His comment
was an articulation of what seemed to him to be so for everyone.
He accepted APx's opposition without concern and at once
abandoned his account. Neither is APy's affirmation of APx a
personal opinion or a declaration of support for APx; it is merely
a docile repetition, opening the matter up for consideration by
everyone present. The production of consensus is dependent
upon the public availability of accounts, and calling for the
consensus is one organizational item which facilitates the
generation of those accounts.

3.3 The serial order of accounts

Summary accounts are objectivities produced to handle tests of
general confirmation. Aboriginal speakers do not necessarily
have any personal investment in the accounts they provide and
frequently are quick to abandon them on behalf of the consensus.

This does not mean that strong personal beliefs do not exist. Frequently the unanimity achieved is predicated upon voluntary silence on the part of some participants, as we have seen. Aboriginal etiquette demands that individuals do not go 'against the grain' of public opinion and that propositional content be sacrificed in favor of preserving congenial relations. Sansom (1980: 1962) characterizes persons who go against the resistance of a consensual judgment as 'pushers.' Of course a genuine consensus is more productive of genuine congenial fellowship.

Summary accounts are provisional 'truths' whose force awaits validation by the ensemble. Seldom will Aboriginal people formulate 'either – or' possibilities for themselves. There is no 'or' in the desert Aboriginal language (although syntactic arrangement can produce a silent equivalent), and generally one possibility is developed at a given time. Instead of formulating simultaneous alternatives, Aboriginal interlocutors utilize a serial order of formulation, whereby the single possibility is developed, carrying the consensus along with it as it matures – or else dying for want of ratifiers. Typically, a summary account (denoted abstractly by 'AB') will be repeated, and once it becomes an established acquisition it may serve as the vehicle for an enlargement of the theme. This may be represented diagrammatically as follows:

APa   AB
APb   AB
APc   ABC
APd   BC
APe   BCD
APf   ABCD

The enlarged account will in turn be taken up and circulate in a repetitive format, like an audible equivalent of the wake of a ship. Sansom (1980: 98) has called this a 'round-the-rally exchange of comments.' The repetition of the summary accounts provides the opportunity for additional public tests of the verdict. The group may produce and circulate several formulations about the theme at hand, gradually consolidating the ground won by way of a final summary account which is accepted as the fact of the matter. Preferably, this final account is as concise as possible. If it is not, yet another speaker may provide a formulation which captures the matter more accurately and in a more capsulized form.

If an account wanes, a call for consensus may occur, and a new summary account may be produced, which is then taken up in a serial format. Discussion of a given theme normally will be concluded before another topic is taken up. Aboriginals complain about the complication of discourse which handles too many topics at once, and, in any case, most of the participants will naturally remain oriented to an original topic which is left undetermined. At a pan-tribal meeting, the assembly was discussing the matter of some negotiations about mineral work being carried out in the area, and the young Aboriginal chairman – realizing that it was already past dinnertime and that many of the men had to return to their home districts – changed the topic to that of the land rights in an adjacent State so that such an important matter could be addressed before too many people had departed. The assembly refused to follow his lead. After three turns of talk, two of them the chairman's, the assembly returned to take up in serial fashion the mining matter which continued to occupy their concern.

This serial procedure often sounds like mass confusion to an unskilled listener because there seems to be no control of turns at speaking; anyone may offer a contribution almost at will. There is no governing board or 'chair' to centralize the accounting – the accounts themselves are the only exhibit of the group's progress.

The phenomenon of the seriality of accounts requires its full presentation in extended transcripts, and so I will save the major part of this discussion for the 'Detailed Transcripts' section which follows this enumeration of organizational items; however, there are some briefer examples which illustrate some of the aspects of discourse involved. Case (42) displays the seriality well. Case (51) is a mundane cumulative account of the form A–AB (lines 1 and 2):

APx And *motorcar too.*
APy *Motorcar to take everyone around.*
APz *That would be wonderful.*   (51)

Case (52) illustrates the tentative nature of some formulations. Instead of formulating at the outset a number of options, a single possibility is offered. Subsequent possibilities, presented one at a time, are produced, until one of them catches on in a repetitive manner. It is not inconsequential that the repetition alternates between the English and Aboriginal forms; that is part of the 'of course' tone typical of much Aboriginal confirmation.

KL   [It would be] very good to get [the government
      ministers] to sleep on the ground one night.
APa   *Yes, like that he says!*
KL   We've got sleeping bags.
*APb Three nights?

APc	Naw.
*APb	Months?
APc	*Like that*
*APd	One week *they'll wait there.*
APe	One week.
APf	*One wiki.*
APg	One week.
APh	One week. (52)

The collaborative production of consensus via the seriality of accounts extends to all communicative issues, including closings:

APa	*Yes, that's all.* Finished.
APb	*Fine, we'll get another one.*
APc	*Yes.*
APd	*Good.*
APa	*That's the meeting.*
APe	[whispered] *I agree with what he's been saying*, this old fellow . . .
APf	*Yes, so it will be like that.*
APg	*Yes, that's all. Finished.*
APh	*Finished.* 10
APb	*The meeting is over.*
APg	*Finished, once more.*
APb	*So yes, that's [the] lot.*
APa	*That's all*, that's [the] lot.
APc	*Yes, finished, isn't it?*
APd	All done.
KL	Finished?
APi	*Yes.* (53)

The initial 'finished' in line 1 is only a tentative beginning of an agreement about concluding the assembly, and it is not finally confirmed until nearly everyone present has validated the closure.

3.4 Traditional models

As in any society, there are traditional axioms which are marshalled to assist the adjudication of typical issues. One observer has commented: 'Aboriginal people frequently invoke the use of traditional explanations according to the degree that the stimulus is perceived as being derived from well-established concepts of social action' (Stanton 1976: 16). My concern here is not to enumerate a list of standard regulations but to identify some of the processual features involved in the production of consensus; therefore I will take up two traditional vehicles for conflict-resolution which are highly organizational in character: the 'Old Men' vehicle and the rule that an assembly must speak 'as one' (*wangka kutjungka*). These vehicles provide formats available for use by interacting parties and are useful in helping to preserve the unanimity of a gathering, particularly during controversial moments.

Much has been written in the anthropological literature about the role of the tribal elders in decision-making. The earliest anthropologists described Aboriginal political life as a gerontocracy, but this characterization has been proven to be exaggerated. The area of life over which the elders have absolute control is the custodianship of the Dreaming, the sacred 'Law' from which all Aboriginal existence is thought to emanate. Because much of the political and disciplinary life of Aboriginal society is associated with sacred matters, the old men (*wati yirna*) do indeed have an inordinate amount of power, but they are in no sense a council of chiefs. As the custodians of sacred sites which are the foundation of camp locations, their influence spreads into secular affairs; however, they are more often the emblems of Aboriginal authority than formal leaders. Most of the everyday direction, particularly in these times of European contact, is provided by middle-aged men of the camp. Occasionally a vocal woman, usually middle-aged, may be influential. The elders are used as vehicles for authenticating proposals. They spend more time passively confirming the work of others than generating their own programmatic notions, although when the elders do get together and take up a proposal affecting the secular life of the camp, their word is rarely challenged.

The authority of the elders is an underlying structural item which rationalizes Aboriginal political life and provides social cohesion throughout occasions of decision-making. When old men speak before a gathering, usually (though not always) the rest of the participants will stop to listen. The summary account of an elder is generally accepted as an appropriate kernel for the developing consensus.

But the authority of the old men is more of an institution available for use by everyone than it is a leadership which imposes itself upon others. One of the most frequent applications of the authority of elders in secular matters is by their nephews who want to undertake a course of action which will benefit themselves. In such instances these persons avoid speaking on their own behalves but speak '*for the old man*,' who himself may not have a very great interest in the matter. The old man may accept the burden of carrying such a proposal out of a sense of family obligation but may choose not to speak on the matter. Another use of the institution is to give the tentative verdict of a group its final confirmation by the announcement that it is what the old men desire (cf. case (46)). As community adviser I was frequently asked to do favors for younger people in the guise of helping out one of the old men. Aboriginals are indeed respectful of the elders and expect Europeans to share such respect; but that respect may become an only apparently non-egoistic device for engineering personal aims.

Achieving the status of an elder is not something which is accompanied by any formal title or investment, other than the gradual accumulation of ritual initiations and responsibilities. Besides ritual status, the most obvious mark of a *wati yirna* (old man) is gray hair. Aboriginal men are proud of their gray beards and occasionally point to them as the mark of authority. When the hair of middle-aged men turns gray, they display it conspicuously, letting the gray portions of hair, beards or moustaches grow long. Elder status is something which one accumulates slowly, as those older people pass away and one finds oneself as one of the emblems of tribal unity.

One's status as an elder has also much to do with the respect others have for one's own strength of character. I encountered many old men who were not held in high regard and did not carry the authority of slightly younger men. Such status may also be engineered, by playing a prominent role in the planning of ritual activities and by a certain self-presence; however, it is very poor etiquette to be conspicuous about claiming such status. Of course, the best way to win the status is to have developed some profundity of outlook, but there exist more manipulative ways. One of these is to begin to speak up when conversation has deferred to elders. For example, when outsiders arrive at an Aboriginal community they will be shown the sacred store of ritual objects which the local community have as their private spiritual treasure. On such occasions a formal presentation of the objects will ensue, after which the old men will lead an informal discussion of the significance of some of the objects. These discussions may involve anything from reminiscences to spiritual hermeneutics. Aging men on the verge of becoming elders in their own right may begin to carry out resolute explication of the objects, thereby creating the grounds for their own high status. Courtesy demands that no one interrupt them, which could lead to disharmony, and the visitors – who may not be cognizant of the local status – will not be able to tell the difference. Such work must be subtle and without any obvious egotism. In fact, on the occasions when it is carried out as a deliberate practice, it is usually not out of a desire for personal benefit but out of the wish to increase the standing of the entire familial group the aging Aboriginal represents. The worst censorship which will take place, and only in cases of patent egotism, is that the other Aboriginals will look away, as if embarrassed. Naturally, this response provides powerful constraints against self-assertion (in all realms of Aboriginal life).

The institution of the authority of elders is able to help resolve conflicts which do not even involve them, as all parties to the conflict will defer to the elders instead of insisting upon their own views. This practice serves to keep order in the community. An old man may be merely the convenient vehicle for a solution by interacting parties, as in a case involving a small remote encampment which was given an automobile from royalties on sales of minerals on Aboriginal lands in the Northern Territory. The arrival of the vehicle, which was to assist them in carrying supplies and with medical emergencies, unleashed a terrific rivalry among the younger members of the community, all of whom wanted to do the driving. As the old men did not know how to drive, the competition was left to those younger. After several weeks of growing tension, a fight broke out between two of the would-be drivers, which by that time involved nearly everyone in the camp. One of the antagonists argued that because his father was the senior elder in the camp he had the rights to the vehicle. The other, who was nearly an elder himself, had the support of most of the camp and argued that by virtue of his status the younger antagonist should defer to him. After a long argument, during which I was called in to moderate, all parties agreed that the car properly belonged to the senior elder and that he would decide who would drive the car. The difficulty was that the elder involved had no great interest in drivers or motorcars, so deferring to him was merely deferring to a symbol of the community, without really settling the dispute; however, the immediate crisis was averted. As a traditional mechanism the authority of the old men was available as a resource for resolving disputes and maintaining accord.

The 'wangka kutjungka' (speak 'as one') vehicle has already been referred to. As a procedure it is invoked to defuse any conflict which appears to be becoming overheated. In the example just cited a climax at an early stage was averted by employment of this device, which rules formal argumentation out of order. APb and APc are the son and aging man respectively:

APa   You fellow good driver and *you're* number two.

Well, *let's not cause troubles for the camp.*

APb   No *arkamin.*

APn   No *arkamin.*

APc   *I'm not doing any arguing. I'm sitting down in the camp without any car . . .*

APd   *Like this, talk if you want but don't argue, try not to argue.*   (54)

What is noteworthy here is that the son (APb) invokes the traditional rule against arguments in an attempt to defuse the attack of his antagonist, which he does successfully. As in any society, the rules of discourse are well known and may be exploited by any skillful interlocutor. Skill in Aboriginal interaction, however, involves highly subtle and inconspicuous moves which never formally oppose the will of the community of speakers. In the best of all possible worlds one may be able to use the will of the community and the proscriptions against disruptive interaction in support of one's personal interests.

3.5 *Letting-it-pass* ('Wanti')

As well as avoiding arguments, where possible Aboriginal people avoid interaction which looks as if it will not flow smoothly. They prefer not to be troubled by unpleasant matters and to avoid troubling others. While persons in all societies share such an aspiration, Aboriginal people are more inclined to withdraw from potential troubles than persons in European societies. Aboriginals provide a great deal of space for each other, and this is accomplished in part by not pursuing the detail of every matter which might be a source of differences. The records of the first European settlers in Australia remark about this inclination to avoid invading the space of others. Hunter (1793: 490) comments: 'None of these people have ever been seen to interfere with what did not immediately concern themselves.' One of the common refrains in ordinary Aboriginal interaction is '*wanti,*' which means, 'Leave it.' '*Wanti*' is the Aboriginal equivalent of the American counter-cultural maxim, 'Don't hassle it,' an invocation to let a matter which is best left alone pass without being considered. '*Wanti*' and its equivalents '*Ngula*' ('Leave it for a while') and '*Paluna ngulaku*' ('Later for that') permeate Aboriginal discourse.

While this organizational item may be used with regard to activities which Aboriginals want to avoid, including painful chores, it is most frequently employed in situations which verge upon some sort of disharmony. '*Wanti*' is an indication to others that they are bearing in too closely upon oneself and that they should 'back off' and allow more space. As imposing one's self upon another is a cardinal error in Aboriginal relations, the invocation will bring about immediate capitulation. Persistence in continuing with a topic, once a '*Wanti*' has been invoked is in most cases evidence of poor character. The discrete interlocutor has no choice but to abandon the topic, at least for the time being.

'Leave it' is frequently invoked on behalf of a third person who is known to have strong negative feelings about a topic being raised. It will be invoked to silence a second party who may be unaware of the problem:

APa   Half a day's work *he'll put in*. Half a day's work *done*, four hours; half work, *nothing*, well, too absent *that fellow*.

APb   *Leave it, [speaking] that way will make things go badly*.

APc   Yes, *over there*, maybe there can be a meeting [later].   (55)

APa   *I've been asking for that* [Toyota], *and in vain I've been waiting*.

APb   *We [all] have been asking for* Toyotas.

KL   *Yes, Yes*.

APc   *Later we can ask, leave it for now*.   (56)

In (56) 'Later' was '*Ngula*.' Another variation of letting-it-pass is '*wantiku*,' the future conditional tense of '*wanti*.' The '*-ku*' so removes the matter from discussion that even its rejection is postponed. '*Wantiku*' has the sense of 'It will leave itself, by itself,' thus it removes any personal involvement with the issue. It is the perfect Aboriginal rejection.

Another method of letting-it-pass is to become silent. In discourse nothing is pushed too far. If an Aboriginal person doesn't care to answer something he will simply do nothing and allow silence to overcome the party. Such silence – which provides communicative content without involving self-assertion – is a recommendation that the matter be dropped. If it is continued, then it will be assumed that the matter is very important, and the person who had wanted to 'let it pass' will assess such importance and the possibility that failure to become involved will be an insult to the person raising the topic. It would be a breach of etiquette to continue with a matter which was only of meagre importance. The device of letting-it-pass forecloses much discussion which threatens the solidarity of a gathering of Aboriginals; however, it also imposes limits upon free discourse.

4.0 Anonymity

I have observed that summary accounts are articulated on behalf of the group as a whole and that summary accounting is an organizational item which allows the group to keep track of its progress. Frequently, speakers have no personal interest in the accounts they offer; rather, their contribution is what 'anyone' would have made – they speak as anonymous persons.

The anonymity of Aboriginal discourse is one of its outstanding features, productive of the collective character of Aboriginal interaction. Comments are mostly impersonal; one does not dwell upon his own egoistic interests; the best discourse is that wherein each person can forget himself and instead identify with the emotional life of the group. Discussion can move along very rapidly in a general public tone, but as soon as the topic reveals the personal side of a participant his speaking becomes radically altered, both slower and more cryptic. The anonymous tone of speech is obvious. The summary accounting sounds something like a corner newspaper salesman hawking his papers – there is a public tone to his voice, an 'anyone' quality which depersonalizes both the call and the reception. Garfinkel (1969: Nov. 14) has identified such a tone among people in a public queue who address each other about organizational matters dealing with the line. The tone has a public character, as illustrated in lines 2 and 3 here:

APa	*So, we will go there?*	
*APb	*↑ O.K., don't you all think? ↑*	
*APc	*O.K., we probably think.*	**(57)**

Such anonymity helps to allay direct, oppositional discussions. As participants' personal involvement is not stressed, it becomes less available for altercations. If one has personal interests, one must find an inconspicuous, seemingly anonymous, way of presenting them. Methods of achieving this include pretending that one is speaking on another's behalf, or to suffix one's remarks with 'they said' or 'it is said' (*watjarnu*).

The anonymous character of utterances is evident in the affirmations. 'Yes' is an approval on behalf of everyone, not merely one's personal evaluation. Vocal gestural forms of affirmation, such as 'HmHm,' carry an anonymous tone, something like 'Of course, we all believe that!' It displays the consensus and by that display makes it visible to the group as a whole. Similarly, if there is no consensus, one's remark 'I don't know' or 'I am ignorant' (*Ngayulu ngurrpalu*) does not mean 'I, as a particular person, don't know'; it means 'I don't know what course of action the group wants to take.' '*I don't know*' formulates and displays the fact that the group has not yet come to a consensus; the personal content is negligible.

The format of syntagma reversed in repetition has a similar anonymous character:

Well you, *one way* one way *must speak,*
speak one way that way.   (58)

Because the reversed structure, once commenced, provides the speaker with an obligatory order of expression, in following that order he is able to passively submit to what is being uttered. The effect is that the speaker is not personally involved; he is only saying 'what anyone would say':

. . .

APa   *Ngura kutjarra nyaku nyaangkara.*
      (camp) (two) (will see) (this way)
APb   Mm.
APc   *Nyaangka ngura kutjarra nyaku.*
      (this way) (camp) (two) (will see)
APd   *Uwa, nyaangka.*
      (yes) (this way)   (59)

An easy method for distinguishing anonymous comments from personal ones is to address the person who has just spoken in a personal way and listen to see if his tone changes once the conversation has been personalized. During a community meeting to select a governing board for the remote Aboriginal community at which I was the community adviser, several people were chosen in typical Aboriginal style. At one point I wanted to confirm a specific 'nomination' with a participant who had already been chosen, and in doing so I made the mistake of calling for his personal confirmation (cf. line 35 below). The participant was dumbstruck, could hardly speak and chose to remain silent; another spoke on his behalf, and on behalf of the assembly:

KL   *Who will be* vice-president and secretary?
      Who will be vice-president? *Who will be* secretary?
WP   Jillian *for* secretary.
APn   Naw.
KL   President, *for* Charlie. Must be vice-president and
      secretary *another*.

APn	*Yes.*	
APx	*Another, some girl.*	
APn	*Yes.*	
APa	*For what?*	10
APb	Secretary.	
KL	And vice-president?	
APn	. . .	
APb	Secretary.	
KL	Which one?	
APc	⎰ Simon.	
APd	⎱ Simon.	
KL	Secretary or vice-president?	
APf	Vice-president.	
WP	Vice-president	20
KL	Vice-president. *Truly?*	
APn	⎰ *Yes.*	
APn	⎨ *Yes.*	
APn	⎱ *Yes.*	
APg	*Yes*, Simon.	
APh	Simon Banks.	
APn	. . .	
KL	And might be =	
WP	= Jillian secretary?	
KL	Jillian secretary?	30
WP	Yes.	
APi	*Yes.*	
KL	*Yes?*	
APe	Hmhm.	
KL	Simon? Jillian secretary? *Yes?*	
APn	Yes.	
APg	*That's it.*	
KL	O.K.	
APi	Put 'em all on the paper.	**(60)**

5.0 Turn-taking in Aboriginal discourse

The anonymous nature of talk is reinforced by the structure of turn-taking in Aboriginal discourse. Sacks, Schegloff, Jefferson, Moerman and others have found that turn-taking in ordinary conversation is a function of the collaborative use of means for arriving at who speaks after any current speaker. They have discovered widespread systems of organizing turns of talk in ordinary European conversation. Among their discoveries are the findings that in a massive number of conversations the current speaker has the right to select who speaks next and that the first person to begin speaking has the right to make an utterance after a subsequent person has finished speaking. While Sacks *et al.* have proposed that these systemic features are universal, I would argue that their features are identifying of Western structures of discourse. While they are not altogether absent in a number of non-Western styles of discourse (including that of Australian Aboriginal people), they are not always predominant.

In everyday Aboriginal group discourse, most discussion is not 'paired' the way Sacks *et al.* have described. The serial order of accounting provides the right for anyone to make a contribution. There are social structural features constitutive of who may speak – for example, a person whose country is part of the topic may find it easier to gain the floor, elders generally take precedence over younger participants, and men frequently have priority over women in a large number of mixed settings – but the discussion is not 'paired off' between addressors and addressees. There are no individual rights; speaking rights are corporate. Since one is speaking on behalf of the gathering, there is no 'turn' that one possesses. A speaker addresses his comments to everyone, and anyone may take up the account in a cumulative manner. Turn-taking in Aboriginal community discourse is serial rather than based upon a structure of 'you–me' pairings.

Generally, a gathering will remain with one topic. When a new topic is proposed before a prior topic achieves its consummate objectification, there will normally be a formal announcement of the impending change, such as, 'Here is some talk about another matter' (*wangka kutjupa ngaanya*). Another structural feature affecting the flow of conversation are announcements which refer to the fact that someone has finished speaking – 'That fellow is finished now' – or that someone else is going to begin – 'Listen' (*kulila*). The latter organizational item is usually something uttered on another's behalf. Occasionally an Aboriginal may announce his own intention to speak, but in such instances it is usually an elder or is a sort of apology-in-advance for a comment which is personal in character.

APe *I have something to say about some sacred items.*   (61)

It is noteworthy that persons of European descent who have learned to speak an Aboriginal language employ the announce-ment of one's intention to speak with a frequency and a casual manner foreign to Aboriginal speakers.

EA *Listen, I have something to say . . .*   (62)

Such an announcement is necessary to break the seriality of the talk and reorient the gathering to extensive personal comments. A European-Australian who fails to make the announcement may suffer the inconvenience of being interrupted by Aboriginals who have failed to note the change in organizational structure. European speakers are frequently calling out 'Hold on!' to prevent the rest of the assembly from running off with the floor. Such invocations against being interrupted are not so frequently employed by Aboriginal conversationalists. Clearly, the 'turn' is a more personal possession in European discourse.

The most announcement an Aboriginal is likely to provide is a short introductory syllable or two, such as 'This' (*ngaanya*) or 'Like this' (*alatji*), and frequently a mere cough will suffice. If there is a common rule of turn-taking it would be that one has more right to speak following a member of one's family group than when members of other groups have been speaking. Younger participants may wait until they can ride on the coattails of a close member of kin before making any substantial comments. In another people's homeland it is polite to remain silent until an elder from one's own country speaks, and by so doing provides a less conspicuous point of entry.

When the character of the conversation is public, Aboriginal people do not mind interruptions. 'Interruptions' here is a misnomer because the comments are part of the normal current of discursive activity. Such 'interruptions' are not usually personal matters but are for the purpose of assisting to make the objectivities of the discourse more observable. It would be poor form to interject a personal matter (which would be an interruption), and others would consider such interjection to be egoistic. Meyers writes (1976: 142): 'On public occasions men avoid interrupting each other – lest they cause "embarrassment." This gives discussions the peculiar quality of a series of discrete, disconnected speeches. The desire to avoid the impression of egotism . . .' Meyers's observation here is correct, but he has not examined carefully enough the variety of modes of ordinary Aboriginal conversation. One of the few researchers even to address such an organizational issue, he nevertheless misconceives the organizational detail. Speakers do interrupt – avidly so; his observation is only true of particular types of discourse, i.e., personal. His description – 'a series of discrete, disconnected speeches' – correctly characterizes the anonymous character of the serial order of accounting, but the proscription against interruption does not apply amidst such discourse, even when elders (APe) are speaking (see also Appendix III, Transcript A: lines 7, 54-6 and 179-81):

APa   *Yes.*
APb   *Yes.*
APc   *They will soon be giving us our own land*
      title =
APd   *= Yah!*
APe   *= Those whitefellas will do this =*
APf   *= They've*
      been speaking about our homeland.
APg   Giles Creek =
APh   = Giles Creek.
APi   = Giles Creek.   **(63)**

As we shall discover, the 'disorderly' character of Aboriginal discourse prompted many European observers to remark about it. Aboriginal people have observed the effect their organization of turns of speaking has upon Europeans and have at times attempted to reform their structure during interaction with Europeans the success of which concerned them. When an assembly was planning the correct approach to use while asking the government for a truck, one of the participants offered the advice, 'Can't be talkin' every way at once,' explaining that white people are unable to understand talk which proceeds in such a manner. Nevertheless, it is difficult for Aboriginal people to institute such an organizational metamorphosis; at an important meeting of a pan-tribal council at which a number of government officials were present, the discussion developed according to the competent system of discourse outlined in these pages. The young Aboriginal chairman observed that the Europeans (some of whom spoke the language) were having a difficult time following the group's deliberation. He announced, invoking European rules for a 'proper meeting,'

Kutju-kutju chairmantakutu wangkama.
(one-by-one) (to the chairman) (be talking)
Address your remarks one at a time to the chairman.

His effort was entirely unsuccessful.

Customary Aboriginal regulation of conversation – openings, turns of talk, 'interruptions' and closings – is entirely corporate, and their attention is centered upon the objectivities being produced by the assembly wherein lies the collective character of their life. There are no leaders (including the 'chairman' instituted by European legal and political structures) who convene and direct discussion. Anyone may participate in the direction, but not 'anyone' as an individual personality – 'anyone' as an anonymous member of the gathering. The turn-taking organization of Aboriginal discourse is productive of an anonymous character of speaking. All decisions, propositional or organizational, must be ratified by everyone, and 'anyone' may participate in the ratification. This holds true for conversational closings:

APa   *That's all.* [*It is*] *a great homeland.*
APb   Right, *that's the* meeting, *that's all.*   **(64)**

The findings regarding the collaborative production of congeniality and consensus are summarized in the following table:

1.0   Facilitators.
1.1   'Yes' and its variants.
1.2   'Good' and 'Wonderful.'
1.3   'That's it' and 'That one.'
1.4   Repetition.
1.5   Vocal gesture.

2.0   Congeniality.
2.1   Congenial rhythms.
2.2   Displaying-the-obvious.
2.3   Objectification of discourse.
2.4   Contentious interaction.

3.0   Consensus.
3.1   Summary accounts.
3.2   Calling for the consensus.
3.3   The serial order of accounts.
3.4   Traditional models.
3.5   Letting-it-pass.

4.0   Anonymity.

5.0   Turn-taking.

Some detailed transcripts

With the organizational features of this system productive of congeniality and consensus in hand, we can now turn to an examination of some detailed transcripts and view their operation in actual discourse. I will present four transcripts:

A   Discrete advocacy
B   A consensus
C   Approving the visit to Star Rockhole (I)
D   Approving the visit to Star Rockhole (II)

The first transcript displays the proper format for personally advocating a course of action: profuse self-deprecation and elevating the status of the corporate body. Transcript B displays the production of a consensus where a difference of opinion exists; the outstanding feature here is the number of opportunities which the gathering gives itself for reconsidering their decision. No single individual dominates the decision-making. Transcript C is abstracted from a lengthy deliberation, and it presents further material regarding the work of reconfirming consensual decisions. Finally, Transcript D presents a lengthy discussion which displays in their natural setting the phenomenon of accounting and other organizational items I have identified.

A   Discrete advocacy

While Aboriginal people are basically humble, they are also concerned to display proper humility when engaged in publicly visible activity. Such 'formal humility' is a common phenomenon of large gatherings, where Aboriginals are particularly careful to be discrete and to demonstrate their consideration for the collective will. It is necessary for Aboriginals to receive warrant from the community before undertaking any activity which might have repercussions upon other community members. This requirement is especially important when the activity will lead to an individual's increased reputation. This sometimes places Aboriginal people in a double-bind: they must deal publicly with matters that make their personal selves a common focus or face the criticism of acting to further one's own interests without being concerned for the welfare of the community. It would be best for all honors to be foisted upon oneself unwillingly, but when one finds it necessary to raise such a matter for oneself, it must be done with great delicacy.

In this first transcript, the Aboriginal (APc) requests permission to accept an appointment on the Northern Territory board of tourism. His presentation of this request and supplication to the gathering is a very skillful demonstration of 'formal' humility and provides us with a model of proper Aboriginal interaction at its best. Complete transcripts of the original language of these transcripts, along with a word-by-word translation, are included in Appendix 2. As before, italics indicate that the original text is in the Aboriginal language.

Transcript A: Discrete advocacy
KL   Do you want to send Kurt up there or not?
APa   *Good*, Kurt, *good.*

APb	*Not at all, that's just fine.*
KL	*Yes, fine,* good idea.
APc	Because *they asked me*, and I want to go up for us and all. Show 'em, *show them.*
APn	*Yes.*
APc	Because *they asked me about this one.* Ken *was the one who brought this up.* =
APn	= *Yes.*

10

APn	*Yes.*
APc	*He spoke to me about it. He asked, and I said sure. Because I can't just speak for myself and go. I have to ask the* council first.
APn	*Yes.*
APc	*In this way I came to talk about it, and I'm waiting for what everyone has to say.*
APb	*This one is fine, isn't it?*
APd	This fellow holds many positions. He's clever.
APc	They gotta Adelaide, Sydney, Melbourne.

20

APf	That's right, they must be *doing this for* next year.
APn	*Yes.*
APc	*That one.*
APe	*That's it.*
APc	And Alice Springs, and Darwin. *We'll have a good position.*
APn	Mm.
APn	Yes.
APc	*That one.* For tourists.
APn	*Yes. Yes.*

30

APc	*And they'll give us a lot,* too. *One Aboriginal* from the North. *One was appointed, and I was asked to sit on the board. And I said no, I have to* ask 'em first. I must see the Docker River people first. And he said *alright,* go ahead and *ask* them.
APg	*Alright, then.*
APc	And we can find out, ring 'em up and let 'em know, later on.
APh	*Fine!*
APc	*Maybe you think that is fine? I don't know. It's your community, you have to decide this one.*

40

APn	*Yes.*
APc	*This is for all the Aboriginal people. We might get some money for the community.*
APn	Yes.
APn	Yes.
APc	*This way.*

APn   *Yes.*
APc   *That way.*
APn   *Yes.*   50
APn   *Good.*
APc   *I'll tell them about our needs. I'll ask about getting houses.*
APn   ⎡ *Yes!*
APn   ⎨ *Yes!*
APn   ⎣ *Yes!*
APc   *And we'll have our own money here.*
APn   Mm.
APi   *That's it, wonderful.*
APc   *And the money will come to the Aboriginal people.*   60
APn   *Yes.*
APn   *Yes.*
APj   That's *houses, for the Aboriginal people.*
APc   *Yah, for all the Aboriginal people.*
APn   [inaudible]
APk   *Fine, Shorty* [KL]. *Good.*

APc left it to KL (myself, alias 'Shorty,' as community adviser) to carry the burden of assertiveness regarding the proposal that he accept the appointment. Europeans are frequently utilized as a means of avoiding potentially embarrassing moments of self-assertiveness. In this instance a good slice of the gathering approves the request at once (lines 2-4). But this is only the beginning – not only must unanimous assent be won, the good fellowship of the group must be assured as well as everyone's positive feelings about the verdict. APc makes very clear to all that at no time did he actively seek the appointment. In lines 8-10 and 12 he explains that others had asked him, and that the first he had heard about it was when KL had raised the matter with him. In lines 13-14 and 16 he expresses his absolute dependence upon the desires of the community ('council' is only a euphemism of the community), displaying the proper attitude toward the general will and a deferential equanimity about their ultimate decision. (He displays his propriety further in lines 32-5.)

  At line 18, APb calls for the consensus on APc's behalf. A short discussion ensues, and the group moves toward a more general approval. APc's '*That one*' in line 23 and '*That way*' in line 49 are remarkable for their anonymous character. In the former case, the rhythm of the utterance is fully in step with the remarks of APf, APn and APe which surround it, as if APc prefers to conduct his participation in as indistinguishable a manner as possible. Because the energy carried by the rhythm of APf, APn, and APe's remarks is productive of group solidarity and fellowship, APc's remarks also have the effect of being oriented to the group's collective life. The utterance on line 49 is rendered even more impersonally, with a crispness that blends in easily with the objective character of the group's remarks. APc almost 'disappears' from the discourse.

APg's assent (line 36) displays the looks of a final confirmation. His utterance, '*wartalpi*', is a phrase of confirmation usually employed only after a consensus has been achieved (another example of the use of '*wartalpi*' may be found in illustration (14), p. 39). APh strengthens this confirmation in line 39, and APc now feels it is appropriate to call for the consensus on his own behalf (lines 40-1), but his call emphasizes his equanimity and lack of self-assertiveness. A third and conclusive general approval is offered in lines 45-51. Note that a consistent rhythm has been produced by the gathering: beginning with lines 31-5 a sequence of comment and response develops, with APc providing the utterances and the other participants providing the chorus of approving replies. Thus, lines 34-5/36, 37/39, 40-1/42, 43-4/45, 47/48, 49/50-1, 52/54-6, 57/58-9 and, in a full crescendo, lines 60/61-3 display a rhythmic achievement which in itself is ratifying of the congenial fellowship and the community's decision.

B A consensus

Transcript B is the record of a discussion about a community's response to a written proposal by an acculturated part-European Aboriginal person to pay the community for captured camels (the camels were to be resold in the Middle East). The community had had difficulties with the proposer in the past and was uncertain about what to do. The text (lines 32-3) demonstrates that the source of their problems was this fellow's ability to play upon the sympathy of members of the community in the past. During the discussion APa and other community members try to brace themselves for the eventual encounter with the fellow. Given the unassertiveness of Aboriginal people, it is necessary for them to deliberately 'psyche' themselves up for the negotiations so that they will not be dominated. Excuses are made which will justify in advance the extraordinary assertiveness they anticipate will be required in order not to be taken advantage of. This preparation requires a group effort, both regarding its approval and regarding the generation of the resoluteness of their posture. Because there is some difference in opinion, the matter comes up for approval on five separate occasions (lines 5-10, 38-42, 60-3, 80-3 and 89-92).

Transcript B: A consensus

KL	What shall we say in the telegram?
APa	Hm?
KL	We gotta send him a telegram saying = he should come or he shouldn't come.
APb	= Tell him to come.
APc	*Have him come.*
APd	*Come!*
APa	*Come*, and talk to the people here about this.
KL	*To talk* = about the camels, but he can have them 10 there, not in the camp.
APa	= *to talk.*
APf	*Leave it! Tell him like that.*
KL	Or *we'll talk about it later.*
APg	*Only one person can come.*
APc	*Tell him like that.*
APh	Camel.

[laughter]

APi	*Tell him to come here a while.*
APa	*Perhaps he should come*, but if he gives us trouble, 20 *we'll just forget about it*, and he can go back. *If we* *tell Arthur Little to come*, what is he going to say = This fellow =
APj	= *I say we should forget* *about it.*

['Rush' of talk]

APe₁	*Listen, I want to talk, Arthur and Friday want us to* *bring them camels, and they'll pay us for them.*
APa	*One*, one way. There's too much *talking*; *we have* *to all be* agreed. *The* old men *will have the final say.* 30
APn	Hm.Hm.
APa	If Arthur Little *gives us these* horses, fine, but if he can't pay *us*, then I won't even speak with him. *I'll* *become angry about it.* =
APk	= *Like that you'll tell him.*
APn	= *Yes.*
APa	*And he'll say, 'I'm just* a broke part-Aboriginal, *I* *have to* sell my family,' you know, two thousand *he'll have to pay for each one*, I'm broke too. *Like* *this, I'll tell him.* I'll be firm, *like this I'll be* 40 *speaking*
APe₂	Alright, *what he says is the right way to speak about* *this – with strength.* Aboriginal people. Arthur.
APl	He's a good fellow.

APa	*Ask him*, we might let him come up and talk *with the old men.*
APe$_1$	*Yes.*
APn	⎡ *Truly*
APn	⎨ ( ) come here, *to speak with all of us.*
KL	⎣ Mm-hm.
APe$_1$	*We'll speak strongly.*
APa	We got some of them quiet camels here too.
KL	Mm-hm.
APa	Quiet camels.
KL	We might *get* a couple of the quiet camels *for* Puta-Puta.
APa	*Yes,* we might also get a lot of horses *for* here, *for* the Docker River area.
APm	Areyona also has camels.
APn	Cows too.
APo	*Lots of* camels.
KL	We might get a lot of horses, *maybe.*
APa	*Maybe* we might get some horses.
APp	Lots of *them.*
APa	*Yes.*
KL	Maybe he'll pay some people to get a lot of camels = and you can get your own camels at the same time and use his horses.
APe$_1$	= *For work.*
APn	*Yes.*
APq	*All for the old men.*
APr	*We will do this.*
APs	*Like that.*
APa	If he brings the horses he can take them to Puta-Puta. He can build a *watering-place*, you know, make a *big camp.*
APt	*I'll ask him for lots of meat.*
APn	*Shhhhh.*
APa	*And he can remain there*, he can sit down there because the children might grab the tail. *The children* have never seen a horse before. They might hurt them, and all the camels. *We'll keep all the* horses *over there.*
APn	Mm.
APu	*So it's alright for Arthur Little to come?*
APv	*We'll get a* windmill *for the camp like Areyonga.*
APn	*Just like that we'll have—*
APa	*We'll get a* windmill *for the camp*, alright.
APw	*Yes, that's it.*

50

60

70

80

APa   *Listen, we've been thinking about this for* too long   90
      anyway. *We have no money. The camels will attract*
      tourism. ↑ *Will we let Arthur Little come?* ↑
APc   *Yes.*
APn   *Yes.*
APa   *Yes, we are all speaking the* same way *about this; he*
      should come. He can talk about *it with all the old*
      men. This uninitiated man can come to speak with
      us. Maybe. Maybe, we'll ask him, 'Are you going to
      keep paying us?' You know!
APz   Pay *us for them. Over there* (   ).   100
APn   *Yes.*
APa   Arthur, *Arthur can come,* ↑ *Arthur can come?* ↑
APn ⎰ *Yes.*
APn ⎱ *Yes.*
APa   *Is this what the* meeting *is saying?* Alright, *that's*
      what we're saying.

In formulating the alternatives for the gathering (cf. line 3),
KL faces the double-bind in which Europeans frequently find
themselves. He does not want to put words into the minds of the
Aboriginal people, so he formulates both sides of an issue;
however, Aboriginal discourse normally proceeds by way of one
formulation at a time. In settings where the European is little
known or thought to be unfriendly, the Aboriginal respondents
will frequently assent to the last formulation uttered, or both, in
order to placate the European; this frustrates the neutral
aspirations of European speakers. In this instance, however, the
participants have no apparent difficulty with KL's formulation
and take up the aspect they favor most; note that they do take up
possible solutions one at a time, building upon a core in serial
fashion. The initial approval (lines 5-9) is very tentative – it is
more an attempt to lay out publicly a possible resolution than it is
an actual decision. If it had been ratified more generally, APf
would not have displayed his disapproval of the proposed
solution (line 12). In line 14 KL, wanting to keep open the matter
for discussion and not wanting to appear to take sides, assists APf
in making the rejection of the part-European's visit observable
for all the participants. APg produces a compromise solution
(line 15), and further formulations of approval – though very
reserved – are voiced in lines 19-20. APf is never heard from
again as he does not want to oppose the developing consensus.

A fine illustration of the ability to produce highly capsulized
summary accounts may be found on line 17, where APh's
'Camela' captures the global purport of the deliberation. APj

83

displays the group's failure to reach a consensus (line 24), when he explains that he doesn't know what to think about the matter. All the participants begin to talk at once in a general effort to produce an efficacious summary account, at which time an elder (APe$_1$, line 27) feels it is time to step in and assist in the production of agreement. It takes him several words to win the floor, one of the few self-claiming turns in the transcript; his comments are not personal but for the purpose of providing a summary account which can assist the group to get ahold of the issue. He provides the first concise formulation of the matter (27-8), which serves as the core formulation to which the group addresses itself. APa invokes traditional ideology and reminds the gathering that they must reach a stage where they are able to speak 'as one.'

Here, APa begins to discuss the need for the group to be resolute and unyielding in their discussions with the person proposing the business arrangement. APk summarizes the obvious (line 35), and the group begins to congeal. The elder speaking at line 42 provides a summary account for APa's remarks, and APa proposes approval of the part-European's visit, though he preserves the tentative character of his proposal (i.e. 'might'). His advocacy is in no way personal; rather, he speaks as a sort of moderator. APa's proposal is given stature by including deference to the tribal elders (line 46). Despite his observation that they must be unyielding, his actual utterance –

tjilpi   *turtangka*
(old men) (all + with)

– provides some interesting linguistic evidence of the Aboriginal conception of public negotiation. The '*-ngka*' implies no transitive activity about the projected negotiations; rather, the activity he envisions is a *passive* one, something which happens *to* them all and which is under the influence of the corporate will of the elders. Deliberation best 'rests' with the participants. The second general approval ensues (lines 47-50), and an elder (51) produces a summary account of APa's remarks about the need to be resolute. A number of serial accretions to the collective formulation of the matter are made, regarding camels (lines 52, 54, 55, 59, 61 and 67), horses (57, 62-4 and 63), cows (60), and the establishment of a camp with a water supply (75, 76, 79, 86 and 87). What is significant is not the amplification which occurs but the public character of the men's talk (cf. especially APo and APp, lines 61 and 64).

A third approval (70-4) is validated with reference to the elders (71), and APr (72) repeats the obvious for the group. The latter's formulation is typically objective and anonymous. Discussion then continues in a serial manner. The group has achieved some solidarity, and (buoyed by the energy which such collective 'effervescence' provides) APt abuses his serial slot with a proposal which is quickly deemed too self-serving. After another turn, APu calls for a final consensus (line 85), but the seriality of the developing decision has not run its course and APv, APn and APa pay it no mind and continue to broaden the consensual kernel.

APa makes a final call for the consensus (92), and his way of doing so is remarkable for its impersonality. Almost like a ventriloquist – and in the middle of his own remarks – he raises the volume and pitch of his speech and, sounding like an auctioneer or some other neutral participant, asks ' ↑ Will we let Arthur Little come? ↑ ' All agree, and this agreement is ratified via traditional forms: *'Yes, we are all speaking the* same way *about this'* (line 95), and *'He can talk* about *it with all the old men'* (96). Despite the positive approval, APa calls for a fifth and final reconsideration (line 102; and receives it. In the last line ('Alright *wangkanyi*': 'Alright, it is said') the decision is objectified as the corporate possession of the gathering.

Approving the visit to Star Rockhole

Transcripts C and D include portions of a very lengthy discussion about a proposal to invite a group of government ministers to a highly sacred site in order to be given some instruction on secret matters normally the purview of only initiated men. The elders are worried over the fact that the government has held that the Aboriginal people do not have legal title to the area, and they wish to demonstrate to the government that they are indeed the proper 'owners' of the site. They have argued that once the government leaders witness the sacred 'law' for the site they will be impressed enough to accept the community's demand for proper title. They also consider the merits of securing newspaper and television publicity on the issue, which has already attracted the interest of the national press. All these proposals are very unorthodox and require absolute unanimity before any of them may be carried out. Besides the members of an Aboriginal community, the speakers include myself (KL) and an Anglo-Australian (EA) employed by the Department of Aboriginal Affairs. As nearly the entire discourse is in the Aboriginal language anyway, I have omitted italicization in order to make the text more readable.

Transcript C covers half an hour of conversation and consists of glosses for eight calls for consensus occurring during the discussion. To have displayed the entire transcript would have been too cumbersome for the reader, so I have abbreviated this display of the length of time Aboriginals take to achieve a consensus. Note the number of opportunities they give themselves to reconsider their decision. As the Select Senate Group cited above remarked, Aboriginal people take a great deal of time to reach a final decision, and it is not unusual for them to reverse a previous decision. The key to their decision-making is that a general consensus must be produced without any coercion; not only must the group achieve unanimity, they must be able to reside within that unanimity without misgivings – the consensus must be sustained by congenial fellowship. Following Transcript C the discussion continued for an additional fifty minutes, part of which is presented in extensive detail in Transcript D.

The first five lines of Transcript C displays three calls for consensus and two traditional forms of organizing discourse: that all must speak 'as one' and that the elders' views carry the most weight. The sixth line displays the first summary account of the discussion, which is not a personal account but is rendered anonymously:

Transcript C: Approving the visit to Star Rockhole (I)
APa   What do people think?
. . .
APa   We must all agree.
. . .
APa   Shall we bring them here?
APe_1 The elders think that those fellows should come.
. . .
APb   Like this, is it?
. . .
APp   We are saying that they should visit Star Rockhole.
APy   I don't know what we should do.
. . .
APc   Not in the houses . . . They shouldn't sleep in the settlement.
APn ⌈ Yes.   10
APn ⎨ Yes.
APn ⌊ Yes.
APp   Yes! Now he's speaking correctly.
. . .
APa   Yes, that one. Now is that what we're saying?
APd   Correct.

APe_1	Yes, good.	
APf	Wonderful.	
. . .		
APg	Alright, so it's settled.	
APh	Settled.	
APi	Mmm. We all agree on this one.	20
APe_2	One way. That way: they will enter the sacred area.	
APj	We are all agreed on that.	
APn	Mm.	
APp	One way, this way.	
APn	Finished.	
APn	That one.	
APn	Mm.	
APk	They'll camp at Star Rockhole . . . They'll come to Star Rockhole.	
APe_1	So—	30
APe_2	Alright, to Star Rockhole.	
APe_1	So to that homeland there . . . From the south, from the south, from the south; all the men, all the men, all the men.	
. . .		
APc	Are we all agreed on that one?	
. . .		
APc	So say the old men. They say we should do it.	
APb	Listen.	
. . .		
APa	The Prime Minister.	
APe_3	Or a lot of important leaders will come.	
APl	A lot of important leaders.	40
. . .		
APa	Is this the way we think? We'll also ask the Prime Minister?	
. . .		
APa	Shall we ask them?	
APn	Mm.	
APa	This one, the Prime Minister.	
APm	Bring him, bring him, bring him, bring him.	
APn	Mm.	
. . .		
APo	Ask everybody.	
. . .		
APp	Bring them here, and we'll all stay at the site.	
APe_4	That's it. Wonderful.	50
APq	Good.	
APr	That's what we all say.	

APs   Correct.

APp   They'll stay there . . .

APe_2 This one, this one, this one, this one, this one, this one, this one.

APy's comment (line 7) is an utterance which objectifies the indecision of the group, making observable the fact that the group lacks a consensus. His assertion is not personal. After the fourth and fifth calls for consensus ensue (lines 14 and 18), the gathering begins to find its footing. Note the confirmatory role of the repetition in line 24. The account is summarized in lines 21 and 30, and that summary is capsulized efficaciously by elders at lines 31 and 32. The elder at line 32 embellishes his remarks with a review of the sacred significance of Star Rockhole, which everyone knows anyway but which is appreciated for its affective value. Still another call for consensus occurs at line 35, and validation via ascribing the verdict to the elders is offered in line 36.

A repetition of an elder's comments (line 40) displays-the-obvious for the group and by so doing helps to maintain the consensual flow of the discussion. Two more calls for consensus follow, and a highly typical conclusive confirmation is illustrated in line 46. The emphatic approval ('Bring him, bring him, bring him, bring him') receives its license by the fact that it does indeed embody the general will. The repetition is really an incantation whose rhythm and energy is founded upon the previous discourse. Although the consensus is quite conclusive, there are other matters to be decided, and the group wishes to have several additional looks at its decision.

The summary account at line 48 is more succinct than the English demonstrates. The Aboriginal rendering ('*paratjapira*') is literally 'around + asking' ('*para-*' is similar to the Latin prefix 'circum-'), and in a single word captures the essence of the course of action which has won favor. This determination is reaffirmed in lines 49-54 and is finally awarded with an elder's most eloquent validation at lines 55-6. The elder's utterance embodies the solidarity which the participants have sought throughout the long deliberation. A younger man may not have been so emphatic; however, the elder's comments are strictly impersonal. They make the consensual decision into an absolute objectivity.

Transcript D is the most extensive and complicated illustration we will examine. Despite the agreement reached during the discussion glossed in Transcript C, the unorthodox character of the proposal leads them to reconsider their decision many times, especially beneath the doubt raised by APb. We are preoccupied here with the organizational character of the deliberation, which produces both consensus and congeniality.

Transcript D: Approving the visit to Star Rockhole (II)

APe_1	Leave it, we won't allow any photographs when they visit Star Rockhole.
APb	Because they shouldn't take photos. They shouldn't take photos. No photos for television. We'll leave that one.
APc	Forget about TV coverage.
APd	I've seen television = . . .
APb	= And you can't get them back. Well Perth, Charles Court he can come for himself.	10
APe_1	Right.
APb	So what should we do about this?
APn	. . .
APb	Just this, we'll allow them just to visit themselves.
APf	So we'll let them come?!
APb	We'll allow them just to visit themselves, that's what we're saying.
APf	Yes!
APb	Just that.	20
APg	All the elders will perform a sacred ceremony.
APb	They'll come and learn the sacred truth, that's what we're saying.
APf	Alright, that's what it will be . . . Mm Hm!
APb	This way. Canberra will come, enter the sacred area and receive the Law, and everyone will find out it.
APf	That's what it will be, just that.
APb	The elders are concerned about their sacred Star Rockhole. It's not just rocks there; it's a very sacred place.	30
APg	That's a very sacred place. We've cried for that one.
APn	Goodness yes.
APb	They don't even know the name for that one, Star Rockhole.
APn	They don't know.
APn	We will tell them about Star Rockhole.
APe_2	My goodness, we will give up the secrets of Star Rockhole, and it may lose its power.	40
APf	This! For the Department of Aboriginal Affairs.

	['Rush' of talk]	
APf	Up to there!	
APn	My goodness!	
APf	They'll see that, from that place they'll receive the Law.	
APh	The whitefellows will have to bring the elders meat.	
APi	Blood.	
APe$_2$	. . . that Star Rockhole.	
APn	Yes	50
APj	The spirit of all the Aboriginal people rests there.	
APn	That's it.	
APn	Yes!	
APe$_2$	Alright-alright-alright.	
APn	We agree on this one.	
APn	This one, on this.	
APb	This is what I'm thinking, if we took the big 'bosses' there, we'll teach them the sacred Law, this I'm thinking.	
APn	Where?	60
APb	The Aboriginals should be keeping that place to themselves.	
APf	Yes!	
APb	Like this, I'm thinking. Two ways.	
APn	. . .	
APm	Just like this.	
APo	Just like this.	
APb	They don't want to show the government people all of the important ones.	
APe$_2$	I want to say something about Promontory Point. The elders say that Promontory Point is *very* important, a men-creative center. We need an automobile to take care of the place properly but none has come for us.	70
APb	You want the car.	
APp	Whitefella come away.	
APq	That's very bad.	
APr	Poor fellow, not even one.	
APs	This one here.	
APe$_2$	Yes, mine.	80
APt	All over.	
APb	That's what he means.	
APu	We gotta go all over.	
KL	Mm hm.	
APv	(Just one man.)	
APw	If we bring them to the men's place and put it in the	

	newspapers... it's alright for all to see, or is it no good?	
APb	O.K., then.	
APx	Of course. The whitefellows will go to see it.	
APb	. . . no.	90
APy	Promontory Point.	
APe$_3$	Two. Alright, two places we'll let the white people enter. They'll enter, they'll enter, and the newspapers will report it after we've finished with the ceremonies.	
APn	Mm.	
APe$_3$	This way.	
APn	Yes.	
APe$_3$	This way!	
APn	Mm. Like that.	100
APe$_3$	So that's O.K. is it? So that's O.K., is it? Goodness!	
APn	Yes this! [laughter]	
APn	Yes.	
APz	That one has a lot of sacred ceremonies associated with it.	
APe$_3$	This one.	
APf	Great ones.	
APaa	For this place.	
APn	That's it.	110
APbb	The government people will see this sacred claypan area.	
APn	[laughs]	
APcc	And all the uninitiated people will see it in the newspaper.	
APb	They'll have it in there.	
APe$_4$	So?	
APdd	Everyone will read about it in the newspaper.	
APn	[laughs]	
APe$_4$	So then, we're saying that we'll let them visit Star Rockhole.	120
APee	But it might be dangerous for uninitiated people to be going about there.	
APe$_4$	How will we take them to Star Rockhole. They'll come to visit the sacred ground?	
APf	It's an important place. They'll hear a little of this place's story, my place. We'll give them the sacred Law.	
	[Everyone begins to speak at the same time. Figures refer to the number of people speaking at the same time.]	130

91

1		
1		
1		
3		
3		
3		
2		
1		
2		140
1		
0	[pause: 2.5 seconds]	
APff	That one.	
APgg	The uninitiated people will be seeing this. This they'll be seeing, those uninitiated people.	
EA	. . . TV newsmen here . . . the Prime Minister. Talk about land rights and everything. Well that film will go =	
APe$_3$	= D.A.A. [Department of Aboriginal Affairs]	
APb	Its power will truly spread everywhere.	150
APn	↓ Mmhm. ↑	
APn	Yes.	
APn	↑ Mmhm. ↑	
APb	What we do will be sent out everywhere, and all will see it. Still, all the sacred knowledge will be sent around everywhere.	
APe$_3$	Yes.	
APn	Yes.	
APb	They should go to see this very sacred ceremony but not send out news reports about it. These secrets were handed down in the Dreaming; they're really very sacred those ones. They caused the water to spring forth from the sandhills!	160
APm	Wonderful, maybe.	
APn	Mmm.	
APn	Yes!	
APn	HmHm.	
APn	Good.	
APb	But they'll be seeing a sacred place. We'll be revealing to them that sacred waterhole, Star Rockhole. =	170
APn	= ↑ MmM. ↑	
APb	We will teach them there?	
APn	Yes!	
APn	Yes.	
APn	This one!	

APb	But still, this is very extraordinary. I'm not sure what we should do. It's very unusual. This one I =	
APn	= Ayi! [to dogs]	180
APb	And the government ministers will come. Stop or I'll hit you [to barking dogs]. And the Minister will come.	
APn	Ayi! [to barking dogs]	
APn	Hoo-hoo!	
APb	I'll hit you all! [to dogs]	
APii	Over here. [to dogs]	
APn	Hee-hee.	
APjj	My goodness! That's my grandfather's home.	
APkk	This council meeting is talking about important things.	190
APn	(laughs)	
['Rush' of talk]		
APll	My goodness! = . . .	
APn	= . . . homeland.	
EA	I'll ask the Minister for Aboriginal Affairs.	
APn	Yes.	
APb	He's going to do that.	
APf	Yes!	
APn	Yes.	200
APn	Yes.	
APnn	He will make a report.	
APe$_4$	Yes.	
APn	So—	
APoo	In one month's time.	
APpp	He'll make a report = HmHmm. ↑	
APn	= Oh yes.	
APpp	The old men will tell about this; it's very important.	
APn	Yes.	
EA	Eyi?	210
APe$_3$	How many week before the secretary comes?	
APn	Yes.	
APqq	We'll ask first.	
APe$_3$	Are you going to ask them to get a permit?	
APn	Yes.	
APb	And Ken, you might find out from Darwin, and by that time, alright we'll sit down [to talk].	
APe$_3$	You'll find out from Canberra!	
APb	I know, that's what = . . . they'll be able to see.	
APn	= . . .	220
APe$_3$	And those there.	

APn	Of course.	
APb	If you get an answer from Canberra, then I'll ask my minister friend and Darwin, if it's agreed.	
KL	Yes.	
APb	We'll wait on that one for the time being.	
APn	Yes.	
APb	So that is what we'll say. We'll ask them for = this.	
APn	= This [inhalated]	230
APb	We'll get newspaper coverage for it. They'll come and we'll show them the sacred place.	
APn	Mmm.	
APb	They'll see the ceremony and we'll have a talk when we're finished.	
APe$_3$	They'll see both places there.	
APrr	Mmm.	
APe$_3$	Over there, two places they'll see.	
APrr	Yes, there.	
APe$_3$	. . .	240
APss	We'll sleep out there.	
['Rush' of talk]		
APb	This, and two nights.	
APe$_2$	The northern people will come for this.	
APn	Mmm.	
APn	Yes.	
APtt	Wonderful.	
APe$_3$	Wonderful, perhaps.	
APb	There are still many important things which we shouldn't allow them to find out about.	250
APn	. . .	
APn	Of course.	
APb	We'll tell the white people about the sacred water-hole.	
APuu	We'll bring them and the old men will teach them the sacred Law at the site.	
APf	. . .	
APvv	Over there.	
APf	So we'll reveal the sacred Law for that place?	
APww	We'll all go to the sacred site.	260
APn	Mm.	
APf	HmHm.	
APb	That one.	
APxx	That one . . .	
APyy	. . .	
APn	. . .	

APf	I live at this site, and I'll give them its sacred Law.
APn	Mmmm.
APf	We'll tell them about the sacred ground there,
	about the world-creative essence which rests at Star 270
	Rockhole.
APzz	The sacred beings who are my ancestors rest there.
APe	This man is truly sacred.
APf	Will we have anything in the newspapers?
APaz	You can go and tell everybody, we all agree.
APn	Yes.
APl	So we will go ahead with it?
APb	They all seem to think so.
APl	So we all think it's alright.
['Rush' of talk.]	280
APby	All the elders are saying it's alright.
APcx	That's fine, everyone is saying.
APn	So yah.
APn	Yes.
APn	Yes, fine.
APe_3	I have something to say about some sacred items.
APn	Yes.
APe_3	I have a little of the sacred material for the
	ceremony.
APn	Yes. 290
APn	Yes.
APn	Oh!
APn	MmHm!
APe_3	This material is back at my home camp.
APe_4	Yes.
APn	Yes.
APe_3	Two of them.
APn	↑ Hm Hm. ↑
APe_3	So this is what we have decided.
APn	This one. 300
APn	Yes.
APn	Mm.

The first calls for consensus in this transcript are to be found on lines 13 and 16, and the first summary accounts appear on lines 17-18, 21 and 22. Particular attention must be paid to the format of the accounts, for they have a public character typical of Aboriginal deliberation: '. . . that's what we're saying' (lines 17-18 and 22-3) speaks on behalf of the objective achievements of the discussion, not on behalf of individual points of view; the orientation is collective. This is equally true for APg's comment on line 21; the public character of his comment is evident in the repetitive structure of his utterance, which translated literally means, 'Ceremony, ceremony, all the elders.' The account has its power as an objective facticity – it provides the gathering with a conclusive summary of its deliberative accomplishment. The concise and poetic form of the utterance is typical of Aboriginal summary accounts. APf repeats-the-obvious at line 24, which reaffirms the objective character of the account.

The basic account consists of these components – the visit to Star Rockhole in order to make a request for land title (I will call this component 'A') and the revelation of a sacred ceremony so that the government leaders will learn the sacred 'Law' and recognize that the Aboriginals are the proper owners of the place ('B'). In order to facilitate our monitoring of the serial development of the account and its approval, I provide here an abstract rendering of the discourse from lines 15 through 142. 'C' here stands for the topic of the spiritual importance or essence of the site; 'D' refers to the proper presentation of fresh meat which traditionally precedes the revelation of sacred lore; and 'E' refers to the topic of newspaper reportage of the entire affair. This abstracted rendition allows us to see readily the evolution of the discussion:

line			
	15: A		81: E
	16: A		83: E
	17: A		86: E
	21: B		92: ABE
	22: B		105: BC
	29-31: AC		108: C
	32: C		111: A
	45-6: AB		114: E
	47: D		116: E
	49: ABD		118: E
	51: C		120: A
	54-6: ABCD		124: AB
	57-9: AB		126: BC
	71: C		144: ABC

Through the discussion, the participants frequently return to accounts of topics which have already achieved consensual approval. This is for several reasons. First, the only public access the gathering has to their previous achievements are the capsulized summary accounts themselves; therefore, they need to be reiterated in order to preserve them as accomplishments-in-hand. Secondly, when during the course of the serial extension of the consensus the discussion begins to enter uncertain territory, reiteration of the previously won consensus will assist the group in maintaining their collective outlook. Third, further repetitions of consensus always provide additional opportunities to correct a decision if it inaccurately reflected the true consensual feelings of the group.

The first commanding demonstration of consensus appears on line 54, with the elder's remark, which has its objective character in its repetitiveness. A difference of opinion at lines 61 and 64 makes necessary a great deal of the succeeding discursive work and is largely responsible for the length of the discussion. The opposition is not strong and is formulated as 'just another' way to look at the question; that is, the opposing position is not bluntly presented but is contributed from the perspective of the outlook of the entire ensemble. The summary account by the elder at line 92 is fairly conclusive; it is more strongly spoken for at line 100 than line 92, after it has received some confirmation, yet the elder carefully presents his account again to the gathering at line 102. The public character of his speech is evident in his tone, which is similar to that of an auctioneer who is completing the bidding on an item ('Going once, going twice . . .'). The elder's remarks (literally, 'That is good? So that is good? My goodness!') are attentive to the corporate will, and his previous formulations are approved.

The anonymous character of APb's remarks (line 116), as he summarizes he previous speaker, well displays the way such a summary account makes objectively available the previous remarks so that they may be observed readily by everyone present. The remarks of the elder speaking at lines 124-5 also have the public character which is identifying of Aboriginal discourse. After everyone speaks at once, amidst tremendous convivial energy APgg (line 144) provides the perfect Aboriginal summary formulation. Not only does the rhythm of the speech – the intensity succeeded by a moment of pause – lend force to APgg's comment, but his utterance has the format of reversed syntagma which is the penultimate conclusive account of Aboriginal discourse:

Nyanga tjitji paluru nyakupayi. Turta nyakupayi tjitjiku.
(this) (children) (they) (are seeing) (all) (are seeing) (children)

('Children' here refers to those who have not yet received the initiations which are the mark of manhood.)

After this, the participants begin to gloat about having produced a verdict and, along with it, congenial fellowship (cf. lines 164-8 and 172). At line 173 there is a repeat call for consensus regarding component B (revealing the 'Law'), which it receives (174-6). APb is still not quite happy with the result (177), and backtracks from B to the ratification of component A (that the government ministers will come) at line 181, but his reservation is drowned out by the barking dogs, and he decides that it is unwise to raise it again amidst such general consensus regarding ABCD. The Department of Aboriginal Affairs representative offers to ask the Minister for Aboriginal Affairs on the men's behalf (196), and following him (197) there is an excellent illustration of displaying-the-obvious: APb's 'He's going to do that' has its role not as the conveyor of information (the information it contains is already obvious) but in keeping before the group's common sight EA's declaration. APb's summary lays the declaration before the group just like a lay-up in basketball, and everyone has an opportunity to concur with it. APnn quickly duplicates the account (202), and so does APpp (206), and it is approved. The salient feature of APnn and APpp's remarks is their public character. They are not their personal remarks; nor are they the calculated presentations of matters for consensus: they are the unreflected, public, anonymously-rendered summary accounts which are produced as part of the basic and general social praxis of the desert Aboriginal people. Keeping the consensus publicly visible assures the success of the consensus, and it is something which everyone participates in spontaneously.

All aspects of the consensus are resummarized in line 234 and validated by an elder according to the reversed syntagma format in lines 236 and 238. Some other mechanical matters are raised, but a final call for consensus by APf occurs at line 259, which it receives (260-4), and APf (one of the main owners of the sacred site involved) capsulizes the consensus (line 269). This in turn receives its final ratification via the validation that 'all' are in agreement (277, 278 and 282) and the validation that the elders approve of it (281). The remainder of the discussion is pure congenial fellowship, and some more mechanical matters are taken up. The transcript concludes with a clear display of the gathering's congenial agreement:

APn ↑ Hm Hm! ↑
APe₃ So this is what we have decided.
APn This one.
APn Yes.
APn Mm.

There are a few other items of note in the transcript. A demonstration of the organizational item 'Leave it' (*Wanti*) may be found on lines 1, 4 and 6. A lack of respect for 'turns' is evident in the way participants interrupt with extraneous remarks at line 7 and lines 70-4. The interruption in lines 211-13 is positive proof that even elders do not hold absolute rights to a turn of talk. The interjection in lines 70-4, fairly extensive, is that of a senile elder whose remarks are readily tolerated by the gathering. Aboriginal interlocutors do not enforce rigid limitations upon participation. In fact, the elder's remarks are provided with a typical summary account in line 75. It is difficult to interrogate the transcript (which, after all, is only a docile record of live discourse) for phenomena indicative of congenial fellowship; nevertheless, the dénouement of the elder's extraneous contribution – lines 75-80 – displays the congenial character of Aboriginal fellowship well. And equally illustrative of the congenial character of the discourse is the spontaneous and abundant laughter about the commotion created by the barking dogs – despite the extreme seriousness of the topics under discussion (nothing could be more grave than exposing the secret and sacred truths of one of their most important religious sites). Such congeniality is predicated upon the production of agreement without argument or acrimony. The public character of remarks minimizes potential personal antagonisms and maintains the social cohesiveness of the assembly. These, then, are some of the components of the collaborative Aboriginal praxis which is productive of congeniality and consensus in a vast number of interactional settings.

3   Consensus and society

The study of ordinary interaction

The competent system of organizational items that is productive of congeniality and consensus is only one of a number of competent systems of interaction which are found in desert Aboriginal society. Other systems include interfamilial controversy, the diatribe, and a number of other highly formalized interactional systems. There are also more personalized varieties of discourse in ordinary conversations. The system I have investigated was chosen because it is exemplary of much that is distinctive about Aboriginal social life.

I have remarked that, despite the collaborative efforts to produce congenial fellowship, Aboriginal social life is not without its share of arguments and violence, and I have attributed some of the violence to disputes which rage between the members of rival families. Since traditionally-oriented Aboriginal people have been living in large settlements constructed by missionaries and by the government, inter-familial rivalries, based largely upon country affiliations, have probably become a more frequent source of everyday conflict in desert Aboriginal societies. In pre-contact times individual families lived further apart from each other and had greater independence than today. They engaged in physical conflicts (well recorded by the early observers) only when proximity and material abundance permitted. Today, dozens of individual families may live alongside each other in a central settlement, and certain political adjustments have been necessary. In a vast number of interactional settings, there is an undercurrent of family and 'country' alliances which transcend many of the mundane relationships which may have developed among the settlement residents. Once one member of a family group commences a quarrel with someone from a rival family or country group, the ill-will is likely to percolate through the membership of both families. I will not display illustrations of such interaction but only comment that the participants are remarkably deaf to reason with regard to the local detail of any interaction and easily find grounds for becoming contrary. These interfamilial conflicts have their own dynamic character, rooted frequently in rivalries which predate Aboriginal contact with Europeans.

Perhaps the most interesting system of non-congenial interaction is the diatribe, or what Sansom has called 'proclaiming' (1980: 89ff.). While normally it is beyond the bounds of acceptability to criticize others publicly or to assert one's self too vigorously, there is an extraordinary interactional method by which one completely loses one's head and rails against the world. The critical characteristics here are that one must exceed the point where one appears to have control over what one is saying and that complaints voiced are in fact ranted and raved to the world at large, a sort of public proclamation of general strife and not only grievances against a single individual. Grievances against others are permitted within the diatribe, but they must be addressed to the group and not at the particular person involved (at least if a spearing is to be avoided). In fact, one is almost oblivious of the audience as well, having the appearance of being entirely absorbed in one's own troubles. The diatribe is high theater, and it employs remarkable rhythmic patterning and oratory which finds much of its energy in its abandonment to its repetitive structures. Until I discovered the propriety of this interactional format I had been unable to voice any of my personal frustrations about problems or individuals (over the years there had been some occasions for complaint); however, once I had developed the capacity to speak the language fluently, I was permitted (at least on two occasions) to voice my complaints by way of the diatribe, and my complaints were considered fairly by the community. In fact, being able to participate in normal Aboriginal systems of discourse was very important in establishing for myself an unremarkable presence in the community. I will not bother to provide a popular psychoanalytic interpretation of the diatribe except to observe that it does serve a useful purpose in everyday Aboriginal society as an outlet for grievances.

A slight variant of the diatribe is what Tonkinson has called 'aggressive sulking' (1978: 122), according to which a person becomes 'very quiet' (Sansom 1980: 212). Here, the person does not speak aloud (frequently for lack of a sympathetic audience) but retreats into silence and angry stares. His or her aim is to draw upon the community inclination to 'feel sorry' for others and to avoid damaging the feelings of other persons. The tactic is usually quite successful. The community 'chairman' discussed above (p. 18) succeeded in turning around his impending dismissal through such aggressive sulking. It really amounts to exploitation of the Aboriginal people's sensitivity to the emotional life of others.

Lest the reader consider Aboriginal society a throwback to an immature inability to control oneself, it should be observed that because Aboriginal people live in outdoor camps their emotional lives are displayed for all to witness; Europeans have the luxury (or misfortune) to suffer their indiscretions in the privacy of their houses and may easily delude themselves that their society is filled exclusively with civilized decorum. Surely the analysis already presented has demonstrated that patience and self-control are skills highly developed in Aboriginal persons; nevertheless, a variety of customary formats are available to members of Aboriginal communities for their less moderate moments.

The number of social encounters which are highly ritualized is high. Interaction within a religious ceremony, formal visitations to distant camps (particularly if one is 'carrying the "Law"') and certain secular relationships based upon marriage obligations provide strict programs for interaction. Descriptions of such systems are easily found in the anthropological literature.

A highly formalized interactional system which closely approximates the system productive of congeniality and consensus is that of the Morning Discourse, described at the outset. Some of the organizational features it shares with the consensual system I have analyzed include the employment of utterances which have the character of formal announcements, a serial development of topic and judgments, and participant orientation to the objective character of the talk.

It is probably apparent to the reader that the system of interaction described in detail in this investigation includes structural features which exist elsewhere in the world. The organizational items productive of congenial fellowship are not altogether unknown in European society. The vital collective life of Western societies which is productive of decisions does not share the consensual and congenial aims of ordinary Aboriginal society, although the social life of some American Indian, Southeast Asian and African societies may give a similar privileged place to such interactional structures. The system of interaction I have discovered and elucidated shares components with typical modes of ordinary interaction found in a number of non-Western societies and also in some subcultural (and counter-cultural) groups in the West.

A colleague (Michael Lynch) has speculated whether the structure of Aboriginal interaction described here in detail could produce congenial and consensual relations in a European society if it were followed as a manual of procedures. It would be an interesting experiment, and I believe that the results would be positive. The important thing to realize is that the structure of which I am speaking here consists of actual practices and so has its 'thing'-like character not as the anthropomorphization of theoretical perspectives but as real activities which are performed in the world. A comparison of these practices with similar ones found in other societies will be of assistance in elucidating this factical character of these interactional practices.

The Kalahari Bushmen share a number of features which are identifying of Australian Aboriginal sociability. According to Marshall (1976) the !Kung Bushmen are very loquacious and allow anyone who wishes to say something to join in the conversation (353). Their ordinary conversation is very animated and full of expression, and members of an assembly frequently repeat utterances several times. Group participation in monitoring the talk is also assisted by facilitators for congeniality and consensus similar to those I have examined above:

> While a person speaks, the listeners are vibrant in response, repeating the phrases and interposing a contrapuntal 'eh.' 'Yesterday,' 'eh,' 'at Deborage,' 'eh,' 'I saw old/'Xashe.' 'You saw old/'Xashe?' 'Eh, eh.' 'He said that he had seen the great python under the bank.' 'EH!' 'The python!' 'He wants us,' 'eh, eh, eh,' 'To help him catch it.' The 'ehs' overlap and coincide with the phrase, and people so often talk at once that one wonders how anyone knows what the speaker has said. (352)

The similarities with the description of Aboriginal discourse are obvious, and no doubt these organizational items are productive of congeniality and consensus for the !Kung. The !Kung share other characteristics with the Aboriginals, such as not attributing status to the accumulation of material goods and general sharing of food and possessions, and they also place a great importance upon preserving harmony in ordinary relationships. Marshall implies that this is in part due to the ferocity of the fights which do take place, a speculation we have considered in the Aboriginal case:

> The !Kung fear fighting with a conscious and active fear. They

103

speak about it often. Any expression of discord ('bad words') makes them uneasy. Their desire to avoid both hostility and rejection leads them to conform in high degree to the unspoken social laws. I think that most !Kung cannot bear the sense of rejection that even mild disapproval makes them feel. If they do deviate, they usually yield readily to expressed group opinion and reform their ways. They also conform to certain specific useful customs that are instruments for avoiding discord.

There are close parallels with the sociability of Southwest American Indian groups, particularly regarding the phenomenon of minimizing one's self-importance. I have witnessed a Navajo elder who spoke extemporaneously before an urban audience for twenty minutes (in his native language, pausing for English translation) without looking at the audience even once. Basso (1979) tells us that the Apaches do not like to be addressed directly by strangers and consider the discourse of Anglo-Americans extremely blunt and unduly harsh (62). Basso examines the joking behavior of the Apache and records an Apache imitation of an Anglo-American ' "Sure it's my Indian friend, L. Pretty good alright." [J. slaps L. on the shoulder and, looking at him directly in the eye, seizes his hand and pumps it wildly up and down]' (46). The Apache make the same criticism I reported above, that white people are too aggressive and argumentative in their speech (55).

Like Aboriginal people, the Apache wish to remain inconspicuous in group settings. Basso describes the Apache displeasure with the forward character of Anglo-American-initiated discourse:

> This can be a source of discomfort because it means that one has been the subject of a close but covert examination. . . As a result, the individual is forced to take notice of himself and is made to wonder if he 'stands out' [-naijaa?], a form of self-consciousness which Apaches are keen to avoid. By comparison, Anglo-Americans do not seem to mind standing out, or causing others to stand out . . . or to be regarded as separate and distinct from other people. (54)

Basso places importance upon the Apache's 'feeling good' (32-3), a condition which he says is stimulated by the lively company of other people and small amounts of alcohol, neither unusual in Aboriginal society.

Gossen (1974) analyzes the speech of the Chamula and uncovers three major forms of discourse strikingly like the

Aboriginal formats I have examined. The three forms are 'ordinary language,' 'speech for people whose hearts are heated' and 'pure speech' (i.e., song, prayer, ritual narratives, etc.). The 'speech for people whose hearts are heated' (*k'op sventa*) is recognized as a separate system of discourse and includes elevated and excited speech as well as angry, emotional address and oratory. It is marked by an increased fixity of form, repetition and parallelism, a degree of verbatim repetition of words, phrases and metaphors which are idiosyncratic, unfixed and relatively unconcerned with performance or the audience's experience (23-4). What Gossen seems to have described is the diatribe, which for the Aboriginals is a socially approved form of publicly voicing complaints; it is unfortunate that Gossen does not mention what relationship *k'op sventa* has with Chamula self-perception or with the interactional practices coincident with 'ordinary speech.'

Not only is it the case that organizational items which compose the competent system for producing congeniality and consensus are part of the interactional practices of other societies, this system is not the only system productive of consensus. Read (1959) describes the organization of consensus in New Guinean society. Like Aboriginal society, Niuginian society is egalitarian. Each participant has an equal opportunity to become influential, and persons who have won some reputation must recognize the rights of others to achieve parity. Members share communicative competence equally and must operate within a system of reciprocal expectations. An essential feature of Niuginian ordinary interaction is that authority is achieved rather than ascribed and, in the absence of political institutions, the consensus is maintained largely through self-regulation.

The similarities end there, however, for authority is usually won through a forceful presentation of self and an aggressive pressing of one's will upon the collective body. The consensus is achieved by way of a locally produced, ephemeral structure of domination and submission; thus, aggressiveness is perceived as strength, and unassertiveness as weakness: 'A man who seeks influence . . . will behave assertively and with swagger. He will exhibit a strong awareness of his individuality, a sense of self-importance' (433). Read's study demonstrates that there are other competent systems capable of producing consensus besides that of the Australian Aboriginal people.

It is important to be mindful of the fact that the particular structures of ordinary Aboriginal interaction I have described are very much the product of my own embeddedness in the perspectives of European sociability. What struck me as note-

105

worthy about Aboriginal interaction was founded deeply upon my experience of human interaction in the modern West; thus, my analysis is not 'pure' description. A Japanese sociologist, for example, may not have been impressed with the novelty of some of the practices I observed, or alternatively, she may have been capable of elucidating them in greater detail, having shared some similar practices. The claim that a description of interactional praxis could be 'pure' and objective is *a priori* impossible. As Gadamer has commented (1975: 358): 'To try to eliminate one's own concepts in interpretation is not only impossible but manifestly absurd.' Western sociology is condemned to viewing the interactional practices of other peoples through the window of its own perspectives. While one can limit the distortion through a frank recognition of the difficulties involved, the worst limitations are those which the analyst never discovers and yet which render him blind to the most strange yet fundamental practices of the people he is observing.

I selected the practices I considered to be distinctive of Aboriginal people by assessing the gap between them and the ordinary European praxis I possessed. I treated the interactive adjustments and work I had to perform in order to get along successfully in Aboriginal gatherings as indicative of what could be identifying about the Aboriginal social praxis involved. That is to say, I was capable of understanding and describing the practices involved because I had to perform them as practical, everyday concerns in order to function adequately as an intimate European resident in Aboriginal society. I sought, so far as I was capable, to make my behavior as unremarkable as possible. Success in this endeavor was indicated by my being able to participate in ordinary affairs without receiving special attention, curious examination or deference of any kind. Being interrupted or being able to perform typical Aboriginal speech acts (such as inhalated speech, self-deprecation, vocal facilitators and even diatribe) without raising curiosity were signs that I had succeeded in mastering some of the practices identifying of Aboriginal interaction. There is a rule of thumb in ethnomethodological research known as the unique adequacy requirement (Garfinkel 1975: June 30; 1980: Jan. 9). This methodological proscription against pseudo-objectivity claims that the best way to be certain of the adequacy of one's descriptions of interactional practices is for the researcher to perform those practices in their infinite practical detail. While I would not assert this methodological proce-dure as an absolute epistemological requirement for all sociology, it is the most adequate method for uncovering local practices that I know of and its heuristic potentialities are extensive.

The practices I have examined here were all practices that I discovered by having to perform them during the two years of my fieldwork in the Australian desert. My method of inquiry was to be as inconspicuous as possible and to seek a practical role in the community which was helpful to the welfare of the people and which they defined for me. Although the people knew I was a sociologist and had even extracted a formal promise from me that I would not make available to anyone sacred details of their ceremonial life (a promise I have honored), they were not aware of the nature or seriousness of my research interests in their secular relations. In this way my presence became as mundane as it was possible to achieve. At no time did I administer prepared sets of questions, and while I sometimes steered a conversation in a direction which interested me, usually I deliberately waited for what direction the people took themselves. My interest was not in content as much as in process. For this reason I believe that the phenomena I have discovered are *natural* phenomena, spontaneous and unelicited displays of Aboriginal social activity. A combination of impassivity, openness and time was the best strategy for uncovering the practices of their ordinary interaction.

Consensus and society

Simmel understood well the operation of congeniality in ordinary fellowship. Unlike Durkheim, Simmel searched for the source of collective feelings not in Society as an abstraction but in the actual practices of human gatherings in all settings:

> To be sure, it is for the sake of special needs and interests that men unite in economic associations or blood fraternities, in cult societies or robber bands. But above and beyond their special content, all these associations are accompanied by a feeling for, by a satisfaction in, the very fact that one is associated with others and that the solitariness of the individual is resolved into togetherness, a union with others. . . . typically there is involved in all effective motives for association a feeling of the worth of association as such, a drive which presses toward this form of existence and often only later calls forth that objective content which carries the particular association along. (1971: 128)

Simmel also recognized the direct relationship which exists between sociability and self-assertiveness (or, in its negative aspect, self-deprecation). He argued that where value is placed upon congenial relations among fellows, participants will tend to

107

minimize the importance of personal status, material wealth and personality. This is certainly true for the Australian Aboriginals.

> The personal traits of amiability, breeding, cordiality and attractiveness of all kinds determine the character of purely sociable association. But precisely because all is oriented about them, the personalities must not emphasize themselves too individually. Where real interests, co-operating or clashing, determine the social form, they provide of themselves that the individual shall not present his peculiarities and individuality with too much abandon and aggressiveness. (1971: 130)

It is obvious here that Simmel recognized sociability to be a social state (elsewhere he calls it an 'empire') which is produced by people in actual settings. Durkheim, on the other hand, presents a much more abstract version of collective life: 'So it is society in the foreground of every consciousness; it dominates and directs all conduct' (1915: 390). It is the moral authority of Society which founds the solidarity of collective feelings: 'In fact [religious forces] are only collective forms hypostatized, that is to say, moral forces; they are made up of ideas and sentiments awakened in us by the spectacle of society' (362). Durkheim addresses himself to the production of collective feelings by actual people when he takes up the ceremonial life of the religious cult, but once the cult has produced Society as the hypostatized collective form, it seems to dictate the character of the moral life of the people; that is, while Durkheim has located a phenomenon of great importance he recognizes the productive role of Aboriginal people only when they are engaging in religious activities and misses entirely the ordinary social phenomena which are productive of collective sentiments:

> So the first effect [of religious ceremonies] is to bring individuals together, to multiply the relations between them and to make them more intimate with one another. By this very fact, the contents of their consciousness is changed. On ordinary days it is utilitarian and individual avocations which take the greater part of the attention. (389-90)

But how could Durkheim have been aware of the collective sentiments which are produced in ordinary Aboriginal social life when he never visited Australia and had to rely upon ethnographers whose investigations were almost exclusively preoccupied with the sacred cults?

Durkheim was forced to invent a scenario where religious activity is necessary from time to time in order to renew the vigor of the moral force of Society, which is then able to endure through the secular period which follows. The gradual abatement of this collective force eventually makes necessary additional cult ceremonies: 'The real reason for the existence of the cults . . . is in the moral regeneration which these acts aid in bringing about . . . social sentiments live on their past, and consequently they would be used up in the course of time' (388-9). This economy of moral force is unlikely, or at least is not demonstrated by anything other than theoretical speculation. Durkheim relies upon the existence of an *a priori* Society in order to prove that such an economy operates. If the emotional energy of a community is to be transferred to symbolic activities which have a transcendental life, then we will need a more precise description of that transfer and also more detail about the functioning of such symbolic orders in the mundane social life of Aboriginals. While I would not deny that notions of Society (or of sacred 'Law' in the Aboriginal case) perpetuated in an abstract sense by members of a society have important moral functions, what is most productive of moral authority and collective sentiments are actual people. The macrosociological phenomena which Durkheim sees in the collective life of the Australian Aboriginals consist of active practices which have their only existence in the local life of the people, both sacred and secular. The joy and confidence which Durkheim finds are produced by their positive rites (434) are also produced by the competent system of ordinary interaction I have examined. Durkheim is not entirely unaware of this shortcoming and presents examples of collective activity from the mundane life of Western societies (which appear to have 'evolved' beyond the stage of primitive religious cults), but he fails to present a concrete picture of social sentiments in the mundane life of Aboriginal people:

> Every feast, even when it has purely lay origins, has certain characteristics of the religious ceremony, for in every case its effect is to bring men together, to put the masses into movement and thus to excite a state of effervescence. (427-8)

Durkheim is fond of speaking of this 'effervescence' (405, 428, 441) which energizes a community and renews their moral unity, but in desert Aboriginal society frequently the production of congenial fellowship is consummated not in an effervescence but in a collective silence which makes further discussion excessive. It is experienced as a sort of quiet bath in the fellow-feeling of the moment. Durkheim was never present to hear this silence and so was not able to consider its importance. It may be that we have located a silence which is the microsociological basis of its own macrosociological presence. It is not Society which produces the harmony here but the people themselves. Durkheim's sociology errs in being almost exclusively preoccupied with macrosociological phenomena. The skills and fascination which Aboriginal people have for an immediate social creativity which is productive of harmonious collective sentiments are evidence enough that we cannot overlook the microsociological praxis of Aboriginal people when we are studying their collective life.

Durkheim considers the religious life of Aboriginal people to be 'elementary,' and his sociology presumes a social evolutionary perspective, the Australian Aboriginal people being one of the early forms of human society. In his study of the Australian Aboriginals, Maddock (1975) discusses Kroeber's views on the progress of civilization. Kroeber located four objective measures of the steady progress of human societies: increasing size, the progressive reduction of superstitious beliefs, a decrease of anatomically oriented cults (e.g. blood-letting), and increasing technology (179-80). Maddock argues that Kroeber conflates progress in the sense of developmental change with progress in the sense of improvement (181), and certainly it is hard to find 'civilization' in Kroeber's criteria in the important sense of the maximization of human freedoms or in the more mundane sense of a gentility which breeds respect for others. Maddock argues that we must consider both freedom from oppression and freedom for positive, humane social relations (183) and that on either score Aboriginal society would rate well, particularly in 'freedom-asserting features' (185), among which he includes a mutual respect for others, a humanitarian anarchy, and egalitarian political relations.

It would seem natural to judge 'progress' by the happiness, wisdom and social justice available in a given civilization, and Kroeber's measures should be evaluated for their success in assessing these. But how does one measure contentment? Certainly wisdom would have to do with the qualitative side of personal relationships, but there is little attention paid to this question. In its preoccupation with the objects of societal life (e.g., material culture, quantitative measurements of behavior, kinship categories, static features of language use: i.e., 'things'), sociology has yet to develop an adequate methodology for the study of human relationships and social praxis.

Habermas has begun to examine the character of concrete human relationships in his consideration of the roots of social justice. He argues that social justice is measured by 'the expansion of the domain of consensual action' (1979: 120), and he places great importance upon the communicative prerequisites of just political relations. In an advanced society, understanding should be achieved without force. Genuine consensual relations, based upon reciprocity between acting subjects and a communicative competence shared equally among participants, should predominate and order conflicting interests, not 'the choice of correct strategies' (1979: 88). The consensual resolution of conflict is predicated upon the general structures of possible interaction; thus, Habermas recognizes the importance of the study of the structures of ordinary interaction.

It would seem, at least from Habermas's viewpoint, that Aboriginal societies would rate very high marks for the degree of social justice in their political life. The reciprocal character of their relations and the consensual formats I have presented appear to meet Habermas's criteria; however, both Rousseau and Marx, who also accept social justice as the major criteria for measuring the progress of human civilization, reject the possibility that a 'primitive' society would be capable of developing institutions which are productive of genuine cooperation and coexistence. Primitive people have yet to realize the freedom which comes from taking their destiny into their own hands, and their myths and superstitions are distortive of genuine freedom. Marx views industrial civilization, the very technology of which Kroeber speaks, as being necessary for peaceful coexistence; however, I am not at all certain that the cases of either the Australian Aboriginal or the California Indian would bear out the truth of this (leaving aside the question of the history of the modern era). Also, we cannot overlook the fact that accompanying the development of technological and industrial capacities has been the monopolistic accretion of power and property which is anything but productive of reciprocal and egalitarian social relations.

Habermas speaks of the rationalization of human conflicts:

> *Rationalization* here means extirpating those relations of force that are inconspicuously set in the very structures of communication and that prevent conscious settlement of conflicts, and consensual regulation of conflicts, by means of intrapsychic as well as interpersonal communication barriers. Rationalization means overcoming such systematically distorted communication in which the action-supporting consensus concerning the reciprocally raised validity claims – especially the consensus concerning the truthfulness of intentional expressions and the rightness of underlying norms – can be sustained in appearance only, that is, counter-factually. (1979: 119-20)

Given this very keen insight into the interactional basis of political domination, it is worth considering in what way the

111

competent system of interaction productive of congeniality and consensus we have described may have incorporated systematically distorted modes of communication. There certainly do exist strategic features which may be exploited – an example of this was provided in our discussion of the debate over the use of the four-wheel drive vehicle in an Aboriginal camp, where one participant muted the case of his antagonist by invoking the proscription against argumentative discourse. In Aboriginal deliberation there is much which goes unresolved through not being said. When the systematic distortions of interaction produced by family and country rivalries is added to this, one would have to conclude that the Aboriginal case is no ideal exhibition of social justice. But neither is it the most deficient of societies. The role of strategic action which Habermas criticizes, i.e., an exclusive concern with one's own successes, plays a relatively minor role in Aboriginal political life, and there do exist structures productive of genuine consensual relations. While Habermas views undistorted communication as exclusively a possibility open to modern, developed, industrial societies, he might find some components of the interactional praxis he is searching for among the variety of forms of interpersonal relations practiced in the non-Western world, among them the Australian Aboriginal people.

Habermas appears to have the right perspective – he wants to avoid maintaining a theory of social justice as abstract theorizing, and in its place he attempts to develop a theory which addresses itself to the concrete interactional praxis of societies. But Habermas has not yet provided himself with enough analytical firepower to reveal the interpersonal praxis in anything but a superficial way. Just at the moment when it comes to specific description of the local work of consensual or strategic interaction Habermas waxes very theoretical, mixing Marx with Chomsky and the philosophy of language. His investigation of the interpersonal component of communication is too narrowly restricted to illocutionary accessories to the message which establish the formal status between interlocutors (demand, request, warning, etc.). Habermas makes it seem as though the interpersonal dimension is something merely added on to the propositional content of an utterance. He writes (1979: 53): 'In speaking we can make either the interpersonal relation or the propositional content more centrally thematic; correspondingly we make a more interactive or a more cognitive use of our language.' Simmel offers support for such an absolute dichotomy between the cognitive aspects of social life, which are concerned with matters of propositional content, and the more interpersonal domains where sociability exists as the primary affective value:

> The decisive point is expressed in the quite banal experience that in the serious affair of life men talk for the sake of the content which they wish to impart or about which they want to come to an understanding – in sociability talking is an end in itself; in purely sociable conversation the content is merely the indispensable carrier of the stimulation, which the lively exchange of talk unfolds. (1971: 136)

But such a schism is unwarranted in the Aboriginal case. Simmel also claims that in sociability the participants 'play' at the forms of society. For Aboriginal people the production and maintenance of a community of feelings *is* something serious; it has a more fundamental role than that of a mere vehicle for superficial entertainment.

Further, Habermas argues that the thematization of content involves only analytical (1970: 122) or propositional (1979: 53) and not interactive uses of language; however, in Aboriginal discourse propositional formulations in public gatherings have important interpersonal functions, namely to provide for the interactants reflexive guides which assist them in monitoring and maintaining the collective progress of the group's deliberations. The formulation of summary accounts are constitutive of both propositional and interpersonal components of the interaction and compose part of the very consensual procedures which make possible undistorted communication. While congenial fellowship may be a primary goal of the interactants, even to the exclusion of the resolution of propositional matters, the interpersonal and the analytical components are not separable when Aboriginal assemblies take up propositional issues; the interpersonal component is integrated in a more deeply constitutive way than Habermas has recognized. In Habermas's writings the interactional basis of communication has its only presence as part of the syntactic life of his theoretical apparatus. I am seeking a more penetrating sociological analysis, which the ethnomethodological research strategies I have employed are better capable of providing.

There may be some clues regarding the level of social 'advancement' of Aboriginal civilization which are grounded in the concrete interpersonal relations which I have examined. Social justice in both Hegel and Marx has been measured by the degree of alienation present in a society. Marx's objections to the factory workers who have become just another commodity, the product of their products, is well known. Sartre writes (1976: 319): 'everyone's action disappears, and is replaced by monstrous

113

forces which, in the inertia of the inorganic and of exteriority, retain some power of action and unification combined with a false interiority.' Alienation in this Marxian sense occurs when one becomes overwhelmed by the societal objectification and objectifying apparatus one has built. It should be obvious that there are no such 'monstrous forces' in Aboriginal society. The anarchism which Maddock includes among their 'freedom-asserting features' militates against their development. While the roots of fascism exist in all societies, the emphasis upon the importance of immediate interpersonal relations and the interactional structures I have identified reduce the possibility of tyranny in Aboriginal society.

However, in the more Hegelian notion of alienation, objectification is a constant result of human thought and activity in all domains. Alienation here is something cognitive, where one's own creative social praxis becomes reified and reappears to oneself as anonymous and objective. Consciousness 'does not recognize in what has gone before its own essence, but looks on it as something quite different' (Hegel 1977: 102). Berger and Pullberg (1965: 200) treat alienation in this Hegelian sense: 'The product now appears to the producer as an alien facticity and power standing in itself over against him, no longer recognizable as a product.' This alienation is present in all objectifying activity which has lost sight of its origins:

> Consciousness . . . does not recognize itself in that reflected object. *For us*, this object has developed through the movement of consciousness in such a way that consciousness is involved in that development. . . But since in this movement consciousness has for its content merely the objective essence and not consciousness as such, the result must have an objective significance for consciousness; consciousness still shrinks away from what has emerged, and takes it as the essence in the *objective* sense. (Hegel 1977: 79-80)

In this investigation we have seen that the Aboriginal people have a chronic case of almost total amnesia of their creative participation in ordinary discourse. Idle comments quickly become social objectivities whose force is absolute. In the anonymous nature of their discourse, Aboriginals quickly lose sight of the very real fact that they are the producers of the perspectives which have come to appear to be substantially existent. If the 'rationalization' of social interaction includes the recognition that one's own conceptual articulation and organization of experience is productive of the meaning of that experience, then it might be concluded that Aboriginal interaction is not as rational as that of people who have achieved and internalized the dialectical insight that the objects of their social cognition are also their own production and have thereby come to take hold of their social praxis in a more fully conscious manner. In this Hegelian sense, one might conclude that there are 'primitive' alienating components to the conventional social relations of Aboriginals. Stanner (1966: 169) has spoken of an 'innocent authoritarianism' in Aboriginal society, by which he refers to their proclivity to accept objectivated social productions as absolute; however, it is an authoritarianism without leaders, and its essence is cognitive rather than exploitative.

Here, then, is an interactional basis for assessing the degree of 'civilization.' But before we can characterize Aboriginal social life as 'backward' according to such a criterion, we must be able to demonstrate that the people of Western civilization have progressively come to internalize dialectical sagacity in their everyday social lives and become cognizant of the reflexive structure of social discourse. Hegel himself describes the false objectification of some scientific theorizing which is equally ignorant of the creative function of their conceptual organization and articulation of experience (1977: 147f.). Merleau-Ponty (1964: xiii) has taught us that everywhere perception masks the fact of its own organization and development and that those features productive of the object are almost always unrecognized, as the object itself comes to be viewed as an independent entity. He calls this 'the prejudice of the world.' It would seem that Aboriginal people only share the identical error we ourselves have mastered. On their own part, we should note that the organizational feature of repeating the summary accounts almost *ad nauseam* provides abundant opportunities for them to repair any objectifications which threaten to prove too 'monstrous.' There is much about the competent system of Aboriginal interpersonal relations I have identified which goes a long way toward providing a basis for social justice, and it would be a misrepresentation for me to assert that these features are 'elementary' while those of contemporary Western civilization are more advanced. Aboriginal fellowship is more accurately presented as merely another variety of human social activity.

As I noted at the outset, what is essential to the phenomenon I have investigated is not only a matter of the regulative forms which have been identified in their social discourse. Aboriginal congeniality and consensus are also a function of the affective concrete human relationships which are commonplace, and this latter may partly transcend the system of interactional detail I have located in their discourse. Simmel (1971: 139) acknowledges this wider concern for us:

> The deep-running source, from which this empire [sociability] takes its energies, is nonetheless to be sought not in these self-regulating forms but only in the vitality of real individuals, in their sensitivities and attractions, in the fullness of their impulses and convictions.

Part II
Through a glass, darkly:
a historical review of
European/Aboriginal interaction

4 Aboriginal appraisals of Europeans

Looking and being looked at

The European sailors and settlers who landed on the shores of Australia during the 17th through the 19th centuries brought with them interactional customs which were very different from those we have just examined. They also brought with them the guns and assertiveness to impose their vision of human reality upon the Aboriginal people, in the name of the fruits of British civilization. One of the diarists of the first English settlement in Australia wrote of the initial approach, in 1788, of the ship bearing the first settlers as it entered Botany Bay and prepared to make its landing:

> For on the Supply's arrival in the Bay on the 18th of the month, they were assembled on the south shore, to the number of not less than forty persons, shouting and making many uncouth signs and gestures. This appearance whetted curiosity to its utmost, but as providence forbade a few people to venture wantonly among so great a number, and a party of only six men was observed on the north shore, the Governor immediately proceeded to land on this side, in order to take possession of his new territory, and bring about an intercourse between its old and new masters. (Tench 1789: 53)

All intercourse with others initiates a necessary and fundamental change in oneself. A person comes to understand himself through recognizing what he has come to be for an other and through incorporating this reflection of himself into his own self-image. It is not necessary that one accept the other's impression of oneself as one's identity; but it is necessary that one cope with the other's impression, if only negatively. Hegel (1977: 111) has

119

written; 'Self-consciousness exists only as being acknowledged.' We are somehow dependent upon others for our own self-awareness. Our consciousness depends upon the consciousness for us of an other who is dependent in return upon our consciousness for him:

> Self-consciousness is aware that it at once is and is not another consciousness, and equally that this other is *for itself* only when it supersedes itself as being for itself, and is for itself only in the being-for-self of the other. Each is for the other the middle term, through which each mediates itself with itself. (*Ibid.*: 112)

Sartre describes similarly the 'look' of an other by which one is transformed – the look is the intermediary which refers me to myself. In the shock which seizes a person when he apprehends the other's look, he experiences a subtle alienation of his world and all his possibilities (Sartre 1956: 265). The other's look initiates a limitation upon one's world which is ultimately a limitation of one's freedom.

This sudden alienation one experiences beneath the other's look is well known by lovers, who naturally prefer solitude: 'it suffices that the lovers should be *looked at* together by a third person in order to experience [their] own objectification' (*ibid.*: 396). Beneath the other's look, one's love becomes an object wholly alienated from its original experience. It is this *looking at* which robs one's own being of its essential life and makes one into an *object* for the other. 'Self-consciousness is, to begin with, simple being-for-self, self-equal through the exclusion from itself of everything else' (Hegel 1977: 113). It is only with the inception of the other that one suddenly witnesses oneself as a phenomenon, i.e., one necessarily joins in with the other in his looking and witnesses one's self for the first time. 'I see *myself* because *somebody* sees me' (Sartre 1956: 160). This recognition is the ontological prerequisite for embarrassment.

Part I presented the Aboriginal inclination to experience shame in the presence of others. This mode of social being towards others was frequently the initial response of the Aboriginal people to the English and French sailors and British settlers in the 17th to 19th centuries.

> The Indians sat down on the rocks, and seemed to wait for our landing; but to our great regret, when we came within about a quarter of a mile, they ran into the woods. (Hawkesworth 1773: 490)

> Those inhabitants also that live on the main, would always run away from us. (Dampier 1729: 469)

However we could know but little of their customs as we were never able to form any connections with them. (Beaglehole 1955: 312)

Flinders (1814: 58) described the Aboriginals as 'shy but not afraid.'

Shame was the appropriate traditional Aboriginal response when encountering strangers. When during their travels Aboriginals enter a locale where another Aboriginal group is residing, they do not march into the camp with their hands extended, offering themselves eye-to-eye, rather, they remain some distance away and wait for the people of the host camp to issue an invitation: 'It was usual for visitors to stop several hundred yards away from the camp they intended to visit. There they would wait until invited to join the residents' (Mathews 1977: 177). The shame which many Aboriginal people experienced during their first exposures to the gaze of white people was a response to the radical transformation of their world beneath the look of those who were radically other. Just as a young child is naturally shy and embarrassed before the entrance of a strange visitor, whose gaze introduces the child to his or her own world in an alien light, many Aboriginals retreated from the entrance of the European explorers.

As I have discussed previously (and as is evident in the accounts of the first European settlers) Aboriginal people always exercise discretion when encountering unfamiliar persons. After coming face-to-face with others, Aboriginals customarily fall into silence for a number of minutes before making any effort to communicate. They do not look at the other directly, but glance aside in a downcast formality, fixing their eyes on the ground. It may take a long while for verbal communication to commence, as I have experienced on many occasions while accompanying Aboriginals paying visits to other encampments. One English explorer recorded this behavior:

I then went forward with him, and was received with the most demure inattention; that is to say, by their sitting cross-legged, with their eyes fixed on the ground, which it appears was their formal mode of expressing respect or consideration for strangers when first received.

Early this morning the cooys of three natives were heard. On meeting them, they went through the usual formalities, an old man fixing his eyes on the ground with due decorum. (Mitchell 1838, I: 201 and 303)

It is as if in the cultural wisdom of Aboriginal life there is instutionalized a recognition of the alienating affect of the other's look and, out of mutual concern, they have the habit of only gradually introducing the painful realignments of worlds necessarily inaugurated by encounters with strangers. Not looking is both shame about being looked at and consideration for the position of the other through the restraint of one's own looking. The Europeans interpreted this mode of interaction as an inherent lack of curiosity (Elkin 1951: 164).

Sociologists are inclined to conclude hastily that the withdrawing character of the Aboriginals was (and is) due to the deferential behavior which is customary among those who are systematically dominated; however, the Aboriginal people's shyness was evident before the Europeans established their dominance and under circumstances which were not altogether unfriendly: 'Yet the aborigine remained aloof, out of reach, elusive, practising a stand-offishness which puzzled and exasperated the bearers of such gifts. They remained shy in the company of the white man, though they had been treated with kindness and loaded with presents' (Clark 1962: 116).

The look of the other is violent in that one's world is usurped. The only adequate responses are to flee (a course of action frequently chosen by Aboriginals), force the other to remove himself (an option the Aboriginals chose occasionally), or to return the look, so that the onlooker also experiences being looked at and its associated alienation. Péron (1809: 74) spoke of the 'obstinacy of these people in avoiding or even repelling strangers,' and two other explorers provide us with impressions of the Aboriginals' immediate discomfort:

> like the generality of people hitherto seen in this country, these men did not seem to be desirous of communication with strangers; and they very early made signs to our gentlemen to return from whence they came. (Flinders 1814: 58)

> They made us understand, by signs, that they did not desire our company. (Hawkesworth 1773: 579)

Hegel's argument suggests that the dominant person is the one who is looking rather than being looked at. In being looked at one loses part of oneself and 'must proceed to supersede the *other* independent being in order to become certain of *oneself* as the essential being' (Hegel 1977: 111). With one's own look one is able to render the other merely an unessential, negatively characterized object (*ibid.*: 113). But this project is doomed to failure, for in such instances one becomes not the master of the other's true being but only the master of the fantasy into which one has made him, 'for one does not see the other as an essential being but in the other sees [only] one's own self' (*ibid.*). In this way one's dominance is an empty dominance.

Authentic social intercourse exists only when one experiences the interior life of the other and one's own being as its reflection; the self-certainty arising from making the other into an object is self-deception, 'For one would have truth only if one's own being-for self had confronted the other as an independent object' (*ibid.*). One cannot escape the fact that the other is also a self-consciousness and that one individual is confronted by another individual with equal ontological status. (Of course, the issue of such ontological equality becomes very significant.)

Sartre follows Hegel's logic in asserting that one must experience the other's interior life, i.e., his essential being, in order for one's mastery to be meaningful in any authentic sense. The other must be more than an unessential object; he must be recognized in his essential subjectivity: 'This relation, in which the other must be given to me directly as a subject, although in connection with me, is the fundamental relation' (Sartre 1956: 253). There is a way in which the Aboriginal interactional practice of shame preserves an authentic respect for this interior subjective essence of the other. In the silence and the downcast formality may lie ultimately a respect for other human beings.

Sartre extends his considerations here to the activity of the look. To achieve genuine social intercourse one must not only do the looking but submit to being looked at; and in order to be looked at, one must suspend one's own looking. Thus, an interminable dialectic is begun where each person alternates between looking and being looked at. The English explorers discovered that their looking was too intense for the Aboriginals, who retreated in front of their gaze. They discovered that to establish any intercourse it was necessary to look aside themselves and submit for a time to being looked at: when one group of Aboriginals in southwestern Australia fled beneath the explorer's look, 'No attempt was made to follow them, for I had always found the natives of this country to avoid those who seemed anxious for communication; whereas, when left entirely alone, they would usually come down after having watched us for a few days' (Flinders 1814: 146). Hawkesworth (1773: 572-3), in southeastern Australia, reported similarly:

> some of our people were for going over to them in a boat, but this I would by no means permit, repeated experience having convinced me that it was more likely to prevent, than procure an interview. I was determined to try what could be done by a

contrary method, and accordingly let them alone, without appearing to take the least notice of them: this succeeded so well, that at length two of them came in the canoe within a musket shot of the ship.

Sartre again illustrates his analysis with the example of lovers. In love, one becomes fascinated with another, but this fascination consists of a positive objectification of her (or his) essential being. In order to win another's love, however, one must in turn fascinate the other; thus, one must also be an object for her. When one succeeds in attracting the other, a transformation occurs; one's objective fantasy of the other is usurped by the reality of the other's interior life and a disillusionment may set in: simultaneously, once the other becomes totally fascinated with oneself, she (or he) no longer seems interesting enough. The dilemma is this: love is meaningful only when it is the embodiment of the other's freedom, but as soon as one succeeds in capturing that freedom, it is no longer free but fascinated, and the fire of one's own love subsides. Thus, lovers engage in interminable contests where each alternates between freedom and fascination, between fascinating and disappointment. The relationship of the Aboriginal people and the European explorers was similar.

The first accounts demonstrate that the Aboriginals had less fascination with the Europeans than the Europeans had with them. The European explorers and first settlers attempted to fascinate the Aboriginals with the aid of bugles, cannon, rockets, mirrors and assorted paraphernalia. But to the disappointment of the Europeans, the Aboriginal people remained something less than fascinated. Although the Aboriginals were curious enough to observe the novel phenomenon with which the explorers presented them, the Europeans complained about their lack of fascination. These accounts are illustrative. In many instances these accounts are those of explorers and journalists who have given their names to much of the Australian landscape, including towns (Dampier), deserts (Simpson), mountain ranges (Flinders) and peninsulas (D'Entrecasteaux). Their records are useful in helping to identify the Aboriginal responses to Europeans before institutional structures of domination became established. The first two citations are from 18th-century explorers, English in the first instance and French in the second, and the last is from the record of a 19th-century explorer of the interior of New South Wales.

They seemed to have no idea of any superiority we possessed over them; on the contrary, they left us, after the first interview, with some appearance of contempt for our pusillanimity; which was probably inferred from the desire we showed to be friendly with them. (Flinders 1814: 66)

M. Freycinet and myself offered various presents to this interesting family, but everything we offered them was received with an indifference that surprised us, and which we had often occasion to observe among individuals of the same country. (Péron 1809: 175)

Nothing seemed to excite their surprise, neither horses nor bullocks although they had never before seen such animals, nor white men, carts, weapons, dress, or anything else we had. All were quite new to them, and equally strange, yet they beheld the cattle as if they had been always amongst them, and seemed to understand the use of everything at once. (Mitchell 1838, II: 112)

Beaglehole (1955: 395 ff.), Hawkesworth (1773) and Tench (1789: 56) in eastern Australia reported finding clothes, mirrors and other presents given to the Aboriginals lying abandoned on the beach or in the woods. King (1827: 46) in northwestern Australia recorded: 'They expressed no pleasure in receiving their presents, or astonishment at their effects'; Dampier (1729: 468) commented: 'neither did they seem to admire anything we had.' The reader of these early accounts frequently receives the impression that the Europeans felt affronted by such casual regard for the effects of Western Civilization (e.g., 'contempt for our pusillanimity').

The reasons for this lack of interest were many. Elkin (1951: 164) has spoken of the traditional lack of curiosity among Aboriginal people. How much their lack of interest had to do with an endemic indifference and how much it had to do with misinterpreted cultural practices is in doubt; besides shame being standard Aboriginal behavior, Aboriginal people are cautious about the potential for sorcery in social intercourse with strangers. Their abandonment of some of the articles given them may have in some cases been due to such fears. King (1827: 214) reported the aversion of one group of Aboriginal people to a clasp-knife, which obviously too closely represented the traditional pointing stick with which a sorcerer visits illness and death upon others, although King had no way of knowing this. The smallpox suffered by those engaging in intercourse with the British settlers may have strengthened such suspicions.

There does seem to have been a genuine apathy toward Europeans, and this is also true today in the regions of Australia where traditional Aboriginals still dwell. Aboriginal people are inclined to mind their own business. Hunter (1793: 490), one of the chroniclers of the Sydney colony, reported of the Aboriginals: 'None of these people have ever been seen to interfere with what did not immediately concern themselves.' The anthropologists R. and C. Berndt have discussed the lack of concern which Aboriginal people show for other Aboriginals' interpretations of traditional religious objects which do not coincide with their own interpretations. Aboriginals provide a great deal of room for others' beliefs: 'The Aborigines do not normally attempt to enforce their own interpretations on other groups' (R. and C. Berndt 1964: 351). It is not extraordinary that since the arrival of the first European settlers, the Aboriginals have shown considerable tolerance of European customs, a tolerance not matched by their partners in the European community.

In this connection it is interesting to note the case of the first Aboriginal 'informant,' Bennelong, who had befriended the first governor of the Sydney colony. After some time, Bennelong was sent to England where he was the object of much discussion and interest. He was given the most stylish wardrobe the royal court could afford and all varieties of presents were lavished upon him; nevertheless, upon his return to Sydney he promptly gave away all of the items and walked off naked into the bush (Turnbull 1813: 94-5), which surprised and disappointed many of the European settlers. An even more penetrating insight into the Aboriginal psyche is provided by the incident which Turnbull recorded (*ibid.*: 95-6) about Bennelong's assessment of his English hosts. It appeared that Bennelong considered their fascination with him a bit foolish. The only Englishman Bennelong spoke of with any degree of respect was an old gentleman who took no interest whatsoever in him, preferring to be occupied with his snuff while the others were gawking with abandon. Bennelong considered that this old fellow had demonstrated good sense.

The Europeans were unsatisfied with the Aboriginals' apathy. Convinced of their own superiority, they pressed their material culture upon them in an effort to fascinate. Gunfire was the most successful here, occasionally demonstrated upon birds but also against the Aboriginals' wooden shields (White 1790: 117-18) and occasionally against the Aboriginals themselves (Pèron 1809: 130). La Billardière (1800: 74) ordered a full display of the cannon, and Mitchell (1838, I: 287-8) sent up rockets to coincide with bugles and volleys. In most instances the Aboriginal people understood the messages. If the recognition of the other's essential being is made possible by an attentive silence and provision of the opportunity for both parties to be both the looker and the looked at, then it is possible that the Europeans' forwardness in imposing themselves upon the Aboriginals straight away may be evidence of their having objectified the Aboriginals in a fundamental way.

I have witnessed many times contemporary Aboriginals who have recoiled in embarrassment for Anglo-Australians who, while visiting Aboriginal people in their traditional homeland settlements a thousand kilometers from the urban centers of European population, came with their heads so full of their own plans and programs (govermental, scientific, or other) that they overlooked the matter of taking into account the actual interior presence of the Aboriginal people. That is, they failed to acknowledge the Aboriginals' essential existence or, in Hegelian terms, mutually to recognize one another (Hegel 1977: 112). This is considered by Aboriginal people to be evidence of poor character, and the oversight is almost always apparent to Aboriginals who, out of embarrassment and consideration, have usually allowed the Anglo-Australians to continue speaking. For their part, the white Australians have been mostly unaware of the effect their interactional praxis was having. This matter will be taken up in more detail in chapter 7, but it should be said at this point that it does not seem that the Europeans were disappointed with the Aboriginals' evasive tactics because of the lost opportunities to engage in genuine communication with them; rather, most of the Europeans were inclined to reduce the Aboriginal people to the status of mere objects, vehicles for their own freedom: 'The natives now always fled at our approach; a circumstance to be regretted, perhaps, on account of the cognomena of my map' (Mitchell 1838, II: 194). Here the Aboriginal people were important only insofar as they could assist the European to complete the nomenclature of his map – both the Aboriginals and the landscape had the status of standing in reserve for European usage.

Touching

Once the Europeans managed to capture their attention, many Aboriginal people enjoyed the novelty which the Europeans provided, at least until violent intercourse recommended a greater distance. Seldom did the Aboriginals organize hostile responses; more frequently, they eventually came down to investigate the Europeans, if only to assure themselves that they were more than apparitions. To indicate their friendship Aboriginal people held their open hands in the air (Hunter 1793:

496). In expression and sensual orientation, Aboriginal people are much more involved with their hands than are Europeans. Not only are all Aboriginals capable of carrying on full conversations by hand signing, they enjoy exploring their surrounding world through the sense of touch. It was natural for them to carry out their looking with their hands.

Several commentators have recorded that the Aboriginals were confused about what sex the Europeans were because the clean-shaven faces of the Europeans gave them the appearances of women:

> These people seemed at a loss to know (probably from our want of beards) of what sex we were, which having under-stood, they burst into the most immoderate fits of laughter, talking to each other at the same time with such rapidity and vociferation as I had never before heard. (Tench 1789: 56)

The Frenchman Péron (1809: 217) reported similarly:

> Presently, however, they wished to pursue their researches somewhat farther: perhaps they might doubt whether we were beings formed like themselves, or perhaps they wished to satisfy themselves of our sex; whichever it might be, they solicited this singular investigation with so much warmth and obstinacy, that we found it extremely difficult to refuse them; when perceiving at length our determined repugnance, they insisted no longer with respect to us, but pursued their inquiry with one of our sailors, who by his youth, and being without a beard, seemed to be the more proper object for verifying their conjectures, or removing their doubts. This youth having, at my solicitation, consented to give them the satisfaction they required, the savages seemed transported with pleasure; but scarcely were they convinced that he was formed like themselves, than they set up a cry of joy and acclamation that perfectly stunned us.

These initial explorations and exchanges included displays and demonstrations of European artifacts which, as I have said, entertained the Aboriginals but did not fascinate them. In their love for dance, the Aboriginals demonstrated their greatest enthusiasm for the songs offered them by their European counterparts:

> [The officer] whistled the air of Malbrooke, which they appeared highly charmed with, and imitated him with equal pleasure and readiness. (Tench 1789: 58)

> We chose the hymn which was . . . likely on this occasion to

produce effect. At first, the savages appeared more affected than surprised, but in a few moments they lent an attentive ear. Their meal was left unfinished, and they expressed their satisfaction by divers contortions – so many odd gestures, that we could scarcely restrain our risibility. (Péron 1909: 177)

One French party even paraded an ape, which they had captured en route to Australia (La Billardière 1800: 65), presumably widening the Aboriginals' scope for the radically other even further.

What is noteworthy about these encounters is that the Aboriginal response, where positive, was characterized by vociferous conviviality and a light-hearted interest in mimicking the songs and words of the Europeans. Previously, we examined how Aboriginal people generate congenial fellowship through vocal gestures and also sustain social cohesion through verbatim repetition. Their verbal enthusiasm and repetition is almost a tactile appropriation of the physical aspects of the other's soundings and is a standard means by which friendship is established and enjoyed. Thus, the Europeans came to report that the Aboriginals were 'amused with everything they saw' (King 1827: 122): 'They opened our clothes, examined our feet, hands, nails, and etc., frequently expressing their surprise by laughing and loud shoutings.' It is important to note that the Aboriginals were not amazed but 'amused.' The light-heartedness characteristic of much Aboriginal interaction, then and now, frequently led to mildly pleasant feelings on both sides (Tench 1789: 54).

The Europeans record with great care and interest the Aboriginals 'mimicking us and indulging in their own merriment' (White 1790: 203; cf. King 1827: 133). Both the English and the French (Péron 1809: 42) reported that the Aboriginals were very adept at pronouncing the European words they heard:

their voices were soft and tuneable, and they repeated many words after us with great facility. (Hawkesworth 1773: 475)

Anything spoken by us they most accurately recited, and this in a manner of which we fell greatly short in our attempts to repeat their language after them. (White 1790: 192)

Such accounts indicate that the Aboriginal people were having a very good time.

But having a good time does not necessarily mean that they took the Europeans seriously. From the beginning the Aboriginals seemed to find the authoritarian attributes of ordinary European social intercourse an absurd mode of social being.

They were to learn quickly that such a social praxis was a very serious matter; however, in their initial lighthearted explorations of the European psyche, the Aboriginals delighted in holding the European rituals up for, not exactly derision but public amusement. Flinders (1814: 61) reports the response of Aboriginals in King George's Sound to the martial display of some of His Majesty's soldiers:

> when they saw these beautiful red and white men [red coats and white crossed belts], with their bright muskets, drawn up in a line, they absolutely screamed with delight; nor were their wild gestures and vociferation to be silenced, but by commencing the exercise, to which they paid the most earnest and silent attention. Several of them moved their hands, involuntarily, according to the motions; and the old man placed himself at the end of the rank, with a short staff in his hands, which he shouldered, presented, grounded, as did the marines their muskets, without, I believe, knowing what he did.

Displays such as this are frequently provided by Aboriginal people, and imitations of tight-lipped and stiff-necked Anglo-Australians are still acted out today. Daisy Bates recorded an illustrative example from a Trappist Mission in Beagle Bay, Western Australia, in 1900. The Aboriginals had just been attending a Sunday Roman Catholic mass – attendance was always a prerequisite for the week's food rations. After the mass, the Aboriginals conducted their own ceremony. Daisy Bates (1966: 37) writes,

> Imagine my mingled horror and delight to find Goodowel, one of the corroborree comedians, sitting on a tree-trunk with a red-ochred billy-can on his head, and a tattered and filthy old rug around his shoulders. In front of him pranced every member of the tribe, all in a line, and each wearing a wreath and veil that were a bit of twisted paperbark and a fragment of somebody's discarded shirt. As they passed Goodowel, each received a resounding smack under the ear with a shout of 'Bag take um!' Hilarious and ear-piercing shrieks of laughter followed each sally. I went back in glee to tell the Bishop. He shook his head. 'Ah, the poor craytures!' was all he said.

Although there were occasions where Aboriginal people responded to the European intruders with violence (Collins 1798: 147; King 1827: 48; Mitchell 1838, I: 270-1) or with threatening gestures (Hawkesworth 1773: 491-3; Péron 1809: 74), the records of the explorers and first settlers are filled with descriptions of the kindness of the Aboriginal inhabitants. White (1790: 117) called them 'friendly and pacific'; Dampier (1771: 359) described them as 'pitiful and courteous to one another'; the French explorer Péron (1809: 174) described two Aboriginal people he met: 'his countenance, as well as that of the young man, was frank and open; notwithstanding some unequivocal signs of fear and disquiet, it was easy to discern kindness and candour'; Collins (1798: 66) spoke of one of their number whom he came to know well as having 'docile, affable and truly amicable deportment'; and a colonial official from Brisbane (Commonwealth 1925, XXIV: 260) called Aboriginals 'naturally a humane – good natured race.' Mitchell (1838, I: 169) wrote of one Aboriginal person:

> His manner was grave, his eye keen and intelligent, and, as our people were encamping, he seemed to watch the moment when they wanted fire, when he took a burning stick, which one of the natives had brought, and presented it in a manner expressive of welcome, and an unaffected wish to contribute to our wants.

The French explorer La Billardière (1800: 61) recorded a most astonishing friendship with one group of Aboriginal people with whom he spent some time. He described his ship's leave-taking in this way:

> When we re-embarked to go on board, these good people followed us with their eyes for some time, before they left the shore, then they disappeared in the woods. Their way brought them at times to the shore again, of which we were immediately informed by the cries of joy, with which they made the air resound. These testimonies of pleasure did not cease until we lost sight of them from the distance.

Most of these accounts were written long before an institutional system of domination had been established, and so such affability, apparently common, cannot be attributed merely to being standard deference behavior.

Perhaps the treatment of Europeans by Aboriginals is best typified by the case of a shipwrecked party stranded in southeastern Australia which attempted to make their way to the colony at Sydney by walking north along the coast (Flinders 1946: 57-63). The full variety of Aboriginal responses to Europeans is evident in the account: while the party was attacked once by a group of Aboriginals, they were fed shellfish and mussels by another, assisted in making a perilous river crossing by a second, and provided a guide by a third. An official colonial report in 1844 reported that the Aboriginal conduct toward convict runaways who were lost in the bush was 'almost uniformly kind' (Commonwealth 1925, XXIV: 260). The pacific nature of the Aboriginals was all the more impressed upon the European explorers by the reception they received when their ships carried on northward to New Guinea, where they faced attacks from warlike tribesmen (Hawkesworth 1773: 657).

While for the most part the Aboriginals did not appreciate strangers, they were very moderate in their responses and dealt with what were intruders in a remarkably considerate way. At least one influential Aboriginal at Sydney attempted to incorporate the Europeans into the traditional system of kinship recognition – Bennelong, while living at the Governor's house, called the Governor 'Beanga' or 'Father' and insisted upon being called 'Dooroow' or 'Son' (Hunter 1793: 405). The chosen relationship is significant because it suggests that Aboriginal people recognized at an early date that the Europeans were in the position to be providers. The Aboriginals quickly took to corn and beef, and later flour, tea, sugar and alcohol (Bennelong himself died a drunkard). Probably accurately, Hunter (208) expressed his admiration for the 'harmony and friendship' Bennelong offered so spontaneously.

As the European settlements grew, and more Aboriginal people were displaced, Aboriginal resentment also grew. Hundreds of Aboriginal people died of smallpox during the early years, and hundreds more were killed by parties of sailors or convicts (Collins 1798: 24 ff.). Retaliation and reprisals began, which justified further violence by the Europeans. As one contemporary Aboriginal person has put it to me, 'The whitefellas were lucky for that gun.' As more of the country became settled, the Aboriginals quickly became a defeated people (Liberman 1980). One Crown Lands Commissioner (Commonwealth 1925 XXIII: 491) summarized in 1843 the period of settlement this way:

> I have had several times last year to be called upon when the
> natives, in distant parts of this district, have been imposed
> upon and when they have come in collision with the settler, but
> in no case have I been able to prove to my satisfaction that the
> natives were not in the first instance the party grieved.

The colonial administrator at Darling Downs in New South Wales attributed the conflicts in his region to Anglo-Australian sexual abuse of Aboriginal women.

The accounts of the Sydney colony reveal that the Aboriginal people were reduced to the status of objects, and obstacles at that. The European settlers quickly lost their curiosity about them in their concern to transform Australia into a European state. The long record of personal abuse in the Australian outback from 1800 to the present (Mathews, 1977; Palmer and McKenna 1978; Liberman 1977) demonstrates that most Aboriginal attempts to express or assert their essential interior lives only presented the Anglo-Australian settlers with a challenge they found a stimulant to further demonstrations of their superiority. As with Sartre's lovers, the expression of the other's freedom enhanced the will to power. The Aboriginals wisely chose to remain within a more sedate subjection.

Aboriginal critiques

The English explorers recorded their complaints about the reluctance of Aboriginal people to offer them anything in exchange for the presents which were given them:

> They had indeed no idea of traffic, nor could we communicate any to them; but never appeared to understand our signs when we required a return. (Hawkesworth 1773: 634)

> We always made them presents of such things as seemed to be most agreeable but they very rarely brought us anything in return; nor was it uncommon to find small mirrors and other things left about the shore; so that at length our presents were discontinued. (Flinders 1814: 58)

This is only a single illustration of the numerous confusions coincident with European-Aboriginal intercourse. The Aboriginal people, for their part, appeared to be taken aback by the selfishness demonstrated by the Europeans. In traditional Aboriginal society it is customary for those entering the homeland region of another group to provide fresh meat for the homeland residents. This is a custom carried out today in the traditional regions, and one in which I myself have participated. Even when one is not a visitor, it is customary to share one's food, especially one's meat supply. As one recent informant, born at the turn of this century in western New South Wales, explains: 'If there was not sufficient [meat] for everyone, the donor must be the first to relinquish his portion' (Mathews 1977: 78). That Aboriginals considered themselves to be extending the privileges of their homeland to European guests is evident in this account from an early 19th-century interior exploration of New South Wales. The explorer in this instance (Mitchell 1838, I: 304-5) fulfilled his obligations: 'I have more than once seen a river chief, on

133

receiving a tomahawk, point to the stream, and signify that we were then at liberty to take water from it, so strongly were they possessed with the notion that the water was their own.'

Nothing was due from the Aboriginal side except the extension of hospitality, i.e., tolerance of the Europeans' presence. Those coastal explorers of the late 18th century who offered the Aboriginals presents were only fulfilling their lawful responsibilities, at least as viewed from the Aboriginal perspective. In fact, the Aboriginals probably did not consider the 'toys' (Tench 1789: 56) and 'trifles' (White 1790: 155) to be satisfaction of the Europeans' responsibilities. They had little use or desire for such articles, and on at least one occasion – during the voyage of Cook in 1770 – they communicated their disdain for the explorers' failure to produce the standard provision of fresh meat. After Cook had left Botany Bay, he sailed north along the Queensland coast and had captured a number of turtles. The Aboriginals he encountered probably naturally expected to be given some of the turtles. Aboriginal people do not worry very much about the future; their temporal life is distinctively present- and past-oriented, and they were unable to appreciate Cook's intention to save the meat for the coming voyage. They were outraged, to their way of thinking justifiably so, and became even more upset when the ship's men attempted to assuage them with some biscuits. Aboriginal people do not consider vegetarian food to be a manly demonstration of one's hospitality; it may suffice when there is no ready supply of fresh meat available and when the sentiment of self-sacrifice is genuine, but when there are fresh turtles ready to be cooked the offering of vegetarian food is a blunt insult. One Aboriginal snatched a biscuit and threw it overboard 'with great disdain' (Hawkesworth 1773: 581).

There was other behavior which the Aboriginals found shocking, not the least of which was the European habit of shooting dingoes. The Aboriginal people do not consider the dingo to be just another animal. Ontologically, the dingo has a spiritual essence closer to that of a human being. The constant companion of Aboriginals, the dingo is treated with love, provided with a portion of the family's diet and often given a human-like funeral. What is more, the dingoes were vital to the Aboriginal owners in assisting them to chase down important game after it had been speared. The shooting of dingoes was akin to the acts of the first European settlers in California, who immediately set to chopping down food-bearing oak trees for lumber, an act to which the Indians responded with horror.

In the early days of the Sydney colony, a dingo who annoyed a settler was shot on the spot (Tench 1789: 83); and only five years after the establishment of one of the missions in the Kimberleys (northwestern Australia), poisoned baits were systematically set in the surrounding bush to remove the district of its dingo population (Perez 1977: 16). During my fieldwork in Western Australia, an Aboriginal council of elders at Wiluna called me into one of their outdoor meetings to complain about the number of dingoes being killed by baits set by the pastoralists. In many cases these were their own dogs, and they were deeply saddened by their loss. They expressed the view that the drought of recent years (1976-7) was due to the sacrilege of murdering the dogs, whose spiritual essence the Aboriginals valued. Barker, the New South Wales part-Aboriginal who grew up in forced confinement in a government mission, has reported the mass killings, without warning, of Aboriginal dogs by local police:

> The man riding in the sidecar would be holding an automatic rifle as the police entered the mission, and as they drove up the street he would shoot every dog in sight, perhaps twelve lying dead on the road. (Mathews 1977: 195)

In two remote Aboriginal settlements at which I have lived, police have carried out the same slaughter, with only the approval of European staff who did not have the authority to issue such orders – and much to the dismay of the Aboriginals.

Along the same lines, in 1791 the Aboriginal residents of Sydney Cove were horrified with the public flogging of a convict (caught stealing from the Aboriginals) which Governor Phillip went out of his way to have them witness (Clark 1962: 126). One of the Aboriginal women began to weep and finally picked up a stick with which she menaced the flogger. Because of such behavior, many Aboriginal people consider white people to be 'hard blokes.' One mild-mannered Pitjantjatjara Aboriginal person held in great respect by his fellows once told me, 'I know *those* whitefellas, them hard blokes, *bad*' (italics indicate use of Aboriginal language). And also, about an angry Anglo-Australian, 'I seen 'im funny feelin' walkin' around, you know, whitefella way.'

While there are 'goodfellas' as well as 'hard blokes' among Anglo-Australians, one of the 'whitefella ways' acknowledged by Aboriginal people is the exercise of an authoritarian attitude (Kolig 1972). In fact 'whitefella' is as much a category which defines a variety of social roles and personality characteristics, one of which is having an authoritarian personality, as it is an indication of race. One Sri Lankan community adviser was introduced by an Aboriginal to his fellows as 'whitefella new one.' It is customary for Aboriginals in the European-occupied

135

regions of Western Australia, South Australia and the Northern
Territory to refer to white people as 'boss.' Bilingual Aboriginals
revert to English when communicating authoritarian messages
such as 'Can't do that,' 'Not allowed' and 'Don't come around
here.' Also the term *'arkamin'* (argument) is reserved for a
distinctively European mode of verbal contest, a mode Aboriginal people caution each other against. Finally, when imitating
Anglo-Australians in conversations, contemporary Aboriginals
raise their voices and speak more loudly than they do in their
normal discourse.

Aboriginal people recognize that forwardness is natural to the
character of Europeans. When the Aboriginal translator and
guide for the Mitchell exploration of the interior of New South
Wales was forced into pressing questions for the Europeans
about the local landscape and for the names of surrounding lakes
and rivers, the Aboriginals residing in the district refused to
answer:

> 'I won't tell you', was the answer (*murry coolah*; i.e., very
> angrily). They then told him there was 'too much ask' all about
> him. (Mitchell 1838, II: 142)

But 'too much ask' is part and parcel of the identifying genius of
European being, a mode of life which has been characterized
elsewhere (Heidegger 1977: 124) as dominated with 'the act of
driving on' or 'ongoing activity' (*Betrieb*). One not very reliable
English journalist who visited Australia in 1841 is perhaps more
dependable in his characterization of Anglo-Australians:

> Rapidity is the grand characteristic of [Anglo-] Australian life;
> and the habits of this country remind me much of what is
> asserted of the Americans. 'They are born', it is said, 'in a
> hurry, educated at full speed, make a fortune with a wave of
> the hand, and lose it in like manner, but only to remake it and
> relose it in the twinkling of an eye. Their body is a locomotive
> travelling at the rate of ten leagues an hour. Their thoughts are
> a high-pressure engine. Their life resembles a shooting star,
> and death surprises them like an electric shock.' (Hood 1843:
> 113)

The intellectual energy of Anglo-Australians is ceaseless, and
this is contrary to the Aboriginal social attitudes of letting things
be and passively attending to events rather than being always
engaged in manipulations. Aboriginals are cautious but insistent
about their criticism of the European peculiarity of 'driving on.'
One elderly Aboriginal told me, 'Whitefellas they goin' past and
don't see land or hills. "Hello, nice pretty hill that one," take a

photo of it and go off. "I took a photo of that one!" ' Aboriginal people recognize that in their hurry to become master of their environment Europeans have missed matters of importance. A personal incident provides a perspicuous example of such European behavior. I was engaged in interviewing three elderly Aboriginal women in Western Australia about their knowledge of the environment, seeking on this occasion to establish whether there were names for particular winds depending upon their character and direction. I became so absorbed with my inquiries that I failed to notice which way the wind was blowing. Asking if the wind ever blew from the southeast, I was informed, 'Blowin' that way now.'

A typical Aboriginal response to questions posed by persons of European descent is silence. I have witnessed this many times, first as a recipient and later as an adviser sitting on the side of the Aboriginal people. When whites press the Aboriginals for answers, they are usually rewarded with a gratuitous 'Yes,' or concurrence with whatever they have said, but the concurrence embodies little or no propositional content. Above all, Aboriginal people avoid forcing themselves upon others; nothing is pushed too far, and the better part of discretion is silence. An early Aboriginal song about the white settlers suggests something about the loudness which Aboriginals have associated with the European presence. The song is from the Wollondilly Aboriginals of New South Wales and was recorded in the year 1832:

> *Morruda, yerraba, turdy kinarra.*
> *Morruda, yerraba, minyin guiny witemala.*
> On the road the white man walks with creaking shoes;
> He cannot walk up trees, nor his feet fingers use.
>
> (Mitchell 1838, I: 302)

The gait of the Anglo-Australian walk is indicative of a mode of being in the world which is distinctively non-Aboriginal. I once sat with some traditional Aboriginal women in an outback town while they were observing a half-Aboriginal young woman walk along the town's only sidewalk. The woman had married an Australian immigrant and had adopted a European style of life, and this was reflected in her walk: whereas Aboriginal women glide more or less silently along the street, Anglo-Australian women have a segmented gait, with the heel emitting a sharp sound with each step. In the gait and its sound there is manifest a distinctively European 'driving on,' an unrestrained expression of self-confidence. On this occasion the Aboriginal women I was sitting with scoffed at the part-Aboriginal, pointing with their lips and chins while evincing both interest and disapproval.

Little attention has been paid to the possibility of a coherent Aboriginal critique of Anglo-Australians. While it is acknowledged that the Aboriginals have been remarkably unwilling to adopt European lifestyles, this intransigence has been attributed to an intellectual deficiency on their part. O'Connell (1836: 83-7) complained about the 'low cunning' of Aboriginals and thereupon placed the blame for the fruitlessness of missionary enterprises. Even a noted Australian historian has accepted the view that the Aboriginals' lack of European acculturation has its roots in their cognitive inabilities:

> the aborigine was also endowed with a tenacious, if not unique inability to detect meaning in any way of life other than his own; and by one of those ironies in human affairs it was this very inability to live outside the framework of his own culture that prevented any subsequent invaders from using the aborigine for their own purposes. (Clark 1962: 5)

Could it be possible instead that the Aboriginal people understood European life and nevertheless concluded that it did not merit their participation?

Dampier's account (1729: 468), one of the earliest (1687), is telling on this score:

> After we had been here a little while, the men began to be familiar, and we clothed some of them, designing to have had some service of them for it: for we found some wells of water here and intended to carry two or three barrels of it aboard. But it being somewhat troublesome to carry to the canoes, we thought to have made these men to have carried it for us, and therefore we gave them some old clothes, and to one an old pair of breeches, to another a ragged shirt, to the third a jacket that was scarce worth owning; which yet would have been very acceptable at some places where we had been, and so we thought they might have been with these people. We put them on them, thinking that this finery would have brought them to work heartily for us; and our water being filled in small long barrels about six gallons in each, which were made for the purpose to carry water in, we brought these our new servants to the wells, and put a barrel on each of their shoulders for them to carry to the canoe. But all the signs we could make were to no purpose, for they stood like statues, without motion, but grinned like so many monkeys, staring one upon another: For these poor creatures seemed not accustomed to carry burdens; and I believe that one of our shipboys of ten years old, would carry as much as one of them. So we were forced to carry the water ourselves.

The weight of a twelve-gallon burden of water, with barrels, would have exceeded a hundred pounds. Far from being monkeys, the Aboriginals were amused with the absurdity of the request and perhaps appalled with the pushiness of the sailors. And they responded in typical Aboriginal fashion – they remained silent and did nothing. The sailors may have interpreted this as evidence of the Aboriginals' pathetic condition, but it is far more likely that the Aboriginals' intransigence was deliberate, just as in the case of Hood (1843: 231-2):

> I am anxious to obtain one of the tribe, as they are desirable in many ways as servants, when removed from their brethren, being faithful, without any motive to leave your service, and causing very little expense. He was to have come today, but has not appeared, and I begin to suspect he is like all his caste – a man of words, and not of deeds.

Turnbull, recording in 1801 in Sydney, approached the truth of the matter more closely:

> Everyday are men and women to be seen in the streets of Sydney and Paramatta, naked as the moment of their birth. In vain have the more humane of the officers of the colony endeavoured to improve their condition; they still persist in the enjoyment of their ease and liberty in their own way, and turn a deaf ear to any advice upon this subject.
>
> Is this to be imputed to a greater portion of natural stupidity than usually falls to the lot of even savages? By no means: if an accurate observation, and a quick perception of the ridiculous, be admitted as a proof of natrual talents, the natives of New South Wales are by no means deficient. Their mimicking the oddities, dress, walk, gait and looks, of all the Europeans whom they have seen from the time of Governor Phillip downwards, is so exact, as to be a kind of historic register of their several actions and characters. Governor Phillip and Colonel Grose they imitate to the life. And to this day, if there be anything peculiar in any of our countrymen, officers of the corps, or even in the convicts; any cast of the eye, or hobble in the gait; any trip or strut, stammering or thick speaking; they catch it in a moment, and represent it in a manner which renders it impossible not to recognize the original. (Turnbull 1813: 87-8)

During the time I lived among Aboriginal people I have frequently heard, and been the subject of, coherent Aboriginal criticism of European behavior. A partly Europeanized but 'full-blooded' and fully initiated Aboriginal man in an outback town in which I lived once criticized the large desk I had in the front room of my house/office which he believed separated me too absolutely from my visitors. I have observed on several occasions the silent criticisms of Aboriginal passengers who, when preparing to enter my automobile, were forced to wait for me to unlock the door on the passenger's side; but this was small-time compared with the Anglo-Australian medical assistant in a remote Aboriginal settlement who had no less than seven locks to open before he was free to trespass upon his own living quarters. The idea of locking anything is anathema to Aboriginal people.

Aboriginals also criticize the ordinary relationships of Anglo-Australians with each other, believing that such sociability is too competitive. I have heard them contrast this with what they have characterized as the mutual supportiveness of their own social relations. Several times I have listened to traditionally-oriented Aboriginal people of the Western Desert satirize European conceptions of objective time and space. When speaking about the distance it might be to an outlying Aboriginal camp, two men joked, 'Ten miles might be, or million trillion miles.' It was all artifice to them, as was the concrete notion of calendrical time I was employing for the Aboriginal who told me in a tone of mockery that the amount of time involved was 'Two years, three months.' Such objectified time and space is not taken seriously by many Aboriginals, while others have considered such notions almost on a par with sorcery, especially when it is invested with a certainty which is uniquely European. Such *certainty* is a mode Aboriginal people have observed as being part of European social life. While Aboriginals may have dismissed it upon occasion, for the most part they have been victimized by it, particularly in environments dominated by European modes of discourse and interaction. A perspicuous case of such an environment is a court of law, an environment I will analyze in detail in chapter 7. Aboriginal people have expressed wonder about the certainty which surfaces at times in the course of customary courtroom activities. They have no explanation for where the license for such certainty originates; at least one observer (Elkin 1947: 176) has commented upon the Aboriginal ascription of magic to courtroom proceedings, and this may be due in part to the certainty about the correctness of words and actions which courtroom personnel demonstrate. Speaking of the official word of legal authority, Sansom (1980: 210) writes: 'police business is the inequality that allows blackfellas only sayings while "that police mob" can dominate each situation with "that word they got." ' Anglo-Australian 'correctness' is one component of the 'hard bloke' personality with which Aboriginal people must contend. Heidegger considers such correctness to be 'merely correct' and characterizes it well (1977: 6): 'The correct always fixes upon something pertinent in whatever is under consideration. However, in order to be correct, this fixing by no means needs to uncover the thing in question in its essence.' When Anglo-Australians become fixed upon something, Aboriginal people make room; but making room does not imply the aspiration to be European, although some Anglo-Australians have viewed it in such a light.

The docility of the Aboriginal accommodation to Europeans perhaps heightened the English disappointment over their failure to 'civilize' (Lachlan, Commonwealth 1925, XXIV: 267) the Aboriginal people. The reports of journalists, missionaries and colonial officers alike recorded the taciturn but persistent adherence of Aboriginal people to their own cultural traditions. It is difficult to assess this stubbornness as anything other than deliberate and intelligent:

> It struck forcibly on my mind as one of the characteristics of the colony, that it is almost the only settlement in the world, in which the residence of Europeans has produced absolutely no change in the manners or useful knowledge among the natives. (Turnbull 1813: 75) [1802]

> With regard to the advancement the Aborigines of this District have made in civilization, I have nothing favourable to state. (Commonwealth 1925, XXIV: 262) [1844]

> Could they be induced to abandon their wandering mode of life, I have no doubt that their services would render the settler comparatively independent of the extortionate demands made by the present class of servants in these remote districts. From my experience as regards the natives, however, I must state my conviction that so desirable an object will *never* be attained; their migratory habits are in my opinion so deeply rooted that their tenure of service cannot be depended upon. (*Ibid.*: 265) [1844]

Accommodation

Despite a century or more of accommodation and submission to Europeans, in many outback districts Aboriginal people have yet to abandon their primary affiliation with their own traditions. They present themselves to station-owners as nothing more than cowboys and satisfy the concerns of missionaries with equal facility. Aboriginals may have been willing to attend church

141

services in order to receive food rations, but in most cases it was just another piece of work done at the missionaries' request and their hearts were rarely in it. In fact, a few Anglo-Australians have entertained a question about who has received the better part of the arrangement. One member of an original family of settlers complained to me, 'Some days I feel I'm just workin' for the blacks.' While this is exaggeration, Aboriginal people were concerned all along to receive from the settlers what they desired with as little interference as possible with their own domestic affairs. They were not altogether successful, but they became very skilled at 'putting-on' the settlers for their own ends. This pattern of exploitation of whites has been called 'intelligent parasitism.'

No sooner had the English established themselves at Sydney than Bennelong asked the Governor, whom he called 'father,' to build him his own hut in his favorite cove. The Aboriginals were quick to take advantage of Europeans and their resources. One missionary reported: 'Watermelon had for long been the great attraction' (Perez 1977: 22), and the Sydney Aboriginals were attracted by corn, flour and other foodstuffs which could be had easily. Aboriginals quickly incorporated introduced items into their own material culture, using glass for spearheads (Hunter 1793: 496) and for circumcision knives, and they were (and are) adept at extracting a variety of other goods from Europeans. Something of an expert on this (from the wrong end), I can verify Elkin's observation when he wrote that Aboriginal people try to presume on a white newcomer before the latter's character has been summed up (1947: 367). The diarist for one of the Kimberley missions had this opinion: 'A good number of Aborigines were born comedians, and all of them experts in deception' (Perez 1977: 62). Once I was visiting my wife in an outback hospital, when a kindly elderly Aboriginal woman in the bed opposite awoke and called out to me with instant pleasure: '*Yamatji mutuka!*' ('*Motorcar friend!*'), apparently considering that she had at last found her ride home. The persistence of Aboriginals in such matters is legend.

> Our friends the blacks had been rather forward during the night, and throughout this day they lay about my tent pointing to their empty stomachs, and behaving in a contemptuous manner, although we had given them most of our kangaroo. At length I determined to send them off, if this could be done without quarrelling with them. I directed our overseer Burnett to take some men with fixed bayonets and march in line towards them. This move answered very well, they receded to

a distance, perfectly understanding our objects, and there sat down and made their fires. Only two came up the next morning, again pointing to their stomachs; but I knew from experience that to feed them was to retain them permanently in our camp, and now I did not want them, and had no food to spare. (Mitchell 1938, I: 317-18)

In the Western Desert there are a number of names with which Aboriginals may baptize Anglo-Australians when speaking to them. If a white person has adopted a subsection classification, then the terms Aboriginals use will be the appropriate family relational term; otherwise, the names are likely to reflect the degree of 'con' present in the relationship or the degree to which the Aboriginal feels intimidated (the latter also a function of the distance of his place of rearing from centers of European population, self-confidence being proportional to distance). When one is called 'boss,' then it is time to be alert for the quiet take; frequently, 'boss' is little more than customary Aboriginal humoring of Anglo-Australians, who tend to view themselves in such a dominant social position – but it is often only rhetoric. It is much better to be called 'kurta,' or older brother, for then the obligations are not quite so severe. Speaking from the male perspective, if one is called 'marlanypa' or 'katja,' younger brother or son, then it is less likely that one will become the 'mark' for an Aboriginal sting operation. And it is a certainty that a sting will occur if one is perceived, rightly or wrongly, to be 'kapamin,' i.e., a government officer.

Aboriginals have found Europeans to be useful for many purposes. The settlements of colonists and missionaries provides a sort of neutral ground to which Aboriginals would run for refuge from tribal conflicts and to escape spearings (Turnbull 1813: 19), and this is still the case. The missions were frequently used as places to deposit the lame and elderly who could no longer keep up with the remainder of the band in their foraging. At times, the Aboriginals attempted to enlist the settlers on behalf of one tribe or another, denigrating rival groups in the effort to strike alliances. Collins (1798: 408) reported a very interesting case of some Sydney Aboriginals who exploited the European belief in Aboriginal cannibalism for their own purposes: 'They assured us, with horror in their countenances, that Gomé-boak was a cannibal' – the hope being that the rival would fall into disfavor. It was once suggested that the Sydney colonists use their guns to destroy a rival band altogether (Hunter 1793: 487-8). Thus the pattern of exploiting the Anglo-Australians, while accommodating their active-aggressive genius, was something established early in the history of Aboriginal-European contact.

Ideas

The Aboriginal people of central Australia refer to the European trait of 'driving on' in one of its aspects as '*i ´tiyas.*' With the accent on the first syllable, '*i ´tiyas*' has the significance of 'quick thinking,' i.e., a unique rapidity of thought and analysis which Aboriginal people associate with persons of European descent. The Aboriginal observance of the phenomenon was best displayed for me by the laughter of an Aboriginal woman who, listening to me speak about her fire, remarked with delight and amazement about how actively my mind jumped around. Similarly, when I was talking over plans for an Aboriginal land rights campaign with an Anglo-Australian community adviser who was visiting from another Aboriginal settlement, one of three men at the settlement to which I was community adviser commented to the other two, 'Don and Ken are like two wirelesses.' A 'wireless' is a radio, and the Aboriginal was referring to the way our talk (and thought) was able to continue without pause, like two radios running at the same time.

This phenomenon which the Aboriginal people have identified has been characterized with acuity by Martin Heidegger (1966: 46), who contrasts 'calculative thinking' with 'meditative thinking' and finds the former to be identifying of the cognitive life of contemporary Western man. While meditative thinking is 'a waiting upon that which regions,' by which Heidegger means to refer to an essential receptivity and openness to the world in its unfolding, calculative thinking arrests and objectifies (Heidegger 1977: 131). Where meditative thinking is an immediate receiving (*Vernehmen*), calculative thinking actively grasps the world, which in turn consists of a variety of equipmentality which stands as fodder for the peregrinations of the calculative mind. The work of the calculative mind is ceaseless, and its energy is that of ever 'driving on.'

The English word 'idea' evolved from the Greek *eidos* 'visual shape,' and in Western history and philosophy ideas and thinking have been associated with sight. Today, one expresses sudden in*sight* with the remark, 'I see.' By contrast, desert Aboriginal people refer to the activity of thinking by calling forth the metaphor of hearing: '*kulira*' means both 'listening' and 'thinking,' the implication being that thinking is a more receptive activity. The Greek '*theorein*,' from which English derives 'theory,' meant literally 'to be a spectator.' 'Looking at' became equivalent to 'contemplating,' and the eye served as the model for the absorption of experiences among Western humankind. While desert Aboriginal people have a word for knowledge (*ninti*), there is no word for 'mind' in the Western Desert Aboriginal language, and it is interesting to note that the discovery of 'mind' was in fact a historical achievement of Western civilization locatable in both time and place:

> At least as far as Western intellectual tradition is concerned, 'mind' was not discovered until about the time of Homer or shortly afterwards (according to historical studies of language). Further, when mental operations or processes were first named by means of a metaphorical use of the terminology of sensation, it was sight which was the metaphor. (Edie 1975: 33)

'*I'tiyas*' refers not to anything objective on the part of Europeans, such as literacy or note-taking, but as it is used by Aboriginal people it refers to an active skill or praxis for engaging the world. This fact is well corroborated by the case of a middle-aged Aboriginal leader who was one of the most conservative and traditionally-minded men in a remote encampment. Despite the fact that he was also illiterate he had, through a period of association with Anglo-Australians earlier in his life, developed the ability to think in a European way, a skill which rendered him valuable in assisting his community to evaluate Anglo-Australian proposals. As this person explained it himself, he was '*walypala* way *ninti*' ('whitefella way intelligent').

Peter Berger (1976: 190) speaks of rationality as everyday praxis:

> It has long been a truism that modernity is the 'age of reason,' but the quality of this 'reason' must be specified. It is not necessarily the 'reason' of philosophers and scientists; that antedated the modern period and is today, at best, the property of a small minority. The rationality of a modern society is 'functional' rather than theoretical . . . Rationality here implies not great sweeps of theoretical reflection, but a certain attitude of calculation, classification, and manipulation of reality.

There being no like phenomenon in pre-European Australia, the Aboriginal people have adopted and pidginized the English word 'idea' when referring to it. Their notion is indicated in this application of its use on the occasion of a group examination of an aerial photographic mosaic of an Aboriginal community's homeland district. The environing landscape and salient geographical features are of tremendous spiritual importance to Aboriginal people, and they are always engaged in reciting the sacred tracks of the world-creative beings of the Dreaming who have passed through the area. Upon gazing at the photomosaic, the first any of them had seen, they immediately began to take delight in identifying all the sacred places representative of their homeland and their lives. As the older men were deeply engaged in their investigation, a highly respected middle-aged Aboriginal man commented:

> I'tiya wiyarringkula tjilpirrinkula. Whitefellas
> (idea)(will become nothing)
> (old men)
> no worries, good i'tiya men.
> (idea)

The old men forget the locations when they get old and senile. But white people are clever and are able to hold on to their ideas.

Aboriginal people express both positive and negative feelings about this massively evident European cultural phenomenon of i'tiyas. I have heard some say, 'We gotta get more i'tiyas,' but I have also heard Aboriginals criticize each other, 'He's too many i'tiyas, well wiya [no].' What is important is that it is an acknowledged European trait. Aboriginal elders speak of the need to become more clever in order to combat Anglo-Australians effectively, but they have not really interiorized such European praxis themselves. One elder from an Aboriginal settlement on the fringe of an iron-ore district told me, while pointing to his ear [his mind], 'Now we got 'em here, we don't fight,' referring to the Aboriginals becoming clever enough to unite together to press for land rights for their sacred homelands. A young Aboriginal man moved to explain the elder's comment for me, 'You see, we use brains now,' and pointed to his *forehead* much as an Anglo-Australian might. The elder did not turn toward me and nod yes, as might be expected, but continued to stare at the young Aboriginal in a quizzical manner. The young Aboriginal had interiorized Anglo-Australian cognitive praxis, and the elder experienced it as something foreign.

The active-assertive 'quick thinking' glossed by 'i'tiya' has been recognized as a trait uniquely European by a great number of peoples with whom persons of European descent have come into contact. The Cahuilla, a Californian desert Indian tribe, referred to Europeans as 'milkish,' which meant 'jabberers' and referred to their being loquacious. A young Tibetan refugee living in Sikkim once told me, 'The Western mind is sharp,' and this assessment is consistent with that of an American black, the administrative assistant to Muhammad Ali, 'The thing about whites is that they are very cerebral. Their mind is never "off", it's always "on," it's always moving. The rational processes are always "on." '

Aboriginal people admire such a genius yet find it to be repulsive. A young, highly regarded traditionally-oriented Aboriginal person had spent a week in Perth, the capital city of Western Australia, representing his people at some meetings called to discuss the protection of sites which were of sacred significance. During the automobile trip back to the remote Aboriginal settlement, he ran into some old acquaintances and proceeded to get drunk with them. We engaged in a long conversation, during which he expressed his exasperation with 'all those i 'tiyas down in Perth.' In particular, it was the 'driving on' character of the meetings which disturbed him. For Aboriginal people, the best social interaction is affective, relaxed and receptive. Another traditional Aboriginal declared that he was 'through with this meeting business' and informed me, 'I just like to sit around.' When I asked him to explain further (my own 'driving on'), he described how he liked to sit against a tree, feeling good 'just looking at the day.'

During my period as a community adviser, I heard frequently the complaint, 'too many wangka [talk]' and 'one wangka at a time.' Meetings had to be short and take up only one or two issues, or else the participants would lose patience for the intensity and mode of intellectual effort required. A common complaint, heard perhaps between the fifth and sixth items of an agenda, was 'Tirtu watjanma' ('Still they're talking on'), very frequently uttered on an inhalation, the sign of true exasperation. After a full season of council meetings, one group of Aboriginals decided to choose a new council, explaining,

These committee blokes 'bin have a full ear already, new
committee change-'imalku wangka kutjupa next meeting.
        (+ future) (next meeting)

Given what we know about the cognitive metaphor of the ear in Aboriginal life, having 'a full ear' is feeling mentally satiated with European cognitive praxis.

Aboriginal people are easily satisfied with what a situation presents them. Their orientation is less assertive and manipulatory, and they are capable of managing harmoniously in most environments. An American Indian's characterization of the passivity of Indian worldly praxis may serve also to contrast the Aboriginal praxis with the European:

Consider the example of the one-eyed Ford. If a Ford loses a headlight, the Indian who owns it might never consider replacing it. It has changed form and has simply become a one-eyed Ford. If the car breaks down altogether, the Indian might decide to leave it as it is, move in and convert it into a home. The car is not just a broken Ford; it has changed form again and now amuses and bewilders the white man but makes perfect sense to the Indian. (Redbird 1973)

I have known Aboriginal people who lived in automobiles. Along similar lines, I have noticed that most Aboriginals do not like to change gears while driving but remain within whatever gear they are in for as long as possible; the most preferred gear is high, in which they will drive at all speeds and in most conditions, even with the load of a dozen passengers. It is as if high gear provides the least assertive, most harmonious ambience available. One partly Europeanized young Aboriginal person who broke the laces on a newly purchased pair of boots continued to wear them for months without laces. Less acculturated elderly Aboriginal men have left their shoes in my car and carried on for weeks barefoot and contented.

A part-Aboriginal described the differences in this way:

One of the basic differences between white and dark people is the ability to worry. White people worry a lot about money and those things they want to possess or do possess. They may commit suicide because of their worries. This does not happen to the dark man. I am sure he is happier when he has nothing. He does not envy the possessions of white people and finds it difficult to care for his belongings. (Mathews 1977: 185)

However, Aboriginal people have come to recognize that if they are to defend their traditional homelands, they will need to sharpen their cognitive skills. An elder on the school board of the only Aboriginal-administered school in Australia told me: 'When whitefellas come to this country, he bin kill 'em blackfella. Now we learn all this *wangka* [talk; literacy], we win the country back.' The irony of their predicament is that the very capabilities they require in order to protect their traditional values are those which, when achieved, will render them more European than Aboriginal; nevertheless, Aboriginals are today insistent upon defining their own Aboriginal modernity without Anglo-Australian interference.

5 Anglo-Australian appraisals of Aboriginal people

When James Cook set sail for the southern ocean in the *Endeavour* in 1768, he carried with the ship's papers the following advice regarding the 'Natives of the several lands where the Ship may touch, given to him by the President of the British Royal Society, one of the sponsors of his voyage to observe the transit of Venus' (Beaglehole 1955: 514):

> They are the natural, and in the strictest sense of the word, the legal possessors of the several Regions they inhabit.
>
> No European Nation has a right to occupy any part of their country, or settle among them without their voluntary consent.
>
> Conquest over such people can give no just title: because they could never be the Aggressors.

On their way, the men of the *Endeavour*, and of the other voyages of discovery, visited a great many coastal and island peoples and came to develop a sophistication regarding the brute reality of European–'savage' encounters which was greater than that of the more sedentary members of the Royal Society.

By the time the British arrived in Australia the various 'inhabitants' of the lands they visited were more or less lumped into one general nuisance, objects of curiosity and even scientific inquiry, but ultimately only natives whose destiny it was to be dominated. The Aboriginal people of Australia, called 'Indians' (Tench 1789: 54), as were most of the American and Pacific inhabitants, were compared with natives of other locales in terms of both strength and material culture. Having suffered opposition from other inhabitants, such as the Mouna tribesmen of the Isles des Navigateurs who attacked some of the British settlers en route to Botany Bay (Collins 1798: 17), the British were inclined to presume danger and were quick to utilize their firepower.

Accustomed to hierarchy in their own society and in societies of the other 'Indians' they had encountered, many of the explorers immediately presumed that the most conspicuous or best 'proportioned' Aboriginal was their 'chief' (Tuckey 1805: 169, 174-5). The explorers and settlers saw little more than their own projections.

With some exceptions (Hawkesworth 1773: 493 and King 1825: 48 among them), the Europeans were surprised with the generally pacific response of the Australian 'Indians' and proceeded to take advantage of such a disposition without hesitation. Notwithstanding the dim prospect of the Aboriginals offering their homeland in exchange for the opportunity to experience British civilization, one of the Port Jackson chroniclers (Hunter 1793: 58) recorded: 'From that appearance of a friendly disposition, I am inclined to think, that by residing some time amongst, or near them, they will soon discover that we are not their enemies.' A number of sailors and settlers were pleased to be able to help the Aboriginals by offering them fishhooks, hatchets and the like; however, the attitude of the British was more accurately displayed in the actions of Royal Society member and botanist Joseph Banks who, upon returning to England, pressed for settlement of Australia on the argument that the inhabitants were 'few and cowardly' (Price 1957: 65).

I have discussed the basis for this assessment, i.e., the proclivity of the Aboriginals to run off at the approach of the Europeans and their customary shame, but the other side of this relationship remains to be examined: while the Aboriginals were less than eager for social intercourse, the Europeans were usually so overwhelmed with curiosity that they chased the Aboriginals on land and sea whenever they saw them or their fires:

> Some smokes being perceived at the head of the harbour, Mr. Brown and other gentlemen directed their excursion that way . . . but like the generality of people hitherto seen in this country, these men did not seem to be desirous of communication with strangers; and they very early made signs to our gentlemen to return from whence they came. (Flinders 1814: 58)

> It was not without the greatest difficulty that Mr. Bedwell succeeded in bringing one on board. On the boat's coming up with the nearest Indian, he left his log and, diving under the boat's bottom, swam astern; this he did whenever the boat approached him, and it was four or five minutes before he was caught, which was at last effected by seizing him by the hair, in the act of diving, and dragging him into the boat, against which

he resisted stoutly, and, even when taken, it required two men
to hold him to prevent his escape. (King 1827: 38-9)

The botanist of the D'Entrecasteaux expedition M. Riche
followed the smokes of fires for many miles through the bush of
southwestern Australia but was unable to catch up with the
Aboriginals and had to content himself with examining their feces
for '*les pepins et les grains*' which would indicate at least which
plants were their major food sources (D'Entrecasteaux 1808:
199). The curious Europeans could hardly have faced a
personality more opposite.

Hegel has investigated the degree to which we are dependent
upon the other for our being. As soon as we are faced with
another self-consciousness we are forced out of ourselves: 'Self-
consciousness has lost itself, for it finds itself as an *other* being'
(1977: 111). The other's exteriority constitutes a challenge to our
own life's totalization because it does not fall within our
totalization's domain; rather, it indicates 'an *elsewhere* which
escapes me and escapes all totalization because it is itself a
developing totalization' (Sartre 1976: 105). The certainty of one's
own world cannot be assured until one has brought the other's
totalization under some sort of control.

The Europeans sought the Aboriginals in order to reaffirm for
themselves their own supremacy. One finds one's being by way of
the other; to be Master one must find a slave. The encounter with
an other must, according to Hegel, lead to a struggle where each
tries to supersede the other, for each 'must raise their certainty of
being *for themselves* to truth' (Hegel 1977: 114). The very
presence of the Aboriginals called for the struggle, which in every
case the British took up at once:

Our first object was to win their affections, and our next to
convince them of the superiority we possessed: for without the
latter, the former we knew would be of little importance.
(Tench 1789: 57)

The metaphysical character of this struggle is revealed by the
care, and even fanaticism, with which English explorers con-
cealed any weaknesses which dim the armor of their superiority.
Mitchell, a 19th-century explorer of the Riverine district of New
South Wales, recorded his concern:

We next yoked the bullocks to the empty drays and cart on the
opposite side, and all were soon brought safely through the
river to our own side. I preferred doing this work when the
natives were absent, because I did not wish them to see what

151

difficulties the passage of a river occasioned to us. (Mitchell 1838, I: 115)

Burke and Wills, the mid-19th-century explorers who were the first to cross the center of Australia from south to north, ran out of food and water near the Simpson Desert on their return but refused to call for help to some Aboriginals they met, even though the Aboriginals could have saved their lives. Their diary records show that they did not want Aboriginal people to see a European in distress but preferred to continue unaided, a choice which proved to be fatal for them.

Hegel notes that the other is not seen at first as an essential being but only as the reflection of one's own self. As I discussed in the cases of Flinders and Mitchell, the Aboriginals were seen as fodder to be utilized, either to act as laborers or as informants; their own totalization was a disturbance at times challenging and at times only annoying: 'The will and hindrance of the natives much impeded my progress [in recording their habits], or rather led to a wasting of labor in profitless wanderings' (O'Connell 1836: 81). The first missionaries at Kalumburu in the Kimberley region of Western Australia arrived by ship at the mouth of the Drysdale River with the Abbot himself in tow – 'The Abbot moved freely among [the Aboriginals], caressing some' (Perez 1977: 10) – completely oblivious to the actual experience of the Aboriginal people he came to save, until one of the lesser monks informed him, 'Father, they want war.' In imposing their own reality upon the Aboriginals, the Europeans only experienced a relationship of themselves with themselves; they failed to recognize the Aboriginal people in their essential being.

After the explorers had spent more time with Aboriginal people, they observed many features of Aboriginal society which they considered to be evidence of their inferiority. They gradually became aware of the fact that Aboriginals had little or no governing social hierarchy, and this was taken to indicate their low degree of societal advancement:

> To me, indeed, they appeared altogether the most stupid and insensible race of man I had ever seen.
> They are wholly without any form of government, or any family or individual whom they acknowledge as their king or chief. (Turnbull 1813: 97)

> Although some personal respect is sometimes paid to a kind of chief among a tribe, it would seem that it is altogether personal and independent of any right, either hereditary or elective. (Welles 1859: 222)

> Excepting a little tributary respect which the younger part
> appear to pay those more advanced in years, I never could
> observe any degrees of subordination among them. (Tench
> 1789: 89)

Surprise was also expressed about the lack of subordination of
youths towards adults (Tuckey 1805: 185). And Collins (1798: 16)
wrote about how they left their spears and other articles 'loose
and scattered about.' All the English officers could do was just to
keep the convicts from taking advantage of their carelessness and
stealing their articles. But the intransigence of Aboriginal
backwardness was perhaps most celebrated in the Aboriginal
reluctance to don the clothes which the Europeans so willingly
offered them. One Sydney colonist lamented; 'however well you
may cloathe them, they generally return naked the next day'
(Hunter 1793: 487). This would serve well as the epigraph for the
first century of Aboriginal-European contact.

Most of the European accounts record with some amazement
the 'vociferous' (Collins 1798: 3) character of Aboriginal
discourse, a phenomenon I have examined in Part I:

> . . . talking to each other at the same time with such rapidity
> and vociferation as I had never before heard. (Tench 1789: 56)

> The manners of these people are quick and vehement, and
> their conversation vociferous, like that of most uncivilized
> people. (Flinders 1814: 66)

> the passions were strongly marked, as they succeeded each
> other in rapid succession, and their whole figure was changed
> and modified with their affections. (Péron 1809: 217)

Far from being uncivilized, the fault of a general inability to
respect the participation of others, Aboriginal discourse (relative
to European discourse) is characterized by humility. The
vociferation and repetitive succession the Europeans noted are
components of the structure of discourse whereby Aboriginals
make ideas and events available for public affirmation – the
discussion is productive of group cohesion. Far from being the
collision of too many egos obsessed with themselves, Aboriginal
vociferation is designed to celebrate the collective life of the
assembly over that of its individual members. A turn of speaking
in Aboriginal discourse is usually not something which is
possessed by anyone. To *possess* talk requires an egoistic
structure of public identity and possibly also a degree of social
hierarchy. What was chaotic for European observers was in fact
orderly interaction for Aboriginals.

The same accounts refer also to the Aboriginal inclination to engage in convivial vocal gesture, a practice which we found to be connected with the production of congenial social relations:

> When anything pleased them, they expressed their satisfaction by a shout. (Collins 1790)

> The whole tribe began to shout and laugh in the most extravagant way. (King 1827: 112)

> They burst into the most immoderate fits of laughter. (Tench 1789: 56)

One explorer (Mitchell 1838, I: 285) took this Aboriginal discourse practice personally, describing the Aboriginals engaged in 'loud laughing to each other at our expense.'

Regardless of the actual function of such conversational practices, the settlers were convinced that the Aboriginal people were uncivilized and saw as the Aboriginals' only hope their capitulation to the civilization of the British Isles. In 1814 Governor Macquarie wrote to Lord Bathurst in London:

> the Aborigines had scarcely emerged from the remotest state of rude and uncivilized nature, that they appeared to possess some qualities which if properly cultivated and encouraged might render them not only less wretched and destitute by reason of their wild wandering and unsettled habits, but progressively useful to the country either as agricultural labourers or a lower class of mechanics. (Clark 1962: 280)

Thus a monumental cultural-political struggle between Aboriginal- and Anglo-Australians was born, a struggle the outcome of which remains in doubt in central and northern Australia in the late 20th century.

The absence of a concern for the future, the convivial spontaneity which Aboriginals preserve in their ordinary social intercourse, the absence of an authoritarian structure of social relations, and perhaps above all the lack of a strictly regulated, reserved self-control (listed by Weber, 1958: 173, as one of the major characteristics of English Protestantism) combined to bring the English settlers to consider the Aboriginal people as children: 'we were amusing ourselves with these children of ignorance' (Collins 1798: 137). Using their own primary socialization as a yardstick, the English settlers associated what was merely the absence of customary English socialization with the status of children. Adults were serious people who dedicated themselves in disciplined ways to orderly tasks, while Aboriginals appeared never to labor beyond what was necessary to satisfy the day's demands and were rarely serious, even on the occasions of their most sacred rites.

Bestowing upon Aboriginal people the status of children is a practice which has characterized Aboriginal- and Anglo-Australian interaction throughout the history of the European occupation of Australia. The records of missions and government settlements are filled with references to 'boys,' even when they are speaking of adults. A letter dropped from an airplane pilot on the Kalumburu mission in 1929 read, 'We trust that you will send out boys if we don't return on flights to be made in a day or two' (Perez 1977: 82). As a recent social and political study of Canada has found (Friedenberg 1980: 129): 'Proper British, and proper Canadians, treat foreigners and those not naturally Anglophone as children.' The attitude persists in Australia to the present day; I can count in the hundreds the number of Anglo-Australians who have summarized their feelings about Aboriginals in this way – 'It's too late. We've spoiled them.' That Aboriginal people may have deliberately and maturely attempted to exploit Anglo-Australian resources without sacrificing very much of their own habits and traditions is seldom considered; rather, the failure to become socialized into Anglo-Australian society is more commonly interpreted as a failure to modernize rooted in the backwardness of the Aboriginal mentality.

The journalists of the Sydney colony (Collins 1798, Hunter 1793, Turnbull 1813) paint the picture of a benevolent and humanitarian governing authority which was unable to restrain the excesses of the convicts and settlers who molested Aboriginals. Petty theft (of spears and other artifacts stolen for barter with supply ships), physical harassment and illicit sexual contacts aroused the Aboriginals' anger, but such offenses were viewed to be the responsibility of a lower-class sort of person (slovenly commoners) and were not seen to reflect upon the high motives of the aristocratic officers who husbanded the early English occupation. This attitude persisted for many years; Mitchell (1838, I: 272) lamented, 'I was indeed paying dearly for geographical discovery, when my honour and character were delivered over to convicts, I could not always rely for humanity.' It was genuinely believed that the colonization of Australia was necessary for the prosperity of the European world and would in the long term also prove beneficial for the native inhabitants; if colonization was desirable, the excesses of some of the early British settlers constituted an unfortunate and regrettable situation, although such failings were inevitable given the innate imperfections of the human species and the scale of so complex a human venture.

However it was, the process of settlement and colonization continued, and very soon a young pastoral industry began to penetrate to more interior regions from the coastal settlements, first along the rivers of the southeast running westward from the Dividing Range and then to every location where the climate and rainfall would permit. The occupation of Aboriginal lands was justified on the grounds that Aboriginals were 'many centuries behind' British civilization (White 1790: 205) and were unable to utilize the land to its considered full potential. A visitor to Australia in the early 19th century (O'Connell 1836: 82) described the Aboriginal people as 'the connecting link between apes and men.' The notion of historical evolution which viewed society as commencing with savages and culminating with British civilization became the organizing ideology justifying the English occupation of Australia. Evidence of such a social evolutionary bias is present throughout Australian literature. Here are three illustrations, from *A Short History of Australia*, *World Book Encyclopedia*, and *Australia's Heritage*:

> They were a people so low in the scale of human development . . . (Scott 1936: 185)

> They had not even developed the bow and arrow. (World Book Encyclopedia 1963, I: 756)

> The Australian natives . . . never advanced beyond the Stone Age. (Sparkes 1970: 52)

A more popular version is demonstrated by these comments from the essay of an Australian university student taking a correspondence course on Australian history in 1977:

> Man had thus grown from an ignorant hunter living a precarious nomadic existence to the development of agriculture skills and the growth of the first cities, to become a more reasoning cosmopolitan being, occupying a certain position in society decreed either by birth or physical ability.

The movement toward British civilization was inexorable. During my field research, the Magistrate for Carnarvon, Western Australia, explained to me that the Aboriginal people's innate inferiority was proven by the facts that they had 'never invented the wheel, never developed agriculture and never colonized.' For the Anglo-Australians there was only one route to civilization, and following that route was a moral obligation which overshadowed responsibilities towards native peoples such as the President of the Royal Society suggested in 1768.

The settlers depended heavily upon Aboriginal people for the successful establishment of pastoral concerns. The Aboriginals living in the districts slated for pastoral development became virtually unpaid labor for the station. Young part-European Aboriginal men raised in mission settlements closer to the coast were 'apprenticed' to pastoral owners for two years or more at a time (Mathews 1977: 93; Western Australian Royal Commission 1974: 11 and 23) and served as indentured laborers. A white Australian born in the Western Australian outback at the turn of the century and sympathetic with the Aboriginal people of that region described the process of establishing a sheep or cattle ranch in this way:

> Now when you started up muckin' [pastoral industry], your blackfellas never knew up from down. They were kind people and you said that you were their 'brother' [according to Aboriginal subsection classifications] and patted them on the back and then circled their wives and daughters, and knocked up a few half-caste kids just to show who the family belonged to. They shepherded your sheep and dug soaks for them so that they wouldn't perish, and then when you sold enough wool – well, you killed kangaroos and brought them in for meat so you wouldn't have to kill your precious sheep too. And then when you sold enough wool to put up wire and windmills, the blackfellas erected those and put the fences up. And they never paid them fuck-all, did they. They used both their labor and their land for nothing.

If there were any considerations of conscience on the part of the English settlers, it was assuaged with the thought that Christian missionaries were providing a more humanitarian introduction to civilization for them. But the work of the missionaries was characterized by the forced separation of children from their parents, fanatic imposition of European religious and sexual mores and generally little tolerance for the perpetuation of Aboriginal customs (cf. Tonkinson 1974). A review of the accounts of missionaries reveals a preoccupation with the details of European life and politics. The record of a missionary in Victoria in the 19th century (Young 1854) reveals an almost exclusive concern with the logistical detail facing the establishment and development of the mission – Aboriginal people are mentioned almost as afterthoughts necessary only as the initial justification. Here again, the essential being of Aboriginal people was represented as merely an unessential objectification, the projection of a European alter ego.

The motivation of the missionaries was praiseworthy, by European standards; only they failed to recognize the Aboriginal

157

person as his own subjectivity:

> Basically the work of the Catholic missionary is to give
> testimony to the truth (objective truth based on reason and on
> God's own revelation, through his Word made man, Jesus
> Christ) to preach by words and action the good news of man's
> salvation.
>
> On this basis the missionary approached the Australian
> Aborigine, not with preconceived scientific or romantic ideas
> of economic or intellectual adventure . . . but as the unfortun-
> ate man of the gospel story, in need of sympathy, love,
> understanding, and a helping hand from the good neighbour.
> (Perez 1977: 56)

The missionaries genuinely wished to bring Jesus Christ's
message of peace to the Aboriginal people, whose apparently
incessant revenge violence among rival groups disturbed the
missionaries. The gentle congeniality which characterizes the
ambience of a great deal of ordinary Aboriginal interaction was
less apparent, with some exceptions (e.g., Bates 1966).

The major concern of the missionaries was religious conversion, although they did provide the Aboriginals some protection
against the worst excesses of the new settlers. A contemporary
piece of literature prepared by the United Aboriginal Mission
(n.d.) explains Christianity to the Western Desert Aboriginals:

> God said: 'If you leave my word you will die.'
>   Have I broken his law?
> Yes, you have truly!
> God said: 'All are sinners. All have left Me.'
>   Is God angry?
> Yes. He is angry because of sin.

The booklet is written in both English and in the Western Desert
Aboriginal language, with illustrations; however, the word 'sin'
does not translate ('*palyamunu*' = 'not good').

The missionaries' notion of success is evident in this passage,
from the annual report of the Rev. William Watson in 1845
(Commonwealth 1925, XXIV: 272):

> When I see these young men dressed in a clean and respectable
> manner, and with their Bibles and Prayer Books coming to
> church, and especially when I behold those, who in their native
> fights have been as ferocious as beasts of prey, sitting meekly
> under the word of God, and tears rolling down their manly
> cheeks, I cannot bring myself to believe that no good has been
> affected by our labours.

The Aboriginals' enthusiasm for Christian forms had to be dampened in some respects, particularly when the Aboriginals' attitude was too convivial in the wrong context. Here is the Rev. Watson's report for 1843 (*ibid.*, XXIII: 495):

> The children frequently sing hymns by themselves; a few evenings ago when they were thus engaged, one of them laughed, another of them immediately said, 'Don't laugh when you are singing, it is mocking God.' These instances show . . . that they are indeed capable of moral culture and of becoming possessed of Christian principles.

The missions did not always meet with such success, particularly in the more remote regions. The records of the Kalumburu mission in Western Australia show that the Aboriginals were considered selfish when they did not assist the missionaries in their projects (Perez 1977: 115); nevertheless, the missionaries were generally determined men:

> 'The story of this mission is the best witness to the progressive tactics used by the Aborigines to carry out their wicked intentions. We believe, therefore, that our neighbours are planning a new attack in their minds. Under such circum-stances so critical for the very existence of the Mission, we are ready, with the greatest sorrow in our hearts, to take the initiative at the slightest sign of treachery, as our only way of self-defence. Toribio has the rifle ready, and we are preparing the other arms for ourselves . . . We are in the chapel saying our prayers, with the Rosary in one hand, and the revolver in the other.' (*Ibid.*: 23-4)

While the missions were concerned with conversion, the settlements constructed by the various state governments, also called 'missions,' were concerned with acculturation. The func-tion of the government missions was to facilitate the settlement of the Australian outback by removing the Aboriginal residents from their traditional locations in the regions being settled by whites. These institutions were especially concerned with part-European Aboriginals, often the progeny of forced copulation in previous generations, in the belief that they could be the most easily civilized; nevertheless, Aboriginals who were as much as three-fourths European retained their Aboriginal identity (having been raised by half-Aboriginal mothers in Aboriginal camps). In the government settlement, they were taught that such an identity was inferior:

> School started early in February . . . It was on this day that I

learnt how unacceptable Aborigines are to other people. The manager told us straight out that we were just 'nothing'. He continued at some length, telling us that Australian blacks were recognized as the lowest type of humanity living today. (Mathews 1977: 56)

'All nations have a flag, but the blacks have not. A blanket would be good enough for you.' (*Ibid.*: 122)

The point here is not to belabor the racist character of the European settlement of Australia (of that there can be no doubt); what is essential is to appreciate that not only were Aboriginal people dominated but that their domination was justified by a consistent rationale which provided for the British settlers verification of the morality of such domination. A contemporary anthropologist (Koepping 1975) calls the perpetuation of such moral notions today 'mental colonialism.'

The confrontation of Aboriginal- and Anglo-Australians was ultimately a cultural and political collision. And Christianity was not the only justifying apparatus. Nineteenth-century Western humankind viewed the mechanically instituted domination of the world as a sacred charge; it was the age of Progress. Heisenberg (1962: 169) well describes the mental attitude of the time:

The nineteenth century developed an extremely rigid frame for natural science which formed not only science but also the general outlook of great masses of people. This frame was supported by the fundamental concepts of classical physics, space, time, matter and causality; the concept of reality applied to things or events that we could perceive by means of the refined tools that technical science had provided. Matter was the primary reality. The progress of science was pictured as a crusade of conquest into the material world. Utility was the watchword of the time.

It was difficult then, and difficult now, to convince the practical-minded Anglo-Australian that the Aboriginals should be permitted to remain on their traditional lands and engage in their inefficient and primitive means of economic pursuits. I once drove an Anglo-Australian windmill engineer to an isolated homeland encampment in order to investigate the possibilities of building a windmill for the Aboriginals residing there. While he was willing to undertake the job for pay, he couldn't see the value of assisting the perpetuation of a traditional lifestyle – it was throwing good money after bad. I explained that the windmill would reduce their dependence on the local settlement and render less frequent their visits to the closest outback towns, where they face the perils of alcohol abuse. He replied, 'But you see, Ken, that doesn't make any difference because they're just sitting down, not engaged in earning any livelihood.' I answered, 'Well, when they're living at these homeland camps, they secure about 70% of their own food; that's almost a livelihood.' He fell into a contemplative silence and appeared to be somewhat intrigued, until we drove up on a couple of the Aboriginals' dogs lying in the road when he remarked (in outback slang), 'Get atta the road ya lazy basstahds.' There was no ambiguity for the engineer about the uselessness of the Aboriginals' dogs. I did not inform him that the dogs were often essential to the success of the Aboriginals' hunt.

In the end the engineer was unconvinced by my argument. The basic problem was that there was no teleology to the Aboriginals' economic praxis. Their 'calling' had no future except more of the same: it led nowhere. What counted for him was evident material advancement; without in some way assisting general progress what could be the value of one's life? Here we have located the metaphysical root of the cultural–political conflict: what makes one's life meaningful for a European is that it is productive. One in some way makes the world a *better* place and redeems one's life with a contribution which has its fulfilment in some *futural* maturation, a future which has benevolently infinite implications. For the Aboriginal person, there is no thought of a future; in such a lived reality the world appears closed upon itself too finally for a European's spiritual aspirations. Of the Aboriginals' spiritual aspirations the engineer knew nothing, and so the Aboriginals' life praxis was characterized only negatively.

The struggle with Aboriginals was necessary – science itself had demonstrated that competition was the way of all life. Drawing upon the sociobiology of aggression, Anglo-Australian folk ideology holds that people are *basically* competitive. Drawing upon scientific theories of evolution, they believed that it was necessary and correct for those most fit to survive. Man is by nature territorial, and the struggles of competing societies only result in the survival of the more able people. It is the victory itself that justifies the victorious. Such folk science provided justification for the Hobbesian nature of British social existence, and the Anglo-Australian personality traits of individualism, competitiveness and egoism were given a scientific basis. The Aboriginals fell victim to 'a bastard melange of pseudo-Darwinism and the assumptions of a stock-breeder' (Rowley 1970: 198).

By the mid-19th century the Aboriginal people were taken for granted. The continent belonged to European civilization, and

161

Anglo-Australians had much work to 'get on with.' An English visitor's Australian travelogue (Hood 1843) mentioned Aboriginal people on only 12 of its 465 pages, and then only after offering an apology for the digression.

But the domination of any people can never be secure and is always subject to the possibility that those subjugated will exercise their freedom. What is more, to the extent that the Anglo-Australian immigrants became something like lords in the Australian outback, the essence of their domination was dependent upon the participation of the Aboriginal people. As Sartre (1956: 237) says, 'The Master is not certain of his being for himself as truth,' but ironically becomes dependent upon the slave for the meaning of his social being. 'To be dependent upon a dependent consciousness is not real independence. It is not to be certain of one's truth' (Olafson 1980). Discussing Hegel, Ogilvy (1980: 202) explains,

> An individual proto-self-consciousness which is not 'recognized' by any other self-consciousness can surely affirm its own individuality as a single, individual existence; but apart from the process of determination through negation vis-a-vis another self-consciousness, that individual cannot gain the determinate characteristics which constitute the essence (and not just the existence) of a particular self-consciousness.

The Aboriginal people had entered without remedy the heart of the Anglo-Australians' own essence, and this failure to secure an independent hegemony impelled many white Australians sadistically to drive their mastery more deeply into their Aboriginal subjects. These were the 'hard blokes' who would tolerate no 'cheek' from the Aboriginals. Here is an Aboriginal's record of one pastoralist's attitude. (cf. also Parker 1978):

> He told me that I was apprenticed to him for four years and I must never try to run away. I must not address anyone by their Christian name, and must do everything I was asked to do. Any refusal or rudeness would be dealt with by him. He stressed that I must not raise my hands to anyone, even in self-defence. (Mathews 1977: 93)

The control exercised by the Anglo-Australians had to be total; the remarkable thing is that its very totality produced a certain self-righteousness about the use of such power, a quality which is not absent among contemporary outback Anglo-Australians who continue to operate their remote ranches as diminutive fiefdoms. The *New Yorker* film critic Pauline Kael (1980: 149-50) well describes the countenance of these masters-come-lately in her

162

review of *The Chant of Jimmie Blacksmith*:

> Irish and Scottish and English men who were at the bottom in
> Europe now command thousands of acres. Scrabbling tight-
> wads, these white landowners got where they are by self-
> denial. Penny-pinching is a moral tenet to them, and they don't
> regard cheating the helpless aborigines as cheating, because the
> aborigines don't know how to save their money anyway . . .
> These isolated farmers are terse, close-mouthed, as if even a
> little companionable chat would be a profligacy, a waste. They
> can't resist finding fault with Jimmie's work and shorting him
> on his pay; thrift and mistrust have become second nature to
> them. Besides, they need to see him fail; it confirms the
> necessity of keeping the savages in their place.

The intensity and personalization of the Anglo-Australians'
dominance was motivated by their desire to raise their mastery to
truth. As a constant task, they had to reassure themselves that
the Aboriginals remained contained within their bondage – the
Aboriginals' subjection had to be reified.

> Thus the Other-as-object is an explosive instrument which I
> handle with care because I foresee around him the permanent
> possibility that *they* are going to make it explode and that with
> this explosion I shall suddenly experience the flight of the
> world away from me and the alienation of my being. Therefore
> my constant concern is to contain the Other within his
> objectivity, and my relations with the Other-as-object are
> essentially made up of ruses designed to make him remain an
> object. (Sartre 1956: 297)

I will examine what these ruses consist of in chapter 7. Within
such a situation there is no incentive for understanding the
Aboriginals' own lived experience; on the contrary, he is to be
denied any interests apart from his own bondage to white
Australians.

A caption for an etching published along with the journals of
an explorer of Western Australia's interior (Carnegie 1898: 241)
reads, 'A Buck And His Gins Camp At Family Well.' The
drawing depicts a traditional Aboriginal family, and the implication is that their status was that of mere animals. Similarly, a
former miner explained to me that during the Western Australian
gold rush there were three sorts of people: 'People in the mining
camps have three categories – "human beings," "wogs," and
"boongs." The "wogs" [i.e., Italians, Greeks, etc.] could come
into the pub so long as they didn't jabber, and the "boongs" had
to get their beer "round the back." ' The ontological essence of

non-Anglo-Australians was objectified within the Australian dialect of English. Safely located as 'coons,' 'boongs,' 'darkies' and 'Abos,' the essential subjective life of the Aboriginal people could be masked. Racist terminology abounded and was frequently employed regarding non-Aboriginals and even Anglo-Australian contexts. Eccentric people were all 'Chinamen,' and a great many orbicular objects were 'round as a Jew's nose.' The Kalgoorlie *Sun* of April 9, 1905, published a typical poem by a miner who refused a billet at Mt Morgans, saying he should go hang rather than toil with 'a blanky 'Ghan.' The camp at Lancefield was like 'a foreign sink,' and at the Gwalia mine the 'Dagos' swarmed like bees (Smith 1977: 73-4):

> From Esperance to Murchison is in their vampire grip,
> It's like a trip to foreign parts to do the Outback Trip.

Many Chinese workers were killed in the Western Australian goldfields; as for Aboriginal people, this comment of an Anglo-Australian defendant is indicative of the attitude prevalent during the initial years of interior settlement: 'We were not aware that in killing the blacks we were violating the law . . . as it has been so frequently done before' (Barnard 1962: 654; cf. Millis 1985).

Anglo-Australians were often inclined to satirize the Aboriginals' accent when speaking English, as if their poor command of English grammar was certain evidence of their low social status, just as it was in the case of members of the English lower class. Such satire was commonplace during the two years I spent in the Australian outback; here is the account of one Anglo-Australian old-timer:

> Squatters used to tell a story about blackfellows years ago and in so doing established in their own minds a sort of prestige, the logic of which was not easy to follow since it was merely a play on words, and the blackfellows were quite unfamiliar with English words. Their bewilderment should have been quite easy to understand, but apparently the squatters needed such things to give them justification for how they held the blackfellows in thrall.
>
> The story went like this: a squatter and a blackfellow had been out shooting but had not done very well, getting only one duck and one crow for their efforts. On the way home the squatter put a proposition up to the blackfellow, and being just and honest with his working man, gave him two options thus – 'Well, Jacky, we haven't done that good so we will make an even split on our bag; you can have the crow and I will have the duck; or I will have the duck and you can have the crow;

make your own choice.' The blackfellow asked the squatter to set it up again so the squatter repeated his proposition. The blackfellow then made the request that the squatter say it again and say it slow since it seemed to him that he got that plurry crow every time.

Most importantly, the Anglo-Australians were very concerned to inculcate in the Aboriginal people a sense for the necessity of regular work and discipline. Most of the early accounts describe the Aboriginals as lazy, an opinion which persists to the present day. Hood (1843: 190) commented, 'These blacks are a curious race: indolent to a degree, and willing to do nothing but baske in the sun.' Stephen Simpson, a Commissioner for Crown Lands, reported in 1844:

They are in general a good-natured, cheerful race, by no means deficient in intelligence, but having few wants; they consider increased comforts dearly purchased by increased toil, and the abandonment of that merry reckless life they lead in the wilds of Australia; hence, though when pinched by hunger they may occasionally consent to labour to supply their immediate wants, these are no sooner satisfied than they return to their usual habits. (Commonwealth 1925, XXIII: 487)

A conflict of values is usually mistaken for indolence. The report for the District of Moreton Bay, Queensland, for the same year expresses the despair felt by many Anglo-Australians about implanting in the Aboriginals a Protestant sense of work:

The Aborigines of Brisbane, Amity Point and Ipswich, from 500 to 600 in number, have for years been within reach of civilized man, but without, I fear, any real improvements in their moral or social condition; they are still as lazy and indolent as ever, preferring with few exceptions, and those old men and children, the joyous life of the bush to earning a scanty livelihood by daily labour from the inhabitants . . . it is to be hoped that the rising generation at least will ultimately learn the advantages of labour. (Commonwealth 1925, XXIV: 258)

And a Catholic missionary moaned more directly (Perez 1977: 118), 'Who can feed so many loafers?'

The correct way to deal with Aboriginal people, most Anglo-Australians believe, is to refrain from giving them any benefits without requiring them to perform some work. A retired miner spoke to me about the head missionary at Mt Margaret Mission in Western Australia:

If they came in from the bush and wanted a feed, he said [pointing], 'Straight to the wood heap,' and they had to chop a pile of wood before they could have a feed . . . That was his prime rule – nothing for nothing – and it should be applied equally black or white. He put hundreds of blackfellows on the right path. Now some say later that they left the path. But if they did, that wasn't his fault, it's their own.

As Barnard (1962: 658) observed, year by year the official reports became more despondent. It was impossible to acculturate them; they were lazy and unreliable. If anything, with government guarantees of equal wages, social security benefits for the elderly and support of duly constituted Aboriginal 'councils,' Aboriginal people have become even less amenable to Protestant notions of work. One contemporary pastoralist bemoaned one July, 'It used to be they'd go corroborrin' two months a year, around Christmas, but now they're corroborrin' all year long. And that's because the government gives them all welfare pensions. They haven't stopped corroborrin' since last September.'

The earliest British settlers observed that the Aboriginals' greatest love was the religious dance of the 'corrobories' (*turlku*, in the Western Desert idiom), and this has changed little in the remote outback. With the increased opportunities for large gatherings made possible by a reliable food supply and access to vehicular transport, some Aboriginals are today engaging in more celebrations than they could have performed in traditional times. This irritates most outback Anglo-Australians, who view the increase of Aboriginal ceremonial activity as a threat. When I was living in Leonora, Western Australia, one nearby pastoral leasee who had arrived only a few years previously heard the Aboriginals' religious chants through the quiet of one night and went to investigate; when he found them engaged in a sacred ceremony, he ordered them sternly to cease at once or be thrown off his property, even though there were Aboriginals present who had been born and raised on the station and had traditional connections to the religious spot on which they were singing.

Because most Aboriginal people in the outback have refused to submit to a work schedule of forty hours a week, white Australians have criticized their lack of dependability: 'Discipline really kills these Aborigines, who find it intolerable to have to go to the Anjo Peninsula every two weeks without fail, even though they are given food in abundance, and many other presents as well' (Perez 1977: 115). The material pleasures of European life are not desired to the point that most Aboriginals are willing to reorganize their lives according to Anglo-Australian ideas of economic productivity. As Turnbull (1813) reported in 1801, 'They still persist in the enjoyment of their ease and liberty in their own way.'

Anglo-Australians have found particularly unnerving the customary free run Aboriginals give their children. Even anthropologists have been critical of the Aboriginal failure to discipline their children: 'The Ooldea children are indulged by their parents to an extreme degree. The good effects of any punishment are immediately nullified by indulgence' (R. and C. Berndt 1942-6, XIII: 251). It is certainly the case that Aboriginal children know few constraints. As one Kimberley Aboriginal elder told me, the 'Aboriginal way' was to allow children to do nothing but play. The almost universal tolerance of Aboriginal people extends most emphatically to children.

On many missions and settlements the Aboriginal children seem to be employed as a political weapon; there are few government and missionary settlements where major buildings of importance to the administration of the settlement have not been seriously vandalized, some costing more than a million dollars' worth of damage. A part-European Aboriginal person recorded his own complaint: 'On the mission I have seen a child breaking windows just for the fun of it. His parents were close but would neither say nor do anything to stop the destruction' (Mathews 1977: 187). While Aboriginal adults do not necessarily approve of their children's actions, the buildings destroyed are symbols of Anglo-Australian authority, and some Aboriginal people are content tacitly to allow the attacks to occur.

Such refusal to discipline their offspring offends the Anglo-Australian sense of order. The comment of one pastoralist is typical: 'They have to learn discipline, these kids. They've got to start spanking them at the age of seven.' Most Aboriginal people I lived with were highly critical of Anglo-Australian attempts to initiate stricter practices of child-rearing, while lack of discipline in childhood is considered by whites to be one of the main causes of the adults' lack of dependability. Another pastoralist explained the indolence of Aboriginal people to me – 'Well, they never punish their kids, now do they?' Here is the politics of culture conflict. The Anglo-Australian assessment of Aboriginal people which best characterizes the second century of European–Aboriginal contact is the appraisal of a young geologist from Perth, Western Australia, who had just arrived in the remote Aboriginal-inhabited outback for the first time. 'They've got to shape up,' he concluded.

Part III
Intercultural communication
in the Western Desert

6 The hermeneutics of intercultural communication

Any politics of culture conflict operates within a specific communicative environment, and it is the task of a rigorous ethnomethodological analysis to appreciate the strategic moves of such a cultural politics just as they are embedded in the particulars of their interactional setting. Though the communicative environment of any intercultural contact is specific in the sense that it provides material possibilities for a mutually confirmed understanding, in most instances this communicative environment has the additional feature of being indeterminate for all participants; that is to say, the communication which is emerging is problematic. Where multicultural contacts occur, the cultural politics which ensue finds itself embedded in pregnant half-formulations, indeterminate senses and miscommunications whose ambiguities are only partly appreciated by the participants themselves. Understanding this indeterminacy – and what it is that parties do with it – is basic to knowing what is occurring in intercultural social interaction.

It is one of the shortcomings of both empiricist and rationalist efforts to explain intercultural communication that an examination of this indeterminacy is omitted. By their reducing the interaction to a collection of favored cultured components which are subsequently re-added to comprise the theorist's version of intercultural communication, they overlook the embedded features of naturally occurring interaction, i.e., what it is that parties to intercultural interaction are actually doing. Because the local orderliness of the interaction is missed, the indeterminacy which is the creative fundament, the growing familiarity and the despair of all intercultural interaction is missed. The phenomenon is missed also by most anthropologists, which is perhaps more surprising since there have been no anthropological field researchers who have not had to work their way through endless naturally-occurring conversations which have the appearance of being intelligible while leaving all parties uncertain about what it was that was communicated. The phenomenon is so universal in intercultural settings and so basic to the material particulars of what it is that can be accomplished that its disregard by social anthropologists can only be an indication of the prominence of professional pressures to turn research notes into objective science, a science that will have no intercourse with indeterminacy, however actual.

It is impossible to understand interaction between Aboriginal people and Anglo-Australians without a deep appreciation of the material consequences of this indeterminacy, and this appreciation is available only when one has captured the open horizon of progressively developing sense to which the parties, as their own enterprise, are addressed. It is the achievement of the ethnomethodological approach to the study of intercultural communication that this open horizon of possibilities of sense is preserved.

Given the cultural differences which are involved, it is to be expected that communication between Aboriginal people and white Australians will be riddled with difficulties. But these impediments to successful communication are not only a function of the different world-views of the two cultures involved. Along with these culturally-based communicative constraints, there are substantial constraints presented by features which are characteristic of all intercultural discourse regardless of who the participants may be. It is impossible to come to a competent understanding of the problems of interaction in central Australia without recognizing the importance which the structural aspects of intercultural discourse have in providing for and constraining communication in ordinary settings.

Despite the problematic character of communication among Aboriginal- and Anglo-Australians, most plans designed by private citizens and officials from various agencies of the Australian government to assist Aboriginal people on a variety of social welfare, economic development and medical matters have treated issues regarding the adequacy of mutual understanding to be something less than consequential, giving no more than token attention to problems of ordinary communication. In actual fact, the practical difficulties of understanding in such intercultural contacts present substantial obstacles to the success of all governmental or other projects. A similar observation could be made about development assistance projects in the Third World undertaken by international organizations or by one of the affluent nations. Whether the projects involve agricultural, medical, educational or industrial development, they face the constraints which accompany intercultural communication as one of the central features of their efforts.

In intercultural communication the basis of much misunderstanding is technical in character, for speaking and listening are indeed technical activities. These technical and linguistic phenomena accompany those cultural differences which may also produce misunderstanding. To arrive at a complete comprehension of the nature of interaction between Aboriginal- and Anglo-Australians, it is necessary to examine such interaction in its structural detail; however, before we can take up aspects which inform us about the technical bases of misunderstanding in such settings, we need to be clear about what understanding itself is.

What is understanding?

Modern European societies have for many centuries labored under the proposal that understanding is always something clear and distinct. An ideal adequation of mental representations with things was accepted as the correct model for understanding. Ambiguity was treated as a deviant case of understanding which required remedies. But such a bias toward exactitude is a view of understanding in theory, not in practice. In practice, understanding may be vague, is a many-levelled phenomenon and may refer to a variety of empirical situations. Habermas (1979: 3) has considered the range of application to which the gloss 'understanding' may be applied:

> We can see that the word *understanding* is ambiguous. In its minimal meaning it indicates that the two subjects understand a linguistic expression in the same way; its maximal meaning is that between the two there exists an accord concerning the rightness of an utterance in relation to a mutually recognized normative background.

Habermas is here speaking of adequate understanding, and so far as he goes, he correctly addresses the range of possible applications of the term; however, his perspective is not radical enough. His view of understanding as shared agreement of some sort is still representational and amounts to a perspective taken from *outside* the interaction: it misses essentially the phenomenon of understanding as it is lived by the participants who are engaging in communicative activity.

Garfinkel (1967: 40) has commented:

Various considerations dictate that common understandings cannot possibly consist of a measured amount of shared agreement among persons on certain topics. Even if the topics are limited in number or scope and every practical difficulty is forgiven, the notion that we are dealing with an amount of shared agreement is essentially incorrect.

Understanding as the hermeneutic work of actual participants in intercultural interaction is a lived praxis addressed to the production of 'a matter talked about' as a developing event over the course of the interaction. Understanding, as viewed from *within* interaction, consists of that practical orientation toward a developing content whose mutual recognition is as much a product of the content which is progressively developed as it is the result of prior meanings which have come to be shared. Merleau-Ponty (1964: xv) writes, 'The germ of universality . . . is to be found ahead of us in the dialogue into which our experience of other people throws us by means of a movement not all of whose sources are known to us.' The essential character of understanding in the radical sense I am employing rests in the *'ahead of us'* as the practical concern of the interaction's participants. This 'ahead of us' is not always grasped with precision. It may be, in Husserl's words (1973: 38), only 'an empty horizon of familiar unfamiliarity'; nevertheless, it is there (it is all that is there) and it is the creative fundament of communication in ordinary interaction.

While communication among members of a given society involves the same structures which are found in intercultural settings, the practical hermeneutic work of understanding involved there is so transparent that it is difficult to recognize. 'The familiar, just because it is familiar, is not cognitively understood' (Hegel 1977: 18). Because communication in intercultural interaction is riddled with so many obstacles and dilemmas, the work of understanding there is more observable and its structures may be identified more easily. Understanding is captured as a field of practical activities having different arenas of application but all of them productive of communication among co-participants. By elucidating the structures of intercultural discourse it will be possible to clarify some of the technical difficulties which Aboriginal- and Anglo-Australians face in their efforts to make sense of each other in every day interactions, while also shedding some light on the nature of understanding in all settings.

Some of the arenas of competence which are constitutive of communication include lexical meanings, paralinguistic and nonverbal phenomena indicative of emotion, context and motivation, and a variety of organizational items which provide for orderly interaction. Of these orders of sensibility, lexical meaning has been examined with the greatest care, but the other arenas play roles which are no less constitutive of successful communication. Gumperz (1978) has observed that 'style and surface form are major means of communicating content,' and the content communicated by style may be grasped without having comprehended the lexical meanings of a message. Face-to-face communication involves *faces*, which are capable of performing endless communicative work. A simple smile-to-smile may bear the major portion of a message. Similarly, a falling intonation may communicate a great deal (Gumperz 1978). Pike (1962: 18) has found: 'A simple change in pitch – a sharp step-up or a step-down warns the hearer that something is happening, but does not of itself tell him what that something may be.' It is possible to arrive at some comprehension of another's talk without that understanding being lexical. Gumperz observes that some paralinguistic phenomena may even carry lexical meaning (1980): 'Children use their own contextualization conventions relying on stress, rhythm and intonation to convey information that in adult talk is commonly put into words.' This is in accord with Wittgenstein's claim (1969: 30) that 'Our talk gets its meaning from the rest of our proceedings.'

The sequential organization of talk and other organizational items provides for systems of reciprocity among speakers without there necessarily being communication of lexical content. So long as there are reciprocal structures, a horizon of potential significance will remain 'ahead of' the participants and the opportunity for mutual understanding will be preserved. An organizational item is any item which parties to an interaction repeatedly utilize in providing order for the interaction. When someone masters the sequential structure of a mode of discourse, he already has won important communicative skills which will allow him to enter elaborate verbal exchanges which may ultimately bear lexical fruit. One may achieve great competence in opening conversations, closing them, replying at moments which facilitate the perpetuation of verbal interaction, etc., without winning any precise understanding, yet such competence is an important arena of communication. The success of all conversation is dependent upon the mutual encouragement of the co-participants. A supportive attitude manifest in the skilled use of phrases of confirmation uttered at appropriate moments is a necessary constituent of all successful ordinary interaction.

While an auditor may be unable to understand the meaning of

particular linguistic signs, he may be able to grasp syntactic or structural relations among them. If, for example, he recognizes the words for 'like,' 'similar' or 'the same,' what he recognizes in the message, 'A and B are the same,' may not be its meaning but it is also not nothing and so is understanding of a kind. Anthropologists have prepared complete treatises on religious ceremonies and rituals which describe only the syntactic relations of the constituent elements and little about their meanings, yet such findings are accepted as valuable contributions to anthropological understanding. Tonkinson (1977) once observed that the associative properties of symbols are easier to grasp than the meaning of the symbols. But understanding the former is an important step on the way to comprehension.

Understanding thus involves a great many competencies besides lexical meanings. As Wittgenstein has concluded, 'Understanding is not a mental process' (1972: 61). Understanding does not occur in the form, 'The formula occurs to me,' but in the form, 'Now I can go on'; that is, understanding is above all practical and worldly and involves systems of reciprocity on many levels. What is essential is not agreement on an ideal plane but what in fact the participants to an interaction are capable of doing, given the practical circumstances which they face.

'Strange' discourse

To gain any competence in understanding intercultural communication it is necessary to address talk's own events. Whatever the cognitive activity of the talk's participants may be, it will always be the case that they will be tied to the detail of their talk throughout their efforts to produce 'the matter talked about' (which in practice is what making sense amounts to). Nowhere is this more evident than in the case of discourse in intercultural settings, whose very strangeness makes utterances and other components of communication into mysterious objects.

One of the outstanding features of 'strange' discourse is that the definition of what falls within the bounds of normal sensibility is left open. To be sure, all forms of social life operate within limits of propriety, but what those limits are remain mysterious for parties to intercultural discussions; therefore, the interlocutors must be prepared for 'anything' and simultaneously must be ready to admit the unremarkable character of that 'anything', to presume that what is strange is natural. Wittgenstein (1972: 8, 88) has argued that a language embodies not merely meanings but, more significantly, a form of life. As such, the utterances one hears are integrated into the life-world of a community, and so one must treat the incomprehensible utterances of intercultural discourse with respect. In 'strange' discourse the net of potential signification is cast very widely, as the parties range freely in search of adequate interpretations, yet their findings are treated with the same customary respect paid to those phenomena which are standard in any social world: 'strange' talk is generous in what it comes to take for granted. It has the remarkable character of waging herculean struggles of eyes and ears and sense while displaying the most matter-of-fact acceptance of its hard-won discoveries. Such a character is necessary and critical to the smooth and orderly development of communication in such settings.

Schutz has analyzed the reciprocity of perspectives assumed in most normal discourse. According to his findings, parties to ordinary interaction presume an interchangeability of standpoints:

> I take it for granted – and assume my fellow man does the
> same – that if I change places with him so that his 'here'
> becomes mine, I shall be at the same distance from things and
> see them with the same typicality as he actually does . . . until
> counterevidence I take it for granted – and assume my fellow
> man does the same – that the differences in perspectives
> originating in our unique biographical situations are irrelevant
> for the purpose at hand of either of us. (1971, I: 12)

This rule of ordinary discourse undergoes a modification in 'strange' talk because the differences in perspective are obvious; nevertheless, parties proceed as though nothing was amiss. Such a state of affairs leaves much room for communicative distortion, however, because the practical contingencies of the discourse (e.g., the desire to preserve congenial interaction, the intention to secure a given outcome or a concern to defuse a potential threat) easily leads to facile communicative solutions which do not accurately portray anyone's perspective. Agreement may be achieved, for practical purposes, without there being any substantial content behind such agreement; what is more, the willingness of parties to accept as 'natural' almost any solution which the talk produces leaves the situation open to manipulation and exploitation. For this reason, there may exist a good deal of paranoia in 'strange' talk as the interlocutors cast doubt upon the reliability of their partners.

Similarly, there is a problem of the incomprehensibility of 'strange' discourse. In most ordinary discourse the parties take for granted that what they are saying is being comprehended. In the case of 'strange' talk such an assumption is problematic. Anthropologists, whose business it is to engage in 'strange' talk, have long recognized the problem; however, while they are familiar with informants who produce solutions whose first purpose is to please the researcher (regardless of the adequacy of communication), the issue of the problematic character of the comprehensibility of 'strange' talk – so basic to the anthropologists' everyday work – is only rarely mentioned and remains for the most part unanalyzed. With the exception of a very few (e.g., Bardon 1970; Moerman 1972) most discussions of the problem have been by amateur anthropologists who are unafraid to admit the insecure basis of their findings. Brokenshaw (1974: 25-6), for example, reports: 'There is a danger of assuming that anything is pregnant with meaning as well as a real problem of understanding and interpretation of meaning.' This real problem is rooted in the enterprise of producing a matter talked about and in the proclivities of parties to sensibly organize an ambiguous body of particulars so that it may come to constitute something comprehended, even if that something is mere projection. The activity of formulating candidate solutions and then attending to their deficiencies is central to engaging in 'strange' discourse.

These candidate solutions to communicative impasses are addressed to more potentialities of signification than can be formulated. They exhaust attempts to grasp them conceptually, and this limitation of logical analysis must be frankly admitted if we are to avoid imposing an alien logic upon the lived course of events of 'strange' discourse. Understanding is 'pre-reflective.' But this only tells us something about what understanding is not. My concern here is with what the study of 'strange' discourse can inform us about the positive, progenerative work of understanding.

'Strange' discourse makes observable the primordial origins of understanding. It reveals the character of meaning as an atmosphere which dissipates when scrutinized closely, or as Husserl has reported (1962: 92), we are led to observe how 'an empty mist of dim indeterminacy gets studded over with intuitive possibilities or presumptions.' Here, understanding is not always precise, yet it is semantically pregnant and bears the temporal character of being oriented to what possibilities may mature 'ahead' in the talk:

AP   *This Dreaming, this Dreaming ( ) munilangari.*
EA   *Muni-, munilangari.*
AP   Yeh, *munilangari.*
EA   What is that?

AP   That's one here, look, all that.
EA   Which one is that, who is that?
AP   North side.
EA [North side.
AP |*Munilangari.*
EA   Is that a name?   10
AP   Yeh, that's the name of that *sacred board.*
     He got a pretty one there, all that, *munilangari.*
EA   What's the English word for *munilangari?*
AP   Oh well, I don't know, see. In the *Aboriginal* way,
     this is munilangari.
EA   MmHmm.   **(65)**

The European-Australian (EA) has not grasped the full
significance of '*munilangari*,' but he has not understood nothing.
His contribution to the talk is supportive of the Aboriginal
person's (AP) explanation: at line 2 he repeats AP as if in saying
the word he could come closer to AP's intended significance; in
line 3 AP reciprocates, bringing the two parties into some sort of
dialogue in progress toward communication; in line 6 EA reveals
that he is unsure whether the object in question is human or is a
material entity, and AP provides him with some (not yet
adequate) detail, and EA repeats the information. There are all
sorts of sensible possibilities, and AP's 'all that' (lines 5 and 12)
directs EA toward a plenum of signification. Here is the empty
horizon of familiar unfamiliarity which Husserl observed, existing
as the horizon towards which the talk will progress.

One researcher in the Western Desert (Bardon 1970) has
remarked, 'We have an impression, yet we don't know exactly
what the clues were.' Elsewhere the same researcher observed
that a candidate sense 'indicates at once the possibility of,
and the demand for, development, although the direction of
that development is not yet understood'. In (65) the
'MmHmm' and the repetition is verbal evidence of the progressive, directional character of the communicative development. Understanding proceeds in a vague and general way, at
first grasping the outlines of the phenomenon. One cannot always
articulate what one understands:

'I know what this is all about.' But what is it all about? I should
not want to say. (Wittgenstein 1972: 143)

It is dangerous, particularly in 'strange' discourse, to attempt to
clearly formulate what one has understood because such attempts
will too severely constrain the global work of comprehension.
Such premature formulations will only result in having a weak

version of the developing meaning impose itself on the significative horizon, which is then made to conform with the hypostatized reduction, as Merleau-Ponty observes (1973: 87): 'Language
contains some significations that are acquired or available and
others that are in the process of suggesting themselves. One
would impoverish language by reducing it to just what is actually
stated.' Communication is achieved when each of the parties to
an interaction follow up each other's tracks to see if they will lead
to anywhere instructive, even if they have only a vague sense of
the direction. In this next example, AP remains with EA long
enough to transform his confusion into certain communication.
'Tjilpa' here is the *Kuwarra* word for 'old man' (*tjilpa*). Through
a linguistic confusion with some Anglo-Australian missionaries
with whom the Aboriginal 'Norman' came into contact, he was
baptized with the family name of 'Tjilpa,' a situation which
produces the confusion in this discussion:

EA What about Norman, uh, Norman Tjilpa?
AP Yeh.
EA Tjilpa, Cosmo.
AP *Tjilpa?*
EA Yeh.
AP Old *tjilpa?*
EA Old Tjilpa.
AP Ahhh. Oh yeh. Tjilpa yah!
EA Would he be the 'boss' of that place? . . .   (66)

There is nothing more characteristic of 'strange' discourse than
the insensible alternation of 'Yeh'-'Yeh' we find on lines 2 and 5.
They constitute a system of reciprocity void of meaning, yet are
part of the production of meaning. After the initial aporia EA
offers the explanation that he is referring to the Tjilpa who
resides at Cosmo ('Tjilpa, Cosmo') but that only begins to effect
communication. Despite his confusion, AP remains with EA's
talk and eventually the talk opens the way to a solution.

The structural aspect of intercultural discourse that I will
analyze may function in serious ways to constrain communication. But these structures, being part of the primordial
character of the enterprise of understanding in such settings, are
the very apparatus which makes possible any communication at
all, and so they are not to be viewed as merely obstructions to
clear understanding. They are what clear understanding consists
of – these structures are unavoidable, and my account here is in
no way remedial. I will refer to these structural aspects not as
obstacles but as 'features,' in the hope of preserving their neutral
character.

Garfinkel has directed the major portion of his investigations to naturally-occurring interaction and has discovered many of the characteristics of the features which concern us here. Perhaps their most intractable character is that the practices which constitute structures productive of clear understanding are *hidden* (1975). Garfinkel says that locating these practices is like having fish locate the water in which they are swimming: the practices are embedded in the practical and the familiar. They are discoverable only in the course of their being used. Having their life only as the familiar equipment which allows parties to proceed to satisfactory communication, they are transparent just as the white cane is the transparent equipment of a blind person when he is engaged in navigating down a customary path. The practices are regularly employed without the parties necessarily being aware of their employment; nevertheless, they are available for mastery only to their practitioners, and the analyst is able to locate them only in and as they are employed: 'Their observability must be wrested from the familiar' (Garfinkel 1979). This makes their exegesis something unique.

Clear understanding

Understanding properly proceeds through a milieu of potential signification which is *indeterminate*. This milieu, as the necessary source of clear understanding, is unavoidable and omnipresent. Merleau-Ponty (1962: 364-5) has written with acuity:

> The truly transcendental is not the totality of constituting operations whereby a transparent world, free from obscurity and impenetrable solidity, is spread out before an impartial spectator, but that ambiguous life in which the forms of transcendence have their *Ursprung* [source], and which, through a fundamental contradiction, puts me in communi-cation with them, and on this basis makes knowledge possible.

Ambiguity is not a popular topic. Dreaded by the foreigner and denounced by logicians, it is avoided by social scientists who already have enough difficulties with producing unambiguous findings. Most persons are unwilling to see indeterminacy as the ground of any clear understanding; this is because they are preoccupied with having solutions-in-hand and not with the developmental origins of understanding. Husserl investigated with great care the indeterminate sources of meaning, calling attention to the fact that 'the individual thing in perception has meaning only through an *open* horizon of "possible perceptions" ' (1970: 162; my emphasis). The indeterminate origins of clear understanding have as their habitat the 'open' horizon of possibilities of meaning of which Husserl speaks.

If we recognize that understanding may lack determinacy, then it will pay us at least to be clear about what we mean by ambiguity. Empson (1953: 1) has defined ambiguity as 'any verbal nuance, however slight, which gives room to alternative reactions to the same piece of language.' Edlow (1975: 424) defines ambiguous speech as 'discourse which admits of (at least) two paraphrases x and y, such that x and y are not paraphrases of one another.' But the phenomenon so described is only a species of the indeterminacy which constitutes the primordial basis of understanding which I have outlined and in which the meaning-content of one or more of the co-existing possible solutions may be unfilled (or which may carry multiple meanings which are not mutually exclusive). Rimmon (1977: 19) makes a distinction between ambiguity and indeterminacy: 'While an ambiguous expression has many meanings in itself, a vague or indeterminate expression does not enter into the full commitment of any determined meaning.' Thus, what we are dealing with in clear understanding is indeterminacy, and ambiguity is only a species which bears confusions of a more technical nature.

In making the distinction between lexical and syntactic ambiguity, Edlow provides the example of 'The pen is construc-ted of metal.' This is a case of lexical ambiguity because the topic may be a fenced yard for animals or an instrument for writing. The utterance, 'The love of God is a pillar of the faith,' is a case of syntactic ambiguity because the ambiguity derives from the alternative possibilities of associating the syntagmic detail in the sentence – the speaker may be referring to God's love for humankind or to our love for him.

These confusions, while common to 'strange' discourse, lack the horizonal character which is identifying of the indeterminacy of intercultural communication. That indeterminacy is the vague yet progenerative medium which *'points forward to* possible patterns of perception' (Husserl 1962: 125; Husserl's emphasis). This 'pointing forward' refers to the open horizon of possibilities from which clear understanding emerges: 'This horizon in its indeterminateness is co-present from the beginning as a realm of possibilities, as the prescription of the path to a more precise determination' (Husserl, 1973: 32). It is this horizonal character which distinguishes indeterminacy from ambiguity.

The very open character of the possible sense of an utterance makes it possible for the participants to take that radical leap toward each other which is communication. Equivocality is the price of gaining new insight. Ricoeur argues (1974: 60):

> The variability of meanings, their displacability and their sensibility to the context are the condition for creativity and confer possibilities of indefinite inventions on both poetic and scientific activity. Here indeterminateness and creativity appear to be completely solidary.

An utterance's indeterminacy is the reservoir of its potential meaning. As Wittgenstein has observed, 'A multitude of paths lead off from these words in every direction' (1972: 143). Far from being an obstacle to communication, indeterminacy is its fundamental ground.

Studies by Gumperz and by Mehan on understanding in the classroom demonstrate that pressing for clear and distinct talk may arrest the progressive flow of communication. To achieve any meaningful communicative results one must abide with the indeterminacy of the dialogue until such time as its course leads to clear understanding. Gumperz, Gumperz and Simons (1979: 26-7) report on the case of the classroom talk of school children: 'The teacher's comments seem to interrupt or disturb the child's flow of thought. When this happens, the child's turn is either cut short or, if allowed to continue, the child often stops trying to formulate detailed description and reverts to one or two word responses to the teacher's questions.' The same dynamic operates in intercultural communication.

In cases of European/Aboriginal discourse in particular, the European logocentric proclivity to establish determinate versions of what is being said severely constrains the success of the interaction. This is true most conspicuously in courtroom testimony where clarity and precision is the burden of the hour (as well as being a discursive tactic). Aboriginal witnesses may be willing to describe in their own terms the circumstances of a matter of testimony, but questioning which is too closely concerned with each and every sensible portion of an utterance can reduce the Aboriginal witness's replies to mostly monosyllables:

EA What did the policeman do?
AP He was gonna do it with me but he grasp me.
    I try to run away.
EA When you were in the station how many officers
    were there?
AP There was more than four there.
EA There was four or there wasn't four?
AP There wasn't more than four.

EA	More than four?	
AP	Yes.	10
EA	In the last part of your evidence you told us that you went to a doctor but that you can't remember the doctor, is that right?	
AP	Yes.	
EA	Were you completely sober at this time?	
AP	No, I wasn't completely sober.	
EA	No, when you went to the doctor, were you sober when you went to the doctor?	
AP	Yes, I was really sober.	
EA	You were really sober then?	20
AP	[No reply]	
EA	And what about on the night you and the constable have given testimony about? Were you really sober on that night?	
AP	No.	(67)

Successful communication is dependent upon tolerating a certain amount of indeterminacy – expression is *necessarily* indeterminate. The signification of an utterance must keep itself open for possibilities which may be forthcoming, or else those possibilities will never arrive. Garfinkel and Sacks (1970) write,

> Speakers do the immense work that they do with natural language, even though over the course of their talk it is not known and is never, not even 'in the end,' available for saying in just so many words just what they are talking about. Emphatically, that does not mean that speakers do not know what they are talking about, *but instead that they know what they are talking about in that way.*

Garfinkel and Sacks are not only saying, along with Husserl (1962: 225), that 'Clearness is quite compatible with a certain margin of indeterminacy'; they are saying that clear understanding is dependent upon that margin.

When Schutz speaks of the prospective and retrospective sense of occurrence, he is referring to the way conversationalists treat many of the unexplicated features of their conversation as matters which are not to be queried. This occurs under the rule that items which are presently unclear will, in due course, receive their clarification; that is, parties presume that subsequent elements of their interaction will provide the context (retrospectively) for what seems indeterminate at a given moment. Thus, the assembly of sense in a conversation involves addressing current elements of the discourse to what it is imagined will come later (the prospective, i.e., the 'ahead of') and subsequent elements to what has come before. Under this procedure co-participants assume that they will come to know that 'the matter at hand' is all about. Frequently what was unclear becomes forgotten, and what becomes clear comes to be what the interaction is – and was – all about. As Merleau-Ponty describes (1962: 179), 'In understanding, the problem is always indeterminate because only the solution will bring the data retrospectively to light as convergent.' Garfinkel (1977) describes the phenomenon in more detail:

> We are able to converse under the following agreement: let there be a term, a phrase, that is initially incomprehensible; we proceed to talk with this understanding – that this matter which is incomprehensible will not call for (for the time being) any attempt to make it definite or to turn it into something available by definition. That is, we will not thematically address such terms or phrases but will continue to use the work they make possible not as if they had precise sense but without questioning whether they could have better sense.
>
> We use them over the course of the talk, with the presumption that if and when it might happen that there could be an issue as to what it is we are speaking of in using them that way, we could then, at that time, pick up just what (in the course of their use and as the course of their use) they were understood to have been meaning from the very beginning, in the very way that we will have come to see they had to have meant.
>
> They are opaque with respect to what they could possibly mean. Yet their very opacity is what it is about them that we are making use of over the course of our speaking. It is *in* that they are incomprehensible, and in fact with their full incomprehensibility over a course of our talk that they have their efficacy. As we are using them we are always willing to wait, and do wait, for that future time when we will have been able to stop to see what it is we could have been talking about 'all along.'

How could it be that the very opacity of our remarks is what it is about them that we are making use of over the course of our speaking? 'The matter talked about' occurs in conversation *before* it has a definiteness of sense, but as the matter at hand it stands there collecting available signification, pointing towards possible interpretations and acting as the focal point for the collaborative energies of the interactants. Here is a graphic illustration of how talk proceeds in this way. Members of a remote Aboriginal community have been speaking with a Sri Lankan community worker whom they are considering for the post of community adviser. The Sri Lankan has been explaining, in an English accent which the Aboriginal people can barely follow, his qualifications for the job and the kinds of community programs he has had experience with. At the end of his explanation, the Aboriginal person most fluent in English translates the Sri Lankan's remarks for the rest of the community. The problem, however, is that the Aboriginal translator himself grasped the purport of the remarks in only a vague and preliminary way. His responsibilities as translator force him to reduce the remarks to a clear and discrete message; nevertheless, his translation is very successful in pointing the audience toward possible contents of meaning which exist as indeterminate possibilities. By employing a gloss (*palunapinypa*: 'That way' or 'like that') for that elusive 'something spoken about' he is respectful toward that developing and yet to be determined meaning which lies at the horizon:

Council*ta wangkara helpinaningi waark. Ngaanya palyala,*
(+ nom.) (says) (will be helping) (work) (this) (does)
He says he will help get more work for the Council, for

yarnangu ngaaku, ngura ngaaku kutjupaku. Nyaraku waarka
(blacks)   (this + for) (home) (this) (another) (there) (work)
Aboriginals, the way he did for another place. He'll do

ngura ngaaku. Palunapinypa watjara nyanga. Paluna muku-
(home) (this + for) (that way) (says) (this) (that)
the same job here that he did there, he says. *That* is

rrikngkula. Palunapinypa palyalkitja nyinalkitjalu, nya-
(wants)   (that way) (work + intends) (sit + in order to)
what he wants. *That* is why he wants to come here. There

ralu palyarntu palupinypartu . . . Palupinypa watjara. And
(there) (did)   (that way)   (that way)   (says)
he did *similar things . . . Similar things*, he says. And

palupinypa palyalkitja mukurringkula palyanya watjara.
(that way) (work + intends) (wants)   (to do)   (says)
that sort of job he wants to do here, he says. But

Ka paluna kuwarripanya palurunya yaratjarra watjaranyi
(but) (that) (later on) (he) (confusing story) (said)
later he added something about what he wants

mukurringkula palunalu watjaranyi mukurringkula paluna,
(wants)   (he)   (said)   (wants)   (that)

He says he wants to do *that*, to get work for Aboriginal

yarnangu waarkakatinyi . . . Palyalpayi, palyarnu palunalu
(Aboriginal) (work + bring) (doing that) (did)   (he)
people . . . He's been doing this, finding

<u>*ngaanya*</u> bin *waark mantjira ngaliya* <u>*palupinypa.*</u>   10
(this)   (work)(secured)(unintelligible)(like that)
jobs *like that* before, but I couldn't understand all of *it.*   **(68)**

The Aboriginal person's talk is a demonstration of how one can carry along a reference (*palunapinypa*) without its meaning being specified. He outlines in a global fashion the domain of his referent in lines 1 through 5 and, so to speak, points it in the directions where it may have some application. The last mention of *palunapinypa* ('*palupinypa,*' line 10) refers to all previous associations and references which the employment of '*palun-apinypa*' had in the preceding talk, and its clear understanding will lie wherever it manages to find practical application. There is an etcetera accompanying the referent, but, in Garfinkel's words (nd.), 'it is not the etcetera that is "left over," it is the etcetera as the inhabitant of the house. And it is not even a mysterious inhabitant. It is not something wistfully waving around in the air – it is the most cogent, practical thing. It is the activity we engage in, the open horizon which inhabits the world.' What is central is that there are *specific* horizons of potential meaning to which the participants are being directed, while there is not yet any definite semantic content. This is what Garfinkel (1967: 40-1) has called 'specific vagueness.' Those realms of possible signification promise everything and justify the conversationalists in carrying on the way they do, as if there was nothing at all indeterminate about the talk.

This is to say, the interlocutors will come to understand what their talk is about by speaking (incomprehensibly). Their talk collects significations as it proceeds and by so doing informs the speakers about what they have come to mean. An original speaker's utterances are abandoned to the other participants who make of them what they come to be. The original speaker must accept such significance as the very field of semantic particulars (syntagma) with which he must operate. This is clear understanding – no more, no less. The participants' talk opens up a field of activity, and they are tied to the equipmental detail of that field and must achieve what communication they can with it. Understanding is doing rather than knowing.

The practical activities of understanding are seldom planned in advance, and even when they are, such plans must give way to the contingent details particular to any conversation. Their character is reflexive. Having spoken, one finds that what one has come to mean could not be fully anticipated – 'the spoken word . . . enjoys available significances as one might enjoy an acquired fortune' (Merleau-Ponty 1962: 197). Expression, as the corporeal presence of thought, is the focal point of the signification it collects over the course of the talk. The speaker finds from where his utterances have already led what real communicative possibilities they can accomplish. The components of his utterances are like pieces of equipment whose utility is defined not by himself but in collaboration with others, i.e., by the situation. Working in a practical way with what the situation presents them with, the participants progress toward communication.

The 'ongoing character' of the talk

Parties to conversation are positively tied to the detail of their talk and to the direction their talk is taking. Talk is not a static phenomenon; as I have observed, its character is to be developing. Their talk has the character of always moving on, and this places important temporal constraints upon the participants. The amount of semantic exploration parties may accomplish is limited, and avenues which participants may have liked to explore become closed off in the inexorable forward movement of the discourse. Particularly in intercultural discourse, much has to be abandoned in the effort to keep pace with the talk, and what is abandoned retreats to the horizon and is quickly forgotten. Much communicative work must be left only half-accomplished:

> Even an experience is not, and never is, perceived in its completeness, it cannot be grasped adequately in its full unity. It is essentially something that flows, and starting from the present moment we can swim after it, our gaze reflectively turned towards it, while the stretches we leave in our wake are lost to our perception. (Husserl 1962: 127)

Most attempts to repair misunderstandings are directed to the environment of detail immediately surrounding the talk in which they occur. As Schwartz (1977) has observed, and also Schegloff and Jefferson (1977), misunderstandings are usually dealt with at once or not at all. A great portion of the efforts to repair conversational errors must be abandoned in face of the ongoing movement of the conversation which erases the contingent environment, as is illustrated here:

EA *What is the name of the homeland of these people?*
AP *Eh?*
EA *The name of the homeland here.*
AP Name.
EA *Of the people who speak Tjupanypa.*
AP *Tjupanypa talk*, yeh. Then there's *Martu talk in the
     east, and Kiyatjarra and Pintupi talk in the north.*
EA *Kiyatjarra* and *Pintupi.*
AP Yeh.   **(69)**

EA never does discover the name of the *Tjupanypa* homeland, but what is important here is the way the talk moved forward to what AP had made of it. Despite EA's concern with a previous topic, he found himself carried into a different environment of talk. Once such a procession was under way it became too awkward for him to force a return to his earlier inquiry. Forcing such a return upon AP would have disrupted the 'natural' flow of the talk, may possibly have been interpreted as too aggressive and would have risked a more serious breakdown in the conversation.

The situation is similar in cases where one's partners have taken one's remarks in a sense which one never intended. Only rarely one asserts something like, 'No, that is not what I meant'; more commonly, one moves forward with the talk and attempts to discretely subvert it back towards one's original intentions without disrupting the temporal integrity of the conversation. The conversation is all that there is for the parties to work with; therefore, it must be treated with respect, even if its growing structure fails in some ways. In brief, the parties end up working with what the significance of the conversation comes to be. If B takes A's remarks in a way differently from that what A intended, in most cases A will accept that as one of the possible meanings he or she has intended all along. Similarly, if A questions B and B's reply signifies more than B intended, B is likely to accept the credit for the broader implications of his utterance. As Schegloff has written (1977), 'The speaker must also attend the possible derivative actions that may be analyzed out of his utterance, for he will be "responsible" for them as well.'

Here is another dialogue which demonstrates the way in which misunderstood exchanges are nevertheless treated with respect, a respect which is forced upon the speaker by the ongoing character of the talk. In this illustration I have been interviewing two Aboriginal people who have traditional associations with an area which was destined to become a uranium mining development. Their interview was part of the Aboriginal component of the Environmental Impact Report I was preparing for the proposed development. It was necessary for me to determine Aboriginal opinions regarding first, the effect the development would have upon sacred sites in the area, and second, possible health problems which a uranium development might create.

KL	What do you think, Billy?
AP	Hm?
BP	*I don't know.* It danger awwright.
AP	We don't know, *we're ignorant about* that one.
BP	Yeh. We don't know. We don't know, *don't know.*
AP	But if they make trouble in the ( ) ( ) it must be dangerous. To man, for the, I mean like a danger to the people.
KL	Mmhm. Well, there'd be two different things. One would be whether it would be dangerous.
AP	Mmhm.
KL	And the other would be whether or not it would be good or bad for the sacred sites. Like =
BP	= Yeh.
KL	*Sacred white ants* like we've been seeing.
BP	Yeh.
KL	Would the – the mining be bad for that or wouldn't it make any difference?
AP	Ohhh. That's pretty – Uh, yes, = I spoze/ it
BP	= I don't know./
AP	would be dangerous to the miners if that people.
KL	If they put the town there.
BP	Yeh.
KL	And *many people came to live there,* and make a lot of houses.
BP	Yeh.

10

20

(70)

KL lays the groundwork in his talk for the question posed at lines 17-18, and he pays close attention to the Aboriginal's answers at lines 19 and 20 with the belief that they are answers to that question; however, it turns out (line 21) that AP has understood a different question (that of the health dangers for the miners). Despite that, KL proceeds along with the talk as if nothing has happened, hoping to return to his dichotomous inquiry later on. The talk as a moving spectacle pulls the attention of the participants along with it, closing off opportunities to clarify misunderstandings which occur in the previous turns. The succeeding discourse presents parties with new communicative tasks, with which they become preoccupied; preceding topics are always falling out of the scene.

Sequential organization

Mastery of the sequential aspects of discourse provides a speaker with tremendous opportunities for sustaining interaction. Parties accept and adjust to the use of words without necessarily knowing their meanings, and competence with the sequential organization of talk is one of the ways in which such communication can begin to emerge. Scharchella (1980) has discussed cases of new immigrants to the United States who are capable of engaging in coherent discussion without knowing what the conversation is about.

Robin Are you studying Greek right now?
Miguel It's very interesting.
Robin Did you study Greek?
Miguel Ye:s.   (71)

In this case Miguel has learned how to get along in conversations at a syntactic level. He knows how to look interested and act like he understands and frequently employs the strategy of changing topics when he has lost the sense of the talk. Above all, he recognizes the importance of maintaining the turn-taking structure of the talk and using his turns to display his 'competence' by either agreeing with his partner, repeating what his partner has said or providing an encouraging comment which has the generality of application of a Chinese cookie fortune. Sacks, Schegloff and Jefferson (1974: 728) have noted, 'It is a systematic consequence of the turn-taking organization of conversation that it obliges its participants to display to each other, in a turn of talk, their understanding of other turns' talk.'

Here is an instance of my displaying an 'understanding' of some talk I had not fully comprehended:

AP   That mean (*parily-parily*) that mean they all sleep on
      TOP of one another. That, that mean (*parily-parily*),
      they all sleep together, you know? (   ) they all TOP.
KL   (*Parily-parily*).
AP   Yeh, that mean (*parily-parily*) all lyin' there.
      And this . . .   (72)

Displaying such competence is critical to the healthy progression of a conversation. Even when the displays are gratuitous, such replies, in maintaining the sequential organization of the prior turn's talk, display at least the recipient's understanding of the prior turn's talk as a command (question, complaint, etc.) which calls for him to say something. This is not so simple a matter as it may appear. The serial order of talk which I examined in Part I and which is so critical to the production of congeniality and consensus in Aboriginal society provides for turn spaces of a particular kind. Competent discourse within that order of talk demands that a non-Aboriginal speaker enter the conversation at just the places and in just the way in which the talk makes provision. Finding those places may be a difficult task for a novice, just as finding the places for one's utterance is sometimes difficult for Aboriginal persons giving testimony in a court of law. While an Aboriginal person may sustain courtroom testimony with nothing more than gratuitous 'yeses,' he or she must also know where to place those 'yeses.' If, as I have witnessed in Australian courtrooms, an Aboriginal witness replies 'Yes' to talk which is not even addressed to the witness (or to comments which do not call for a reply), then the Aboriginal's talk is exposed as being vacuous. Similarly, if one confuses the sequentiality of a story within some discourse with the discourse itself, then the lack of comprehension will be exposed. Such problems are not far fetched; rather, they are the abiding practical concerns of speakers in intercultural interaction.

This illustration, taken from the courtroom testimony of an Aboriginal person, demonstrates the importance for successful communication of producing a clearly recognized sequential order for the talk. As early as line 5 the prosecutor begins to try to set up both a temporality for the events and a sequential order for the talk, but he does not succeed until lines 82-100:

Prosecutor: And what happened then?
Aboriginal witness: He bin' beltin' 'im up.
P: They were pushing each other?
A: Yes.
P: After they've been wrestling a bit, what happened then?
A: They 'bin pushin' and fightin'.
P: And what happened then?
A: He pulled a pocket knife.
P: Who pulled a pocket knife?   10
A: Toby.
P: And what happened then?
A: Ø [No reply]
P: Who hit who?
A: Toby.

P: Who did he hit?
A: My father.
P: What did he hit him with?
A: Shoulder [points to shoulder].
P: No, *what* did he hit him with? 20
A: Neck.

. . .

P: What did you say Toby did?
A: Lay down.
P: No, that's your father.
A: Ø
P: What did Toby do?
A: Run away.
P: What position was your father in at the time of the argument?
A: Night time. 30

. . .

P: Now, was your father sitting around the fire . . . at the back?
A: Ø
P: You told us your father was sitting around the fire. Was your father sitting around the fire?
A: Ø
P: What happened then?
A: Told him to go away.

. . .

P: Can you describe the fight to us?
A: Ø 40
P: Can you describe the beginning of the fight to us?
A: Yes.
P: You told us Toby was standing up.
A: Yes.
P: And that your father was sitting down.
A: Yes.
P: What happened then?
A: [indistinct]
P: When did Toby hit your father with his hand?
A: Fightin' with hands. 50
P: When did Toby hit your father?
A: He hit 'im with his hand and then grabbed his pocket for his knife.
P: You told us . . . after your father told Toby to go away and sit with someone else, you told us that Toby hit your father with his hands. What did your father do then?

A: Picked up the nulla-nulla [club]
P: So he got the nulla-nulla after Toby hit his father?
A: He got the pocket knife from his pocket. 60
Magistrate: Perhaps if he was asked about one and the other and then see if they are associated or not?
P: You told us . . . when did your father get the nulla-nulla? Did he get it before Toby got the pocket knife?
A: Before.
M: How did your father hold the nulla-nulla?
A: He hold 'im like he was gonna kill 'im.
M: He held the nulla-nulla as if to kill him?
A: Ø 70
Court translator: No, he hit 'im with the nulla-nulla, and then 'bin kill 'im.
P: What did your father do next?
Defense counsel: Objection. He already asked that question.
P: You've told us that your father was sitting down and that . . .
Translator: [Explains sequence to witness.]
P: What happened after Toby hit him with his hand?
A: He stood up.
P: And what happened then? 80
A: Toby was arguin'.
P: And what then?
A: Fightin' now.
P: Can you tell us what happened in the fight?
A: Stood up.
Translator [to P]: He went back to the start.
A: They were fightin' with their hands. He got the big stick, nulla-nulla.
P: Who got the big stick?
A: Father. 90
P: And what then?
A: He hit him with it.
P: And what then?
A: Threw the stick down and 'bin wrestlin'.
P: And what then?
A: Fightin' and got pocket knife.
P: And what then?
A: He cut 'im.
P: And what did your father do then?
A: He lie down now. 100
P: And what did Toby do then?
A: He hit 'im and ran away. (73)

The prosecutor experiences difficulty at the start, in part due to miscommunication which has its origin in the sequential organization of the talk – at line 19, the Aboriginal witness has determined his sense of the question not from the lexical meanings but from the place in the conversation where the prosecutor's question falls; for him, after it has been established whom it was that was hit, the syntax of the examination points to the issue of where the person was hit. An attempted repair by the prosecutor at line 20 is unsuccessful, as the Aboriginal person's account of the talk continues to organize the data.

The prosecutor utilizes a skillful strategy for setting up an order of talk at lines 34-5 and again at line 45. His technique amounts to asking the witness an obvious question in order to receive the obvious reply and thereby begin a sequential exchange which can become the basis of an order of talk for the more complicated examination to follow. But more problems arise when the witness incorrectly cues off from 'hand' in line 49 and again misjudges the sense of the question at line 51 by presuming content from the place of the talk instead of word-meaning. In lines 40 to 82 and 91 to 99 the prosecutor finally meets with success, using 'And what happened then?,' 'And what then?,' etc., to order the talk. The first indication of success is at line 83, where the witness's 'now' demonstrates that he has mastered the dialogue; unfortunately, the sequence of events is lost again at line 85, and the translator quickly jumps in to repair the damage. But by line 94 the local order is reestablished, and the talk proceeds smoothly. The witness conclusively demonstrates his competence at line 100.

The comments of a speaker collect the sequential environment in which they are located. The meaning of a 'Yeah,' for example, depends upon what the speaker's partners believe it is the response to, and these contents are selected largely on the basis of sequential proximity. As Schegloff (1977) has found, 'The analysis that is operative for a party will turn on the sequential structure he sees it to be embedded in.' This is illustrated here:

EA   This bird has a *ceremonial song* too?
AP   Yes!
      [sings:]
      A man is passing by,
      'tira-tirala' [bird call + imperative]
      A man, he tells.
EA   What does that mean?
AP   That means that bird give a man a notice. He tell
      the man, see?

195

EA   What does he tell the =   10
AP   = That's a word, now he tell 'im '*tira-tira-tira*,' see?
       He tell the man.
EA   Tell the man what?
AP   To watch out.
EA   For what?
AP   For bushranger's coming. *Footprints* coming.
       That's all. An' he watch out. Get ready. Get all the
       spears. Wait, you know. Walk around all a' time.
EA   What do the words mean?
AP   Hm?   20
EA   The words. The – what do the words mean?
AP   '*That's all*,' that means, 'That's it.' *This* bird tell 'im
       there's a man around there somewhere, you know?
EA   Uh-huh.
AP   Because the old people they singin' . . .   **(74)**

At line 22 AP refers EA's question about what the words of the song mean (sung on lines 3-6) to AP's previous turn of speaking. It is common, especially in intercultural discourse, for utterances to be related to the turns which immediately precede them. The 'noise' created by communicative confusion reduces the circumference of the horizon of meaning and causes participants to concentrate upon the immediately surrounding detail. On many occasions, participants will miss obvious solutions available only three or four turns previous, as in our example. I would hypothesize that this is because in 'strange' discourse one has to cope with more potentially meaningful phenomena than one can handle. Faced with what amounts to a swarm, one becomes nearsighted. But Sacks, Schegloff and Jefferson (1974: 728) have discovered that such nearsightedness occurs in ordinary conversation also (the difference, I would argue, is only one of degree). They write, 'A turn's talk will be heard as directed to a prior turn's talk unless special techniques are used to locate some other talk to which it is directed.' Misunderstanding resulting from utterances collecting the wrong portions of their preceding sequential environment are a common sort of communicative failure in intercultural conversations.

A remark may also collect what *follows* its utterance, in this fashion: in the case of a 'Yeah' which comes second in a sequence of three utterances. It may be applied to the utterance which follows it as well as to the one which preceded it. This is particularly the case in congenial talk, much to the dismay of those who find themselves committed, by the sequential course of the talk, to something they hadn't intended. Another version of this is when a succeeding speaker obviously misinterprets what a previous speaker has said while enthusiastically concurring with it, leaving the original speaker to suffer in silence or (by way of 'special techniques') risk disturbing the harmony of the inter-action. This again operates under the feature that once the talk has moved on, it is almost impossible to retrieve it for the purposes of repair.

Conversation, though an intersubjective activity, is an entity. Utterances exist in the world as things and so are available to others for all sorts of work their speaker may not have planned for. Words are not merely the results of meanings, they are able to establish connections of meaning; these semantic connections are influenced by the sequential features of the talk. The co-participants in a conversation deal with a display of linguistic particulars which, though generated by themselves, are directed toward horizons of possible meanings which are handed to them by the situation (cf. Liberman 1982).

Gratuitous concurrence

An elderly one-eyed Aboriginal man at Wiluna is joking with me, speaking of the upcoming ceremonies where *tjitji* (children; young boys) will be made into full men by subincising the 'child's' penis. The conversation suffers from the 'noise' typical of intercultural communication – we are never absolutely certain of what his broken English and my newly acquired Aboriginal mean. The old man jests, 'We can't have the government blokes goin' 'round as *tjitji*' (i.e., not subincised). His face is dead-pan, his eye searches my face for content. I think, 'He looks serious. But is this a joke? What does it mean? Which government blokes? Am I taken to be a government bloke?' I look to him for some indication of what he can mean: all this in an instant. It suddenly strikes me as humorous, and I break out laughing; and just as suddenly his eye breaks into a grin: it *was* a joke all along, but he wasn't prepared to show himself until he was sure that I would comprehend him correctly. He is happy to be 'with me,' but if it had turned out that I wasn't 'with him,' he still would have been 'with me.'

Trust is an important characteristic of all successful conver-sation. It provides the solid foundation for an enduring interaction, and in the case of intercultural communication it is frequently the only thing the parties have going for them. That is why 'strange' talk is packed with phrases of affirmation and concurrences of every kind. It is important to display for one's partner that one is 'with him,' and the appearance is as important as the fact.

Intercultural conversation is crowded with concurrence which is rendered gratuitously; that is, the agreement or confirmation has no basis in anything semantic being understood. Such concurrence is rendered as a structural feature designed to encourage the development of the conversation. It may in part be a way to fill the empty space of a turn of talk or it may be one method for producing an ambience of congeniality in the interaction, but its primary function is to permit the conversation to continue toward its communicative result without an interruption which would place the anticipated solution in jeopardy. Also, gratuitous concurrence is a frequent strategy of oppressed peoples, who utilize such facile assent to placate those they fear and to avoid confrontation.

'Yes,' 'MmHmm,' 'Sure!' and also repetition of a portion of the remarks uttered in the preceding turn of talk are all types of gratuitous concurrence. Aboriginal people in particular are expert at rendering gratuitous replies with incredible and disarming enthusiasm (e.g., 'Oh yah, I know! I know that one'), and sometimes it is very difficult to separate such gratuitous concurrence from phrases which indicate genuine comprehension. What is more, gratuitous concurrence itself may be deliberate or done entirely without reflection; it may involve brilliant artifice or be as innocent as the good-will of a child:

American: Excuse me, but we're just trying to find the right
bus that takes us to the boat for Upolu. We were told
that it stops here in front of the village store, but we've
been waiting since 9 o'clock this morning and we'd like to
know if there is going to be a bus before this evening or if
we'll have to wait until tomorrow for a bus.
Samoan: Yes. (75)

Gratuitous concurrence is a pervasive phenomenon of intercultural conversation. An Aboriginal representative from Western Australia was attending a meeting on land rights with some officials of the State government. He was engaged in some intensive discussion which I followed. After the discussion concluded, I walked over to the tea tray with the Aboriginal representative, who was a friend of mine, and asked, 'Did you understand that?' He gave a 'Hm' with a nod, and then quickly looked away: he had not understood (as a subsequent discussion revealed beyond a doubt), but none of the government officials was aware of the fact. His 'Hm' reply to me – another case of his praxis of gratuitous concurrence – was almost half-way between

THE HERMENEUTICS OF INTERCULTURAL COMMUNICATION

yes and no, presented in the likely hope that I would make of it what I required. Clearing one's throat or stammering similarly allows one's partner to take the communicative initiative, thus relieving oneself of the possibility of making an improper reply.

A young Aboriginal once drove up to my camp to pass the time. His car had no silencer and the idling was stuck, so his motor was very loud, making conversation difficult. (He couldn't stop the car because it would not start again without a push.) I asked him about when a community meeting was going to begin that day. He only smiled. Although he understood English fairly well he couldn't hear me over the roar of his engine (which was not unlike the 'noise' of 'strange' talk). I asked again, 'Is the meeting going to be soon or in a few hours?,' and just at that point his car, in its turning, showered me with its maximal noise. He gaily replied 'Yes' and drove off.

The simple gratuitous concurrence is capable of solving all varieties of communicative impasses. Even where it fails to satisfy the requirements of the discourse, it will rarely give offense; and such a positive production, as a thing out there in the world, is easily adapted to whatever a listener wishes to make of it. For example, Michael Ne Yin, a recent Vietnamese immigrant, visited an all-night pharmacy to get a doctor's prescription for sleeping pills and pain-killers filled. The pharmacist asked him if he understood the directions. Not understanding a word of English, Michael smiled and nodded his head. Gratuitous replies such as this frequently meet with success.

While it is an important structural feature of intercultural (and all) discourse, gratuitous concurrence is responsible for some of the most infuriating vagaries 'strange' talk can produce. It is so plastic that it at once suggests myriad solutions without guaranteeing the existence of any of them. Accompanying its presence is the massive task of determining whether or not it indicates or portends a matter successfully communicated as well as the problem of locating what in the talk it should be applied to:

EA   Where should we go first – go shopping or go see Barber?

AP   Ye:::s.   (76)

KL   and were you on Tarmoola?

APx   Yeh.

KL   Which way from =

APx   = Tarmoola Station.

APy   That way from station.

KL   That way. *Far?*

APx   Yeh. (On the other side) that we campin' there.
KL   On the other side?
APx   'Nother side.
KL   That *place*, special one or just any place? ·
APx   No. APz's camp.
KL   MmHm.
APy   From Apz's camp, that way [points].
KL   Is it a special *ceremonial place*?
APx   Yeh.
KL   That you sing at?
APy ⌈ Yeh.
APx ⌊ Yeh.
KL   Or is it just any place that you happen to sit down?
APx   Yeh! And we got =
APy   = We got to sit down at Leonora
      now.   (77)

The gratuitous replies here are equivocal. It is not that they are
without any semantic content, but there is no justification for
applying the concurring replies to the utterances which precede
them.

   But .this is not to claim that gratuitous concurrence always
constitutes deception; frequently, it is the most direct route to
communication. Here is an example of gratuitous concurrence
employed in a manner productive of communication:

APx   *They sat in the cave.*
KL   *Yes.*
APx   *In the cave they sat. The Tirutiru men there* tell 'em,
      'Oh, you fellows stop here. *Stop a while at this place.'*
      Marry *their women.*
APy   *At that place.*
APx   I, I *have seen this place. They went on to the east, the
      Two Men announced.*
KL   Oh.
APx   *So they say* =
KL   ⋡ *Yes.*
APx   'You fellows stop here, and I'll keep goin'.' Goin' to,
      goin' to what's his name, *Nguranya.* To *Nguranya*
      mob. *Those two* traveling.
KL   *The Two Men went to Nguranya.*   (78)

KL never understood the full import of APx's remarks, but
because he offered his uncomprehending concurrence at lines 2,
9, 11 and 15 (the last via repetition), he sustained the talk until
he was provided with enough detail to make some sense of the

story. Were he to have stopped APx to ask for explicit elucidation at each point, he would probably not have been taken into any communicative realms radical enough to be worth his efforts.

Gratuitous concurrence has the peculiar feature of allowing a person to offer agreement while simultaneously being oriented to what that agreement might consist of. A gratuitous 'Yes' faces directly the swarm of potential meanings which have yet to mature into something discrete. The best of hopes, it is frequently a more accurate response than a negative reply would be because something may have been grasped in a vague and general way. It is a sign for that 'familiar unfamiliarity' which has all of its force in its character as a developing sensibility.

Anger, impatience, or such innocent utterances as 'Of course you know . . .' or simply 'You know . . .' are apt to force concurrence. More often than not, such attitudes are conveyed by way of vocal gesture rather than with words. The very frustrations endemic to intercultural discourse may lead one of the parties to impatience, which his partner may placate via the use of gratuitous concurrence. Such episodes are self-inflicted traps: one's eagerness to communicate insures the failure of the communication, yet the presence of such incidents in intercultural interactions is massive. The irony of the phenomenon is that upon occasion the facile assumption of being understood may be just the force needed to jostle one's perspective in the right direction:

AP   *Do you understand?*
KL   *No.*
AP   *Yes you do.*
KL   [shrug of shoulders: dunno]
AP   [to his son] *He knows.*
Son: No, he said he *doesn't know.*
AP   [Staring right through KL] But you *know.*
KL   *Oh, I see!* [KL understands]
AP   *Now you understand?*
KL   *Yes, I understand.*
AP   [to son] See, I told you he *knew.*   **(79)**

But more commonly the pressure of anger or frustration will distort the conversation by constraining the normal hermeneutic inquiry. In (80) AP describes a mysterious substance to KL who was never able to inquire deeply enough to discover that AP was talking about fog because AP is at first so certain that quick agreement will be forthcoming (lines 8-11) and then so impatient when it does not occur (line 18) that KL's inquiries are constrained. KL's gratuitous responses to AP take the form of repetition (lines 11, 13, 15 and 19). At another moment AP's certainty that the impasse is a simple one to resolve might have become the very clue which could propel KL to comprehension [another instance of non-lexical communicative work], but in this case KL misses the matter and abandons his efforts after settling for a gratuitous accord ('Mmhm'-'Mm') at lines 19 and 20:

AP	*Nyinga, nyinga up there.*	
KL	*Nyinga up there.*	
AP	Nyinga up there.	
KL	And what is that?	
AP	Well, that's when, you know, some time in the morning you see hills up trees and everything up.	
KL	You see it. Do you see trees too?	
AP	Yeh, trees come up to, and tree, what you call 'em, hills in the hair in top. [voice of certainty]	10
KL	In the top. Like	
AP	It grows sort of.	
KL	It grows.	
AP	Then it goes away after.	
KL	Then it goes away.	
AP	Mmm.	
KL	Is it like a reflection?	
AP	Nah, nah, when it's just, you know, SHOW UP!	
KL	Mmhm.	
AP	Mm. Hill, anything like that.	**(80)**

Repetition

Repetition such as occurs in (80) is a very common method of providing gratuitous concurrence; but, as Sacks has observed (1969), repeats are equivocal as demonstrations of understanding. Nevertheless, they are surprisingly successful in convincing co-participants that one is following the talk, and thus are very important in maintaining the uninterrupted development of the talk's possibilities. Because repeats are taken directly from utterances whose worth have been proven by their previous use, they offer safe passage in most situations of near or total aporia. What is more, repeats are useful in eliciting more information about what they are in fact about. Repeating an utterance focuses attention upon it and recommends its further use, which provides more opportunities for a party to witness its field of application. In (81), KL employs the word '*greenery*,' which KL discovers more properly refers to any vegetation at all, including a location's latent but recognized potential for vegetative growth. After being surprised by an Aboriginal woman's (WP) assertion that there was plenty of '*yukiri*' in a location where all of the vegetation was parched by the desert sun, KL continues to repeat the word in order to discover its correct use. While his repeat in line 5 is gratuitous it has a bona fide hermeneutic function:

KL *This place ever have any yukiri?* There is no *yukiri* here.
WP *Oh yes, it has yukiri.* Over there plenty *yukiri.*
KL *Yukiri.*
WP *There is yukiri here.*
KL *Yukiri* finished?
WP *Yukiri* there. Plenty. Big rains come, all come up then.   (81)

'*Yukiri*' becomes here a sort of hollow expression which KL employs in order to discover its correct usage. Once again, we encounter the equipmental character of utterances – the components of an utterance have their power in concert with other expressive components; what one is able to do with words in the systems in which they operate is more significant that the words' formal definitions. Through witnessing the kinds of work the particles of utterances (syntagma) perform, one learns their meaning: the meaning of a word lies in its use. But in order for utterances to be seen in the context of their use they must be spoken, and repetition is one way of keeping them before the interacting parties as the equipment of their practical significative work.

As we witnessed in the case of '*palunapinypa*' in illustration (68), an utterance may serve as the index for a broad field of indeterminate yet burgeoning sense; such an indexical utterance is a device for allowing the speakers to retain their focus upon that indeterminate field which may yield the effective solution to their interaction. Repetition, in preserving the prominence of an indexical expression, preserves as well the field of developing significance to which the expression refers. In this next illustration, well-populated with repeated concurring phrases, KL has been trying to procure the literal definition for '*Ngamuru*' and employs five repetitions of '*Ngamuru* Rockhole' (including line 17) in order to generate more discussion about the phenomenon for which '*Ngamuru* Rockhole' is the indexical expression. As is all too common in intercultural conversations, his effort meets with no success, as AP finalizes the exchange with his own repeat. This leaves KL's inquiry unresolved, another casualty of the structure customary to intercultural communication:

AP	We goin' to *see Handprints Cave*, we're goin' to 'Ngamuru' Rockhole.'
KL	*Ngamuru* Rockhole.
AP	Yeh.
KL	*Ngamuru.*
AP	*Ngamurunya.* ['*nya*' = nominalizer]
KL	*Ngamuru.* Who-wh-what does that mean '*ngamuru*'?
AP	That's a rockhole, big one.
KL	Big one.
AP	This way, *fire dreaming.* 10
KL	Mm.
AP	*Fire.*
KL	⌠ *Fire.*
AP	⌡ Fire.
KL	Fire.
AP	Yeh, fire been comin', and *then heads south.*
KL	*Ngamuru* Rockhole.
AP	Yeh, *Ngamuru* Rockhole. **(82)**

Repeats are by no means certain devices for eliciting clarifying utterances. When one's partner is ready to concur with whatever one says, a repetition may elicit only another gratuitous concurrence. Faced with two consecutive confirmations which have little basis in fact, the interlocutors have some serious work to perform if they are to save their conversation. And when one of the parties is anxious to satisfy whatever he or she imagines the other is inquiring about, the situation is something like the blind leading the blind:

KL	From where does the road start?
AP	What?
KL	From where does it go?
AP	He go Empress Spring.
KL	Where does it start from?
AP	Start from (new road).
KL	*Nirruru.*
AP	Yeh.
KL	Is that a *waterhole?*
AP	*Waterhole* might be. 10
KL	*Nirruru.*
AP	Well the – *that one.*
KL	That's in Richard's Hill, *Nirruru?*
AP	Richard's Hill different, he got a *sacred watersnake* there, *in the waterhole.*
KL	*A watersnake.*
AP	Yeh, big water there. **(83)**

AP incorrectly keys off the syntagmic particular 'go' in line 3, not grasping the significance of the previous 'from,' and makes of KL's question what he can. KL repairs this but himself misinterprets AP's accented utterance of a poorly articulated English phrase (line 6: '(new road)') to be an Aboriginal place-name, 'Nirruru.' 'Nirruru' has a persisting life in the conversation, having received approval gratuitously at line 8 (AP may have considered that whatever the whitefella's pronunciation of his word was, it was probably close enough). KL's question about whether 'Nirruru' was a 'waterhole' may have suggested that there was a lack of communication about 'Nirruru,' but since AP had already assented to its use it was probably awkward for him to retract his approval. While AP must have found it difficult to understand how KL could have thought a '(new road)' could be a waterhole, he was evidently confused enough to grant the possibility that whatever KL had in mind might indeed be a waterhole and so replies – gratuitously – that it 'might be' a waterhole (line 10); in any event, since KL was so interested in waterholes AP volunteers some information about waterholes in lines 14-15. KL, aware that something was amiss, repeats 'Nirruru' at lines 11 and 13, but the repetition fails to bring AP to employ the utterance in any fashion and generates no constructive clarification. What is so interesting about this dialogue is that it fails despite (and perhaps because of) AP's willingness to be a good partner. Although there is both the repetition (line 7) and confirmation (line 8) productive of competent communication in other settings, on this occasion it presents the participants with an impossible problem, made only more enigmatic by AP's gratuitous concurrences at lines 10 and 12.

Some of the difficulty with repeats is that they have so many uses. A repeat may genuinely display a party's understanding of a preceding utterance; it may function as the vessel for a vocal gesture which displays participants' congenial feelings (cf. chapter 2); occasionally, it may merely be an attempt to have one's partner repeat the utterance to allow oneself another opportunity to hear the correct pronunciation of the words in the utterance or to hear a subsequent part of the utterance which was missed when first heard. All of these uses of repeats differ from the use of a repeat as a method for satisfying interactional demands in situations where one has understood precious little; indeed, the success of this last strategy is dependent upon the repeat being confused with one of the other functions.

One of the discouraging contingencies of the employment of repeats is to have a repeat which was intended as a frank and uncomplicated call for more information come to be considered by one's partner to have one of the other functions typical of repeats (e.g., evidence of what one understood most clearly). In circumstances where one's partner is exhausted, bored or feels threatened by the conversation, a repeat leaves the way clear for him to treat it as 'conclusive' proof that real communication has occurred, thereby being the legitimate grounds for closing off the conversation, as in (82). Gratuitous concurrences such as 'Yes,' 'Hm-hm!,' etc. are excellent ways to close conversations which have become hopelessly confused.

Other possible trouble with repeats may occur when one's partner selects and repeats part of a formulation one has uttered and applies it in a sense which is his own concoction. Because he or she is repeating the very words one has employed, there seems to be adequate grounds for such use of the utterance. Occasionally such a repeat is accompanied by an 'of course' tone which further compels one to resign oneself to the confusion, even when the repeat was intended as a call for verification. In this next dialogue, AP's repeat in line 6 makes out of EA's stumbling comment in the previous line something more coherent than EA was capable of knowing. Fortunately, in this case EA asks a direct question about the matter.

AP   Yes, one more place that I know just over here, and er, it's a big what you call 'em. He's a heap of stones again, and he's a big cock-eyed bob.

EA   Yes. What, made in the stones –

AP   Made in the stones.

EA   What was that place for?

AP   He cock-eyed bob that one. Now olden days, early days, they used to have a sort of hole. Killing one another people. They can make any of 'em things to kill a people. They can make that big cock-eyed bob, to kill a lot of people.*   **(84)**

One can ask questions, but there are limits to how many questions one is able to ask and also maintain an orderly conversation, particularly with partners who are of the opinion that there is 'too much ask' about one's style. Repeats are a less conspicuous though equivocal way to make inquiries. Gratuitous repeats may take the form of verbatim repetition of the trouble source, a phrase of concurrence ('Yes') plus verbatim repetition,

---

* The official report and subsequent entry in the government register reads, 'Cock-eyed Bob. Caused death of enemies.' Thus, the practical understanding of EA – which was part of a developing yet partly undefined sensibility – became 'official information' and part of government records. Much of the official knowledge about Aboriginal people is based upon such practical understanding.

or verbatim repetition with an ascending termination signifying a (mildly) interrogative mode.

Nothing is more damaging to competent interaction (because it is so personally debilitating) than to have a repeat which was uttered in order to elicit once again the proper pronunciation of an unfamiliar phrase come to be accepted by one's partner as that very part of the conversation which one has understood best. In such cases, the repeated utterance is treated by one's partner as an island of communicated sense amidst a sea of confusion, and he or she is likely to return to the utterance time and again when the conversation is in danger of falling apart – never realizing that the repeated utterance itself is the heart of the problem. The situation is complicated by one's natural willingness to admit that the very words which one's partner has taken as the basis for his or her confidence that one is adequately attending to the talk are in fact nothing more than mysterious syllables, nothing more than the signs for what they could be about (which is to say, they are not nothing but might as well be should one's partner discover the extent of one's knowledge about them). The task which one is faced with on such occasions is to carry on speaking as though one knows what one is saying, hoping that one's partner will let slip what the utterance means without having to ask directly for an explanation. Of such stuff is communicative competence made.

Strange silences

Intercultural communication is populated by some very peculiar silences. In all conversation there exist certain 'spaces' or 'gaps' where transfers of turns at speaking occur. Occasionally there are longer 'gaps' when there is hesitation over whether the first party has actually completed speaking and one's own turn has arrived. Silences due to turn-transition gaps may be confused with intra-turn silences which are rhetorical or merely pauses in a party's thinking and with inter-turn silences where the co-participants are engaging in deliberate reflection necessary to the discussion (cf. Sacks, Schegloff and Jefferson 1974: 706). It is essential that parties pay close attention to the silences in talk if they are to avoid blundering into the conversation at places which reveal their lack of competence. Here again the mastery of the sequential structure of the conversation plays a critical communicative role.

Because parties to intercultural conversations may not comprehend everything that is being said, utterance recipients frequently exercise caution in evaluating silences. This extends the length of turn-transition silences, making them longer than those of ordinary conversation. Turn-transition silences may also be extended on occasions where the meaning of an utterance is ambiguous, in the hope that the speaker will provide additional clarifying talk. The pause here is an effort to give an indeterminate phenomenon time to 'clear,' either in one's own thinking or during ensuing interactional events. This is not altogether different from the silence reported by Schegloff and Jefferson (1977: 374) as occurring in the turn directly following possible errors in speaking. They describe what occurs during the initiation of repairs of mistakes in a conversation:

> Indeed other-initiations [of repair, as opposed to self-initiated repairs] regularly are withheld a bit *past* the possible completion of trouble-source turn; not only does a withhold get them specifically positioned in next turn, but it can get 'next turn' itself delayed a bit. In such cases, other-initiations occur after a slight gap, the gap evidencing a withhold beyond the completion of trouble-source turn – providing an 'extra' opportunity, in an expanding transition space, for speaker of trouble-source to self-initiate repair.

The recipient here allows the speaker the maximum opportunity to give his best possible utterance. The difference with silences in intercultural discourse is that their significance is more enigmatic.

Occasionally silences will be overlooked, and the conversation will continue as though no interruption of its rhythm occurred. The sequential order of the talk may make a reply out of a pause, in this fashion: there is a variation of gratuitous concurrence where the utterance recipient is uncertain whether a 'yes' reply is properly called for; a solution to the dilemma is to pause, in hope that the speaker will be so preoccupied with the momentum of his own remarks that he will presume that a gratuitous reply appropriate to his comment was uttered in the recipient's turn slot. The gambit consists of letting the rhythm of the sequential order produce the appearance of a reply, relying upon the speaker's 'natural' expectations to do the work, as in this example:

Clerk: Do you swear that the evidence you shall give will
        be the truth, the whole truth and nothing but the
        truth, so help me God?
AP: [no reply]
[Court prosecutor proceeds with testimony.]   (85)

The problem of silences in 'strange' discourse becomes massive when their length becomes so extensive as to present the parties with another aporia: when does a potential inter-turn or intra-turn silence become 'just plain silence,' with no possibility of being interpreted as part of the sequential structure of the talk? And what consequences does such a conversational breakdown have for the communication? What is so impossible about such situations is that the longer one has waited for an end to the silence, the more reluctant one is to admit that it is a breakdown in communication. Parties are able to treat even these silences as natural parts of the conversation. Since long silences have been allowed to persist through the tacit approval of the participants, the speakers are implicated in the silence and may be reluctant to treat them frankly as the communicative failures they are. Moreover, such a resolution preserves the formal integrity of the interaction while sacrificing the communicative adequacy of the talk; nevertheless, the talk is left free to continue forward. Such occurrences are by no means rare in intercultural communication, however disheartened they may be.

Inquests

Repairs of misunderstanding in intercultural communication involve serious diagnostic work. Initially there is the problem of determining unambiguously that a misunderstanding has in fact occurred. Schwartz (1977) has observed that the interpretation of talk to have involved a misunderstanding must compete with possible interpretations of the same talk as irony, insult, change of topic, etc. If one has any doubts about whether an utterance is evidence of a misunderstanding, one is likely to just 'let it pass.' Given the willingness of parties to go along with possible references which their co-participants' utterances may have but which are not yet clear, many utterances which are suspect are allowed the opportunity to 'prove' themselves. By the time the communicative status of the utterance is determined, enough turns of speaking may have occurred to make a repair very awkward. Should one elect to make the repair, one must first successfully communicate *where* in the talk the misunderstanding has taken place. The work involved in explaining this location to one's partner may be as difficult as making the repair itself. Once the utterance which is the trouble source is mutually acknowledged, the trouble itself must be explained. Most instances of misunderstanding have a history which is observable, and many of the problems have their origins in the sequential order of the talk. For example, the misunderstanding may have been the result of applying an utterance to the wrong referents in the preceding turns of talk. To successfully repair the trouble all of this must be uncovered and made explicit for the parties.

Because repairs of communicative confusions are often so complicated and elaborate, they threaten to disrupt the conversation itself. Persistent and thorough diagnostic inquests risk being interpreted as aggressive. It takes a positive effort to force a refocusing of the communicative energy of the interactants upon an utterance which has already passed and is difficult to locate, and such efforts may place the congenial basis of a conversation in jeopardy. It is probably for this reason that repairs are either initiated at once or not at all.

Habermas considers such diagnostic inquests to be a major transformation of the discursive mode of a conversation (1979: 57): 'If in some communication there is a breakdown of intelligibility, the requirement of comprehensibility can be made thematic only through passing over to a hermeneutic discourse.' It will be necessary for the participants to work out a satisfactory system of reciprocal interaction to handle this new mode of discourse which is a metadiscourse about the adequacy of the discourse itself. Once the co-participants have embarked upon such a hermeneutic enterprise, they become engaged in producing collaboratively structures for making inquiries – they teach each other collaborative skills for asking and answering questions, distinguishing types of questions (say, asking for definitions from asking for repeated pronunciation), and in fact are engaging in building a system of talk. This work, while performed in the context of their conversation, is really structural work addressed to the technical apparatus of the talk itself. Once parties have worked out an adequate system of hermeneutic discourse, it becomes easier for them to attend to the communicative adequacy of their talk; however, the effort required to produce this additional format of discourse may compete with the time and energy available for dealing with the topics which originally motivated the discussion.

This is not to say that a discussion about the actual topics may not be carried on while simultaneously being addressed to producing structural matrices for expanding the talk. While at first there may be very little communication (where caution and confusion reign), as structures begin to develop they multiply the possibilities of the conversation. Clearly understood topics generate structures, and those structures generate more topics. But when there is a breakdown, and one of the parties has elected to repair the structures involved (so that they do not become the basis for a 'longitudinal' error), then an elaborate hermeneutic discourse may commence, presenting the parties with an additional task. If all the parties are not willing to engage in that hermeneutic discourse, if they become impatient or feel threatened, paranoid, etc., then the disruption may place the entire interaction in jeopardy. Because the repair of most misunderstanding in conversation is a collaborative enterprise, the person initiating the repair must pay attention to the willingness of his partner to participate; otherwise, it is better to leave the conversation alone and let it depend upon its own developing resources. Allowing a misunderstanding to pass unrepaired is not always a form of dishonesty (as much gratuitous concurrence appears to be) but may be the very best way of handling the interaction.

For all of the places in conversation where one party does not notify the other of a lack of intelligibility, a large proportion may not even be acts of deliberate obfuscation (benevolent or otherwise) but (and this is no 'merely') the result of the other speakers not giving a participant a chance to say anything. The conversation may not provide, in its temporal flow, an opening (i.e., a turn) for initiating an inquiry about the intelligibility of the talk. Once a party has been forced, by the sequential organization of the talk, to let some portion of the conversation pass by without repair, he is less likely to take advantage of subsequent opportunities which the talk may provide him. Since a lack of intelligibility has been allowed to persist already, there is an understandable reluctance to sacrifice the ongoing rhythm of the talk for what may be a minor confusion or one which has long since passed. By the time the talk provides him with a chance to do something, the confusion may be too great or elaborate for him to attempt to resolve. In this way misunderstanding may have a sequential basis.

One of the unfortunate contingencies of such unresolved confusions is that a party may nevertheless find himself implicated in the confusion and become enmeshed in protecting the apparent intelligibility of the talk which he was unable or unwilling to repair. Once one has let some confusing talk pass by without repair, or has not admitted one's failure to comprehend part of the discussion, it becomes necessary to preserve the appearance of being a competent partner by acting as if everything was comprehensible. The work involved in maintaining the 'natural' character of the talk in such instances may be more extensive than the work of making the repair would have been in the first place. To illustrate what sort of work is involved, consider the case of a conversation I had with three elderly Aboriginal men. I offered some advice to one of them who was attempting to apply for an old age pension. Though he was at least 70 years of age, he was born in the 'bush' and so did not know his age, and there were no birth records for him, disqualifying him for an old age pension. I instructed him to answer the community welfare officer's question, 'How old are you?' with 'I dunno, must be somewhere around 70.' A few minutes after giving him this instruction, I tested his comprehension of the recommended strategy and asked, in the tone of an officious community welfare officer, 'AP, how old are you?' The old man replied directly, 'I dunno.' His younger brother and a friend, both 'full-blooded' Aboriginal men but slightly more acculturated, caught my gambit correctly and fell into broad laughter as the old man dead-panned, still engaged in 'serious' discussion. Their laughter was treated by the old man as an unkindly nuisance to his pulling off being a competent listener with me, and he became annoyed. He went on as if he knew just what we were talking about anyway, but this only caused the laughter to grow louder, and eventually he was forced to accommodate it by laughing aloud himself (otherwise his seriousness would have been too incongruous for him to maintain his front of being communicatively competent). Laughing 'along with us' (incomprehensibly), he persisted to act as though he understood everything which was taking place, while simultaneously attending to possible interpretations which could explain the situation. The longer he attempted to maintain that he was competent to the interaction, the deeper the mess in which he found himself.

The work involved in protecting the illusion of competent communication is very subtle, and on most occasions it is very successful. Frequently, one can bluff one's way until one sees what is really going on or at least until one's partner is convinced of that fact. One may not catch the sense of a word or phrase until many turns of talk have transpired, yet one may act as if he was 'with' the meaning all along. Pressing a hermeneutic inquest when one of the interlocutors is undertaking such protective work can lead to embarrassment and seriously damage the conversation and the relationship.

Much of the work performed in intercultural conversations succeeds because it has the character of being unremarkable. Successful inquests are those which are performed calmly, as though they were the most 'natural' of things to do. Discoveries that a conversation means something different than what one thought are usually unheralded. Most talk is characterized by frequent and often subtle shifts in focus (Gumperz 1980), and such shifts are usually accommodated inconspicuously. And the appearance of comprehending 'strange' talk while hardly fathoming a word is achieved in part by treating all the conversation's events as unremarkable.

Parties to intercultural conversations are preoccupied with producing 'the matter talked about.' The difficulty of communication results in there being the abiding challenge of producing something communicated, that something being communicated clearly and certainly. This effort is necessarily a collaborative one. 'The matter talked about' may not be the matter which motivated the conversation in the first place (that may have been submerged in the confusion of the communication), but it is what the parties have made of the talk for the practical purposes which they have faced. 'The matter talked about' may be fatuous (something about the weather), but the co-participants are anxious that the conversation not result in nothing and so therefore are actively addressed to the task of producing something which can be mutually recognized as bona fide communication.

Where parties are more skilled and have developed better discursive means, 'the matter at hand' may more closely approximate the chief topic attempted, but it may yet fall short of that in one or more ways; it is characteristic for the parties to be satisfied with something less than perfection. Communication is not always the most rational thing in the world. This is because there are far too many local contingencies to plan for and the conversation always has a way of subverting the original intentions of its participants. Once one engages in making utterances, those utterances open up a field of local detail which is more than the participants can account for, and so their 'accounting' has to be a practical one which arranges a 'matter talked about' which will do for the time being. For example, after a lengthy attempt to explain a delicate matter of Buddhist logic, a Tibetan refugee confessed, 'I'm not sure what I'm saying.' It was not that the Tibetan speaker did not know what he was saying; he was simply aware that the words he was employing opened up a plenum of possible meanings and associations which was broader than he himself could appreciate – the local detail of his explanation became too complicated for him to handle. And so he proceeded to lower his expectations and made of his talk a 'matter talked about' which was good enough for the situation at hand. Intercultural communication proceeds in such practical ways.

Political strategies

Intercultural communication is a collaborative activity which depends upon the constructive participation of the interacting parties for its success. Where one of the partners is not anxious to communicate, the features of intercultural communication I have presented provide abundant opportunities to sabotage the communication in ways in which the saboteur can remain undetected. We have observed that a great deal of indeterminacy surrounds the production of 'the matter talked about.' A skilled partner may utilize this indeterminacy to shield him from discussing matters he prefers not to consider.

> He accompanied us during the rest of the day's journey, and I gave him a tomahawk, and a seventh part of my old sword blade. He continued at the camp and asked for all he saw, but we took care not to understand him. (Mitchell 1838, II: 241)

A simple strategy is to pretend not to comprehend something for which comprehension may have undesirable consequences. Since conversations in intercultural settings are usually on the verge of collapse anyway, all that one needs to do is to extend a confusion or vagary at an appropriate moment and the entire attempt at communication will be thrown into turmoil. What is more, it will appear that the indeterminacy natural to the talk was responsible for the failure. Since indeterminacy exists as a thing in the conversation just like other things such as words, silences and anger, it may be exploited at convenient moments for political purposes.

Another strategy is willingly to concur with whatever is being said. The ambiguity which results from the excessive use of gratuitous concurrence may become so great as to foreclose the possibility of meaningful conversation, despite providing a front of congenial and willing association. Similarly, one may employ silence in an innocent way, responding to an utterance with a 'natural' silence, which usually will result in one's partner giving up any hope of communicating. Malcolm (1979: 437) reports that grade school teachers in Western Australia have complained about Aboriginal children 'using silence' to protect themselves when conversations with teachers become too perilous.

One may wish to allow the ongoing character of the talk to submerge topics which one prefers to leave unclarified. Or one may allow a misunderstanding to remain unrepaired.* Intercultural interactants may be engaged in a number of gambits where their primary concern is not communication but survival. These political dimensions must be integrated into the analysis, not by fiat but by locating them in the actual strategic moments in which they are embedded.

What communicative solutions do unfold are usually provided reflexively by the material environment of the conversation and are not the exclusive result of deliberate rational-deductive reason. By locating ourselves in the real world, we secure the natural antidote to the subjectivizing common to some phenomenological thinkers. Interacting parties stumble into 'the matter talked about' without having planned for it in advance, yet they quickly exploit its appearance to expand or contract communication as the situation demands. There is a genius in the idiocy, and it is this genius – embedded in and open to the temporally unfolding sense – that must be observed if one is to understand intercultural communication. Let us take this insight into our examination of cases of contemporary Aboriginal/Anglo-Australian interaction.

*An incident involving an American and an Iranian gas-station attendant in Claremont, California, well illustrates the political work to which the structural aspects of intercultural communication may be put. After pulling up to the pumps, the American stepped out of his car and looked around. The Iranian, who was serving another customer, asked him, 'Do you want Regular?,' to which the American replied that he did. 'This one is Regular,' the Iranian told him, referring to the pump which was already in use; however, the American did not understand because the rhythm and tone of the Iranian's utterance was unfamiliar and it was spoken at a volume considerably lower than that of most American discourse. The American simply replied 'Oh' (a case of gratuitous concurrence, most likely) and pulled out the hose opposite the pump already in use, which was Premium. At this, the Iranian informed him, 'That is Su´-per'; but, being a few feet further away, the American hadn't heard this any better than he had the previous utterance. The Iranian was unwilling to bellow out in the more assertive tones of average American discourse and perhaps felt that if the American was unwilling to listen to him in the way he normally speaks (as the form of life he lives), he was under no obligation to inform the American of his error. The Iranian allowed the interaction to take its course without repair, and the American filled up his car with the more expensive gas. In this case the communicative failure was not deliberate, but merely presented itself as an opportunity in the conversation. It was not a 'shared understanding' gone awry but an event done and experienced and having practical effects. One of the practical effects was that of being available for the Iranian to do nothing about. When the American discovered his mistake, the Iranian could not be blamed; but he was not entirely blameless. The political work available in intercultural interaction is just this subtle, and is easily hidden beneath the indeterminacy of the interaction.

7 Concrete relations between Aboriginal- and Anglo-Australians

Some political consequences

A recent study of Western Apache assessments of Anglo-Americans (Basso 1979) describes in detail the joking behavior of the Southern Arizonan Apache. It seems that 'Whitemen' find their way into a good many Apache jokes, which Apaches use as a vehicle to consider the minute interactional detail which typically occurs in their everyday relations with whites. In the scenes the Apache jokers stage, Western Apaches invariably get 'run over' by Anglo-Americans, whose forward and aggressive style shows little sensitivity to the more silent presence of the Apaches (Basso 1979: 55). Through these mimes the Apaches hold up typical Anglo-American behavior to public satire and criticism.

In central Australia, Aboriginal people are similarly 'run over' by the more forward and self-assertive Anglo-Australians. As I presented in Part I, a degree of introversion and the minimization of one's self-presence constitute correct social behavior in central Australian Aboriginal society. While Aboriginal people adhere to a 'strict refusal to force one's way upon a social ensemble' (cf. pp. 12-13), Anglo-Australians are accustomed to a more extroverted and assertive interactional style. This interactional asymmetry produces serious consequences for Aboriginal/Anglo-Australian relations.

Western Desert Aboriginal people avoid unpleasant interaction and social confrontation with much skill and determination. On most occasions, the establishment of an agreeable ambience is a primary consideration for all parties. In contrast, some argument and difference of opinion is considered natural and unproblematic for much Anglo-Australian social intercourse. Disagreement is a mark of one's individuality and ability to think for oneself, and frequently it is considered an asset to be 'a good competitor'; moreover, members of European societies consider a certain degree of argument and contest within discussion to be a healthy dialectic conducive to stimulating fresh thinking and reasoned judgments. Interaction between Aboriginals and Anglo-Australians involves people who have different interactional skills appropriate for different structures of social interaction. A result of the concrete relations between Aboriginal people and white Australians is that the Aboriginal partners frequently give way to the more forceful Anglo-Australians. Although Aboriginal people are not without interactional resources, founded upon their unique social skills, a pattern of Anglo-Australian domination has developed. This domination is not a domination in theory (whether the theories are economic or political), it is a domination which is effected in the actual and local structures of ordinary interaction between Aboriginals and whites in central Australia.

Anglo-Australians are accustomed to interaction of an impersonal nature, interaction which operates within highly formal, rule-governed domains. These domains – relations with government bureaucracies, with the police and court systems, with members of the public concerned over particular issues, etc. – are increasingly affecting the lives and future prospects of Aboriginal people, yet most Aboriginals are poorly equipped to account for themselves in settings which call for skills in such autonomous interaction. Western Desert Aboriginal people, accustomed to more spontaneous and intimate interaction, find the more impersonal interaction of whites, especially in official contexts, very difficult. Even within their own society, as we witnessed in the case of Aboriginals attempting to speak before Aboriginal communities other than their home community (cf. p. 29), Aboriginal people find it difficult to rally a confident and firm presentation of their perspective. The success of their interaction among their fellows very much depends upon their being unassertive and remaining open for the collective will of the group. During interaction with Anglo-Australians, especially in formal settings, Aboriginal people are often at a loss as to what to do, find it difficult if not impossible to express their feelings and are easily coerced into going along with whatever resolution is being pushed by their Anglo-Australian partners. The very behavior which is appropriate in the context of Aboriginal affairs leaves them vulnerable to exploitation in their relations with Anglo-Australians.

It would be foolish to assert that the domination of Anglo-

Australians is not effected in part by means of their superior physical force. To a very large degree, Aboriginal people were subdued with the use of guns, and today the police and judicial system serves to maintain the power of the whites in central Australia. But brute force is not the mode of domination which Aboriginal people experience on a daily basis. The prevailing mode of domination is something much more personal and occurs in the local interaction they have with neighboring Anglo-Australians. Basso (1979: 81-2) reports a similar situation in the American Southwest. The mode of domination which most concerns the Western Apache jokers is that domination which is effected within local interaction:

> To be sure, Whitemen have stolen land, violated treaties, and on numerous other fronts treated Indians with a brutal lack of awareness and concern. But these are not the messages communicated by Western Apache jokers. Their sights are trained on something more basic, and that is making sense of how Anglo-Americans conduct themselves in the presence of Indian people.

Much of the interpersonal domination is unintentional. Although there are occasions where a white person may try to bully an Aboriginal, for the most part the Anglo-Australian is unaware of the constraints his style of sociability places upon Aboriginal people; unaware, because it is a function of his natural participation in social intercourse. Throughout the Australian outback, on the sheep stations, in the towns and even on the Aboriginal reserves, well-intentioned as well as not so well-intentioned Anglo-Australians unknowingly and inevitably dominate the Aboriginal people they encounter. This is a common, everyday event, and so I offer here at the outset some common illustrations. At a remote settlement in the Western Desert, one known for the militancy of their Aboriginal leadership, one of the members of the community's governing council decided that it would be a good idea for him to drive some Aboriginal visitors back to the main center of the settlement for lunch so that they would not have to wait in the hot sun for the rest of the visitors to finish their business. This council member approached an Anglo-Australian employed by the council and asked, 'What about lunch?,' gesturing to the group of visitors who were with the councilor. The Anglo-Australian staff member replied, 'Oh, no need to worry. We can take them all down when we take the others down for lunch.' Instead of proposing the alternative plan of action he had worked out – which probably would have been accepted happily by the staff person – the councilor elected to defer to the staff person's confidence and replied simply, 'O.K.' The Anglo-Australian was unaware even of the existence of the wish of the councilor (who in fact was his employer). In situations where the protagonists are not on such amiable terms, these 'O.K.'s are proffered even more readily, and the intentions of the Aboriginal participants more opaque to their Anglo-Australian partners.

Such interactional asymmetry may also be witnessed among children. Again, this example is mundane – a phenomenon which is repeated endlessly throughout central Australia. But such domination occurs in the most mundane fashion imaginable, and it is as such that its effects are so devastating. On a picnic for seven people (an Aboriginal lady, her three Aboriginal children, my wife and two Anglo-Australian children), the white children pressed strongly for public recognition and spoke proudly about themselves and their activities (how well they could camp, etc.), while the Aboriginal children offered my wife only quiet looks which seemed to ask for assurance. The white children ordered the Aboriginal kids around, instructing them how to make a fire (of all things), and when the Aboriginal lady cooked the meat and potatoes directly on the fire (according to Aboriginal custom), the white children complained that such a method was too dirty and confidently advised their playmates that the use of tinfoil was superior. In European societies, the parent who attempts to keep her child away from friends who are domineering is nearly legend. For the Aboriginal people of central Australia interaction with Anglo-Australians continually involves encounters where the Aboriginals must contend with a people more assertive than they.

There are additional problems for Aboriginal people which involve certain structural needs of the Aboriginal community which constrain their interactional potentialities. Some requirements of Aboriginal society may make it difficult or impossible for Aboriginal people to deal aggressively with Anglo-Australians on matters of importance. In the first chapter, I presented the case of a visit by the Governor-General of Australia to a remote Aboriginal community. In the absence of the community's elders, no Aboriginal person was willing to step forward to greet the official party disembarking from the plane because no one wanted to be placed in a situation where they could be subject to the criticism that they thought too much of themselves. There was not even a question of the community being able to put forward effectively its deepest concerns to the Governor-General: they were unable to put forward anything at all. While their behavior was puzzling to members of the official party, it was consistent with the rules of interaction in central Australian Aboriginal society.

In most intercultural settings Aboriginal participants are more preoccupied with the protocol and vitality of their own local relations than they are with their relations with Anglo-Australians. White people usually do not remain among their number for very long and so it is considered unwise to build effective communicative structures with whites if it means sacrificing some harmony among Aboriginal fellows. Successful negotiations with whites often require decision-making which is too hasty and forced for an Aboriginal community. As we have seen, decision-making in desert Aboriginal society is a step-by-step process founded upon consensual interaction. It is important that the congenial fellowship of the group is preserved, and this is assured by making certain that everyone present participates and concurs in the developing decision. Such processes poorly prepare Aboriginal people for negotiations with whites. Where Europeans are skilled at formulating plans, Aboriginal communities must appropriate each aspect of a proposal concretely, one-at-a-time; moreover, throughout the Aboriginals' deliberations the congenial character of the assembly is of overriding public concern.

Aboriginal people occasionally find themselves in formal negotiations with government officials about land rights, social welfare, mining, civil rights, etc. During these negotiations opportunities to propose forthright and effective solutions to critical issues may be passed over because there is insufficient time in the context of the negotiations (say, a one-day visit by a government minister) to achieve the necessary unanimity of purpose. Constructive plans proposed at a meeting by the members of one Aboriginal community may be too much for other participating communities to assimilate all at once, and the proposing community may defer to the developing objective consensus of the gathering (a process which can take many months). Many fortuitous opportunities (where all the government principals were present) have been lost. What makes matters worse for Aboriginals is that the government officials have been inclined to assume wrongly that Aboriginal people lacked the concern to press seriously for the political demands involved.

As I described in Part I, Aboriginal people function best when the interaction does not require a focusing of collective attention upon a single participant in a personal way. Where the interaction individualizes the participants, Aboriginal people feel embarrassed and self-conscious, limiting their effectiveness; yet, much European interaction is characterized by a highly individualized style, and unobtrusive people tend to be dismissed easily. The Australian school classroom is a setting where Aboriginal 'failure' to perform may be traced to the interactional structure of the setting. In a survey of schools in the Western Australian outback (Malcolm 1979: 377ff.) 128 teachers of Aboriginal children were interviewed. Among the most frequent communicative problems mentioned by teachers were the inadequate volume of Aboriginal speakers, failure to respond to questions, failure to look up or to look the teacher in the eye and the offering of single-word responses. The problem here is obvious: Aboriginal children are uncomfortable with the attention they receive when they are called upon to deliver formal remarks to the class. As I have noted, in Aboriginal society it is impolite to look one's speaking partner in the eye too directly, yet failure to do so was considered by teachers to be a shortcoming. Many teachers complained about short responses, explaining that such 'condensed' and 'abbreviated' 'shorthand' constrained communication. While shortened replies are surely the result of natural embarrassment, our review of traditional Aboriginal discourse has demonstrated that abbreviated summary accounts are a standard feature of Aboriginal discussion. When viewed in the context of a network of interlocutors collaborating in a serial manner to produce the discussion, such summary accounts are appropriate; however, in the context of the strictly regulated turn-taking of a European classroom such ways of speaking are inappropriate and unsuccessful.

What is most interesting about Malcolm's teacher interviews is that while the teachers were concerned about the Aboriginal children saying too little when called upon to speak, they also complained that the children talked too much when they were not being addressed and that such talk was characterized by a failure to wait for each other to finish speaking, i.e. a 'failure to take turns' (Malcolm 1979: 399). Ordinary Aboriginal discourse is characterized by a great deal of 'chatter' (we have considered the complaints of the first European explorers on this score). Once the environment becomes more informal, the Aboriginal children are prepared to take off as part of a collective praxis, a praxis which has a looser turn-taking structure than does European discourse. Aboriginal children are able to express themselves well when the discourse is of a type with which they are familiar. Teachers need to develop some facility with Aboriginal forms of social discourse if they are to communicate with their Aboriginal students. When the teacher insists upon formal European models of discourse, Aboriginal children find it difficult to communicate well.

What is true for the classroom is true for other intercultural settings, including encounters with Anglo-Australian welfare officials, representatives of mining companies, contacts with police and interaction in Australian courts of law. Oriented to the collective 'ownership' of the talk, Aboriginal people find it difficult to assert their personal views straightforwardly. Once a discussion has included the firmly presented wishes of their Anglo-Australian partners, such wishes take on a corporate life which Aboriginal people are reluctant to repudiate. The more extreme is the self-assertion which is required to oppose such wishes, the less it is likely that any opposition will be attempted. Where Aboriginal people seek unanimity, Anglo-Australians desire that their own wills prevail, and the structural outcome is that the former defer to the latter. The intense arguments and oppositional structure of the Anglo-Australian courts overwhelm Aboriginal participants who do not understand such opposition as merely a structural feature of Australian courts.

All too frequently Aboriginal persons incorrectly assume that such forceful interaction is evidence of anger or aggressiveness. While Aboriginals do cope with a good deal of anger in their relations with Anglo-Australians, much innocent and well-meaning interaction is misunderstood. Malcolm has remarked (1979: 502-3): 'Where Aboriginal children read into teacher behaviours an aggressiveness which is not intended, the cause may partly lie in sociolinguistic interference,' i.e., an asymmetry of interactional styles. Here is an illustration of an occasion during which Aboriginal friends of mine deferred to what they considered to be my growing anger:

KL   *No, ask later. Later, later* this one. And *the govern-*
        ment will read it and may say no. But you can always
        ask! Anything you want you should put down here.
APa   *Yeh,* that's why he askin'.
APn   Mm.
APb   Too full now though.
KL   Might be this, might be this time they'll say no.
APb   *Yes.*
KL   But they'll have this piece of paper in their files.
APn   Yeah.   10
KL   Might be next year, two year's time.
APa   *Later I think. That's alright.*
APc   *Yes.*
KL   They get another request, and they get another
        request, and they see it's on the files that they 'bin
        askin' time and time again.

APa   *Later yes, leave it.*
APe   *Leave it, let's go on.*   20
APf   *Yes.*   **(86)**

The Aboriginal participants wrongly interpreted my effort to provide them with relevant information as opposition to their desire to ask for assistance on some matter from the Department of Aboriginal Affairs. At line 4. APa is trying to assuage what he considered to be my critical attitude, but as community adviser I was only trying to be thorough in providing them with all the details necessary to making an informed decision; however, such a thorough and informative attitude had an officious character which was taken to be something close to anger. My utterance at line (9) was delivered in an officious staccato, and receives a gratuitous concurrence in line (10). While I was about to suggest that making the request would provide good grounds for a successful request in the subsequent year's application, APa concluded that the matter had gone too far and that the conversation risked losing its harmonious character. He employed the Aboriginal strategy of 'later' (*wanti*; cf. organizational item 3.5, chapter 2). At this point I tried to repair the misunderstanding, but that only placed an additional burden upon the conversation, and the Aboriginal participants emphatically closed off the matter, deferring to my 'wishes.'

To have labored further to repair the conversation would have placed the entire interaction in jeopardy (one of the structural constraints that accompanies intercultural communication), and I had no choice but to assent to what had been made of the conversation. Such occurrences, where Aboriginals defer to problems which do not actually exist, frustrate Anglo-Australian participants because a resolution of matters which they consider to be important may be prevented. Non-Aboriginal participants must wait until a more amicable interactional format can develop; indeed, had I exercised enough care at the start I would have been able to communicate my information to my friends, *but only in an interactional format they would experience as familiar and appropriate.* Once the fear of anger spreads over an interaction the opportunity for communication is lost.

The Aboriginal response to genuine anger is similar – they are ready to oblige the angry person and will assent to almost anything that is proposed, though they will not feel obligated to fulfill any of the commitments so made. In such a fashion Aboriginals with the reputation among whites of lacking both decisiveness and dependability. For their own part, central Australian Aboriginals are exhausted with what they consider to be aggressive or overly assertive Anglo-Australians. In their desire for harmony their solution is to attempt to avoid interaction with whites. One Aboriginal (Mathews 1977: 121) reports, 'My wish was for a little security and freedom from trouble with white people,' and his feelings are widely shared.

The Aboriginal acquiescence to Anglo-Australians is an interactional pattern which functions more absolutely when conversation is in the English language. What Aboriginals are willing to be more forthright about in their own language is moderated when the linguistic code is changed. On many occasions I found myself switching into English when I wanted to impress upon Aboriginals the importance of their following my suggestion, a strategy which had some effectiveness. Part of such a response is a deference which is based upon the politics of Aboriginal/Anglo-Australian relations, and this deference has become a structural feature of interaction which is encoded in English language-usage: a switch of language code implies a switch in interactional status. Witness this testimony by an Aboriginal man who was opposing a mining town being built adjacent to an Aboriginal sacred site. In the Aboriginal language his opinion is forceful ('*Mayawanti*': 'All you leave it alone'), but when he is asked to translate his remarks into English (the only language his Anglo-Australian auditors can follow), his remarks are more docile:

AP *Walka tjina.*
(mark) (feet)
He left his footprints.

That means he put his foot there, and hopped away. That's his track there forever and ever. That's the song. That's a big History, from this mark. And he – I can say a little bit words [to tape-recorder]?

KL That's alright.

AP That's alright. From kangaroo *tjina, tjukurpa*
(feet) (Dreaming)
These footprints [ancient carvings on a granite slab] *were made by* kangaroos *from the*

tjina walkatjunu. Mayawanti. That's a *tjukuratja!*
(feet) (put marks) (all you leave it alone) (Dreaming)
Dreaming. All you leave it alone. Those are

Marlu tjina. Ngaanya palunya tjukurrpa.
(kangaroo) (feet) (this) (one) (Dreaming)
kangaroo footprints! These are from the Dreaming.

Marlu, maru,   marlu, karlaya tjina, marlu tjina 10
(k'roo) (Aboriginal) (k'roo) (emu) (feet) (k'roo) (feet)
Kangaroos, emus, and a world-creature Aboriginal
person's prints were left: emu's footprints,

Marlu tjina, wangkatji   mara   tjunkupula,
(k'roo) (feet) (Aboriginal) (hand) (those two put)
Kangaroo's footprints and the handprints of the Two
Men they left [future conditional tense].

tjunkumartu, tjunkumartu, tjunkumartu. Paluna.
(would be putting) (would be putting) (that's all)
They would be putting, would be putting, would be
putting [again, the future conditional tense used for
events of the Dreaming]. *That's all.*

      Talk English way?
KL   *Yuwa*, alright.
      (yes)
AP   Yah. Well, all you people from Western Mining
      [Company], no harm to come and see the cave. And
      that's a History place. Two Histories – cave and a
      main one there, kangaroos tracks and emu tracks
      and you're welcome, but as long as you don't bring,
      make a mess, or put a shot in or bore 'em and put   20
      the shot in and make a mess of that History.
      (Indistinct). Don't do that. You, no harm to come
      and see this ground.   **(87)**

In such a fashion Anglo-Australian domination of Aboriginals
is overdetermined. It is a result both of the political relations
which exist between them and of the asymmetry of the
interactional systems they employ. The interactional asymmetry
provides whites with many opportunities for maintaining political
dominance. The collective orientation of Aboriginal parties,
whereby they look to the situation to provide them with their
solutions, leaves openings for Anglo-Australians to assert their
preferences. Aboriginal parties may be lured into accepting
'positions' by the congeniality of the setting. One gratuitous
'Palya!' ('good') may provide the basis for a congenial band-
wagon, so that one *'Palya!'* inadvertently becomes everyone's. A
notable feature of Aboriginal/Anglo-Australian interaction is that
the Aboriginal participants do more 'rubbernecking' in their
efforts to check to see what their fellows are thinking. By
contrast, Anglo-Australian participants pay less attention to their
fellow whites; that is, the Anglo-Australians' opinions are more

personal and less corporate. One Aboriginal speaker's confidence is contagious, and should an Anglo-Australian have an Aboriginal partner when making a proposal, the articulation of opposition will be muted.

Equally important is the fact that frequently Anglo-Australians are impatient to reach decisive resolutions. They unintentionally force Aboriginal people to make decisions which have not received the customary validation which can come only from the serial articulation of summary accounts we have examined. With insufficient time for such a system of deliberation, Aboriginal assemblies are pressed to make premature decisions. Under the concern to preserve the cordial character of intercultural communication, Aboriginal participants may accommodate their Anglo-Australian partners and forgo the authoritative structures of their own decision-making processes.

The confusions endemic to intercultural communication operate here as well. Commonly, there is such a hurry to collaboratively produce 'the matter talked about' that a faulty 'resolution' will become objectified and be acceded to. With the best of intentions, Anglo-Australian welfare officers are quick to presume in a discussion what Aboriginal people may be wanting (e.g., a motorcar ride, pension money, a cigarette). The officer will present their Aboriginal partners with a possible formulation of what it is they want, expecting some sort of confirmation or denial. But the Aboriginals are likely to accept the Anglo-Australian's formulation as indicative of *his* wishes or intentions in the matter, and they will agree with it in order to satisfy him. This leaves the Anglo-Australian to conclude that his erroneous solution was the correct one. Similarly, Aboriginal parties may be forced to accept as sufficient the poor reduction of their message which their Anglo-Australian partners are capable of making simply because they are not able to better communicate their outlook in a communicative context controlled by whites.

Generally speaking, Anglo-Australians are blind to the interactional life of Aboriginal people and view them exclusively through European standards. Thus, a poor mastery of English or too strong an accent will be judged to indicate lower-class status, just as if the Aboriginal person were an English 'commoner' from a down and out section of London. As in the case of Hawaiians in American public schools described in detail by Gallimore, Boggs and Jordan (1974: 19ff.), Anglo-Australians are inclined to employ 'deficiency explanations' for communicative failures rather than explanations which correctly locate the problems in the structures of intercultural interaction. For example, when one elderly Aboriginal called in at a small town's police station to ask where I lived, his pronunciation of 'Ken' was 'Kin,' and the police failed to understand him (though I lived only across the street). To make himself more clear, the Aboriginal employed the nominative marking suffix '-nga' to let them know he was speaking about a person: 'I am looking for Kin-nga.' The police officers derisively told the Aboriginal that all the kings live over in England. Rather than invest energy in deciphering Aboriginal communicative structures, many Anglo-Australians dismiss Aboriginal talk as foolish or ignorant. Whites merely substitute their own ethnocentric constructions for the actual interior lives of Aboriginal people, and the most ordinary Aboriginal ways of expression never become visible for the whites' witness.

In the course of their relations with whites, Aboriginal people have made certain compromises in their behavior, as do all persons who find themselves in intercultural contexts. For example, Aboriginal people found in 'the bush' for the first time don clothing in order not to offend the sensitivities of Anglo-Australians. Similarly, styles of greetings and terms of address (e.g., 'boss'), topics and tempo of conversation, etc., are adapted by Aboriginals to facilitate interaction with whites. While such adaptations mean very little, the behavior is viewed as grounds for a much more wholesale cultural conversion than is actually the case. Never taking the pains to apprehend the Aboriginals' interior life, such surface conformity is taken to be evidence of a more total acculturation. A missionary writes in 1935 (Perez 1977: 91) that the monks did not 'object to the Aborigines going away for a time in the bush,' as though the time the Aboriginal people spent at the mission was their paramount reality and not the time they spent in the bush. Present-day pastoralists share such an outlook. These presumptions may lead to feelings of betrayal when Aboriginal people eventually follow their own aspirations.

Interaction in Australian courts of law

The innate desire of Aboriginal people to avoid being exposed personally in public settings is confounded when they are forced to appear in Australian courts of law. Either as witnesses or as defendants, Aboriginals must contend not only with a body of interactional procedures which are strange to them, but they are at the same time placed under that close public scrutiny which constrains their abilities to communicate. The agony of Aboriginal people during court appearances is easily visible. For the most part they have one goal in mind, and that is to bring the situation to a speedy conclusion in whatever way they can. Their usual praxis is to acquiesce to whatever placates the Anglo-Australians in the courtroom, even if it means pleading guilty. It is not unusual for an Aboriginal witness to agree with what both the prosecution and defense counsels suggest, thus contradicting him- or herself. Under the current structure of procedures in Australian courts of law, the juridical value of much Aboriginal testimony is practically zero.

Besides this, there are some serious questions about the fairness of court practices in cases involving Aboriginal defendants. The legal significance of almost everything is lost to Aboriginal people. The courtroom personnel engage in a dispensation of the cases without explaining to Aboriginal defendants the legal issues involved. Sometimes courtroom activity seems like sorcery to Aboriginals (indeed, the costumes, oaths, etc., have their origins in extra-legal ritual and customs). Aboriginals find confusing some of the instructions the court gives them; for example, an Aboriginal witness is told he must tell the truth but also that he doesn't have to say anything if he doesn't want to (i.e., if he or his spouse is the accused). The better part of the courtroom strategies which Aboriginal people learn are heard from fellow Aboriginals outside the courtroom before and after the hearings. For example, one Aboriginal was advised to be sure to ask for 'time to pay,' so that he would not have to spend time in jail for lack of funds. When the prosecution and defense had completed presenting their cases, this Aboriginal defendant was asked if he had anything further to say before the judge considered his verdict. He replied, 'Time to pay.'

Many of the replies of Aboriginals are incorrectly understood by the court, and a greater adequacy of communication of meaning is presumed than actually exists. Most Aboriginal testimony is terse, and their inclination to answer 'Yes' to questions, regardless of whether the questions were comprehended, passes unnoticed by most lawyers and magistrates; or, more accurately, while legal personnel are aware of the possibility that Aboriginals may answer 'Yes' without understanding the question, in actual practice they miss the overwhelmingly gratuitous character of the Aboriginal responses and unthinkingly apply the Aboriginal replies to their preceding question as though they were competent answers. When an Aboriginal's difficulty does become observable, the magistrate is likely to become irritated with the hermeneutic burden it imposes, and the court's efforts to clarify the meaning of a piece of testimony may become aggressive. This only leads the Aboriginal witness to feel less secure, reducing the volume of his or her replies and shortening them further, often to the point of silence. What is more, the Aboriginal is then more likely to concur with whatever he believes the court wants (whether his belief is correct or not). Such interactional-communicative failures are taken to be the result of the intellectual deficiencies of the Aboriginal witness. Here is an illustration, taken from the trial of an Aboriginal person (my transcription):

Magistrate: Can you read and write?
Aboriginal defendant: Yes.
Sergeant: Can you sign your name?
AP   Yes.
M   Did you say you cannot read?
AP   Hm.
M   Can you read or not!?
AP   No.
M   [Reads statement.] Do you recall making that
     statement?   10
AP   Yes.
M   Is there anything else you want to add to the
     statement?
AP   Ø
M   Did you want to say anything else!?
AP   No.
M   Is there anything in the statement you want to
     change?
A   No.
M   [Reads second statement.] Do you recall making that   20
     statement?
AP   Yes.
M   Do you wish to add to the statement?
A   No.
M   Do you want to alter the statement in any way?
AP   [slight nod]
M   What do you want to alter?
AP   Ø
M   Do you want to change the statement?
AP   No.   30
        (88)

At line 8 the Aboriginal defendant presumes the negative response is being called for because of the emphasis the magistrate places on 'not' in line 7. This makes the task of accommodation difficult, as the Aboriginal must pay attention to the real possibility that *either* a positive or negative response will satisfy the magistrate (cf. lines 14-24). What is important to observe here is that what the Aboriginal has in mind primarily is his strategy of gratuitous concurrence and only secondarily the facts of the matter. At line 19 he replies 'No,' possibly relying upon the success of his negative reply in line 16; but by line 26 he becomes uncertain about what reply the judge would prefer. He feigns a gratuitous nod, hoping for the best (rule: when in doubt, an affirmative reply is safer), but this is unsuccessful and must wait until line 30 to be repaired. The magistrate, who is close to losing his patience, is unaware of the facile nature of the Aboriginal's testimony.

In this case, where the main evidence is a 'statement' taken by the police out of court, there is little likelihood that it reflects the Aboriginal person's true beliefs. Prosecuting police officers who remain in outback regions and have daily interaction with Aboriginals are more cognizant of the Aboriginal praxis of acquiescence, and not infrequently they exploit it for the purpose of improving their case. Eggleston (1976: 37) tells of one police detective who under cross-examination admitted about his method of interrogation, 'It is probably a habit to suggest an answer that is logical.' And such suggestions are readily accepted by Aboriginal defendants.

In this next case the Aboriginal defendant is partly deaf:

Magistrate: Stand up.
Aboriginal defendant: [Remains sitting; is motioned to stand; stands up.]
M   Can you hear me?
AP   Yes.
M   Do you understand what I am saying?
AP   Ø
M   Do you know the difference between truth and untruth?
AP   Yes.
M   . . . but you must speak the truth.   10
AP   Yes.

. . .

Prosecutor: Do you remember the accident?
AP   Ø
P   Is it all right to talk like this, sir?
M   Well, you can't lead too much.   **(89)**

The Aboriginal's praxis of accommodation works for him successfully at lines 5, 9 and 11, even though he was probably unable to hear the questions. In another case a partly deaf Aboriginal person saw everyone in the court turn to look at him at the same time, and uttered 'Yes,' even though no question was being directed to him.

Two varieties of this strategy are mumbled replies and silence, both normally executed with some skill. I have labeled these practices 'Marcel Marceaux.' A simple instance of a gurgle as a confirmative utterance is that of the Aboriginal defendant who is uncertain about whether a yes or no answer is being sought and replies halfway between them – 'Hm' (Cf. illustration (88), line 6). In another case the Aboriginal defendant successfully received the oath by repeating the words of the court very softly, trailing off into utter silence well before the conclusion, and then nodding. It was accepted by the court without observation because it fell so quietly into the pace of the court ritual.

During this trial the same witness replied to a question of the magistrate in the affirmative – 'Yes, he (mmklpff)' – as he skillfully wiped his mouth while replying. The magistrate did not make the indeterminacy public but merely incorporated the witness's gratuitous reply into his testimony. The testimony was later read back to the witness, as it was hand-copied by the magistrate, and the witness was asked if it was a correct rendition of what he said. The answer was 'Yes.' The next step in the process was for the Aboriginal witness to sign each page of his testimony. This signing also was acceded to gratuitously:

Mag.   Have him sign the bottom of each page of his deposition.
Mag.   Can you sign your name?
AP   Ø
M   Can you sign your name?
AP   My name [repetition, with gestural tone of assurance].
M   Can you sign your name?
AP   You want me to sign my name?
M   Yes. Officer, will you please take him to the back   10
       and have him sign his name?   **(90)**

Eggleston has written (1976: 159), 'To hear a court accept as a plea of guilty the mumbled assent of a defendant to the question whether he was drunk yesterday is to observe incomprehension in action.'

Elkin (1947: 177) observes that the mumbled reply may be a skilful means of dodging an issue. Many times I have observed Aboriginal people successfully exploit their *alleged* ignorance to win excusal from having to give testimony which may have incriminated relatives, and Aboriginal people have learned how to use to their advantage the indeterminacy of the local detail of the communication. Elkin comments,

231

'Pidgin' is a most convenient means of dodging or confusing the issue. How often is the answer to a question 'Might be!' But what does that mean? That the native does not understand the question; or that he is not sure of what sort of answer or information is required; or that he knows the answer is in the negative, but does not want to disappoint or offend the questioner. All these are possibilities.

Their praxis of accommodation is an obstacle to justice when Aboriginal people are giving testimony against white defendants, who frequently live locally and are in a relationship of dominance with the Aboriginal witness. In this next case the defendant was the owner of the sheep station on which the Aboriginal witness lived in an open camp; the defendant, who had been drinking, had run over her husband with his automobile, killing him.

Defense counsel: You live at A?
AP   Yes.
D   Can you read and write?
AP   Yes.
D   Whose fault was it?
AP   Ø
D   You spoke to Mr X?
AP   Yes.
D   Could you smell alcohol on Mr X's breath?
AP   No.   10
D   How did Mr X appear to you after the accident?
AP   Ø
D   Was Mr X driving too fast?
AP   [Hardly audible] No.   **(91)**

The Aboriginal witness was unwilling to risk condemning her 'boss', who could have made it difficult for the Aboriginal people living on his station. In addition, the courtroom principals (police, prosecuting magistrate) were anxious to find justification for dropping charges. The defendant was released by the inquest with no charge of manslaughter being made.

Not having access to Anglo-Australian traditions of legal behavior, Aboriginal people address themselves carefully to the local contingencies of the unfolding interaction in order to ascertain the topicality and the places in the sequence of talk appropriate for their own speech acts. Aboriginal replies to questions may be gratuitous, as we have seen, but in order for these gratuitous answers to retain an unremarkable character they must meet the sequential requirements of the talk. Finding the correct place to begin one's own explanation is a problematic matter which turns on the local organization of question and answer sequences. Here is a simple case of a (pre-trial) interrogation by a police constable:

Constable: Jimmy, I am going to have to talk to you about what happened yesterday, do you understand that?
Jimmy: Yes.
C   I want you to understand that you do not have to speak to me if you don't want to, do you understand that?
J   Yes.
C   What I will do is type on this paper what we say, and it may later be shown to the magistrate in court, do you understand that?   10
J   Yes.
C   Do you have to speak to me? [Translator translates.]
J   Yes.
C   What do you want to talk about?
J   We bin camping we go ask 'im Leo what happened last night . . .

                             (*Legal Aid Bulletin* 1976: 116-19) **(92)**

Although the constable is careful to explain to the Aboriginal defendant what he is doing and what rights the Aboriginal person has, it is not certain whether J appreciates the options available to him. Jimmy replies 'Yes' to what the constable suggests, but there is no indication that Jimmy is more than a passive and uncomprehending participant in the exchange, waiting-searching for an indication of the place where he can begin to tell his story. It is highly unlikely that he has appreciated his legal right to remain silent.

Before a person's testimony may be accepted by a court, Anglo-Australian law provides that the witness understand the nature of the commitment involved in making an oath to tell the truth. Oaths are administered to Aboriginal witnesses on a regular basis, but much of the time their significance escapes Aboriginal participants who may be prepared to swear to anything. Illustration (89) displayed how a partly deaf Aboriginal witness was able to take the oath without his ignorance of its meaning becoming apparent. On occasions the court takes the time to make some sort of effort to explain the meaning of the oath to Aboriginals. In (93) the court employs an Aboriginal translator who attempts to explain the oath to the Aboriginal witness:

Magistrate: Does he know what it is to swear to tell the
                  truth to the court?
Translator: *Wangka tjukurala!* [Talk straight!]
Aboriginal: Ø   (93)

'Talk straight!' is an inadequate translation of the oath. The
tense employed is that of a command, which is contrary to the
voluntary nature of an oath, and it is likely to intimidate further
an already insecure Aboriginal witness. An Aboriginal witness
hearing such a command will understand that he must provide
the Anglo-Australian members of the court with the answers they
are seeking without creating any disharmony. On other occasions
the oath has been translated as '*Wangka palya*,' which means
literally, 'Talk good.' '*Wangka palya*' is employed frequently by
Aboriginals among themselves and may mean, 'Let's keep our
talk harmonious.' Such an utterance is a maxim of Aboriginal
social interaction, but it serves to inhibit testimony which would
create argument in the court. Here the basically non-contestual
character of ordinary Aboriginal discourse handicaps Aboriginal
people in the highly contestual domain of Australian courts of
law.

The Aboriginal strategy of acquiescing to the suggestions of
their court interrogators is displayed clearly in illustration (73),
pp. 192-4, and such a strategy may operate while the Aboriginal
witness is comprehending only portions of the prosecutor's
questions. The Aboriginal's 'time' (line 30), 'hands' (line 50) and
'before' (line 66) are all selected from the prosecutor's utterances
in the previous lines. On several occasions the witness fails to
reply at all (lines 25, 36, 40 and 70), certain evidence that he is
operating in an interactional milieu where his testimony is
probably not reliable. His silence is identical to that of Aboriginal
school children who fail to respond when called upon to speak.
Unsure of what to make of the events, he says nothing at all,
even if it means that his reply will be understood incorrectly
(lines 68-72). His hope, according to the rule of intercultural
communication we have examined, is that the court will make of
his testimony what it requires. If it were not for the court
translator (most courts do not employ translators), the error
would have passed undetected. The prosecutor displays a
disinterest in the witness's failure to understand what is
happening and quickly proceeds with his questioning (line 73).
The testimony from line 61 through line 75 is highly technical,
following the strictly rule-governed procedures of taking evidence
in Australian courts. While the magistrate, prosecutor, defense
counsel and translator are engaged in silent collaboration about

the details of this procedure, the Aboriginal witness is unaware of what is taking place. The court makes no effort to explain the meaning of the defense counsel's objection (line 74); rather, the prosecutor merely continues his examination, and it is only during the translator's explanation of the prosecutor's question (line 75) that any summary at all is offered the witness of what has been happening.

In this next case, the witness is an Aboriginal elder who is appearing as an expert on Aboriginal custom and who tries his best to please the court, although he is never aware of the legal ramifications of his testimony. The issue here is the extent to which an Aboriginal was acting under Aboriginal custom when he hit his wife, who was engaging in affections with another man:

Defense counsel: If a man finds his wife in a hotel
    kissing some other fellow, would Aboriginal people
    say the husband is doing the right thing if he hits that
    wife for kissing that fellow in the hotel?
Aboriginal witness: Yes. You get wild for somebody
    taking your wife.
D   You would get wild if you found that going on. If you
    hit that wife, would Aboriginal people say that is the
    right thing to do or the wrong thing?
AP   For Aboriginal people that is the wrong way.   10
D   What is the right way for Aboriginal people?
AP   I don't think that is the right way because they get
    wild and kill them.
D   They could kill them if they found them in that?
AP   Yes, they catch them something about his wife.
D   Are you allowed to kill her?
AP   Yes, that is the Aboriginal way.
Magistrate: I think Mr X is concerned about the
    conduct towards the man who is engaging in some-
    thing about his wife. [To witness:] Mr X, what you   20
    are being asked about is what happens to the wife if
    she does something with another man? Is the husband
    allowed to punish her?
AP   No, he gets wild.
M   He gets wild with the man but what about the wife?
AP   For wife–
M   What is he allowed to do with the wife? What do
    Aboriginal people say he should do to the wife?
AP   He should punish them.
M   He should punish them?   30
AP   Yes, punish them once.

M   But not kill them?

AP   Not kill them. Some people – like bad men, he get wild quick and kill them, not like we lot.

M   And what would a good man do?

AP   He would let his wife go – he would catch 'im another time when he catch them more.

D   If he catch them more, what would he do then?

AP   He could kill them, that's a law.

D   If he found his wife there, would he be allowed to give   40 her a hiding?

AP   You can give them a hiding.

D   But he is not allowed to kill them?

AP   No.

D   What if he caught them again?

AP   He would be allowed to give her a hiding first time.   **(94)**

Just as in illustration (73), the Aboriginal witness is keying incomprehensibly off of his interrogator's questions. At line 10 the witness cues on the defense counsel's 'wrong' in the previous line; at line 12 he employs the defense counsel's 'right way,' but fails to correctly understand the sense of its employment. 'Wife' (line 26), 'should' (line 29) and 'kill them' (line 33) are similarly borrowed from the utterances of the magistrate.

The massive unintelligibility of lines 24 – 'No, he gets wild' – and 26 – 'For wife' – confounds the court, motivating the magistrate to labor carefully to repair the confusion. While such linguistic confusion may pass unrepaired in ordinary intercultural conversation, in the context of legal testimony the court is under a greater obligation to clarify the miscommunication. Malcolm (1979: 463) has reported similar confusions in the conversations he has had with Aboriginal schoolchildren:

Linguist: What would you do if you saw a snake?

Child: Bite us.   **(95)**

Linguist: What things do you get into trouble for?

Child: Get the cane.   **(96)**

While patient at the start, the magistrate begins to lose his temper and in lines 27-8, in a rapidly delivered tempo, asks for clarification of the legal issue which concerns the court. The witness replies, but it is problematic whether his reply is sincere or only his best guess at what the magistrate preferred to hear. The magistrate repeats his question (line 30), which warns the witness that perhaps his answer was not satisfactory (if his reply was satisfactory, then there would have been no need for another question), and the witness bends to the magistrate's weight, qualifying his reply with 'once' (line 31). At line 32 the magistrate (mercifully) indicates to the witness just what answer he has been searching for, and the witness gratuitously obliges: 'Not kill them.' Such acquiescence, when added to the fact that the legal significance of customary Aboriginal behavior to the case (obvious to the barristers and magistrate) is mostly lost on the witness, produces an intercultural context in which the Aboriginal person is seriously disadvantaged.

Interaction in Australian schoolrooms

Aboriginal children lead a life relatively free of constraints. In their own home camps they are rarely scolded and almost never disciplined. That 'proper decorum' required by Anglo-Australian parents and perpetuated in Australian schools is something new and strange for Aboriginal children, and the rules administered by Anglo-Australian teachers – and already internalized by white children – are difficult for Aboriginals to acquire. Aboriginal children must learn an alternative system of competent inter-action in order to get along in the most mundane tasks, and many teachers are unaware of the extent of the adaptation which is involved or the degree to which Aboriginals are disadvantaged relative to their white schoolmates.

Interactional skills such as nominating and bidding for a turn to speak and other speech formats compose a structure of interaction which must be learned before Aboriginal pupils can participate in the most basic educational activities of the class. Gumperz (1980) has described how critical the mastery of classroom interactional strategies are to the success of students in American schools. Similarly, behavior which is standard inter-action of Aboriginal children becomes rule-violations in the perception of the Anglo-Australians who administer the schools. Collectively oriented talk is considered to be interruption, and congenial discourse unruliness. Malcolm (1979: 477) describes the difficulty Aboriginal children have in learning how to bid for a turn to speak: 'Aboriginal children characteristically share the initiating function with each other, overlapping and extending one another's turns, echoing and concurring with one another's comments, and performing multiple informing acts to make sure they get a hearing.' Malcolm's description of the structure of Aboriginal discourse is accurate, although the motive he ascribes to their discourse style is incorrect (Aboriginals are not concerned to get a hearing but to support the collective and anonymous development of a consensus). The repetition common to so much of ordinary Aboriginal discourse, what Malcolm calls 'restatement' or 'returns' (465), is out of place in Australian classrooms and severely inhibits the participation of Aboriginal children in the class. Similarly, Aboriginal requests sound like statements, imperatives or observations (Malcolm 1979: 395), a consequence of the style of summary accounts traditionally employed by Aboriginals. The sense of address in this discursive format may not be comprehended by white teachers. Aboriginal children must learn Anglo-Australian interactional structures or not participate at all, and frequently they choose the latter course of inaction.

But inaction or silence, themselves common responses in Aboriginal interaction, may be interpreted by teachers to be insolence. Standard forms of Aboriginal embarrassment, such as giggling when being addressed in too public a fashion, can get children into trouble. Malcolm (1977) writes about an Aboriginal student who replied in 'typical Aboriginal fashion, giggling, looking down and trying to hide her face with her hand. The teacher, clearly, is not prepared to tolerate this as classroom behaviour: "Oh, put up your head and talk to me properly." ' Such a response is the worst possible strategy for coping with Aboriginal withdrawal. Yet there is a further consideration, in that as one of a very limited number of interactional strategies Aboriginal school children know how to employ, communicative withdrawal may indeed be used in political ways. Even a skilful teacher may be unsure whether such withdrawal indicates shyness, insecurity or stubbornness. The only thing for certain is that in such instances communication is minimal.

Malcolm (1979: 421) discovered that some teachers considered the interactional adjustments to be up to the Aboriginal child alone, and in fact Australian teachers are capable of becoming very self-righteous about the necessity for Aboriginals to learn 'proper' behavior. There is a widespread feeling throughout central Australia that Aboriginal people should be made to learn English, and this feeling is shared by some of the Aboriginals' own employees on their remote reserves. I met a missionary of seven years' tenure, employed as a handyman in a remote Aboriginal settlement, who refused to learn the Aboriginal language, claiming that it would discourage them from learning English. This attitude places a great deal of pressure upon Aboriginal children, for it adds a moral invocation to the situation, adding to the children's discomfort. Typically, teachers assume that Aboriginal children are more familiar with Anglo-Australian interactional structures and the English language than in fact they are. Just as in Australian courts, more comprehension is presumed than is actually the case. This carries the additional consequence in the schools that the learning achievements of Aboriginal children tend to go unrecognized, leading to a devaluation of their capacity as learners (*ibid.*).

Frequently, the participation of Aboriginal children will proceed in the collaborative, collective fashion which is their habit, yet the degree of mutuality which is the basis of their participation may pass unrecognized by the teacher who is accustomed to perceiving the class as a gathering of individual members. Malcolm (1979: 478) informs us that Aboriginal students 'will be monitoring their behavior very carefully with regard to other Aboriginal children in the class; the decision to participate or to respond may be taken jointly, not individually.'

In fact, the secondary socialization of Aboriginal children in Australian schools may be viewed to be an effort to individualize their formerly collective modes of self-perception and social interaction, and Anglo-Australian educators view this to be a commendable achievement:

> School helps the child to move away from collective to individualistic orientation. This is the movement for autonomy. By acquiring knowledge the child begins to acquire a status. Increased internal control helps a child to live as an individual, and as a person. Development of personal autonomy – freedom to choose a life and freedom to live it – is a necessary function of school. However, this may increase competitive orientation in the child. He may have problems of working together with other members. This problem may be a realistic one. (Pareek 1976: 106)

The difficulty is that few Anglo-Australian educators have come to understand customary Aboriginal interaction well enough to appreciate the seriousness of the 'problem.' Malcolm comments similarly (1977):

> The school seems to anticipate in the Aboriginal child, as in other children, a sense of individual identity, yet he cannot sense an identity orphaned from his people . . . he likes to do things cooperatively, and the school anticipates individual effort and a sense of competition.

The larger social and philosophical issues merit full consideration but there can be no question that such a conflict of interactional structures places severe constraints upon Aboriginal children.

Interaction with pastoralists

The same ignorance of Aboriginal experience is found among the pastoral owners who raise sheep and cattle on land formerly occupied by Aboriginals. Today, Aboriginal people occupy their country in these regions only on the basis of being employees of the white graziers who have the government pastoral leases. These Anglo-Australians are very practical-minded and have little time for entertaining strange Aboriginal customs and sensibilities. The Aboriginal people are permitted to remain so long as they assist the pastoralist in his work, and their relationship is entirely on the basis of Anglo-Australian structures of interaction.

Pastoralists supervise the smallest details of the lives of Aboriginals who reside on their stations. Visitors must be approved by the pastoralists, child-rearing is supervised by the pastoralist's wife, use of the Aboriginal language is discouraged, and relations with outside whites are mediated by members of the pastoralist's household. Pastoralists maintain a policy of firmness with Aboriginal worker-residents, and the Aboriginal response is to acquiesce to the pastoralist's demands while trying to keep away from him as much as possible. The universality of the deference which Aboriginal worker-residents show their 'bosses' serves to make the actual beliefs and aspirations of the Aboriginals invisible to the pastoralists. The Aboriginals become docile objects fit for whatever play-world an Anglo-Australian designs, but the truth of their experience remains hidden.

Yet the Anglo-Australian dominance makes it impossible for Aboriginal people to protect their own self-interests. Even in contexts where Anglo-Australians may be willing to be partly sympathetic to Aboriginal aspirations, the style of the pastoralist's interrogation causes the Aboriginals to submit to what they believe to be the pastoralist's wishes. During the course of my work protecting Aboriginal sacred sites, I have witnessed Aboriginal people, who were desperate to receive protection for a sacred place, deny all such concern when confronted by local pastoralists.

On one occasion I accompanied an Aboriginal elder to a remote site which he wanted the government of Western Australia to protect. The site was the Dreaming for an important edible species in the elder's home country and was also a location where he was raised before the Europeans settled the interior of Western Australia. On the way to the site we stopped off at the pastoralist homestead nearest the site to inform the leasee of our presence and to explain to him the purpose of our trip. After some conversation, the leasee (EA), who had an interest (unknown to the elder) in a supplementary cattle lease in the area of the site, asked the elder to explain his interest in the place.

EA   Now, AP, there wouldn't be any Aboriginals who'd
        have any concern for that place, would there?

AP   Nope. She'll be right, I reckon.   **(97)**

The Aboriginal elder was entirely unwilling to challenge the pastoralist, a member of the very family from which the elder had taken his last name.

Pastoralists have learned that their bullying is almost always successful, often observing that 'You can get a blackfellow to say anything you want him to say.' Aboriginal people acquiesce on the most vital and delicate matters. Palmer and McKenna (1978: 49-50) describe an occasion where McKenna was undergoing some of the most important sacred training an Aboriginal youth can receive. His employer, who valued his strength and willingness to work, walked directly into the middle of the camp where the Aboriginal elders were preparing the sacred rituals and insisted on having McKenna come back to work for him. McKenna was not interested in returning to work until his *maliki* education had been completed, a process which would take many weeks; but McKenna was hidden away in the bush, and the elders capitulated on his behalf:

EA   Where's Clancy McKenna? I saw him here only the
        day before yesterday. I got a job of work for him.

AP   He's bush.

EA   How far bush? What you mean, gone walkabout?

AP   No, he's a man long time now.

EA   By Christ, I know he's a man, but I want him now,
        for a job. You reckon you might find him?

AP   He's just over there, *maliki* line business.   10

EA   Well can you go and get him for me.

[Discussion among Aboriginal elders.]

AP   You get him tomorrow.   **(98)**

Aboriginal people have few defenses against such forwardness.

Other settings

This pattern of interactional domination and exploitation is found in almost all Aboriginal/Anglo-Australian contact in central Australia. An effort by a major American petroleum company to convince Aboriginals to allow mining on their traditional lands met with success in the following way. Some representatives of the company showed a topographical map to an Aboriginal elder, who congenially told them there would be 'no objection' to their drilling at the location they pointed out. When asked to sign a statement to this effect, he unwittingly obliged, and the company was then able to report that they had the approval of the Aboriginals to drill at the location involved (Reece 1980:1).

In a more unscrupulous effort, a group of Western Australian Liberal Party members conspired to disqualify Aboriginal persons from voting in a close race for a rural State parliamentary seat in the Kimberleys. Their plan was simple: they prepared a series of questions all but the last of which required a 'Yes' response to avoid disqualification. Since the Aboriginals would say 'Yes' to anything, their self-disqualification on the last questions was guaranteed. The *West Australian* reports (July 29, 1977): 'The instructions also gave details on asking questions under Section 119 of the Electoral Act and said that some of the questions would be wrongly answered by an elector because they did not understand the questions and were prepared to say "Yes" to anything.' Their strategy was successful, and the Liberal Party candidate won by a very small margin. To add to the affront, the State premier (also from the Liberal Party) appointed the victor Minister for Community Welfare, the post which administers most of the state's Aboriginal policies.

Complaints about the ruse ultimately led to a Court of Disputed Returns' investigation, the first of its kind in the State's history. The Court interviewed many Aboriginals as well as the Liberal Party lawyers who devised and initiated the scheme. The testimony of one of these lawyers was reported in the *West Australian* (September 17, 1977):

Dixon told the court today that he did not find it unusual or embarrassing that a middle aged Aboriginal was asked whether he was of voting age. He also said it did not strike him as odd that Aborigines at Derby and Mowanjum were asked if they were born in Australia. Dixon denied a suggestion that the 'string of yeses' to the first five questions would get the Aborigines to say 'Yes' to the next questions which related to having voted previously that day.

Even persons from governmental institutions which are sympathetic to Aboriginal people place serious constraints upon them. Officers of the Australian Institute of Aboriginal Studies have pressured remote Aboriginal communities on matters of sacred importance. Legalistic formalities, common during visits by government officials, tend to intimidate Aboriginal people, and the authoritative character of government delegations inhibits Aboriginal participation. I once heard a chairman of the Aboriginal council of a remote settlement unsuccessfully warn his fellows, 'We all gotta talk!' In recent years pan-tribal councils have been formed with the assistance of Anglo-Australian advisors in order to lobby the various State governments in central Australia (South Australia, Western Australia, Northern Territory) for political, legal and land rights. The whites involved have viewed the effort as a successful Aboriginal-initiated step forward; however, all but the younger Aboriginals perceive these pan-tribal councils to be a friendly imposition of Anglo-Australian interactional structures, and the Aboriginal elders permit their continuance on an experimental basis only. At a meeting of one of these councils, an Aboriginal elder announced to the assembly, 'Alright, so we go along with this council whitefella way, not *wangkatja* [Aboriginal].'

Even on their own reserves Aboriginal people are dominated in their local interaction with whites. At each Aboriginal settlement, European 'employees' live in a mini-suburb of portable houses, surrounded by high fences. The majority of Europeans do not speak the Aboriginal language and know little about Aboriginal life. In most cases they remain for only one or two years, and yet they are actively involved in establishing administrative policies for the settlements. It takes only a few months for the newest European nurse or school teacher to begin to attempt to influence the policies of community management. These whites are usually supplied with an automobile, propane-powered refrigerator, air-transported food and beer, etc., by their government departments, and they use these to influence the community politics. Aboriginals appreciate having access to such material supplies and services; however, throughout central Australia they have been requesting a reduction in the number of Anglo-Australians in residence because it has become too difficult for the local community elders to influence decision-making.

Those settlements run by missionaries are characterized by a more total domination of Aboriginals. Stanner (1966: 149) has described the political relations in such settlements: 'The pressures to bend before a new, single authority, against which there was no appeal, were too insistent to be resisted, except by a common front for which the men had no genius.' It is the 'insistence' of Anglo-Australians which assaults the consensual structure of Aboriginal interaction before it is capable of generating an effective response. I have witnessed Aboriginal

243

people newly arrived from the desert wilderness contend with autocratic Anglo-Australian administrators, nurses, etc. They were so overwhelmed with the forceful intensity of the whites that they laughed in near disbelief, while willingly granting them any request the Anglo-Australians were able to communicate.

An irony of Aboriginal- and Anglo-Australian interaction on the settlements is that the white 'employees' recognize the inability of Aboriginal people to adequately defend their interests and so presume to speak on their behalf. Despite phenomenal problems of communication and culture conflict between the teaching, nursing and administrative staff and the members of the Aboriginal community, there is a certain paternal affection some whites have for Aboriginal people. Much of this affection is a result of the Aboriginals' congenial sociability. The difficulty is that Aboriginals tend to agree with whatever the whites want, and *the more forceful the interactional style of the Anglo-Australians, the more quickly an Aboriginal person will concur.* Conversely, the less self-assertive the white person is, the more frank will be the Aboriginal response.

During part of a national campaign to reduce the high rate of trachoma in Aboriginal communities, a volunteer arrived at a remote settlement to initiate a medicine drive to overcome the eye disease. She met with some success, but most of her pills were accepted politely and then fed to the Aboriginals' dogs. The results were identical to a contraception program in South Asia (Mamdani 1972: 205):

> When the villagers saw that the experimenters would not listen, they told them what they wanted to hear – and they threw the contraceptive tablets away. Thus an early report stated that 90 per cent of the villagers were in favor of contraception: the report assumed (falsely, it turned out) that a similar percentage was using the tablets. Here is how one villager explained his 'acceptance' of the tablets (needless to say, he never used them): 'But they [the staff] were so nice, you know. And they even came from distant lands to be with us. Couldn't we even do this much for them? Just take a few tablets?'

The case of the trachoma worker had a peculiarly Australian twist. The worker (an Australian university student) had become so shocked at the political situation of Aboriginals in their own community that she began to give advice to members of the Aboriginal council. While normally Aboriginals are opposed to such interference, in this instance the advice she gave was thought by the people to be helpful, and the Aboriginal council had thought that they had won an ally among the Anglo-Australian staff. Her advice upset the head nurse, however, and she was dismissed. When it was suggested to the Department of Health supervisor in the capital city that the volunteer nurse was removed against the wishes of the Aboriginal community, the head nurse took a survey of Aboriginal opinion; naturally, all those she asked gratuitously concurred with her decision, and she was able to report to her supervisor, 'The Aboriginal people wanted her out.' In such a fashion the wishes of Aboriginals are registered in the offices of those making governmental policy. The local Anglo-Australian staff translates most of the data upon which the decisions of Anglo-Australian bureaucrats are made. Here again the communicative distortion, a function of political relations, intercultural confusions and an asymmetry of interactional structures, prevents Aboriginal people from successfully defending their interests.

Aboriginal secrecy

Aboriginal people have a deliberate and successful policy of keeping their white neighbors in nearly total ignorance about their most deeply held beliefs. The thoroughness with which their private lives have remained secret is awesome to consider, given almost a century of contact in some areas and the exposed and dependent character of Aboriginal outback camps. Much of their success can be attributed to traditional Aboriginal prohibitions against revealing their sacred knowledge to uninitiated persons. Aboriginal women, children and uninitiated males are strictly forbidden to share knowledge of a sacred character, to handle or view sacred objects, hear certain songs, visit specific sites or witness sacred ceremonies. These prohibitions prevented the original European settlers from discovering the knowledge basic to the Aboriginal cultural and economic organization of the central Australian deserts.

But it would seem likely that over the period of a century adult European males eventually would have learned the lore of the sacred societies: however, the white settlers were positively unwilling to take seriously any aspect of Aboriginal religious life and held the Aboriginal beliefs in contempt. The attitude of most pastoralists is characterized by the remark of the president of a town shire in the Western Australian outback: 'I thought the main ritual of these fellows was to pile up heaps of broken glass,' referring to the flotsam of the town-dwelling drunks. After I discovered the extent to which the local Anglo-Australian population had been kept ignorant about the Aboriginals' life, I asked an old fellow why they never let them know that they had such beliefs. He replied, 'How we gonna make him believe if they never take notice?' For the last century the Aboriginal people have been leading a religious life about which the Anglo-Australians have been only marginally aware.

Such secrecy amounts to a praxis for reducing the Aboriginals' exposure to whites. The more cognitive distance that is placed between blacks and whites, the less opportunity there is for Anglo-Australians to exercise domination. Annett and Collins (Collins 1975: 216) have observed, 'Deference and demeanor rituals are produced by a combination of social density conditions and authority relationships. The more unequal the power resources and the higher the surveillance, the more often acts of petty ritual deference are demanded.' The best strategy in such circumstances is to reduce the surveillance, and that is what the Aboriginals have done.

From the very beginning of European settlements, the success of the Aboriginals' praxis of secrecy has been evident. Hunter (1793: 413), one of the chroniclers of the Sydney colony recorded, 'No signs of religion have been observed among them.' Hood (1843: 159) reported similarly, 'Their religion is very singular: they worship no idol, nor have they any religious ceremonies whatsoever.' During this century, missionaries who discovered some of the Aboriginals' sacred boards denied that the boards played any genuine role in Aboriginal life:

> But when in July 1947 the secret Kranganda boards arrived in stages at the mission from Derby, they went completely wild. It was disgraceful to discover that the instigators of the unhealthy unrest, the guardians of the boards – *which are not emblems of native culture, but symbols of a most degrading practice* – were Christians from the mission. The 'boards' in their possession were destroyed before their own eyes, for them to see that none of the feared punishments from the 'gods' were experienced by anyone anywhere.
>
> The missionaries could not take lightly this misbehaviour of their Aboriginals, and announced in good time that there would be no sports and no distribution of gifts of clothing in the forthcoming Christmas of 1947. (Perez 1977: 122)

While Anglo-Australians recognized the existence of 'corroborees,' they considered them more of a social affair and viewed them as having a role in Aboriginal life similar to that of Christmas, thus failing to grasp that they constituted the fundamental reality of Aboriginal people. Whites, even when sympathetic, are inclined to think of the Aboriginal beliefs according to Hollywood-styled versions of American Indian or South Pacific islanders' superstitions. As one cooperative mining engineer commented, 'Well, I can show you a map and see which areas are *taboo*.' The Aboriginals prefer to let such ignorance continue and choose not to enlighten whites about the correct character of their ritual life. A dialogue recorded in the fictional film *The Last Wave* is very accurate: after a tribal killing involving an Aboriginal who had violated sacred custom, the Aboriginal defendants were willing to plead guilty and be punished rather than reveal the fact that there was a vigorous secret religious life among urban Aboriginals; when asked directly if the killing was related to sacred Aboriginal 'Law,' the Aboriginal protagonist replied, 'No tribal people in city,' exploiting the erroneous belief of the white population so that the secrecy of their ritual life could be preserved. But let us examine some actual cases.

Pastoralists are unaware of the Dreaming on their own stations, even when the namesake of their station or closest town originates from the cosmology of the Dreaming; e.g., a resident of sixty years of the former mining town of Nannine was unaware that its name came from the word '*nganiny*,' which means 'fat,' and refers to the place where the world-creative Dingo took a bite out of the Emu (the only prominent cliff in the district). The station name 'Weebo' comes from '*wipu*,' a euphemism for penis, meaning 'tail'; the station-owner there was unaware of the existence of the sacred site on his station which was its namesake. Yakabindie Station comes from '*yakamunti*' ('*yaka*': 'female' and '*munti*': 'male') which is the name for Lake Miranda on that station and is where the Two Carpet Snakes copulated. Milly Milly Station received its name from the Aboriginal term for 'secret-sacred' ('*mily-milypa*'); presumably the Aboriginal person questioned long ago wished to withhold its true sacred name and provided a substitute which was a description rather than a name.

Aboriginals encourage this ignorance today by reverting to sacred sites by their European name when in mixed company. Aboriginals feel superior to Anglo-Australians who are ignorant of the 'basis' of the land's existence. The sacred site on Weebo Station is generally called 'Ockerbury Hill,' and a sacred site of outstanding significance near Cosmo-Newbury is called 'Minnie Creek.' Similarly, *Ngaanyatjarra*-speaking Aboriginal representatives east of Cosmo-Newbury requested that I record a highly sacred site for protection under its European name – which was unknown to them until I found it on one of my maps. A justice of the peace, born thirty miles from the town of

Leonora, once announced, 'I want to point out right now that this is the first time in my life, in my sixty odd years, that I've ever heard of a native sacred area.'

It is not uncommon for a pastoralist to be unaware of the extent to which Aboriginal people speak their local dialect. One pastoralist once assured me that a 'full-blooded' Aboriginal I had yet to meet no longer spoke the Aboriginal language and was more white than black: 'The only thing black about him is his skin. Inside his mind is as white as yours or mine.' The pastoralist's wife told me that this Aboriginal 'would be insulted' if I spoke to him in the Aboriginal language. The pastoralist had grown up with this Aboriginal man and, as the case in an earlier example (97), the Aboriginal had taken the family name of the pastoralist. When I first approached the Aboriginal in the town of Meekatharra, I began speaking in the *Kuwarra* Aboriginal dialect straightaway and found him responding readily. Quite the opposite of being 'insulted,' he insisted that the conversation be kept in the Aboriginal language at moments when my vocabulary began to fail. We carried on a long conversation, by the end of which I had probably learned more of the Dreaming of the area than the pastoralist had learned in his lifetime.

Despite the widespread use of Aboriginal place-names among Aboriginal people, the pastoralists derided my own usage of these names, convinced that they had fallen into disuse. Indeed, the 'disappearance' of such usage was seen to imply a final European victory over the cultural traditions of the indigenous Aboriginal people. But such a state of affairs is artifice. Mathews (1977) tells of an Aboriginal man who explained that the Anglo-Australian settlement supervisors 'never wanted to hear a word of any Aboriginal language' (56); yet, 'Quite a few Muruwari still spoke the language when the manager could not hear them' (72). It was my habit to keep discussions with Aboriginal people entirely in the Western Desert Aboriginal language, especially when the topic was the existence of sacred Aboriginal sites endangered by mineral development. I believed that this assisted in providing an honest exchange of information. I once interviewed an elderly Aboriginal lady who had lived as a nomad on the site of the proposed Yeelirrie uranium development as a young child. Her pastoralist 'boss' (a justice of the peace in the district) had followed me to her camp and stayed with me during the interview. After the interview was completed, the pastoralist angrily informed me that I had no business using the Aboriginal language and that English was good enough for any discussion.

Even when one is trusted by the Aboriginals, as is the case of this next illustration, Aboriginal customs may prevent any revelations of a sacred nature from being made. In this example, the sacred site fell under the custodianship of an Aboriginal elder I hadn't met, and so the Aboriginals were reluctant to give me details about the site's 'legal' custodian:

KL   *APe, does he know the sacred Law for this place?*
APa *Yes.*
KL   *He knows its Dreaming?*
APa *Its Dreaming he knows.*
KL   *He knows the ceremony for it?*
APa *The ceremony for it might be he knows.*
APb Yes, he *knows. He knows everything* that one.   **(99)**

Although APe would certainly be master of the Law for the site, my friend (APa) was willing to grant only that he 'might' know about it, leaving it possible for APe to feign ignorance with me if he thought that would be advisable. On other occasions information which would have helped to gain protection for Aboriginal sites was withheld because it was not the right of the Aboriginal person I was interviewing to reveal its truth. Unless the 'proper' custodian could be found, according to tribal Aboriginal custom, the truth of an endangered site would not be revealed. Traditional rules such as these inhibit the ability of Aboriginal people to defend forcefully some of their sacred places because many of the Aboriginal people concerned are obliged to maintain a discrete silence. Lobbying for the protection of a sacred area is often interpreted to be a display of excessive egotism, and this restricts Aboriginal people from speaking out about endangered places in their own homelands. Anglo-Australian officials, who must make political decisions about the sites, are mostly unaware of such constraints.

For nearly a century of Aboriginal/Anglo-Australian contact, Aboriginal people have preserved the strength of their sacred 'Law', and their success in doing so has helped to prevent them from becoming Europeanized. Contemporary Aboriginal people are proud of their sacred life and sincerely consider that it makes them superior to white people. As one Aboriginal remarked to me, 'Our Law is *too* strong. Whitefellas only got paper. Our Law is up here [points to mind].'

In recent years the national government of Australia has been more sympathetic to the traditional beliefs of Aboriginal people, and much of Australia's urban population has been giving a kind of sentimental support to some Aboriginal efforts in central Australia to secure a degree of self-determination and control over their traditional homelands. At the same time, the interest of international mining consortia in a variety of minerals (oil, uranium, nickel, gold, iron-ore, zinc, etc.) in central Australia has increased greatly, and the amount of exploratory work in the remote regions where traditionally-oriented Aboriginal people still dwell has grown to boom proportions. With increasing public and governmental concern about Aboriginals, the tribal elders have been more willing to reveal the existence of their sacred areas in order to save them from being destroyed. While their efforts have been only partly successful, their revelations have had a peculiar effect upon the local Anglo-Australian residents, for whom these revelations have come as a surprise.

It is almost the universal opinion of Anglo-Australians in the outback of Western Australia that Aboriginal people have been inventing sites in order to block mineral development. Their argument is that the Aboriginal people are hoping to secure financial rewards in exchange for withdrawing their opposition to the development of sites. The whites believe that no sacred sites exist and that they are only being contrived by greedy Aboriginals with the advice of interfering outsiders. One pastoralist in the Kimberley region of northern Western Australia wrote a letter to the State's major newspaper (*West Australian*, September 11, 1980) denying the validity and importance of sacred sites. He had been a resident in the area for 40 years and had never heard about the existence of such sites before. He suggested that many of the sites had been thought up by prehistorians and anthropologists who have gathered up information and then put suggestions in the minds of old Aboriginal people. (This is not inconsistent with the opinion of the magistrate of a major outback town who told me that anthropologists had a harmful affect upon the assimilation of Aboriginal people because they reinforced the false belief that there was something valuable about their traditional beliefs: the notion that Aboriginal people were capable of legitimizing their beliefs on their own had not occurred to the magistrate.)

The week that I commenced several months of research in connection with the ethnographic component of the proposed Yeelirrie uranium development's environmental impact statement, the member of the Western Australian House of Representatives for the region announced that pastoral residents in the area of Yeelirrie Station were certain that there were no sacred sites on Yeelirrie Station (*Western Australian*, week of October 10, 1976). My research proved beyond any doubt that there were legitimate and traditional sacred associations with the site where the town for the development was to be built. The main sacred site included some unique life-sized carvings in granite of the footprints of a Dreaming kangaroo hopping across a twenty-meter stream bed, carvings which showed extensive signs of weathering and water erosion. The local pastoralists, who were strongly opposed to any official recognition of Aboriginal sacred affairs, were furious with me because of my findings and argued that the Aboriginal people were making up the sites. What was most identifying of the intensity of the cultural-political struggle between whites and Aboriginals in central Australia was evident in the opposition of the one pastoralist whose own station was to be destroyed by the proposed uranium development. Despite the fact that he would just as soon the development not be built, he became enraged at the thought that some Aboriginal sacred beliefs would delay the project's approval. His outrage was over the government taking seriously Aboriginal beliefs which his forebears had been suppressing self-righteously for decades. As I have noted, the master's superiority is always limited by the possibility that the subservient other may renew the struggle; it is for this reason that the pastoralists have preferred to make the Aboriginal people into mere objects. The possibility that these docile objects might rise to reassert their own subjective life is not only disconcerting, but in this case it threatened to expose the fundamental deception which has been the basis of decades of social relations.

From the evidence I have presented, of course, Anglo-Australian awareness of sacred sites must be dismissed as a criterion for the valid existence of sites which are truly connected to Aboriginal beliefs. The station's original settlers, for example, also asserted that at the time they arrived, there were no Aboriginal people living in the area; yet my field research uncovered three persons who had lived within the station boundaries as nomads during its occupation by those Anglo-Australian pastoralists (they had not shown themselves for fear of being harmed, and especially for fear that their children would be taken away by police, a common practice during the early years of European settlement).

What is interesting about the skepticism of local whites is that their belief that Aboriginal people are engaging in a clever ploy to earn some financial reward is only too obviously an admission that if they were in the position of the Aboriginal people *they* would employ such a deceit because financial profit happens to be one of their central motivations. The advocacy of such beliefs is nothing more than projection. The plain truth of the matter is that traditionally-oriented Aboriginal people care more about their sacred Law than they do about money. I interviewed one Aboriginal elder about the possibility of accepting money in exchange for a sacred site:

KL How much money would Aboriginal people take for
that?
AP No money shall buy it. That stays in the ground, it'll
stop there. Aboriginal people live without money
anyway.   **(100)**

The very success of the Aboriginals' secrecy has worked
against them now that they are anxious to win protection for
some sacred areas. In an internationally celebrated case at
Noonkanbah, Western Australia, an American mining company
succeeded in drilling an exploratory well at an Aboriginal sacred
site (Los Angeles *Times*, August 13, 17 and 31, 1980). Doubt was
cast upon the authenticity of the Aboriginal people's claim
because they had kept the existence of the site secret until it was
about to be drilled. A historian of Aboriginal affairs (Reece
1980: 10) writes, 'One of the reasons for the state government's
unwillingness to accept the genuineness of the Noonkanbah
people's stand was the relative quiescence of Aboriginal people
in Western Australia until recent years.' While their strategy has
succeeded in guaranteeing the perpetuation of their sacred beliefs
undisturbed by Anglo-Australian interference, it has made the
defense of their sacred places more difficult in this era of
increasing mineral exploration.

The case of another sacred site in Western Australia reveals a
great deal about the success of the Aboriginals' strategy of
secrecy. Associated with this sacred site were extraordinary
stones which contained a very attractive marble design formed in
almost perfect circles. One of the local Anglo-Australians
decided that he could sell the stones to tourists and others and so
took some of them to sell in the neighboring town. The stones
were placed in the windows, and the Aboriginal people protested
to a local community welfare officer. The townspeople had never
heard the Aboriginals speak of the stones before and believed
that no interest in them was shown until they proved to have
some commercial value. In fact, the Aboriginal people objected
to the display of the stones in a place where women and children
could witness them. The viewing of these sacred stones was
considered a sacrilege which could possibly lead to the death of
the viewer, and the Aboriginal men kept all their women and
children off of the town street until the stones were removed.

On the report of the community welfare officer and a visiting
anthropologist, an official government delegation was sent to
investigate the matter. During their investigation they spent
several days with the Aboriginal elders and satisfied themselves
that the stones and the site on which they were found were

indeed sacred to Aboriginal people. Afterwards, they took testimony from local pastoralists and townspeople and discovered that not a single Anglo-Australian in the vicinity was aware of the sacred character of the site or, for that matter, of any other Aboriginal sites in the region. The pastoralist who had the lease for the station on which the stones were found had no knowledge of anything sacred being located on the station, and the same was true for a man who had been living on the station for twenty years. The testimony of the shire president, who had been living in the district since the 1930s, was the most revealing:

Chairperson: During the whole of this period you have been
    here have you ever been aware of the existence of a
    sacred area/
Shire President: /No, no.//
C   //on XX
    Station?
SP   No.
C   When did you first become aware that some people
    said there was a sacred site on the station?
SP   Oh, it might have been twelve months ago.   10
C   I see.
SP   No, not that long ago. When they had the stones in
    the window.
C   Can I also ask you if you thought this was surprising,
    that you didn't know the existence of this area?
SP   Well I do, and for this reason – we were connected
    with a station a couple hundred miles north of here.
    And I was a sort of general manager of it from this
    end of the place.   20
C   Yes.
SP   I used to travel up there once a month and camp fre-
    quently at the camp by the salt lake, which is about
    14 or 15 miles from the sacred stone area. And I was
    associated with old niggers that were camped around
    there and [indistinct] and different camps along there,
    and I've never heard of it. And I was associated and
    used to camp frequently at night with old prospectors
    that were around that district who'd been living at the
    lake and had just gone into a camp and lived in that   30
    camp, and I've never heard it mentioned. No mention
    of it at all.
C   Did they mention any other sacred area in this/
SP   /No.//
C   //area to you?

SP   No, not at all.
C   So that in fact you know of no sacred areas at all?
SP   No, not at all.
C   Do you think that there's really any substance in this
story that there's a sacred area?   40
SP   No, I don't think there is any substance at all.
C   Well, so that in fact you don't think the natives are
genuinely concerned about this problem?
SP   I tell you, I questioned a lot of the old natives-um-I've
known. They've known me for, oh, over thirty years,
and I've questioned a lot of them. They're old chaps
now, but they don't know. Like APx, but you can't
get anything from him. He's one of the old local
blokes; and APy, but he's in the same condition, and
they only tell you, now, what they think you wanted   50
them to tell you.
C   I see . . . So you're of the opinion that some lot of
people might get one story from them and another lot
of people might get another.
SP   Oh, I'm aware of that story from them. Natives are all
like that, too.
C   I see.
SP   They tell you the story they think you want to know.
C   I see.
SP   That's my experience with them.   60
C   Yes. Now, but, in addition to this I think we can say
that you know of no sacred areas in this particular
area here. That you believe that the *wangkayi*
[Aboriginal people] talk fully and freely to you?
SP   Oh yes.
C   In other words you don't think they're holding any-
thing back?
SP   No. I don't think they're holding anything back, no. **(101)**

Despite the ignorance of Anglo-Australian residents, it is not uncommon for them to believe that they know everything there is to know about Aboriginal people. A couple who were held in unanimous contempt by the Aboriginal people who had regular relations with them told me in frankness one day, 'We've worked with colored people all our lives, and we understand them.' But the truth is closer to the remarks of an Aboriginal elder who summarized Aboriginal/Anglo-Australian relations for me. 'The curtain hangs between them and has never been unveiled.'

8   Cultural politics

The 'curtain' which shields the private lives of Aboriginal people is only one aspect of a long-term cultural struggle between Aboriginals and Anglo-Australians in the central desert. The struggle is remarkable in that the two sides' munitions are in no way commensurate, and each side concentrates its efforts upon different battlegrounds. The ultimate objective – cultural hegemony for the whites and secured cultural survival for the blacks – has escaped both parties; and it may be said that this struggle, where the issues, resources and consequences are cultural, has so far been a stalemate.

The members of one culture tend to be extroverted in their social personalities, search ceaselessly for ways to overcome nature and are not opposed to dominating their fellows in the process. Jung (1975: xlvii) has described the typical 'White Man's mental equilibrium' as 'the sort of extroversion that is always seeking security by dominating its surroundings.' The members of the other culture are more introverted, uninterested in domination, and, rather than being concerned to invent new ways to transform their world, have developed the more passive ability to adapt to the world in which they find themselves. The critical battles of the struggle do not take place in the open. Because all major public combat is won by the Anglo-Australians, their Aboriginal contestants have sought less conspicuous arenas in which to wage quiet campaigns.

One advantage the Aboriginal people have in the struggle is that they have no interest in dominating the whites, personally or politically; they strive only to free themselves from the whites' dominance and to lead their own Aboriginal lives. While their very disinterest in struggling to dominate has been partly responsible for their being casually dismissed as members of a civilization of no consequence, such moderate aspirations have had the surprising result that major Anglo-Australian political conquests have made little difference to the fundamental allegiance of Aboriginal people to their own reality. Somehow, their lack of interest has rendered them less vulnerable to European power in that the emotional and cognitive coherence of their lives has never depended upon the outcome of their cultural struggle with whites. Just as the Aboriginals showed little fascination with the Europeans who first landed in Australia, today's Aboriginal people are content to mind their own affairs, at least when Anglo-Australians are willing to leave them alone. For Aboriginal people cultural superiority is not a function of a struggle for recognition, and without the recognition of the Aboriginals – as Hegel has told us regarding the slave and the master – the cultural victory of the Anglo-Australians can never be consummated.

But the white population of central Australia will not leave the Aboriginal people alone. It is not enough that Aboriginals have offered them the appearance of submission: the whites require and demand that recognition which is essential to the security of their cultural victory. Accordingly, members of Anglo-Australian society are engaged in what amounts to a moral reeducation of Aboriginal people. Welfare workers, shopkeepers, court officials, pastoralists, teachers and missionaries provide constant instruction as part of their everyday contact with Aboriginal people. The value of work, the importance of economic progress, the need for discipline, the virtues of ambition and other Protestant-European values are impressed upon Aboriginals by Anglo-Australians in the most bizarre contexts. The cultural-political struggle in central Australia has taken the form of an attempt to make the formal domination of Aboriginal people meaningful on a subjective level, and it is here where the European advance has been stalled.

The Aboriginal people have a second advantage in this struggle of cultures: the desert of central Australia is their ancestral home. The very presence of its salt lakes, sandhills, waterholes and breakaways reaffirms the truth of their life because they are living evidence of the reality of their Dreaming. The Aboriginals roam their countryside freely, while this same desert is a foreign and sometimes threatening wilderness to Anglo-Australians who spend most of their life indoors where they can avoid the 120°F summer temperatures and the desert's overpowering sun (skin cancer in the region is widespread among whites). While the whites are dedicated to the care of ten by thirty meter plots of green lawn (reminiscent of England), every bush and tree reaffirms the Aboriginal person's reality in providing not only his food and fire but by having a sacred relationship to the totality of which the Aboriginal is also a part. The central Australian deserts confirm the truth and adequacy of the Aboriginals' cognitive life, and throughout the cultural-political struggle the Anglo-Australians are cognizant of this pervasive ally which nurtures Aboriginal people while being for the whites a vacant and formidable antagonist.

Work-and-wages

One of the outstanding characteristics of Anglo-Australian civilization is the separation of one's occupational work from the household and its concentration into well-defined and obligatory units of time. Much of the cultural-political struggle in central Australia has been over the attempt of whites to force Aboriginal people to conform to this Protestant-European notion of work, yet their efforts during nearly a century have not been successful. In the regions of central Australia where temperatures and rainfall permitted the European settlers to establish sheep and cattle stations, the Aboriginal residents were incorporated (as indentured laborers) into the workforce which established the Australian pastoral industry; however, the ideology of work, with some exceptions, never won the acceptance its white proponents desired. In the regions beyond the limits of European settlement, where Aboriginal people continued to live a traditionally-oriented life, the ethic of work has made even fewer inroads. Today, many of the policies of the Australian government, and the informal policies of whites in the region, are designed to implant this ethic among Aboriginal people. As a governmental commission in Western Australia (Laverton Joint Study Group) once summarized, 'The Study Group believes that a positive approach has to be adopted to motivate the Aboriginal people to embrace a new work ethic.'

To this end the Australian government has devised all sorts of strategies. In the central reserves of the two States and the Northern Territory, Aboriginal people have for millennia fetched water, collected wood for their fires and cooked meals for their children and elderly. Removed from some of their tribal lands by government officers in order to allow atomic testing in the desert by the British after World War II and forbidden by the State government in Western Australia to resettle their homelands outside the reserve boundaries, the central reserves Aboriginal people today survive on government welfare. In 1977 the government reorganized their payment procedures and in some areas now require (on a 'voluntary' basis, the details of which are too extensive to enter into here) that work be performed on an hourly basis before subsidies are given. So today water is fetched, firewood collected and meals for the children and elderly cooked by Aboriginals 'employed' to do so; and for such services these employees receive a 'paycheck,' which they must then cash at a proto-bank which is next door to a one-room store where they can purchase the material goods they require. For those outside the local money economy the same tasks are performed without compensation, and they are forced to draw upon kinship associations or gamble for the cash to provide the flour, sugar, tea, tobacco and refrigerated soft drinks which supplement their daily needs.

It is a very baroque and expensive exercise, but it is perpetuated in the belief that Aboriginal people are learning how to handle money, an ability without which a capitalist ideology cannot take root. As Weber (1958: 72) has observed: 'The capitalist system needs this devotion to the calling of making money.' Along with this education, customary Aboriginal enterprises are being bureaucratized to some extent (e.g., the rationalization of wood collecting, the feeding of children en masse) which may make European inroads into their traditional life. But for the most part the Aboriginal people consider the exercise a game they must play as in former years they attended church services as a necessary prerequisite to being given their weekly allotment of flour and sugar. The effect of the contemporary system is hardly greater than that of former years because in both cases the European world is a finite province of activity divorced from the Aboriginals' essential social reality.

Along with this system of wages and monetary exchange, the government sends films to these communities which glamorize work and portray acculturated Aboriginal people as mechanical engineers and clerk/typists busy-at-work in a European fashion. Wherever these films have been shown, they have been greeted by central Australian Aboriginals with squealing whoops and raucous laughter: there is nothing more unlikely nor less desired by these Aboriginals than working nine-to-five five days a week. The incongruence of expectations produces a levity in which the Aboriginal aspirations are very plainly revealed.

Aboriginal people do not reject work-and-wages because they are lazy, although their desert-adapted industry has conditioned them to exert themselves only when its immediate necessity becomes apparent. When motivated, Aboriginals can perform physical tasks which are awesome; for example, any of them is capable of walking several hundred miles across the desert without complaint. Aboriginal people resist the ideology of work because it interferes with the spontaneity of their lives and, above all, with the natural sociability of their ordinary personal relations. Aboriginal people are unwilling to sacrifice the spontaneous and egalitarian character of their social relations for the material benefits of work-and-wages. Marx (1967: 297f.) has described the distortion of human relationships which the relations of production of capitalism bring about. Aboriginal people, without any ideologizing, are unwilling to abandon their customary human relations. What is more, their entire social life militates against their participation in a capitalist economy. Success in a capitalist economy depends upon accumulating capital. In Aboriginal society it is an embarrassment to have excess wealth: one must share what one has with friends and relatives; indeed, there are formal rules of exchange which require that one's goods pass into the hands of specific relatives. Accordingly, an Aboriginal person must share his food, his home, his car, his clothes, etc., with his people if he is not to lose the respect they have for him. In addition, it is the binding custom of Aboriginal society to destroy by fire or breakage all the worldly possessions of a person upon his death. Many of the new houses built for Aboriginals by the government in the last decade are uninhabitable because of the death of a member of the household (a consequence hardly considered by government planners), and eventually all will be so. If it becomes impossible to accumulate capital, it is senseless to attempt to do so, and it is certain that one will never attain success in capitalist terms.

Similarly, Aboriginal laborers avoid promotion to positions which have a supervisorial responsibility because they have no aspiration to issue orders to other Aboriginals. It is not so much the absence of a desire for social power as it is a fear of the social consequences of their appearing to presume that they are better than their fellows. Such a person is likely to be universally rejected as one who is overly conceited, a reputation Aboriginal people take pains to avoid. In response to political pressure to improve the 'economic condition' of Aboriginal people, the government has sought to increase the number of Aboriginal people in roles of authority; however, many Aboriginals involved in work-and-wages activity prefer to have European supervisors because such an arrangement will leave the egalitarian basis of their ordinary relations undisturbed. This response has confounded Anglo-Australians, who are moved to deliver long lectures on ambition and self-improvement to promising Aboriginal laborers. There are few provisions in a capitalist economy for the more egalitarian social inclinations of the Aboriginal people. Given the opportunity, Aboriginals might evolve a modern economic praxis for themselves which would be more compatible with their structures of social interaction.

A good deal of Aboriginal reluctance to adopt a work-and-wages economic orientation is that they do not see the relevance of European projects for their own lives. Sympathetic Anglo-Australians have devised all sorts of economic programs, but they have failed to first determine whether Aboriginal people wish to be so 'developed.' A missionary (Perez 1977: 143) recorded a typical complaint about the lack of Aboriginal enthusiasm for an economic scheme developed by the mission: 'Much to the missionaries' regret, none of the able-bodied Aborigines had shown the interest, capability, constancy and responsibility necessary for them to be relied on exclusively to carry out the comprehensive plan.' For these missionaries, the value of the 'comprehensive plan' was accepted as a given, and there was little effort to determine the Aboriginals' motivations – all that was necessary on the part of the Aboriginals was that they be 'able-bodied.' This is only another occasion of the Anglo-Australians' practice of turning Aboriginal people into objects which are merely some variant of being European, and it is no wonder that their programs have failed:

> The Aborigines have not shown interest in anything connected with the enterprise. More recently, as an experiment, fifteen acres of land was given them with the use of machinery. It failed to produce any results, and they gave up all efforts to prove their capability to look after even a small concern which would gradually form the basis for their desired independence. (*Ibid.* 149)

The Aboriginal people were already independent in their own terms and saw no need to acquire European skills. As one Aboriginal lady told R.M. and C.H. Berndt (1964: 93), why should she bother about growing food when the wild plants provide it for her in abundance without any cultivation. Instead, the Aboriginal people have become skilled at taking advantage of Europeans as an additional source of material support, and this ability is one which whites have found very disconcerting:

> It cannot be said that the enterprise gave new inspiration to the Aborigines, most of whom took long holidays, up to five months in the bush, where they would not be engaged in handling stones, mortar, or heavy timber. They gradually made their appearance again, to coincide with another arrival of

cargo in Pago and in good time for their Christmas at
Kalumburu. (Perez 1977: 98)

What for Aboriginal people is their natural life is conceived by
whites to be 'holidays.' In this instance the Aboriginals have won
the cultural-political skirmish on two counts – they have reaped
material benefits while adopting nothing of the whites' work
ethic.

In a quiet and unassuming fashion Aboriginal people have
repeated this victory throughout the desert. At some isolated
reserves, European missionaries or government workers carry the
Aboriginals' firewood, run electric generators, provide transport,
cook meals, repair automobiles, refrigerate soft drinks and carry
out most of the functions that lie within the European economic
domain. In local interaction, the very strength of the whites'
work ethic occasionally results in their being exploited by
Aboriginals. For example, when a car containing a number of
whites and blacks received a tire puncture (a frequent occurrence
in the desert), the whites attended to fixing the tire directly, as
the responsible thing to do; they even competed with each other
in demonstrating their responsibility and reliability regarding the
matter. Meanwhile, some of the Aboriginal passengers happily
observed the whites' efforts while others wandered off to spend
some time hunting goannas. The irony here is that the self-
assertive personality of the whites resulted in their performing
work from which the less assertive Aboriginals benefited.
Aboriginal people participate in such tasks when they see there is
a need for it or if they are forced to do so by Europeans (the
latter usually being accompanied by an invocation of the ideology
of the work ethic). In another context, some Aboriginal people,
under my supervision and engaged in European sorts of tasks for
which they were being paid, showed enthusiasm for work only
when I told them, '*We must work*' ('*Wuuku palyalkitja*'). Their
praxis was one of pandering to the European work ethic without
any sincerity of purpose. They responded because they recognize
the moment when whites will become self-righteous about work.

The success Aboriginal people have had in avoiding work-and-
wages has prompted most outback Anglo-Australians to advocate
a policy of forced labor for wages. To their way of thinking the
government is making it 'too easy' for Aboriginal people and
causing them to become convinced that their praxis of exploiting
the white economy while participating only minimally in work-
and-wages is a winning strategy. The whites' concern is not so
economic (the economic costs are paid mostly by the coastal
urban regions) but motivated by their concern about the

perpetuation of the Aboriginal culture and social structure the success of the Aboriginals' strategy allows. This aspect of the struggle has to do with cultural rivalry.

Legalism

Anglo-Australians have long prevailed in the contest for control over land in central Australia, although the struggle is not yet over. The basic strategy of the whites from the very beginning of settlement has been to rule Aboriginal people out of contention by legal fiat. Such a strategy has provided the European expropriation with a moral propriety which it otherwise would have lacked. The dispossession of Aboriginal people has always been legal, and, so the logic goes, therefore justifiable. This began with the initial royal proclamation which made British subjects of all Australia's Aboriginal inhabitants. This excluded the possibility of the Aboriginal people pressing for treaties as sovereign nations, as some of the American Indians were able to do; instead, all of the Aboriginal homelands became Crown Land, which the Crown dispensed to leading English and Scottish aristocratic families.

In 1971 an Australian court ruled that Aboriginal claims to lands (on which they had been residing for as long as 40,000 years) were invalid because they were unable to show the court formal written title to it. At the same time, Anglo-Australian law has provided whites with the proper legal instruments for lands they have expropriated in the last two centuries. As Friedenberg (1980: 22) has observed with regard to the case of the Canadian Indians, 'Law and order, Canadian schoolbooks say, preceded the settlement of the frontier, begging the question of whose law and order it was.'

Since 1971, the national government of Australia has attempted to grant traditional Aboriginal people in the Northern Territory some degree of land rights (the national government's jurisdiction over Western Australia and South Australia is limited). But its effort is presently being emasculated by the northern territory assembly, which is adding a variety of local regulations to minimize the degree of self-determination available to blacks. For example, a section of the Northern Territory Land Rights Act of 1976 provides that no land claims may be made for any portions of towns. The provisional assembly responded by redrawing the boundaries of Darwin, the territorial capital, declaring a new city having a size four times that of London though only 120,000 people reside there (Howard 1980: 2).

In Western Australia, where no lands rights legislation has passed (as of this printing), the only method by which Aboriginal people can gain control over their traditional homelands is to secure a pastoral lease; however, since 1977 the State government has refused to lease any land to Aboriginal people under the regulation that no more than a million acres may fall under the domain of a single corporation. Since the State government requires that all Aboriginal land be held by the Aboriginal Lands Trust, a body which is largely controlled by the State cabinet, and because the Lands Trust has reached its million-acre limit, registration of all new Aboriginal leases has been frozen.

Similar legal strategies have served Anglo-Australian interests in other ways. In 1974 a Warden's Court in Western Australia took away a mining lease from an Aboriginal person who went by the name of 'Munding' because the original paper was written out to 'Moonding' twenty years earlier. Despite the fact that the Aboriginal person lived in an oral culture, his claim was invalidated on the technicality and awarded to a friend of the justice. When the Aurukun Aboriginal people in the Northern Territory were opposed to the use of their name in the title of an Anglo-Australian firm, 'Aurukun Associates,' the consortium informed them that it had the legal right to the name because it had duly registered it (Aboriginal *Identity* 1976: 8).

Mathews (1977: 67) tells about the case of one Aboriginal settlement where the Aboriginal residents were prohibited from having a garden. Her Aboriginal informant reports: 'We were not allowed to grow any vegetables. This seemed peculiar, but it was impressed on us that we could not grow them because it was a government station and not our land.' Similarly, a Western Australian pastoralist scolded an Aboriginal worker-resident who had taken me to a sacred site on the station which merited protection under Aboriginal sites' legislation. She told the Aboriginal elder, 'You have no right giving anybody information about places on our station. All the places on this station belong to [her husband].' The domination of Aboriginal people is thus reinforced with the rhetoric of legal ideology. Even more extraordinary is the report of one of the Liberal Party lawyers who conspired to prevent Aboriginal people in Western Australia from voting (*West Australian*, September 17, 1977): 'Dixon said that it was not his duty to question the legislation [regarding questioning voters]. It was his right to exercise it.' In other words, morality rests not in what is just but in what is legal.

This is consistent with the 'contractual-legalistic orientation' which Habermas (1979: 90) claims results in an individualization of social interaction. The customary obligations of corporate groups are individualized and competition among individual members is encouraged. The constraints of such a rationalized order of interaction are obvious when in outback towns Aboriginal people face legal charges for allowing too many friends and relatives to dwell in one house. While the resocialization of Aboriginal people is for the most part an unintended by-product of the legal system, it has at times been more deliberate. A case in point is the Citizenship Rights Act of 1944 (W.A.), which made the emancipation of Aboriginal people contingent upon certain conditions, one of which was that a 'citizen' (with the privileges of voting, drinking, freedom of travel, etc.) must not associate with Aboriginal natives other than his kin of the first degree.

Anglo-Australian legal rights promote individualism. Along with imposing a system of interaction which produces competing and autonomous participants, the Australian legal system requires Aboriginal people to reconceptualize their world in the same utilitarian and objective terms as the whites if they wish to take advantage of any of the legal prerequisites the law provides them. Aboriginal people are concerned to protect their sacred sites from destruction by mining developers (who are generally unaware of the existence of sacred sites). Legislation has been passed in Western Australia providing protection for any 'Aboriginal site' which can be shown to be of legitimate sacred importance; however, the Western Australian government considers the Act to be a token gesture which is not meant seriously to deter in any way mineral development in the Western Desert. Consequently, the government has interpreted the Act, which placed no limit on the size of the 'protected areas,' to refer only to individual 'sites' a few acres in size and not to large domains of land which Aboriginals may claim on the basis of sacred associations. On two occasions when an area including a number of sacred sites was proposed for protection, the government ordered it to be divided up into the 'individual' sites and be proposed as separate reserves. In one case the Aboriginals were requested to modify their presentation of the sacred area involved. The area was one wherein the same world-creative beings encountered each other in a number of locations, so the locations are not experienced as separate units but as one and the same event. The area is experienced in its Dreaming essence as a single totality, not divisible into separate objects without distorting the Aboriginal cognition. Should the protected areas be approved on the basis of individual objectivated sites which satisfy the unique perspective of the Western Australian government, subsequent mining development could ensue which would translate the European objectivated conception of the landscape into concrete reality. In the meantime, the government has succeeded in instructing Aboriginal people how to interpret the land in a European fashion, a cognitive innovation which may one day have profound implications.

Moralism

The system of legalistic legitimation employed by Anglo-Australians to justify their domination of Aboriginal people is not merely political – it is the basis of a self-righteousness which provides Anglo-Australians with a sense of moral superiority at the very moments they are dispossessing Aboriginal people. Weber (1958: 142 and 165-6) has spoken of the self-confidence, self-righteousness and sober legality peculiar to the men of the heroic age of capitalism, and it is this personality which Anglo-Australians have brought into their relations with Aboriginals. This self-righteous tone is apparent in many of the public remarks of Australian leaders about Aboriginal policies. In 1971 the then Australian Minister of the Interior announced the position of his government on Aboriginal land rights:

> The government believes that it is wholly wrong to encourage Aborigines to think that because their ancestors have had a long association with a particular piece of land, Aborigines of the present day have their right to demand ownership of it.
> (Aboriginal *Identity*, January, 1977)

In 1980 the Western Australian Minister for Community Welfare summarized his government's land rights policy in a similar tone: 'Calls for compensation in a generalized sense for the past wrongs against former generations are misguided, unrealistic and would be totally unjust to many Australians – black and white.' Essentially, the dispossession of central Australian Aboriginal people is a *fait accompli*, and it would be 'wholly wrong' and 'totally unjust' to grant legal title to Aboriginal people who have occupied their land for some 40,000 years.

Such self-righteousness was a component of the effort to prevent Aboriginals from voting in Western Australia which I discussed above. A polling officer (the wife of a local pastoralist) refused to assist six elderly Aboriginals who swam across a 30-meter-wide river 4–5 feet deep in full flood – 'She said that the old people were not supposed to be helped' (*West Australian*,

July 15, 1977). Two of the potential Aboriginal voters asked the polling officer for assistance, without success: 'a couple of Aborigines had approached her inside the polling area but because of instructions to all scrutineers she had put her hand to her lips to indicate she was not allowed to speak' (*West Australian*, July 27, 1977). Not only wouldn't the polling officer assist Aboriginals, but she was 'not allowed' and 'not supposed to,' an Anglo-Australian attitude with which Aboriginal people are familiar. The *West Australian* (July 22, 1979) reported that the interrogation of one of the Aboriginal voters was continued despite the fact that tears were pouring down the Aboriginal person's face – 'She would not answer and did not seem to know what she had to do,' a typical Aboriginal response to the exercise of Anglo-Australian moralism.

In recent years the national government of Australia (with an urban mandate) has been paying attention to some of the moral consequences of the treatment of Aboriginal people, and this has led to certain legal and social reforms designed to improve the conditions of Aboriginals in the Northern Territory, give them some rights to limit the access of multinational corporations to their tribal lands, provide some economic assistance and promote Aboriginal self-determination. These reforms have been strongly opposed by the Anglo-Australian residents of central Australia, but in their opposition the force of the ideology of racial equality (borrowed from the civil rights struggles in America) has not been lost on them. Today, these whites of Australia's desert regions oppose the reforms on the grounds that such legislation is unfairly prejudiced in favor of Aboriginal people. Before the Aboriginal people have even come to understand these contemporary notions of racial justice, the white people of central Australia have mastered its rhetoric in detail and are using it to add a moral force to their defense of their dominant status. The chairman of the Northern Territory branch of the Progress Party sent a telegram to the Prime Minister of Australia asking him to give landholders 'the same rights' as Aboriginal people in land rights reforms which recognized traditional occupancy as a basis for limited title; the Young Liberal (Party) Movement of Western Australia has called on the government to treat all Australians 'equally under the law' (*West Australian*, June 3, 1980); the Western Australian Chamber of Mines president issued a statement asserting: 'We believe territorial and mineral rights should be equal for all Australians' (*West Australian*, May 22, 1980), meaning that the government and corporations should have access to all minerals on land owned by Aboriginals and Anglo-Australians alike; and a South Australian pastoralist sent this letter to the Adelaide *Advertiser* (August 2, 1978):

> As an owner of freehold land in south Australia, I have no control over mining or prospecting other than in small areas around houses, and would receive no royalties for any minerals found.
>
> Why are the Aborigines such a favoured race? They have, either individually or collectively, done little towards Australia's development. If the white man had not colonized the country when he did, some other race would have, and the Aboriginal would have received far worse treatment than he has ever received from us.
>
> Perhaps if we all painted our faces black we would get equal rights.

The utility of such a self-righteous pseudoegalitarianism has not been lost upon Anglo-Australian school children in central Australia. A class of 15-year-olds in one Western Australian outback town heard a lecture on Aboriginal culture: 'In a question and answer session after the lecture the children contended strongly that there was discrimination against white people in their town and that race relations could be improved by giving whites more' (*West Australian*, July 6, 1979). Throughout the history of Aboriginal/Anglo-Australian relations, white people have utilized morality to their every advantage.

Aboriginal strategies

The Aboriginal people's chosen response to such moral right-eousness has been to provide whites with a formal acquiescence which amounts to very little in substance. Gratuitous concurrence – that universal and incomprehensible 'Yes' – is the common chord of Aboriginal/Anglo-Australian interaction in central Australia. Aboriginal people know how to leave a white person satisfied without really coming to comprehend what it is he wanted in the first place or what led him to depart satisfied. Assisted by the whites' own skills at rendering Aboriginal people as mere objects of their own projection, Aboriginal people are able to employ the Anglo-Australian's self-confidence to prevent their own interior life from being witnessed.

Anglo-Australians may become so occupied with their own prejudices that these prejudicial views fill up the world, restricting perception. That is, one of the consequences of an assertive personality is that there is less opportunity for observation: the imposition of one's own world upon events is too successful. Aboriginal people exploit such prejudices as a smokescreen behind which they are able to preserve their privacy. While such a praxis has unfavorable consequences for Aboriginals, in the long run it has made it possible for them to perpetuate their Aboriginal life with a minimum of interference.

I have examined some occasions of this praxis of acquiescence in contexts (such as courtrooms and schools) which are threatening to Aboriginal people, but this praxis has become so routinized that it amounts to a systematic distortion of communication even in contexts which are harmless. Witness this friendly conversation between an Anglo-Australian and an Aboriginal friend of mine who was being employed in a sites protection training program sponsored by the Western Australian Museum:

EA What are you doing here?
AP Working in a training program for the Museum.
EA Doing what, learning how to recognize fossils and things?
AP Yeah.   (102)

In this case AP didn't know what a fossil was. Although the Anglo-Australian was only being friendly, Aboriginal people have learned to minimize their communication as a structural feature of their communication with whites. The gratuitous concurrence of another Aboriginal friend of mine is typical of conversations where an English-speaking person asks an Aboriginal to choose between alternative answers:

KL *Is that good or bad?*
AP Ø
KL *Is that good or bad?*
AP *Good.*
KL Mm.
AP Or bad.   (103)

In such instances, the participation of the Aboriginal partner is so plastic that Anglo-Australian efforts to communicate are frustrated entirely. But this is the intention. Aboriginal people know how to exploit that 'natural' indeterminacy available in intercultural conversation in order to force their Anglo-Australian partners to remove themselves from conversation which is too personal and intense for an Aboriginal person's comfort. While such discourse may be standard in European societies, Aboriginals consider that persons who do not know each other well should be more withdrawn.

Aboriginal people occasionally prefer a conversation not to become intelligible. At a remote settlement I have witnessed

Aboriginal people who speak English well feign ignorance when Anglo-Australian tourists who seem to them too smug asked where gasoline could be purchased. Similarly, Aboriginal people will force government officials to work through the confusions which exist 'naturally' in intercultural communication in order to force them to make some adjustments to the Aboriginals' world. If the official appears too conceited or if the Aboriginals are uninterested in what he has to offer (e.g., an anthropologist), the factical presence of confusion will loom (naturally) as a major communicative obstacle. Aboriginal people may 'talk to rule' in providing police officers the names of Aboriginal persons by employing the actual Aboriginal pronunciation of the European names, a pronunciation which is capable of rendering a name like 'Friday Finley' as 'Bridee Benelli.' Such clever strategies offer Aboriginals a degree of protection, but at the price of reaffirming the Anglo-Australian (mistaken) conviction that Aboriginal people are stupid.

No cheek

The Aboriginal praxis of acquiescence fits well the interactional demands which white people place upon Aboriginals. Aboriginal people have explained to me that Anglo-Australians want 'no cheek' from blackfellows; such an attitude succeeds in limiting the amount of argument an Aboriginal person will offer. As one Aboriginal person tells it, 'I suffered less than the others from ill-treatment by managers. My attitude was that they were in charge, and if they told me I was wrong or had incurred their disapproval I did not argue' (Mathews 1977: 160). A favorite story of Aboriginal people in the Wiluna era (cf. Parker 1978) tells of a white station-manager who attempted to punish an Aboriginal person for insolence. The Aboriginal's wife counsels him:

> Jimmy Missus tells him, 'See that now? He's tryin' you out
> with every bloke. You got to watch yourself now and no cheek.
> When they tell, don't say nothin', don't give them answer. Just
> say, "Yes boss, you good man alright." '

This acquiescence appears to be identical to the deference behavior of oppressed people throughout the world, and there is evidence to support such an interpretation. The response of an Aboriginal lady my wife and I took to a drive-in theater in an outback town is illustrative. During the movie *Hello Dolly*, a subservient Negro opened the door of a prestigious New York night club for Ms Streisand and assisted her with her coat and hat, engaging in some friendly small talk, to which our Aboriginal companion remarked, 'He's talking *wangkayi* [Aboriginal].' At an outdoor showing of a Bill Cosby movie to Aboriginal people at a remote settlement, Cosby spoke to his white boss over the short-wave radio, 'Ye-e-s-s Missuh Harry, I wi-il-ill – you son of a bitch,' to which the Aboriginal audience responded with tremendous enthusiasm indicative of their having experienced similar feelings.

But the explanation of Aboriginal acquiescence as standard deference behavior is too facile. While there surely are structural consequences of domination which produce certain kinds of interaction, such consequences are not exclusive, and perhaps not even primary, in determining the components of local interaction in individual cases. It is fashionable for sociologists to explain such 'shyness' as a function of political domination, but this is a universalization of Western interactional prejudices to the extent that there is the assumption that a vigorous and aggressive self-defense would be the immediate response of all parties; Aboriginal interaction differs from European interaction in some major ways which are for the most part unrecognized by Europeans. These differences have resulted in some of the unique and specific characteristics of Aboriginal/Australian intercourse.

The Aboriginal practices of acquiescence, secrecy and limiting the intelligibility of conversation are overdetermined; they are strategies Aboriginals are well suited to carry out and also ones that are appropriate to the political realities they face. The fact that shyness was the response of Aboriginal people when the first Europeans arrived, before any structure of domination was established, demonstrates that the 'withdrawn' social personality of Aboriginal people preceded the establishment of a European regime. That most Aboriginal people fail to admire the self-confident personality of those who dominate them and instead consider the character of their own social relationships to be evidence of their cultural superiority is proof enough that such introverted social characteristics are indeed Aboriginal and cannot be accounted for exclusively by a sociology which fails to master the interactional detail of the local relationships of domination.

Conclusion

The outcome of this cultural–political struggle is still uncertain.

Where Europeans have been able to settle permanently, the traditional Aboriginal civilization is suffering a decay from which it may not be able to recover; however, in the remote regions where the heat and aridity have protected Aboriginal people from European settlement, a traditionally oriented Aboriginal life is being perpetuated and appears to be full of vitality. The preservation of an orthodoxy of traditional ritual in the remote regions serves to slow the acculturation of Aboriginal people in the regions of European settlement, and even in these latter areas traditional Aboriginal values may exist long after the formal ritual life has disappeared. Hiatt (1965: 151) has observed that Aboriginal people who for years had observed the hierarchical structure of Anglo-Australian social relations remained unaffected by it. It is not likely that such modes of interaction will impress Aboriginal people, and only where the Aboriginal people were killed or removed from the region has their culture disappeared altogether.

Those who have survived continue to lead an Aboriginal lifestyle, only much of the Aboriginality is unavailable for the witness of whites. In the long run, the Aboriginals' passive strategy has succeeded to a surprising degree. Offering little opposition to whites, Aboriginal people have adapted to new situations without relinquishing what is most dear to them. The words of one missionary, offered at the end of his career, report the Aboriginal people's success:

Had I been posted to a parish in South America it would probably have been peopled by ten thousand, and inside of six months I could have converted half of them. Instead I came here to Kalumburu where there are some two hundred Aborigines, and after 37 years only a handful have become Christians, even though most are baptized.

When I die and proceed through the gates of heaven, there – just inside the gates – will be seated the departed souls of people from Kalumburu, because we may have pushed them through the gates but it is unlikely that on their own they will have gone in any further.

The persistence of Aboriginal people in the regions where Anglo-Australian people have settled is evident in these two observations about the contemporary Aboriginal relationship to the sacred Law of their Dreaming. The first remark is that of an acculturated Aboriginal lady and the second that of an elderly Aboriginal man:

They still hangin' on to the Law. Young people they chasin'

271

the Law. Drop everything for the Law, put Law before work, before wife even. Law been goin' on for years. Lots of people reckon in this modern age there no place for Law, but it's still goin' on. I don't think it's going to stop. Too strong.

It'll still be in the History [his translation for '*tjukurpa*' or 'Dreaming'], *brother*. Never change. They still carry on what the people did. They carry on that, young people . . . That *tjukurpa* still stop. Still we remember it. We like to see all the young people to remember what's been happened. We got to follow it, *tjukurpa*, we have to follow 'em and we have to fall back on it; otherwise, they'll let go like Europeans. They've got no *tjukurpa*, nothing.

Whether the growing international consensus on human rights will be able to secure the cultural survival of Aboriginal people before multinational mineral consortia overrun their traditional homelands for precious minerals is uncertain, but international opinion is indeed redefining the Aboriginals' worth. The Australian Commissioner for Community Relations reported to the Australian people the impression that Aboriginal delegates to the United Nations Subcommission on Human Rights made in Geneva: 'Europe was fascinated because here was 40,000 years of continuous tradition suddenly appearing formally for the first time' (*West Australian*, October 13, 1980). While international opinion may increase the reputation of Aboriginals in urban Australia, it is unlikely that contemporary outback Anglo-Australians – who have yet truly to know Aboriginal people – will ever question the morality of their regime. For whites in central Australia, Aboriginal people are useless, slovenly people of no account, and it is unlikely that any guilt will be experienced about the treatment of people who are not respected.

In the remote Aboriginal reserves, Aboriginal people are determined to preserve their relative independence from Anglo-Australians. In both these areas and in the regions of central Australia occupied by Anglo-Australians the cultural–political struggle continues unabated. Aboriginal people who are partly acculturated to European life in these latter areas have expressed concern about their future: 'All us old people are gonna die one day, and we gotta put something together to leave for the young people in the time we got left. We can't leave them with nothing!' And so they hope to make something of the opportunity which the new ideas of social justice have given them. But less acculturated Aboriginal people in the European-occupied regions are not as concerned, and for all that they have suffered they show remarkably little bitterness.

One day I spent an afternoon with three very elderly Aboriginal ladies who were the last survivors of an Aboriginal dialect group which had occupied some 30,000 square miles in Western Australia and which today consists of sheep stations owned exclusively by Anglo-Australians. The ladies were telling me about life 'in the early days,' about areas where nutritious plants were located, about places formerly very sacred to Aboriginal people and the like. In the middle of their conversation, they reflected upon the fact that their people had almost entirely died out. To my surprise, they began to laugh, and one of them announced, 'There's no more old people. All finished. Only three now!' to which they fell into a hysterical fit of laughter. One has to admire these ladies for whom their friendship was fulfilling enough to allow them to live without hatred. It was as if the burden of resentment was too heavy for them to bother about and would destroy that lightness and spontaneity Aboriginal people value in their social relations. While these ladies were living in a hovel made of apple-crates and unwanted bits of corrugated iron, they were satisfied with each other and their lives, and had remained Aboriginal in the most characteristic sense of the term.

Appendix 1

Original text of illustrations (1) through (64)

Key

italics	Italics indicate that the original utterance was spoken in the Western Desert Aboriginal language (*Pitjantjatjara*, *Ngaanyatjarra*, and *Pintupi* dialects).
⎰ *Yes.* ⎱ *Yes.*	Open brackets indicate that the remarks were uttered simultaneously.
Half = = Not . .	An equals sign indicates latching, i.e., that there is no interval between the conclusion of a first utterance and the beginning of a second. It may not constitute an 'interruption.'
[ ]	Closed brackets include descriptions of audio materials other than actual utterances, or other explanatory material.
↑ ↓	Arrows indicate syllable stress.
( )	Parentheses indicate that the audio tape is ambiguous. Occasionally, a most possible hearing will be incorporated in the brackets.
Fine—	A dash indicates sudden cessation of a piece of talk.

NB: AP: Aboriginal person (male); WP: Aboriginal woman; EA: Anglo- or European-Australian; APn: anonymous Aboriginal; KL: author; APe: Aboriginal elder.

Original texts

(1) APx . . .
APe *Palya munta. Palya munta.*
APy *Uwa.*

APz   *Uwa.*
APa   *Turlku pirnitjarra.*
APb   This, *parna ngaanyaku.*
APc   *Alatji.*

(2) Original transcript in text, p. 34.

(3)   APx   *Mani yarnangu pirnikutu pitjalu.*
       APa   *Yuwa.*
       APb   *Uwa.*
       APx   *Nyaaku.*
       APc   *Uwa.*
       APx   *Paluna.*
       APd   *Uwa.*
       APe   *Palya.*
       APx   *Wangka ngayunya turta, palunyangka*
             tjapirnu warli mantjilkulan.
       APn   ⎡ *Yuwaoh!*
       APn   ⎨ *Yuwaoh!*
       APn   ⎣ *Yuwaoh!*

(4)   APx   *Uwa, wangka tjuku-tjuku alatji.*
       APy   *Palya paluna.*

(5)   APe   *Nyangatja!*
       APa   *Wirunya.*
       APb   *Uwa.*
       APc   *Wiruku wangkanyi.*
       APe   *Palya palatja?*
       APn   ⎡ *Uwa.*
       APn   ⎨ *Uwa.*
       APn   ⎣ *Uwa.*
       APx   *Wiru.*
       APy   *Palya.*
       APz   *Uwa.*

(6)   APa   *Yuwa palya.* 'Cause, the can't talk,
             argument, *palya.*
       KL   *Yuwa palya.*
       APn   Mm.
       KL   *Uwa.*

(7)   APa   *Ka nyaapalu panya,* anyway, *ankuna*
             holidays. *Nyuntu katinma. Wantitja wiya palu*
             nyinama. Anybody, *ngula* 'bin *paluru,*
             tjungku kulira ngula katinyi. Like this.
       APb   *Alatji.*
       APc   *Alatji.*

(8) APa   *Yuwa.*
    APb   *Paluna.*
    APc   *Nyanga alatji.*
    APd   *Yuwa, paluna.*

(9) Original transcript in text, p. 37.

(10) APx   If you =
    APy   = *waark wiya.*
    APx   *Waark wiya.*
    APy   *Waark wiya.* Half pay.
    APx   Half pay, *yungantji*, every time.

(11) APx   *Paluna mapungku katiranyingi nyaranya*
           Wolman Rocks.
    APy   Wolman Rocks.

(12) APx   Money*panya ungku ngananya waarkaku,*
           waarka maniku waarkatintjaku.
    APy   Money *kutjupa nyaratja.*
    APz   Money *kutjupa nyaratja.*

(13) Original transcript in text, p. 39.

(14) APa   *Nyarangka* Areyonga*la.*
    APb   Areyonga.
    APc   ⎰Areyonga.
    APd   ⎱*Nyaapalu.*
    APe   Areyonga *katijaku.*
    APf   Areyonga *katitjaku.*
    APg   Areyonga*kutu.*
    APh   [inhalated whisper:] Areyonga.
    APi   Areyonga*kutu.*
    APj   *Ka* Areyonga *yungku.*
    APk   *Wartalpi*, Areyonga *languru.*
    APl   *Nyaa wartalpi.*

(15) APx   Oh, it's *nyuntu.*
    APy   Hey?
    APz   Hey.

(16) APx   *Mununya* white*pala palatjangka*, 'Hey, look
           here. We got no house, and you gonna come
           up here for nothing. *Warli wiya ngananya**
           nyinanyi.' *Warli wiya*, we got no good house,
           wiyatja, nyaratja warli wiya. Nyaa papa
           turtaku nyinanyi.
    APy   *Mm. Papaku turtala.*

(17) APy   *Tjakultjunkunya kuwarri.*
              Mm ↑ Hmm ↓ !

(18) APe   *Wangka kutjupangkayi ngaanya pirayi.*
      APx   *Uwa.*
      APe   *Tjuku-tjuku ngayu ma* ( ) ( ) *ngura*
              tjanampa, nyaatja.
      APn ⌠ *Uwa.*
      APn ⟨ *Yuwa.*
      APn ⌡ *Oh.*
      APy   Mm. Hm!
      APe   *Palunyangkatja ngaanya nyaraku.*
      APa ⌠ *Uwa.*
      APb ⌡ *Yuwa.*
      APe   *Kutjarra.*
      APb   ↑ Hm Hm ↓ !
      APe   *Ngaalu kulilku.*
      APc   *Ngananya.*

(19) APe   *Panya ngayulu nyinanyi nyaangka nyina.*
      APa ⌠ *Uwa.*
      APb ⟨ *Uwa.*
      APc ⌡ *Uwa.*

(20) APe   *Yuwanya, nyaranya, nyangka nyaranya,*
              purtu ngananya, wati nyara tjinguru, paluna,
              mawantjarrpa.
      APa   *Mawantjarrpa.*
      APb   *Mawantjarrpa.*
      APe   *Mawantjarrpa.*
              . . .
      APx   *Uwa.*
      APy   *Wangka kutju.*
      APz   *Alatji.*

(21) APa   Proper wayl*a mantjinyi.*
      APb   *Tjilpi turtangka anutjaku* Laaw truck *paluna.*
      APa   *Minyma, wati yirna.*
      APe   *Tjilpi,* Ernabella meeting *purlkaratjarra.*
      APc   Meeting, meeting *mularpa kuwarri.*
      APb   We got to get, *wiya*, different way.
      APa   Different way.
      APb   Different way, *wiya. Nyangaku,* anyway, ( )
              properly *wangkatja.*
      APa   *Arnangutjaku.* Properly*la nyinalku watjara.*
      APb   Mm. *Wangka kulila.*
      APa   *Walypala.*

	APd	*Uwa.*
	APf	*Tjinguru tjilpiku tjapilku* Laaw truck.
	APn	( ) *paluna.*
	APi	*Uwoah.*
	APf	*Munta alatji wangkara.*
(22)	APa	*Papunyitjarrpangu* Areyonga.
	APb	*Uwa* Areyonga*la watjara.*
	APa	Areyonga*la tjarrpangu.*
(23)	APa	*Marnkurrpa tjitji.*
	APb	*Tjitji marnkurrpa.*

(24), (25), (26), (27), (28) and (29): Original transcripts in text, p. 45.

(30)	APa	*Wiya, warlikupanya nyaapala.*
	APb	*Walpapukanya warlingka.*
	APc	*Warlingka palyara.*
	APd	*Warli palyanyi wangkaku.*
(31)	APa	*Ayi! Kulila!*
	KL	Um, if you want to choose a new council.
	APb	Council*ta ngaatja.*
	APc	Council.
	KL	So you have to decide who you want to put on the council.

(32) Original transcript in text, p. 47.

(33)	APx	Hmm.
	APy	*Ka ngananya palu ngananya.*
	APz	*Yini turtapayi ngaartu tjuralata yiniputa nyanga waarkatirrinkula.*
	[. . .	38 turns of talk]
	APa	*Yinila nyanganya tjunama.*
	APb	*Arnangu kutjupa tjinguru nyaratijarra.*
	APc	Good idea, Aboriginals.
	APd	*Munta.*
	APe	*Tjuratjarra.*
	APf	{(laugh)
	APg	{*Yuwa.*
	APh	*Tjuratjarra.* Mm ↓ Hm ↑ !
(34)	APe	*Arnangu,* every *ngura pakara,* every settlement *ngka nyinanyi . . . yaaltji paka arnanguku kulinyi.*
	APa	*Palya.*

APe   *Walpalaratjapa, arnanguratja kutjurringkulpa*
         nyinantjaku.
APb   *Ohh.*
         Nyina kutju.
APd   *Nyinantja* one.
APf   *Alatji wangkatja, kutju.*
APg   *Alatji.*
APh   ⌠ *Uwa.*
APi   ⌡ *Uwoah!*

(35)   APa   DAA *pitja nyangka nguru kuwarri*
               wangkatjaku.
      APb   *Uwa.* [gestural tone of finality]
      APc   *Turta wangkama mularpa.*
      KL   *Uwa.* So =
      APd   = *Ngananyartu.* . . whole lot.
               Ngayulu, nyuntu and all.
      KL   So maybe we'll sit down next week, and we'll
               go through the whole list. We should have a
               big meeting, let everybody know.
      APd   ⌠ *Uwa.*
      KL   ⌡ *Parawatjalpayi.*
      APe   *Parawatjalpayi.*

(36)   APx   Meeting council*nga, wangka purlka turta.*
      APy   Meeting council*nga wangkarringkupayi.*

(37)   APa   Docker River *tjura.*
      APb   Docker River *ankunyi parna wartalpi.*
      APc   *Docker River wangka!*

(38)   EA   I'll ask the Minister for Aboriginal Affairs.
      APa   ⌠ *Ngananya kuwarri nganalu.*
      APb   ⌡ *Uwa.*

(39)   KL   He's trying to bring a little drilling thing.
      APa   *Yuwanya.*
      KL   He might bring up, he doesn't know yet.
      APb   *Palu ngaanyanya ngurrpa.*

(40)   KL   *Tjuku-tjuku tjapilkurna.* Alright for the con-
               struction bloke to *warli tjarrpa?*
      APx   *Yuwa.*
      KL   *Palya.*
      APy   Yeh.
      EA   No, no worries?
      KL   And, *ngaanya, warli kutjupa, kutjarra tjarrpa*
               palya munta?

	APy	Two.
	APz	Oh.
	EA	Yeh, two.

(41) KL *Warta ngura ngayukulanguru. Ngayulu ninti.*
     APa *Uwa.*
     KL *Ngayulu, tjitji nyangu, nyakupayi.*
     APb *Uwa, tjitji. Nyangu nyakupayi.*
     KL Jojoba, Indian*ku warta.*
     APc Hm.
     KL And you get the seeds.
     APa *Uwa.*
     KL You crush the seeds and, ohh, lovely oil. Smells wonderful, and put 'im in the hair and everywhere. Put 'im on the face.
     APn [laughs]
     KL And *walypala mani purlka payipungku* seeds *nyanga.*
     APc Mm.
     APd *Uwa, palunanya.*
     APe *Uwa.*
     KL ⌈ Now this oil is very similar to the oil that they get from whales.
     APe ⌊ *Walypala parna Tjungku.*
     APf *Parna yaarltjitja?*
     APe *Nyarakutu.*

(42) KL Well, *wangka kutjupa tjuku-tjuku,* um, *nyaa* houses *tjunkutu.* We've got ten thousand dollars for sheds and houses, mostly for the outstations.
     APx Outstations *turtaku.*
     APy ⌈ Hm.
     APz ⌊ *Kuliltju.*
     KL . . . Wherever people stopping, we can put a shed, a closed shed that you can lock 'im, or we can just put up a shade, just a big top, anything you fellows want, but you've got to decide yourselves what it is you want.
     APa *Watjala warli mantjila.*
     . . .
     APb *For the outstations turtaku.*
     APc *Warli kutjupa ngura.*
     APd *Warli purlka.*
     APe *Uwa.*
     APf *Yuwa,* outstations*ku.*

(43) APa   *Palya mularrpa.*
      APb   *Paluru mularrpa.*
      EA   *Nyangka nguru nyanga alatjiku*
             mukurringanyi.
      APc   *Palya.*
      EA   Well, *ngura(uti) (purlka) kulinma. Nyangatja*
             secretary *waark*, chairman*ku waark. Palu*
             waarka turtangku purlka (ngatjinyi) ( )
             katitjaku munu store *katitjaku munu* mail*aku*
             ( ), *Wati turtangka witu (ngatjinyi)*, well
             secretary *purtu waark nyinanyi, munu* chair-
             man, ( ) *waark palyanyi. Ngura purlka*
             kulinma? Ngura alatjiku mukurringanyi, well,
             ngura council*nguru* backup*amala, palya?*
             [Pause: 4.0 seconds.] *Kirti-kirti makatinytja*
             wiya, kutjupa-kutjupa ( ). Palya?
      APn ⎡*Uwa.*
      APn ⎨*Uwa.*
      APn ⎣*Uwa.*
      APd   *Uwuaoh!*
      APe   *Kirti-kirti makatinytja wiya.*
      APf   *Kirti-kirti makatinytja wiya.*
      APg   *Uwa, paluru.*
      APh   *Tjukarula.*
      APb   *Palu mularrpa.*
      APi   *Uwa. Ngaanya katinytja wiya.*

(44) KL   *Walypala tjitji kanilyku, tjitji nintilpayi.*
      AP   *Tjitji.*

(45) APa   *Ka paluru* Peter*lu nguntirrangu.* He shouldn't
             do that, you know. Must be listening all the
             blackfellas. They gonna say.
      APb ⎡ He got to listen to the council.
      APa ⎣ Council, Not, not, not come up here for
             whole lot of talk, this way. People don't like
             like that way, you know.
      APn   *Yuwa.*
      KL   *Nyaa?*
      APc   *Pikapayi pungarnu.*
      APb   Should be listening to the council. To the
             council.
      APa   He gotta, yeah, he gotta listen, you know.
             And he gotta tell 'im. 'Me and what's her
             name 'bin arguin' from this.' He should tell
             like that, out, you know, straight out talk.

That little bit, you know. People not happy about that. That mechanic little bit too rough rough for you whitefellas.

APb   *Ngura*Aboriginal*ku.*

KL   He, he =

APa   = He's a good bloke, waarkin'. Good.

KL   He's a good workin' bloke but, but *tjinguru tirtu nyinalkitja.* =

APa   = *Uwa nyinamalkukitjanku,* well he should*tu!*

KL   Mechanic shop.

APa   Mechani*ca, nyinalkitja paluru,* he gotta, talk silly way, you know. Some of the people might go, 'Ohh, that bloke fuckin' rough that bloke.

APb   rough

No, good, people, *wiya.*

(46) APa   *Palya muntaya?*

APb   *Palya muntanya kulira?*

APc   *Yirnaya yuwanmaranya.*

APd   *Palya wiru.*

(47) APa   *Tjinguru tjarrpatjunku* or *tjinguru wanti?*

APb   *Tjarrpatjunku.*

APc   *Tjarrpatjunku munta?*

. . .

APd   *Walykumunu muntayan?*

APe   *Yuwa.*

APf   *Palya.*

(48) APa   *Wirutja nyangatja, ayi?*

APb   *Tjinguru wiru kulira? Ngurrpa palyalkitja yungara ngura ngaangka.*

(49) KL   EA *pitjangu* permit *wiya, yapu ngurrilkitja.* Permit *wiya, nintilku* police*lakutu?*

APa   *Yuwa! Yuwa, yuwanmara, yuwankara.*

APn ⎧ Mm.

APn ⎨ *Uwa.*

APn ⎩ *Uwa, nyaratja wangka.*

APb   We don't want him.

APc   No, *Kulila.*

APd   *Munta, wantikun.*

APe   *Yuwa.*

(50) APe   *Nyaangurna kulinyi.*

APx   *Nyaangkun nyangatja wiya.*
APy   *Nyangatja wiya.*

(51)   APx   And *mutukayiku* too.
      APy   *Mutuka nyangakutu* run*imalku.*
      APz   *Palya munta mularrpa.*

(52)   KL   [It would be] very good to get them to sleep on the ground one night.
      APa   *Nyara pinypa watjalayi!*
      KL   We've got sleeping bags.
      APb   Three nights?
      APc   Naw.
      APb   Months?
      APc   *Ajatji.*
      APd   One week*patjalu.*
      APe   One week.
      APf   *Wiki kutju.*
      APg   One week.
      APh   One week.

(53)   APa   *Uwa, kala.* Finished.
      APb   *Wiru wati kutjupa ( )*
      APc   *Uwa.*
      APd   *Palya.*
      APe   [whispered] *Uwa palurunya watjapayi.*
            Nyanga ( ) tjilpinya . . .
      APf   *Uwa, alatjirtu.*
      APg   *Uwa, kala. Wartalpi.*
      APh   *Kala.*
      APb   *Meetingku wiya.*
      APg   *Wartalpi, pirukuku.*
      APb   *Uwatjan,* that's lot.
      APa   *Wiyarringu,* that's the lot.
      APc   *Uwa, wiyartu, munta?*
      APd   All done.
      KL   Finished?
      APi   *Yuwa.*

(54)   APa   You fellow good driver and *nyuntu* number two. Well, *ngura pike wiya nguratjarra.*
      APb   No *arkamin.*
      APn   No *arkamin.*
      APc   *Arkamin kutjupatja ngayu nothing. ( ) pupanyi nyarangka ( ) . . .*
      APd   *Alatji tjinguru wangka arkamin wiya, tjinguru arkamin wiya.*

(55) APa Half a day *waark katinyingkala tjunanyi*. Half
           a day *waarkatinya*, four hours; half work
           wiya, well, too absent *palu nyinanyi*.
      APb *Wantirtu alatji kurarringku.*
      APc *Uwanya, nyaranguru*, meeting must be.
           Wantirtu.

(56) APa *Ngayulu 'bin tjapirnu paluna. Purtu
           nyinanyinaku.*
      APb *Tjapinyingu* all the Toyotas.
      KL   *Uwa, uwa.*
      APc *Ngula tjapiltjaku, wanti.*

(57) APa *Ankukitja munta?*
      APb *Palya muntaya?*
      APc *Palya muntanya kulira.*

(58) Well you, *kutju* one way *wangkanyi, wangka kutju paluna.*

(59) Original transcript in text, p. 71.

(60) KL   *Nganalu* vice-president and secretary?
           Nganalu vice-president? *Nganalu* secretary?
      WP   Jillian*ku* secretary.
      APn Naw.
      KL   President, Charlie*ku*. Must be vice-president
           and secretary *kutjupa*.
      APn *Uwa.*
      APx *Kungka kutjupa.*
      APn *Uwa.*
      APa *Nyaakuya?*
      APb Secretary.
      KL   And vice-president?
      APn . . .
      APb Secretary.
      KL   Which one?
      APc ⌈ Simon.
      APd ⌊ Simon.
      KL   Secretary or vice-president?
      APf Vice-president.
      WP   Vice-president.
      KL   Vice-president *Mularrpa?*
      APn ⌈ *Uwa.*
      APn ⟨ *Uwa.*
      APn ⌊ *Uwa.*
      APg *Uwa, Simon.*
      APh Simon Banks.

APn	. . .	
KL	And might be =	
WP		= Jillian secretary?
KL	Jillian secretary?	
WP	*Uwa.*	
APi	*Uwa.*	
KL	*Uwa?*	
APe	Hmhm.	
KL	Simon? Jillian secretary? *Uwa?*	
APn	*Uwa.*	
APg	*Alatji.*	
KL	O.K.	
APi	Put 'em all on the paper.	

(61) APe   *Wangka kutjupangka ngaanya pirayi.*

(62) EA   *Kulila, ngayulu wangka . . .*

(63) APa   *Uwa.*
      APb   *Yuwa.*
      APc   *Paypa ankula parna yunganya*
             ngayulu =
      APd   *= Yuwaoh!*
      APe   *= Walypala palu*
             palyara =
      APf   *= Ngurakutu watjarnu.*
      APg   Giles Creek =
      APh   = Giles Creek.
      APi   = Giles Creek.

(64) APa   *Wartalpi. Ngura purlkanya.*
      APb   Right, meeting*alpi, wartalpi.*

NB Illustrations were selected from 20 hours of transcribed tape recordings.

Appendix 2

Full texts in the original language of transcripts analyzed in the section, 'Some Detailed Transcripts': A through D (chapter 2)

A Discrete advocacy

KL Do you want to send Kurt up there or not?
APa *Palya*, Kurt, *palya*.
    (good)   (good)
    Good, Kurt, good.
APb *Wiya, wiru palya*.
    (no) (fine) (good)
    Not at all, that's just fine.
KL *Uwa wiru*, good idea.
    (yes) (fine)
    Yes, fine, good idea.
APc 'Cause *tjapirnurna*, and I want to go up for us and all.
        (asked + me)
    Because they asked me, and I want to go up for us and all.
    Show 'em *nintijununyi*.
        (show them)
    Show 'em, show them.
APn *Uwa*.
    (yes)
    Yes.

10

APc 'Cause *tjapirnurna   palu   nyanga. palunartu ngaa Kentu*
            (asked + me) (this one) (this)   (this one) (this) [-emphasis])
     Because they asked me about this one. Ken was the one who
     watjarnu =
     (said)
     brought this up.

APn = *Uwa*.
        (yes)
        Yes.

APn *Uwa*.
     (yes)
     Yes.

APc *Palunalu watjarnu*. And *tjapirnu karna   watjarnu yuwa*. 'Cause
            (he) (spoke)   (asked) (and + I) (said) (yes)
     He spoke to me about it. He asked, and I said sure. Because first.
     I can't *ngarnmanpa watjarnurna ankurna*. Council *tjapilku*
              (just)   (speak + me) (will go + me)   (will ask)
     I can't just speak for myself and go. I have to ask the Council first.

APn *Yuwa*.
     (yes)
     Yes.

APc *Ngaanyangka pitjalu   watjarnu*, and *waitingtja watjara*.
     (this + [abla- (come + (spoke) (-[emphatic]) (says)
      tive]) [transitive])
     In this way I came to talk about it, and I'm waiting for what everyone has to say.

20

APb	*Wirutja* *nyangatja, ayi?* (fine + [emph.]) (this) ([interrogative]) This one is fine, isn't it?
APd	Office *wiru pirninya kaninyi. Nintitja paluru.* (fine) (many) (holds) (clever) (he) This fellow holds many positions. He's clever.
APc	They gotta Adelaide, Sydney, Melbourne.
APf	That's right, this must be next year *palyalku.* (will do) That's right, they must be doing this for next year.
APn	*Uwa.* (yes) Yes.
APc	*Paluna.* (that one) That one.
APe	*Alatjingka* (that's it) That's it.
APc	And Alice Springs, and Darwin. *Palya* office *palu ngarala =* (good) (this one) (stands) And Alice Springs, and Darwin. We'll have a good position
APn	= ⎰ Mm.
APn	⎱ *Uwa.* (yes) Yes.

30

APc   *Paluna.* Tourists
   (that one)
   That one. For tourists.

APn   *Uwa. Uwa.*
   (yes) (yes)
   Yes. Yes.

APc   *Ka   nintiltjanu   wirutju,* too.   *Yarnangu   kutju,* top end.
   (and) (give + from) (fine + [emph])   (Aboriginal) (one)
   And they'll give us a lot, too. One Aboriginal from the North.
   Nyinanyi kutju. Ka nyinanyi ngayulunya tjapirnu karna
   (sit)   (one) (and) (sit)   (myself)   (asked) (and + I)
   One was appointed. And I was asked to sit on the board. And
   ngayulu watjarnu wiya. Ask 'em first. I must see Docker
   (I)   (said)   (no)
   I said no, I have to ask them first. I must see the people
   people Council first. And he *yuwanmanku,* alright *tjapilkutja*
           (alright)   (ask + [emph])
   at Docker River first. And he said alright, go, ahead and ask
   mawatjalkulitju.
   (go + speak + future + we two)
   them.

APg   *Wartalpi.*
   (alright)
   Alright, then.

APc   And we can find out, ring 'em up and let 'em know, later on.

APh   *Wirutju.*
(fine + [emphatic])
Fine!

APc   *Tjingurun   wiru   kulira? Ngurrpa. Palyalkitja   yungara ngura ngaangka.*
(maybe + you) (fine) (think) (ignorant) (do + [purposive]) (own) (camp) (this one)
Maybe you think that is fine? I don't know. It's your community, you have to decide this one.

APn   *Yuwa.*
(yes)
Yes.

APc   *Yarnangulankuyan.*   *Mani   yarnangu   pirnikutu   pitjalu.*
(Aboriginal + we + you you all + you) (money) (Aboriginal) (many + to) (come + to) (come + [emph.])
This is for all the Aboriginal people. We might get some money for the community.

APn   [*Yuwa.*
(yes)
Yes.
APn   *Uwa.*
(yes)
Yes.

APc   *Nyaaku.*
(this + for)
This way.

APn   *Uwa.*
(yes)
Yes.

APc   *Paluna.* [gestural tone: crisp, anonymous; hardly audible]
(that way)
That way.

50

APn   *Uwa.*
     (yes)
     Yes.

APn   *Palya.*
     (good)
     Good.

APc   *Wangka ngayunya turta, palunyaangka   tjapirnu warli   mantjilkulan.*
     (talk)   (I)   (a lot)   (that one + about) (ask)   (houses)   (we will get)
     I will tell them about our needs. I'll ask about getting houses for us.

APn   *Yuwaoh!*
     (yes)
     Yes!

APn   *Yuwaoh!*
     (yes)
     Yes!

APn   *Yuwaoh!*
     (yes)
     Yes!

APc   *Ka   pitjala   ngarrira mani   yungkulan.*
     (and) (come) (to lie)   (money) (our own)
     And we'll have our own money here.

APn   Mm.

APi   *Alaji   wiru.*
     (that's it) (wonderful)
     That's it, wonderful.

APc   *Yarnangukutu mani   mapitjalu.*
            (Aboriginal) (money) (will come)
            And the money will come to the Aboriginal people.

APn   *Yuwa.*
            (yes)
            Yes.

APn   *Yuwa*
            (yes)
            Yes.

APj   That's a *warli,   arnanguku.*
                       (house) (Aboriginal + for)
            That's houses, for the Aboriginal people.

APc   *Yuwaoh, yarnangu   pirniku.*
            (yes)   (Aboriginal) (many + for)
            Yah, for all the Aboriginal people.

APn   [inaudible]

APk   *Wiru Tjungku. Palya.*
            (fine) (Shorty) (good)
            Fine, KL. Good.

B   A consensus

KL   *Nyaa watjalku   telegram ku?*
            (what) (say + future) (+ to)
            What shall we say in the telegram?

APa   Hm?

KL   We gotta send him a telegram saying =] *ngalya-pitja* or *pitja   wiya.*
      (here-come)   (come) (not)
      he should come or he shouldn't come.

APb   *Pitjala   wangka]*
           (come + command) (tell)
           Tell him to come.

APc   *Ngalya-pitjantjaku.*
      (here – come + [purposive])
      Have him come.

APd   *Pitja!*
      (come)
      Come!

APa   *Pitja*, and talk about all this people here.
      (come)
      Come, and talk to the people here about this.

KL   *Wangka* =] camels, uh, *nyaratja* but *ngurrangka   wiya?*
      (talk)   (there)   (in the camp) (not)
      To talk about the camels, but he can have them there, not in the camp.

APa   = *Wangkaku]*
           (walk + to)
                To talk.

APf   *Wanti-wanti,   alatji   watjala.*
      (leave it-leave it) (like that) (tell)
      Leave it! Tell him like that.

KL   Or *ngula watjalku.*
      (later) (will talk)
      Or we'll talk about it later.

20

APg   *Wati kutju.*
(man) (one)
Only one person can come.

APc   *Alaji   watjala.*
(that's it) (tell)
Tell him like that.

APh   Camela.
Camel.

[laughter]
APi   *Watjala   ngarrinyi.*
(tell him) (lie down)
Tell him to come here a while.

APa   *Pitjala tjinguru, wanti   kala* ( ) hard fellow. He can go back.
(come) (perhaps) (leave it) (that's all)
Perhaps he should come, but if he gives us trouble, we'll just
Pitjaku Arthur Littlenya   ngananya   yarltingu.
(will come) (+ nom. marker) (this one) (call)
forget about it, and he can go back. If we call Arthur Little
Little is gonna say. He *paluru* =
to come, what is he going to say. This fellow =   = *Ngayulu,*
(I)
I say we

APj   *wantiya* ( ) ( ) ( ).
(leave it + all you)
should forget about it.
['Rush' of talk]

30

APe₁ Kulila, ngayuku, Arthurnya Fridaynya, Fridaynya palu palu
(listen) (my) (+ nom.) (+ nom.) (+ nom.) (he) (he)
Listen, I want to talk, Arthur and Friday want us to bring
watja nyanga tjura you want 'em tjungurringi panya ( )
(says) (this) (puts) (bring) (same)
them camels, and
camela. . ( ) kanyiratja payimalalku.
(keep) (pay him + command + future)
they'll pay us for them.

APa Kutju one way, ( ) way. Too many wangka yanku, one waypanyala.
(one) (talk) (go + future) (+ nom + command)
One, one way. There's too much talking; we have to all be agreed.
Kala old mentjaku.
(alright) (+[purposive])
The old men will have the final say.

APn Hm.Hm.

APa ( ) whole lotanyi. If Arthur Littleanya horseku ngananya
(+ nom.) (+ to) (this)
( ) +[verbalizer])
If Arthur Little gives us these horses,
utira, well he can't pay (ngananyanyi) wiya, and wangka wiya
(give) (this + to me) (no) (talk) (no)
fine, but if he can't pay us, then I won't even talk with him.
ramala nyaapala-nyaapalamalarni =
(anger) (this one one-this one + me)
I'll become angry about it.

40

APk	= ( ) *alataji wangka*
	(like this) (tell)
APn	= *Uwa.*
	(yes)
	Yes

APa '*Ka ngayulu* 'bin broke half-caste, *ngayulu* family sellimal-
(and) (I)   ([+ pur-
And he'll say, 'I'm just a broke part-Aboriginal, I have to
kitja,' you know, two thousand*palu ala-alaji alalkukitja*,
posive])   (+[emphatic]) (this way) (this way + intend)
sell my family,' you know, two thousand he'll pay for each
I'm broke too. *Alatji wangkatja*, I'm gonna say firm way,
                      (like this) (speak + [emphatic])
one, I'm broke too. Like this I'll tell him. I'll be firm,
alatji wangkapayi.
(like this) (speak + [continuous])
like this I'll keep speaking.

APe₂ Alright, he *mularpa purlkanya*. Aboriginal people. Arthur.
              (truly)   (big one)
What he says is the right way to speak about this – with strength.

APl He's good bloke.
He's a good fellow.

APa *Tjapila*, we might, he might come up and talk, *tjilpi turangka*.
(ask)   (old men)
Ask him, we might let him come and speak with the old men.

50

60

APe₁	*Uwa.*	
	(yes)	
	Yes.	
APn	*Mularrpa.*	
	(truly)	
	Truly.	
APn	( ) come here, *nyanaka turta ngarrinyi*	
	(this) (all) (lie down)	
	to speak with all of us about this.	
KL	Mm-hm.	
APe₁	*Wangka witulakutu.*	
	(speak) (strong + toward)	
	Speak strongly.	
APa	We got some of them quiet camels here too.	
KL	Mm-hm.	
APa	Quiet camels.	
KL	Might be two, might be *ka-*, a couple quiet camels *kanilkitja*	
APa	(+ for)	
	Uwa, Docker River*ku* we get 'im. He might got a lot of horse.	
	(yes) (+ for)	
	Yes, we might get a lot of horses for Docker River.	
APm	Areyonga camel again.	
APn	Cow too.	

297

APo   Camel *kutjupa turta*.
       (others) (lots)
       Lots of camels.

KL   Might have a lot of horses, *tjinguru*.
       (maybe)

APa   We might get a lot of horses, maybe.
       Tjinguru might come back with a horse.
       (maybe)

APp   Maybe we might get some horses.
       Big mob, *nyanganya*.
       (this one)
       Lots of them.

APa   *Uwa*.
       (yes)
       Yes.

KL   Might be, he might pay some people to get a lot of camels = and you can get your own camels at
       the same time
       and use his horses.
       = *Waarkutjarra* ( ) ( ) ( ).
       (work + for + having)
       For work.

APe$_1$ is the label for the above "= *Waarkutjarra*..." line.

APn   *Yuwa*.
       (yes)
       Yes.

APq   *Tjilpitjianguru*.
       (old men + from)
       All for the old men.

80

APr   *Nyaapalulan.*
(this + [transitive] + we all)
We will do this.

APs   *Nyaa paluru.*
(this) (that one)
Like that.

APa   Come up with the horse, he can stop off at Puta-Puta. Make
kapi, you know, make 'im a little bit damp, *purlkakitja.*
(water)   (big + [intentional])
water, you know, make it damp so it can become a big camp.

APt   *Kuka ngayulu wangkaku.*
(meat) (I)   (speak + for)
I'll ask him for lots of meat.

APn   Shhhhh.

APa   *Ka nyinanyi,* he can sit down there, for them *nyaratja, tjitji*
(and) (sit)   (there)   (children)
And he can remain there because the children
might grab the tail. *Tjitji* never seen a horse before, all
(children)
might grab the tail. The children have never seen a horse
these *tjitji* might *pika palu.* Camel *turta.* Come lot a
before. The children might hurt them, and all the camels.
horses *nyaapatjan.*
(this-there)
We'll keep all the horses over there.

APn   Mm.

299

APu   *Arthurla palya = munta?*
(+so)(good) ([interrogative])
So it's alright for Arthur to come?

APv   = Windmill*ku* Areyongan*ya* *nguratjarra* ( ).
(+to) (+nom.) (camp+having)
We'll get a windmill for the camp, like Areyonga.

APn   *Nyangkala palyal—*
(this+[ablative])(do+)
Just like this we'll have—

APa   Windmill ( ) *kati nguratjanu* ( ) alright.
(bring)(camp+for)
We'll get a windmill for the camp, alright.

APw   *Uwa, alatji,* anyway.
(yes)(that's it)
Yes, that's it.

APa   *Kulila, ngananyapa* too long *nyinara* anyway. *Mani wiya.*
(listen) (this one) (sit) (money)(without)
Listen, we've been thinking about this for too long anyway.
Touristakupatja ↑ *Arthur Littlenyakitja?* ↑
(+to+[emph.])(+nom.+[purposive])
We have no money. The camels will attract tourism. Will we
let Arthur Little come?

APc   *Uwa.*
(yes)
Yes.

APn   *Yuwa.*

APa
(yes)
Yes.
Uwa, one way *yala wangkanyi, nyanganku watjanyi pitjantjaku.*
(yes) (we all) (are saying) (this + for) (speak) (come + to)
Yes, we are all speaking the same way about this; he should
(he) (talk) about *tjilpi turiangka ngananyala wangkanyi.*
(old men) (all + [ablative]) (this) (speak)
come. He can talk about it with all the old men. This
tjitji paluna wangka here, well right. *Tjinguru. Tjinguru,*
(child) (this one) (talk) (maybe) (maybe)
uninitiated man can come to speak with us. Maybe. Maybe,
watja palu tjinguru ask, 'You goin' to *payimalalku wanananya?'*
(say) (him) (maybe) (+ future) (follow)
we'll ask him, 'Are you going to continue to pay us?'
You know!

APz
Payimalalkupanya. Nyarakula( ).
(+ future + [nominalizer]) (there + for)
Pay us for them. Over there

APn
Yuwa.
(yes)
Yes.

APa Arthur, *Arthurnya pitjanyi,* ↑ *Arthurnya pitjanyi?* ↑
APn { *Uwa.*
APn { *Uwa.*
APa Meeting *wangkara?* Alright *wangkanyi.*
(is saying) (say)
Is this what the meeting is saying? Alright that's what we say.

C Approving the visit to Star Rockhole (I)

APa   *Kulira?*
       (think)
       What do people think?

. . . APa   One way *kulilpa*.
             (think + [nominalizer])
             We must all agree.

. . . APa   *Katikitjalu   wangka tjura?*
             (bring + want) (talk)   (put)
             Shall we bring them here?

APe₁   *Nyaangka ngaaluijarra tjilpilu   kulira nyara paluru pitjalu.*
       (this-of) (this-having) (old men) (think) (there) (he)   (may come)
       The elders think that that fellow should come.

. . . APb   *Alatji   munta?*
             (like this) ([interrogative])
             Like this, is it?

. . . APp   *Pintirinya   nyinankitja watjara.*
             (place-name) (sit-in order to) (talk)
             We are saying that they should visit Star Rockhole.
       [Discussion of whether the ceremonies should be televised occupies the gathering.]

10

APy   *Ngayulu ngurrpalu.*
       (I)   (ignorant + transitive)
       I don't know what we should do.

. . :

APc   *Warli wiyangka, no . . . Settlement munta ngarri paluna.*
       (house) (no)   ([interrogative]) (sleep) (they)
       Not in the houses . . . They shouldn't sleep in the settlement.

APn   *Uwa.*
       (yes)
       Yes.

APn   *Uwa.*
       (yes)
       Yes.

APn   *Uwa.*
       (yes)
       Yes.

APp   *Yuwaoh! Nyaraku tjukura   watjanma.*
       (yes)   (there) (correctly) (is speaking)
       Yes! Now he's speaking correctly.

. . :

APa   *Yuwa paluna.   Palyan-palya   watjara?*
       (yes) (that one) (good + you - good) (saying)
       Yes, that one. Now is that what we're saying?

APd   *Tjukarula.*
       (correct)
       Correct.

303

20

APe₁   *Yuwa, palya.*
       (yes) (good)
       Yes, good.
APf   *Walykumunu.*
       (wonderful)
       Wonderful.

. . .
APg   *Wartalpi, wartalpi.*
       (settled) (settled)
       Alright, so it's settled.
APh   *Wartalpi.*
       (settled)
       Settled.
APi   Mmm. *Kutju alatji.*
       (one) (like this)
       Mmm. We all agree on this one.
APe₂   *Kutju paluna, palu nyanganya tjarrpatjunku.*
       (one) (that one) (that) (this one) (enter + put + future)
       One way. That way: they will enter the sacred area.
APj   *Kutju paluna.*
       (one) (that one)
       We are all agreed on that.
APn   Mm.
       Mm.
APp   *Kutju nyangatja.*
       (one) (this + [emphasis])
       One way, this way.

30

APn	Finished.
APn	*Paluna.*
	(that one)
APn	That one.
APk	Mm.
	Pintiri ngarrinyi . . . Pintirinya pitjaku.
	(place-name) (lie down) (place-name) (come + future)
	They'll camp at Star Rockhole. . . They'll come to Star Rockhole.
APe₁	*Panya—*
	(so)
	So.
APe₂	(alright) (place-name + to)
	Alright, to Star Rockhole.
APe₁	*Panya ngura ( ) . . . yulpari, yulpari, yulpari; wati turta,*
	(so) (camp) (south) (south) (men) (all)
	So to that homeland there . . . From the south, from the south,
	wati turta, wati turta.
	(men) (all) (men) (all)
	from the south; all the men, all the men, all the men.
∴	
APc	*Paluna munta?*
	(that one) ([interrogative])
	Are we agreed on that one?
∴	
APc	*Watjala tjilpi. Watjala ngaalu.*
	(say) (old men) (say) (this + [transitive])
	So say the old men. They say we should do it.

305

40

APb   *Kulila.*
       (listen)
       Listen.

...
APa   The Prime Minister.
APe₃   *Or purlka turta pitjantjaku.*
       (big) (a lot) (come + [purposive])
       Or a lot of important leaders will come.
APl   *Purlka turta.*
       A lot of important leaders.

...
       nyangkanya, nyangkanya.
       (this one)   (this one)
       this one, this one.
APa   *Kulira munta.* Prime Minister
       (think) ([interrog.])   (asl + intend to)
       Is this the way we think? We'll also ask the Prime Minister.

...
APa   *Tjapira munta . . . .*
       (ask)   ([interrogative])
       Shall we ask them?
APn   Mm.
APa   *Ngaanya* Prime Minister.
       (this)
       This one, the Prime Minister.

50

APm	*Kati*	*kati*	*kati*	*kati.*

APm   *Kati kati kati kati.*
(bring him) (bring him) (bring him) (bring him)
Bring him, bring him, bring him, bring him.

APn   Mm.

. . .
APo   *Paratjapira.*
(around) (ask)
Ask everybody.

. . .
APp   *Ngalya-pitja ngurrangkalatju nyinaku.*
(here-come) (site-at-we all) (will sit)
Bring them here, and we'll all stay at the site.

APe₄   *Ajaṯi wiru.*
(that's it) (wonderful)
That's it. Wonderful.

APq   *Palya.*
(good)
Good.

APr   *Alaṯi watjara.*
(that's it) (say)
That's what we all say.

APs   *Tjukarula.*
(correct)
Correct.

APp   *Nyinalku palurutjanu . . .*
(will stay) (there)
They'll stay there . . .

APe₂   *Nyangkanya, nyangkanya, nyangkanya, nyangkanya, nyangkanya.*
      (this one)   (this one)   (this one)   (this one)   (this one)
      This one, this one, this one, this one, this one.

D   Approving the visit to Star Rockhole (II)

APe₁   *Wanti* photograph *wiya.*
      (leave it)   (no)
      Leave it, no photographs [when they visit Star Rockhole].

APb   'Cause *nyanga* photo *mantjintja wiya.* Photo *mantjintja*
      (this)   (take)   (not)   (take)
      Because they shouldn't take photos. They should not take
      wiyangka.   *Ka ngaanya, wiyangka. ngka, wantiku kuwarri* . . .
      (not + [ablative]) (and) (this)   (not + [abl.]) ([abl.]) (leave it) (now)
      photos. No photos for television. We'll leave it for now . . .

APc   TV *wanti.*
      (leave it)
      Forget about TV coverage.

APd   *Nyaa paluna nyangu* = . .
      (this) (that one) (saw)
      I saw that one . . .

APb   = And you can't get them back. Well Perth,
      Charles Court he can look for himself.

APe₁   *Uwa.*
      (yes)
      Yes.

20

APb   *Ngaanyalatju munta?*
(this + we all) ([interrogative])
So what should we do about this?

APb   *Kutju, kutju pitjatjaku.*
(one) (one) (come + [purposive])
Just this, they'll only come.

APf   *Pitjakutja paluna yaka?*
(will come) (they) (exclamation)
So they'll be coming will they?

APb   *Kutju paluna pitjaku* because *palunalu, palu-palunakutu*
(one) (they) (will come) (that one) (that-that one + to)
They'll only come because of that, that's what we're
wangkapayi
(are saying)
saying.

APf   *Yuwoah!*
(yes)
Yes!

APb   *Kutju paluna.*
(one) (that one)
Just that.

APg   *Turlku turlku yirnaluya.*
(ceremony) (ceremony) (all the old men will do)
All the elders will perform a sacred ceremony.

APb   *Pitjala nintirriku palu watjara.*
(come) (to learn) (that) (say)
We're saying that they'll come to learn the sacred truth.

APf   *Yuwa ka paluna. Waiya ngaanya nyaaku,* mmhm!
     (yes) (and) (that one) (men) (these) (for this)
     Alright, that one. That's what these men say.

APb   *Ngaalu* Canberra *wangkaratjaku piijala tjarrpa parararrikula*
     (this)   (talk + intending) (come) (enter) (everywhere)
     This way. The people from Canberra will come, enter the
     wangaratjaku.
     (talk + intending)
     sacred area, receive the sacred Law and talk about land rights.

APf   *Palunakutja palunaku kutju.*
     (that one + for + [emphatic]) (that one + for) (one)
     That's what it will be, just that.

APb   *Ngaalu Pintirinya yirnaya ngura tjapirarnin, purli wiya*
     (this) (place-name) (elders) (ground) (ask + I + you) (rocks) (no)
     The elders are concerned about their sacred Star Rockhole.
     ngalanyi miily-miilypa purlkanya.
     (standing) (sacred) (big one)
     It's not just rocks there; it's a very sacred place.

APg   *Mily-milypa paluna purlkatja nyinara. Yulangu paluna.*
     (sacred) (that one) (important) (sits) (cried) (that one)
     That's a very sacred place. We've cried for that one.

APn   *Nyangkarpa.*
     ([exclamation])
     Goodness yes.

APb   *Palu yiniya ngurrpalu Pintirinya.*
     (that) (name) (ignorant) (Star Rockhole)
     They are ignorant of the name of Star Rockhole.

40

APn | *Ngarala ( ) kulira watjaranyi Pintirinya   Pintirinya.*
(stands) (hear) (speak)   (Star Rockhole) (Star Rockhole)
They will hear the name of that place.

APe₂ | *Pintirinya   utira wiyarriwa makaninyijarra yakayiku!*
(Star Rockhole) (give) (will)   away + inside) (my goodness)
becoming nothing)
We'll give away the sacred secrets of Star Rockhole, and it may lose its power, my goodness!

APf | *Nyangkatjuku DAAku*
(in this one)   (for D.A.A.)
In this,   for the Department of Aboriginal Affairs.
['Rush' of talk]

APf | *Katu kutu!*
(up) (to)
Up to there!

APn | *Nyangarrpa!*
([exclamation])
My goodness!

APf | *Palu nyaku,   nguraltjanu   mantjira nyinaranya (puri).*
(that) (will see) (place + from) (get)   (sit)
They'll see that, from that place they found.

APh | *(Whitepala) kuka   mantjinyi ngura.*
(+ fellow) (meat) (get)   (place)
The whitefellas will have to bring all of us meat.

APi | *Manuri.*
(blood)
Blood.

APe$_2$	*Ngayulurna ( ) Pintirinya palunalu.* (I) (place-name) (that one + [transitive]) I . . . that Star Rockhole.
APn	*Yuwa.* (yes) Yes.
APj	*Aboriginalku (winkilu) ngaraltju.* (+ for) (all) (stand + we all) The spirit of all the Aboriginal people rests there.
APn	*Alatji.* (that's it) That's it.
APn	*Uwaoh.* (yes) Yes!
APe$_2$	*Nyaapa-nyaapa-nyaapa.* (this) (this) (this) Alright-alright-alright.
APn	*Kuju paluna wangkaku.* (one) (that) (talk + to) We agree on this one.
APn	*Palu palunyangka.* (that) (that + this + [ablative]) This one, on this.

60

APb But *ngaalu kulira, anurna nyara bossanya, nyaapangka,*
(this) (think) (went + I) (there) (+ [nom.]) (this + [ablative])
This is what I'm thinking, if we took the big 'bosses' there,
ngaalu kuliranyi if he = ( ) one *palu ninti tjura.*
(this) (thinking) (them) (show) (put)
this I'm thinking, we'll teach them the sacred Law.

APn *Wanytjanguru?*
(where)
Where?

APb *Palunartu yarnangu yungarra yungarra selfama.*
(that + [emph]) (Aboriginal) (own) (+ continuous)
The Aboriginals should be keeping that place to themselves.

APf *Yuwaoh!*
(yes)
Yes!

APb *Alatjiku ngayulu kulira.* Two way.
(like this) (I) (think)
Like this, I'm thinking. Two ways.

APn ( ) ( ) ( )
APm *Nyanga pinypa.*
(this) (like)
Just like this.

APo *Nyanga pinypa.*
(this) (like)
Just like this.

70

80

APb   They don't want to show the most important ones. All the
kapamin ( ).
(government)
government people.

APe₂   *Wangka nyangka Purlipurlkanya nyanganya wangka yirna*
(talk)   (this)   (place-name)   (this one)   (talk)   (elders)
I want to say something about Promontory Point. The elders
Purlipurlkanya purlkanya ↑*watirringkulawu* ↑ *mutukayi*
(place-name)   (important)   (men + creative)   (motorcar)
say that Promontory Point is very important, a men-creative
mungarrtu   *pitjantja wiya liwarrpa.*
(extinguished) (came) (not) (no + emphatic)
place. We need an automobile to take care of that place, and none has come!

APb   You want the car.
APp   Whitefella come away.
APq   *Panyakula kura-kura nyinara.*
(so) (then) (bad-bad) (sits)
That's very bad.

APr   Poor bugger *wiya kutju.*
(not) (one)
Poor fellow, not even one.

APs   *Ngaanyapa ngaanya.*
(this one) (this)
This one here.

APe₂   *Uwarna.*
(yes + I)
Yes, mine.

90

APt	All over.
APb	That's what he means.
APu	We gotta go all over.
KL	Mm hm.
APv	(Just one man.)
APw	*Ngura nyangka kati ( ) palya paperngka watikutja ( )))* (place) (at this) (bring) (good) (in the newspapers) (for the men) *Nyakulinyi palya Pintirinya? Kura munta?* (we will see) (good) (Star Rockhole) (bad) ([interrogative]) If we bring them to the men's place and put it in the newspapers . . . it's alright for all to see, or is it no good?
APb	*Yuwa.* (yes)
	O.K., then.
APx	*Uwanpa whitepala ankulananyi.* (yes + nom.) (+ fellow) (will go) Of course. The whitefellows will go.
APb	*( ) ( ) wiya.* (no) . . . no.
APy	*Purlipurlkanya.* (place-name) Promontory Point.

315

APe₃   *Kutjarra. Wartalpi, ngura   kutjarra matjarrpaku walypala*
       (two)   (alright)   (places)   (two)   (will enter)   (whitefellas)
       Two. Alright, two places we'll let the white people enter.
       and all. *Matjarrpara, matjarrpara,* finishoffariku
               (will enter)   (will enter)   (+ [future])
       They will enter, they will enter, the newspapers will
       ngaanyakutjanytja newspaperkutjanytja pilari.
       (this one will be) (+ will have it)   (spread around)
       report it after we've finished the ceremonies.

APn   Mm. Like that.

APe₃   *Ngaatja nyaaku.*
       (this)   (for this)
       This way.

APn   *Uwa.*
       (yes)
       Yes.

APe₃   *Ngaapa yakaku.*
       (this)   ([exclamation])
       This way!

APn   Mm. *Ala- palyatja.*
            (like-) (that)
       Mm. Like that.

APe₃   *Nyaratja munta   palya. Ngaapanya munta palya. Yaka ( ) ( ).*
       (there)   ([interrg.]) (good) (this one)   (int.)   (good) (exclam.)
       So that's good, is it. So that's good, is it. Goodness!

APn   *Nyangatja uwa.* (laughs)
(this + emph.) (yes)
Yes this! [laughs]

APn   *Uwa.*
(yes)
Yes.

APz   *Turlku   pirni   palumpa.*
(ceremony) (many) (that one)
That one has a lot of sacred ceremonies associated with it.

APe₃   This one.

APf   *Puntu.*
(great)
Great ones.

APaa   This, *nyaaku parna.*
(for this) (ground)
For this place.

APn   *Alatji.*
(that's it)
That's it.

APbb   Claypan *nyangka nyaratja, purli nyaratja kapamintu ( )*
(at this) (there) (rock) (there) (government people)
The government people will see this sacred claypan
nyaku nyaratja nyinanyi.
(will see) (there) (sit)
area.

APn   (laugh)

120

APcc | Tjitji. (newspaper). (laugh)
(children)
And all the uninitiated people will see it in the newspaper.
(laughs)

APb | Palu ( ) he wantitja wangka ngarala.
(he) (leave it) (talk) (stand)
They'll have it in there.

APe$_4$ | Panya?
(so)
So?

APdd | Pappangka newspaperku listenku.
(in the paper) (+ n) (+ for)
In the newspaper everyone will read it.
(laugh)

APn |
APe$_4$ | Yaltjitjanu Pintirinya watjanyiparnya. Nyakuntjaku palu
(what will we do) (place-name) (saying) (will see) (that)
So then, we are saying that they will come to witness
wangkanyi, ngaanyaparnya.
(are saying) (this one)
Star Rockhole.

APee | Ka tjitjilu ngarala ngurlu kutipitjapayi.
(but) (children + [transitive]) (there) (fear) (going about)
But it might be dangerous for uninitiated people to be going about there.

APe₄   *Pintirinyakutu   yaarltji-yaarltji nyanga. Nyangatja.*
    (place-name + to) (where-where) (this) (this + emph.)
    How will we take them to Star Rockhole, in order to
    nyakutjaku   parna   nyangatja. (+ rna) watjarnu.
    (in order to see) (ground) (this)   (+I)   (said)
    see this sacred ground. ( ) they said.   130

APf   *Purlkanya (katjara) kulira wapar ngaalu yakayi*
    (big)   (hear) (story) (this) ([exclamation])
    It's an important place. They'll hear a little of this
    tjuku-tjuku ngaa ngayunyarna. Pirapiralayi ngaanya yutinya.
    (little)   (this) (me + me)   (sacred) (this)   (give)
    place's story, my place. We'll give them the sacred Law.

[Everyone begins to speak at the same time. Figures refer to the number of people speaking at the same time]
1
1
1
3
3
3
2
1
2   140
1
0 [pause: 2.5 seconds]
APff   *Paluru.*
    (that one)
    That one.

150

APgg   *Nyanga tjitji   paluru nyakupayi. Turta nyakupayi tjitjiku.*
(this) (children) (they) (seeing) (all) (seeing) (for children)
The uninitiated will be seeing this. This they'll see, the uninitiated people.

EA   ... TV newsmen here ... the Prime Minister. Talk about land rights and everything.
Well that film will go =

APe₃   = D.A.A. [Department of Aboriginal Affairs]

APb   *Wirtu-wirtu   mangarala   mularrpa.*
(strong-strong) (stand there) (truly)
Its power will truly spread everywhere.

APn   Mm ↓ hm. ↑

APn   *Uwa.*
(yes)
Yes.

APn   ↑ Mmhm. ↑

APb   *Ngaanyala yarltingu   watjalkitja munu paranyinara ka*
(this + to) (everywhere) (will talk) (and) (sit around) (and)
This will be sent out everywhere, and all will see it.
mapitjaku. Still. Paluna palurna   kawaku   parawirrtja
(go away)   (that)   (that + I) (together) (hurry around)
Still, all the sacred knowledge will be sent around
parawirrtjala.
(hurry around)
everywhere.

APe₃   { *Uwa.*
{ (yes)
{ Yes.

160

APn   [*Yuwa.*
     (yes)
     Yes.

APb   *Nyawa purlkanya ( ) again, nyakuya wangka* again. That's
     (look) (big one)   (they'll see)   (talk)
     They should go to see this very sacred ceremony but not
     all. *Ngaanya watjarnu mungantjarra mularpa mily-milypa*
     (this)   (was said) (Dreaming + having) (truly)   (sacred)
     send out news reports about it. These secrets were handed
     purlkaku yatjananya (muurrku)tjarra mularpa warla   katiku
     (big)   (those ones) (+ having) (truly)   (spring) (brings)
     down in the Dreaming; they're really very sacred those ones.
     talikalu. Kaiirna kulilku yaka.
     (sand hill + [trans.]) (bring + me) (will think) ([exclamation])
     They caused water to spring forth out of the sandhills!

APm   *Wiruijuku tjinguru.*
     (wonderful) (maybe)
     Wonderful, maybe.

APn   Mmm.
APn   *Uwoah.*
     (yes)
     Yes!

APn   HmHm.
APn   *Palya.*
     (good)
     Good.

170

180

APb   *Ka ( ) nyakula palumpa nyaku.*   *Ya   palu-palunaya*
         (but)   (seeing) (their)   (will see)   (They) (those)
         But they'll be seeing a sacred place. We'll be revealing
         Pintirinya   yini   watjarlpayinya   kapiku. =
         (place-name) (name) (will be telling) (the waterhole)
         to them that sacred waterhole, Star Rockhole. =
                                           = ↑MmM. ↑

APn
APb   *Nyaraku   nintipungku nyaku. ( ) ngarala   kulila?*
         (there + to) (teach)   (will see)   (stand + we) (think)
         We will teach them there?

APn   *Uwaoah.*
         (yes)
         Yes!

APn   *Yuwa.*
         (yes)
         Yes.

APn   *Nyaampatja.*
         (this + for + [emphatic])
         This one!

APb   But stillpanya,   *yaka-yakalku. Ngurrpangka* ( )
         (+ nominalizer) (exclamation) (in ignorance)
         But still this is very extraordinary. I'm not sure what
         Yaka-yaka stillpa.   *Ngaanya ngayulu* = ( )
         (exclamation) (nom.) (this)   (I).
         we should do. It's very unusual. This one I =

APn   = *Ayi* [to barking dogs]

APb   *Ka minister yanku*   *paluna kapamintu* ( ). *Wiya pungkaku!*
    (and)   (will come) (that)   (government)   (stop) (I'll hit you)
    And the government ministers will come. Stop or I'll
    Ka minister yanku.
    (and)   (will come)
    hit you [to barking dogs]. And the ministers will come.

APn   *Ayi!* [to barking dogs]
APn   *Hoo-hoo!*
APb   ( ) *pungkaku.*
           (will hit)
    I'll hit you all! [to dogs]

APii   *Ngaanyakutu.*
    (here + toward)
    Over here. [to dogs]

APn   *Hee-hee.*
APjj   *Panya, tjamutjan*   *larrapuija!* [laughs]
    (so)   (grandfather's) ([exclamation])
    My goodness! That's my grandfather's home.
APkk   Meeting Council*nga*   *wangkarrinkupayi.*
    (+ nom. marker) (speak + will become + continuous)
    This Council meeting is talking about important things.

APn   [laughs]
['Rush' of talk]
APll   *Nyangkarpa*   *ngayuku* = . . .
    ([exclamation]) (my)
    My goodness.

APn   = ... *ngura.*
            (homeland)
            ... homeland.

EA   *Ngayulu, Ministerku, Ministernya tjapiltjuku.*
      (I)   (+ to)   (+ nom)   (will ask)
      I'll ask the Minister for Aboriginal Affairs.

APn   *Yuwa.*
      (yes)
      Yes.

APb   *Ngananya kuwarri ngaalu.*
      (this)   (now)   (will do this)
      He's going to do this.

APf   *Yuwaooah.*
      (yes)
      Yes!

APn   *Yuwa.*
      (yes)
      Yes.

APn   *Yuwa.*
      (yes)
      Yes.

APnn   *Tjakultjuranya.*
      (report)
      He will make a report.

APe4   *Uwa.*
      (yes)
      Yes.

APn { *Panya—*
(so)
So—

APoo One monthatja ( ).
(+ emph.)
In one month's time.

APpp *Tjakultjunkunya kuwarri* = HmHmm ↑
(will report) (now)
He will make a report. HmHmm. ↑
= *Munta uwa.*
(oh) (yes)
Oh yes.

APpp *Tiilpilu tjakultjunu nyaa paluna purlkari.*
(old men) (report) (this) (that one) (important)
The old men will report on this; it's very important.

APn *Uwa.*
(yes)
Yes.

EA *Eyi?*
APe3 How many weeks is secretary?
APn *Yuwa.*
(yes)
Yes.

APqq *Tjapilku* first.
(will ask)
We'll ask first.

APe₃   Permit*ku*, you gonna ask 'im?

APn   *Uwa.*
(yes)
Yes.

APb   And Ken, you might find out from Darwin, and by that time, alright we'll sit down.

APe₃   *Canberratu nyuntu kulinyi.* ↑
(+ emph.) (you) (hear)
You'll find out from Canberra.

APb   I know, that's what = ( ) *palu   nyakutjarra.*
(they) (see + having)
they'll be able to see.

APn   I know, that's what   = ( ) ( ).

APe₃

Ka   palurutjanya ( ).
(and) (those there)
And those there ( ).

APn   *Yuwaputja.*
(of course)
Of course.

APb   If you get an answer, *ngura kutjarra tjingururna*
(sites) (two) (perhaps-me)
If you get an answer from Canberra, then I'll ask my
mawangka kutjurna yutilu.
(go tell)   (one-me) (if it's decided)
minister friend from Darwin, if it's all agreed.

KL   *Yuwa.*
(yes)
Yes.

230

APb *Wantiku   paluna nyinaku.*
     (leave it + fut.) (that) (will sit)
     We'll wait for that for the time being.

APn *Yuwa.*
     (yes)
     Yes.

APb *Nyaputja   watjalku.* And *ngaalu, tjapilku paluna = nyaapa.*
     (that + emph.) (will say)   (this) (will ask) (that)   (this)
     So that is what we will say. And we'll ask them this.
                                            = [on inhalation:]
                                                Nyaapa.
                                                (this)
                                                This.

APb *Nyaralu* paperpangka.   *Pitjaku   wantirralpi palu   nyinaku.*
     (there) (in the newspaper) (will come) (having left) (they) (sit)
     We'll get news coverage. They'll come and we'll tame them there.

APn Mmm.
APb *Nyaku   watjara finisharri, kuwarri. Wantjawara.*
     (will see) (talk) (+ will) (now)   (where)
     They'll see the ceremony, and we'll have a talk when we're finished.(?)

APe₃ *Ngura kutjarra nyaku   ngaangkara.*
     (places) (two)   (will see) (there)
     The'll see two places there!

APn Mmm.
APe₃ *Ngaangka ngura   kutjarra nyaku.*
     (there) (places) (two)   (will see)
     There two places they'll see.

327

APrr	*Uwa, nyaangka.*
	(yes), (there + [ablative])
	Yes, there.
APe₃	*Manjirartu kuijupangka.*
	(get + [emph.]) (another + [ablative])
	We're getting another. (?)
APss	*Nyarangka mangarinya.*
	(there + [ablative]) (sleep out)
	There we'll sleep out.
['Rush' of talk]	
APb	*Nyaaku,* and two nights.
	(this)
	This, and two nights.
APe₂	*Pitjaku, X ala pitjatjala, Nyangaku ( ) ( ).*
	(will come) (X + to) (come + to) (this + for)
	The people from X will come for this.
APn	Mmm.
APn	*Yuwa.*
	(yes)
	Yes.
APtt	*Wirunya.*
	(wonderful)
	Wonderful.
APe₃	*Wirunya, tjinguru.*
	(wonderful) (perhaps)
	Wonderful.

APb *Munkara tirtu kulila, munkararnin purlkara kulitja-*
(further) (still) (listen) (further + I + you) (big) (hear)
maaltjura (kurlpu)
(don't allow)
allow them to find out about.

APn ( ) ( ) *kutipitjaku.*
(come across)

APn ( ) ( ) come across.
Uwaputja ( )
(of course)
Of course.

APb ( ) *kapirantjananyi nyaranyi watjalkurni walypala.*
(water) (there) (there) (tell + I) (whitefellows)
We'll tell the white-fellows about the sacred waterhole.

APuu *Nyuntu nyaapa, nyuntu ngaa pitjanku, ngayulu ( ) ( )*
(you) (this) (you) (this) (will come) (I)
We will bring them and the old men will tell them
tjilpi nyarangka.
(old men there)
there.

APf ( ) *nyinanyi ( ).*
(sit)

APvv ( ) ( ) *nyarangka. ( ) ( ).*
(there + [ablative])
( ) ( ) over there. ( ) ( )

APf *Nyakulan paanya ( ) ngarala yutalu?*
(will see + we all) ( ) (so) (stands) (reveal)
So we'll reveal the sacred Law for that place?

APww *(Rurrurr) purlka ngarrira nyaratja. Ankutjukulan.*
[sacred?] (big) (lies) (there) (will go + we all)
We will all go to the sacred site.

APn Mm.
APf HmHm.
APb *Paluna.*
(that one)
That one.

APxx *Paluna tjuku-tjuku* . . .
(that one) (little)
That one, a little . . .

APyy *( ) wiya, tjuku-tjuku.*
( ) (not) (little)
Not ( ), little.

APn ( ) ( ) ( ).
APf *Nyaatjatjinya.*
(this + emph. + nominalizer)
This is the one.

APyy *Yuwa, paluna.*
(yes) (this)
Yes, this.

APf *Ngayulurna nyinangu (yutiri)ku nyaangka.*
(I + I) (sat) (wil; give) (about this)
I live at this site, and I'll give them its Law.

APn Mmmm.

APf *Ngaalulatju   ngura   wangkariku nyaariku   parna   nyarakulan*
(this + we will) (place) (will speak) (this + fut.) (ground) (there +
We will tell them about the sacred ground there.
pupanyirnartu Pintirinya   paluna nyinangka.
we all) (crouch) (place-name) (that) (sit + [ablative])
about the world-creative essence which rests within Star Rockhole.

APzz *(Mutu-mutu) (mutu-mutu) ngayulu nyinaranyina.*
(sacred beings) (I)   (sit + sit)
The sacred beings who are my ancestors rest here.

APe *Wai   mularpa.*
(man) (truly)
This man is truly sacred.

APf And *nyaapa (walypala)   nyaangka paper nyaku   wiya?*
(this) (whitefellow) (this)   (will see) (not)
And will we have anything in the newspapers?

APaz *Mawangkala   mapakala   (kulira).*
(go + tell + [command]) (go + get up + [command]) (think)
You can go and tell everybody, we all agree.

APn *Uwaoh!*
(yes)
Yes.

280

APl   *Ankukitja munta?*
(will go + intends) ([interrogative])
So we will go ahead with it?

APb   *Palya muntayc.*
(good) ([interrogative] + you all)
They all seem to think so.

APl   *Palya muntanya kulira.*
(good) ([int.]) (think)
So we all think it's good.

['Rush' of talk.]

APby   *Yirnaya   yuwanmaranya.*
(the elders) (saying yes)
All the elders are saying it's alright.

APcx   *Wirunyara ( )   wangkara ( ) paluna.*
(wonderful + there) (say)   (that one)
That's fine, everyone's saying.

APn   *Paanya ( ).*
(so)
So yah.

APn   Yes.

APn   *Uwa, wiru.*
(yes) (fine)
Yes, fine.

APe₃   *Wangka kutjupangkayi ngaanya pirayi.*
(talk)   (another + [abl.] + [continuous]) (this)   (sacred items)
I have something else to say about some sacred items.

APn   *Uwa.*
(yes)
Yes.

APe₃   *Tjuku-tjuku ngayu ma ( ) ( ) ngura tjanampa, nyaatja.*
(little)   (I)   (home) (there)   (this + emph.)
I have a little bit of the sacred material for the ceremony.

APn   *Uwa.*
(yes)
Yes.

APn   *Yuwa.*
(yes)
Yes.

APn   *Munta.*
(oh!)
Oh!

APn   MmHm!

APe₃   *Palunyangkatja   ngaanya nyaraku.*
(that+this+emph.)   (this)   (there + over)
This material is back at my home camp.

APe₄   *Uwa.*
(yes)
Yes.

APn   *Yuwa.*
(yes)
Yes.

APe₃   *Kutjarra.*
(two)
Two of them.

APn   ↑Hm Hm.↑
APe$_3$ *Ngaalu*   *kulilku.*
   (this + [transitive]) (what we think)
   So this is what we have decided.

APn   *Ngananya.*
   (this one)
   This one.

APn   *Yuwa.*
   (yes)
   Yes.

APn   Mm.

Bibliography

Anonymous 1976, 'Aboriginal and Islander', *Identity* 2, no. 8 (April).
  (1977), 'Aboriginal and Islander,' *Identity* 3, no. 1 (January).
Anonymous (1976), 'Record of Interview,' *Legal Aid Bulletin* (of
  Australia) 2, no. 4 (December).
Bardon, Garrett (1970), 'Modes of Consciousness,' unpublished
  mimeograph, Canberra: Australian Institute of Aboriginal Studies.
Barnard, Marjorie (1962), *A History of Australia*, Sydney: Angus &
  Robertson.
Basso, Keith (1979), *Portraits of the Whiteman*, Cambridge University
  Press.
Bates, Daisy (1966), *The Passing of the Aborigines*, London: Panther.
Beaglehole, J.C. (ed.) (1955), *The Voyage of the Endeavour 1768–1771*,
  Cambridge University Press.
Berger, Peter (1976), *Pyramids of Sacrifice*, Garden City, N.Y.: Anchor
  Books.
Berger, Peter, and Stanley Pullberg (1965), 'Reification and the
  Sociological Critique of Consciousness,' *History and Theory* 4, no. 2.
Berndt, Ronald, and Catherine Berndt (1942-6), 'A Preliminary Report
  of Field work in the Ooldea Region, Western South Australia,'
  Oceania 13, no. 1, pp. 51-70, no. 2, pp. 143-69, no. 3, pp. 243-80; 17,
  no. 3, pp. 239-75.
Berndt, R. and C. (1964), *The World of the First Australians*, Sydney:
  Ure Smith.
Brokenshaw, Peter (1974), 'Report on Preliminary Fieldwork,' mimeo-
  graphed report (May-June), Canberra: Australian Institute of Abori-
  ginal Studies.
Burridge, Kenelm (1973), *Encountering Aborigines*, Oxford: Pergamon
  Press.
Carnegie, David (1898) *Spinifex and Sand*, London: C. Arthur Pearson.
Clark, C.M.H. (1962) *A History of Australia*, vol. 1, Cambridge
  University Press; Melbourne University Press.
Collins, David (1798), *An Account of the English Colony in New South
  Wales*, London: T. Cadell & W. Davies.

Collins, Randy (1975), *Conflict Sociology*, New York: Academic Press.

Commonwealth of Australia (1925), *Historical Records of Australia*, Series I, *Governors' Dispatches to and from England*, Canberra: Library Committee of the Commonwealth.

Dampier, William (1729), *A New Voyage Round the World*, London: James & John Knapton.

Dampier, William (1771), *A Voyage to New Holland*, London: John Sparrow.

D'Entrecasteaux, Bruny (1808), *Voyage de Dentrecasteaux*, vol. II, Paris: Imprimerie Impériale.

Durkheim, Emile (1915), *The Elementary Forms of Religious Life*, New York: Free Press.

Durkheim, Emile, and Marcel Mauss (1963), *Primitive Classification*, University of Chicago Press.

Edie, James (1975), 'Identity and Metaphor,' *Journal of the British Society for Phenomenology* 6, no. 1 (January).

Edlow, Robert Blair (1975), 'The Stoics on Ambiguity,' *Journal of the History of Philosophy* 13, no. 4, pp. 423-35.

Edlow, Robert Blair (1977), *Galen on Language and Ambiguity*, Leiden: Brill.

Eggleston, Elizabeth (1976), *Fear, Favour or Affection: Aborigines and the Criminal Law in Victoria, South Australia and Western Australia*, Canberra: Australian National University.

Elkin, A.P. (1938), *The Australian Aborigines*, Sydney: Angus & Robertson.

Elkin, A.P. (1947), 'Aboriginal Evidence,' *Oceania* 17, no. 3.

Elkin, A.P. (1951), 'Reaction and Interaction: a Food-Gathering People and European Settlement in Australia,' *American Anthropologist* 53, pp. 164-86.

Empson, William (1953), *Seven Types of Ambiguity*, New York: New Directions.

Ernabella Mission (n.d.), *Pitjantjatjara–English Vocabulary*, Alice Springs: Institute for Aboriginal Development.

Flinders, Matthew (1814), *A Voyage to Terra Australis*, 2 vols, London: G. & W. Nicol.

Flinders, Matthew (1946), *Matthew Flinders' Narrative of His Voyage in the Schooner Francis, 98*, London: Golden Cockerel Press.

Friedenberg, Edgar Z. (1980), *Deference to Authority*, White Plains, N.Y.: M.E. Sharpe.

Gadamer, Hans-Georg (1975), *Truth and Method*, New York: Seabury.

Gallimore, Ronald, Joan Boggs and Cathie Jordan (1974), *Culture, Behavior and Education*, Beverly Hills, Calif.: Sage.

Garfinkel, Harold (1967), *Studies in Ethnomethodology*, Englewood Cliffs, N.J.: Prentice-Hall.

Garfinkel, Harold (1975), 'The Boston Seminar,' unpublished manuscript, UCLA.

Garfinkel, Harold (1977), 'University Lectures,' unpublished manuscript, UCLA.

Garfinkel, Harold (1979–80), 'Formatting in Queues,' unpublished manuscript, UCLA.

Garfinkel, Harold and Harvey Sacks (1970), 'On Formal Structures of Practical Actions,' in John C. McKinney and Edward Tiryakian (eds), *Theoretical Sociology*, New York: Appleton-Century-Crofts.

Geertz, Clifford (1973), *Interpretation of Cultures*, New York: Basic Books.

Gossen, Garry H. (1974), 'To Speak With a Heated Heart,' in Richard Bauman and Joel Sherzer (eds), *Explorations in the Ethnography of Speaking*, Cambridge University Press.

Gould, Richard (1969), *Yiwara: Foragers of the Australian Desert*, London: Collins.

Gumperz, Jenny Cook, John Gumperz and Herbert Simons (1979), 'Language at School and Home,' Berkeley, Calif: Language Behavior Research Laboratory.

Gumperz, John (1978), 'The Role of Dialect in Urban Communication,' *Language and Society* 8.

Gumperz, John (1980), 'Conversational Inference and Classroom Learning,' in Judith Green and Cynthia Wallet (ed), *Ethnography and Language in Educational Settings*, vol. 5, Norwood, N.J.: Ablex.

Habermas, Jurgen (1970), 'Towards a Theory of Communicative Competence,' in Hans Peter Dreitzel (ed.), *Recent Sociology, No. 2*, New York: Macmillan.

Habermas, Jurgen (1979), *Communication and the Evolution of Language*, Boston: Beacon Press.

Hawkesworth, John (1773), *An Account of the Voyages Undertaken by the Order of His Present Majesty for Making Discoveries in the Southern Hemisphere*, vol. 3, London: W. Strahan.

Hegel, G.W.F. (1977), *Phenomenology of Spirit*, Oxford: Clarendon Press.

Heidegger, Martin (1962), *Being and Time*, New York: Harper & Row.

Heidegger, Martin (1966), *Discourse on Thinking*, New York: Harper & Row.

Heidegger, Martin (1977), *The Question Concerning Technology*, New York: Harper & Row.

Heisenberg, Werner (1962), *Physics and Philosophy*, New York: Harper & Row.

Hiatt, Lester R. (1965), *Kinship and Conflict*, Canberra: Australian National University Press.

Hood, John (1843), *Australia and the East*, London: John Murray.

Howard, Michael (1980), 'The Selling of Australia,' *Anthropology Resource Newsletter* 4, no. 4 (December).

Hunter, John (1793), *An Historical Journal of the Transactions at Port Jackson*, London: John Stockdale.

Husserl, Edmund (1962), *Ideas*, London: Collier-Macmillan.

Husserl, Edmund (1970), *Logical Investigations*, London: Routledge & Kegan Paul.

Husserl, Edmund (1973), *Experience and Judgement*, revised and edited by Ludwig Landgrebe, Evanston, Ill.: North-western University Press.

Jung, Carl G. (1975), 'The Difference Between Eastern and Western Thinking,' in W.Y. Evans-Wentz, *The Tibetan Book of the Great Liberation*, Oxford University Press.

Kael, Pauline (1980), 'Australians,' *New Yorker* 56 (September), pp. 148-58.

King, Phillip P. (1827), *Narrative of a Survey of the Intertropical and Western Coasts of Australia*, London: John Murray.

Kockelmans, Joseph (1972), *On Heidegger and Language*, Evanston, Ill.: Northwestern University Press.

Koepping, Claus-Peter (1975), 'From the Dilemma of the Ethnographer to the Idea of Humanitas,' *Occasional Papers in Anthropology*, no. 4, Brisbane: University of Queensland.

Kolig, Erich (1972), 'An Australian Aboriginal Model of the European Society as a Guide in Social Change,' *Oceania 43*, no. 1 (September).

La Billardière, Jacques-Julien (1800), *Voyage in Search of La Pérouse*, London: John Stockdale.

Laverton Joint Study Group (1975), *Report*, Perth: Western Australian Government Printer.

Liberman, Kenneth (1977), 'Eastern Goldfields Aboriginal People and the Proposed Yeelirrie Uranium Project: a Supplement,' Perth: Department of Aboriginal Sites (Western Australian Museum).

Liberman, Kenneth (1980), 'The Decline of the *Kuwarra* People of Australia's Western Desert: a Case of Legally Secured Domination,' *Ethnohistory*, vol. 27, no. 2, pp. 119-33.

Liberman, Kenneth (1982), 'The Economy of Central Australian Aboriginal Expression: An Inspection from the Vantage of Merleau-Ponty and Derrida', *Semiotica* 40, no. 3/4, pp. 267-346.

Maddock, Kenneth (1975), *The Australian Aborigines*, Ringwood, Victoria: Penguin (2nd ed., 1982).

Malcolm, Ian (1977), 'Verbal Interaction in the Classroom,' mimeograph, Perth: Mt Lawley College.

Malcolm, Ian (1979) '*Classroom Communication and the Aboriginal Child*,' PhD. dissertation, Perth: University of Western Australia.

Malinowski, Bronislaw (1923), 'The Problem of Meaning in Primitive Language,' in C.K. Ogden and I.A. Richards, *The Meaning of Meaning*, New York: Harcourt, Brace & World, London: Routledge & Kegan Paul.

Mamdani, Mahmood (1972), *The Myth of Population Control*, New York: Monthly Review Press.

Marcuse, Herbert (1964), *One-Dimensional Man*, Boston: Beacon Press.

Marx, Karl (1967), *Writings of the Young Marx on Philosophy and Society*, ed. Lloyd D. Easton and Kurt H. Guddat, Garden City, N.Y.: Anchor.

Marshall, Lorna (1976), 'Sharing, Talking and Giving,' in Richard B. Lee and Irven Devore (eds), *Kalahari Hunter-Gatherers*, Harvard University Press.

Mathews, Janet (ed.) (1977), *The Two Worlds of Jimmie Barker*, Canberra: Australian Institute of Aboriginal Studies.

Meggitt, M.J. (1962), *The Desert People*, Sydney: Angus & Robertson.

Merleau-Ponty, Maurice (1962), *Phenomenology of Perception*, London: Routledge & Kegan Paul.

Merleau-Ponty, Maurice (1964), *Sense and Non-Sense*, trans. Herbert and Patricia Dreyfus, Evanston, Ill.: Northwestern University Press.

Merleau-Ponty, Maurice (1973), *Consciousness and the Acquisition of Language*, Evanston, Ill.: Northwestern University Press.

Meyers, Fred (1976), 'To Have and To Hold,' PhD. dissertation, Bryn Mawr: Bryn Mawr College.

Meyers, Fred (1979), 'Emotions and the Self,' *Ethos* 7, no. 4, pp. 343-70.

Millis, Roger (1985), 'How the North was Won,' *National Times*, March 28, pp. 25-7.

Mitchell, Sir Thomas Livingstone (1838), *Three Expeditions into the Interior of Eastern Australia*, 2 vols. London: T. & W. Boone.

Moerman, Michael (1972), 'Analysis of Lue Conversation,' in David Sudnow, *Studies in Interaction*, New York: Free Press.

Moerman, Michael and Harvey Sacks (1974), 'On "Understanding" in the Analysis of Natural Conversation,' in *Festscrift for E. Voegelin*, The Hague: Mouton.

Mountford, Charles P. (1948), *Brown Men and Red Sand*, Melbourne: Robertson & Mullens.

Mountford, Charles P. (1976), *Nomads of the Mullens, Australian Desert*, Adelaide: Rigby.

O'Connell, James (1836), *A Residence of Eleven Years in New Holland and the Carolina Islands*, Boston: B.B. Mussey.

Ogilvy, James (1980), 'Mastery and Sexuality,' *Human Studies* 3, no. 3, pp. 201-19.

Olafson, Frederick (1980), University lecture, University of California, San Diego.

Palmer, Kingsley and Clancy McKenna (1978), *Somewhere Between Black and White*, Melbourne: Macmillan.

Pareek, Udei (1976), 'Orientation Toward Work and School,' in G.E. Kearney and D.W. McElwain, *Aboriginal Cognition*, Canberra: Australian Institute of Aboriginal Studies.

Parker, Anne Z. (1978), 'A Story of Wongowol Station: Aboriginal and Islander,' *Identity* 3, no. 6, pp. 16-18.

Perez, Fr. Eugene (1977), *Kalumburu*, Wyndam, Western Australia: Kalumburu Benedictine Mission.

Péron, François (1809), *A Voyage of Discovery to the Southern Hemisphere*, London: Richard Phillips.

Pike, Kenneth L. (1962), 'Practical Phonetics of Rhythm Waves,' *Phonetica* 8, pp. 9-30.

Price, A. Grenfell (ed.) (1957), *The Explorations of Captain James Cook, 1768–1779*, New York: Limited Editions Club.

Read, K.E. (1969), 'Leadership and Consensus in a New Guinean Society,' *American Anthropologist* 61, no. 3 (June), pp. 425-36.

Redbird, Duke (1973), 'Declaration for Understanding,' *Macleans* 86, no. 26 (May), pp. 68ff.

Reece, Bob (1980), 'Two Kinds of Dreaming,' paper presented at the 22nd Annual Conference of the Australiasian Political Science Association, Canberra (August 27-29), mimeograph, Perth: Murdoch University.

Ricoeur, Paul (1974), 'Creativity in Language: Word, Polysemy and Metaphor,' in Edwin W. Strauss (ed.), *Language and Language Disturbances*, Pittsburgh: Duquesne University Press.

Rimmon, Shlomith (1977), *The Concept of Ambiguity*, University of Chicago Press.

Rowley, C.D. (1970), *The Destruction of Aboriginal Society*, Canberra: Australian National University Press.

Sacks, Harvey (1969), 'Lecture 9, March 5,' unpublished mimeograph, University of California, Irvine.

Sacks, Harvey, Emanuel Schegloff and Gail Jefferson (1974), 'A Simplest Systematics for the Organization of Turn-taking for Conversation,' *Language* 50, no. 4, pp. 696-735.

Sansom, Basil (1978), Personal correspondence.

Sansom, Basil (1980), *The Camp at Wallaby Cross*, Canberra: Australian Institute of Aboriginal Studies.

Sartre, Jean-Paul (1956), *Being and Nothingness*, New York: Philosophical Library.

Sartre, Jean-Paul (1976), *Critique of Dialectical Reason*, London: NLB.

Scharchella, Robin (1980), 'Negotiating the Accomplishment of Understanding Across Utterances,' unpublished manuscript, UCLA.

Schegloff, Emanuel (1977), 'On Some Questions and Ambiguities in Conversation,' Pragmatics Microfiche, Cambridge University Department of Linguistics.

Schegloff, Emanuel and Gail Jefferson (1977), 'Preference for Self-Correction in Organization of Repair in Conversation,' *Language* 53, no. 2, pp. 361-82.

Scheler, Max (1954), *The Nature of Sympathy*, London: Routledge & Kegan Paul.

Schutz, Alfred (1967), *The Phenomenology of the Social World*, Evanston, Ill.: Northwestern University Press.

Schutz, Alfred (1971), *Collected Papers*, vols I and II, The Hague: Mouton.

Schwartz, Howard (1977), 'Understanding Misunderstanding,' *Analytical Sociology* 1, no. 3.

Schwartz, Howard (1980), University lecture, University of California, San Diego.

Scott, Sir Ernest (1936), *A Short History of Australia*, Oxford University Press.

Senate Select Committee on Aborigines and Torres Strait Islanders (1976), *Environmental Conditions of Aborigines and Torres Strait Islanders and the Preservation of their Sacred Sites*, Canberra: Australian Government Publishing Service.

Simmel, Georg (1971), *On Individual and Social Forms*, University of Chicago Press.

Smith, Beverly (1977), 'Bards of the Backblocks,' *Westerly* 22, no. 1, pp. 66-76.

Sparkes, M.E. (1970), *Australia's Heritage*, Adelaide: Rigby.

Stanner, W.E.H. (1966), *On Aboriginal Religion*, Oceania Monograph no. 11, Sydney University.

Stanner, W.E.H. (1969), *After the Dreaming*, Sydney: Australian Broadcasting Commission.

Stanton, John (1976), 'Research Report 5/75–3/76,' Department of Anthropology, University of Western Australia.

Summer Institute of Linguistics (1977), *Pintupi/Luritja Dictionary*, Alice Springs: Institute for Aboriginal Development.

Ten Raa, Eric and Susan Todd Woenne (1974), *Research Dictionary of the Western Desert Language of Australia*, Perth: Department of Anthropology, University of Western Australia.

Tench, Watkin (1789), *A Narrative of the Expedition to Botany Bay*, London: J. Debrett.

Tonkinson, Robert (1974), *The Jigalong Mob: Aboriginal Victors of the Desert Crusade*, Meno Park, California: Cummings.

Tonkinson, Robert (1977), Remarks, Annual Meeting of the Association for Social Anthropology in Oceania, Calif.: Monterey.

Tonkinson, Robert (1978), *The Mardudjara Aborigines*, New York: Holt, Rinehart & Winston.

Tuckey, James Kingston (1805), *An Account of a Voyage to Establish a Colony at Port Phillip in Bass's Stait*. London: Longman, Hurst, Rees & Orme.

Turnbull, John (1813), *A Voyage Around the World in the Years 1800, 1801, 1802*, London: A. Maxwell.

United Aborigines Mission (n.d.), *Katungkatjanya*, Kalgoorlie: U.A.M. Language Department.

Wallace, Noel (1976), 'Pitjantjatjara *Wiltja* or White Man's House?,' Australian Institute of Aboriginal Studies *Newsletter*, no. 6 (June), pp. 46-52.

Weber, Max (1958), *The Protestant Ethic*, New York: Charles Scribner's Sons.

Welles, C.M. (1859) *Three Years Wanderings of a Connecticut Yankee*, New York: American Subscription Publishing House.

Western Australian Royal Commission (1974), *Report*, Perth: Western Australian Government Printer.

White, John (1790), *Journal of a Voyage to New South Wales*, London: J. Debrett.

Wittgenstein, Ludwig (1969), *On Certainty*, Oxford: Basil Blackwell.

Wittgenstein, Ludwig (1972), *Philosophical Investigations*, Oxford: Basil Blackwell.

World Book Encyclopedia (1963), *World Book Encyclopedia*, vol. I, Chicago: Field Enterprises.

Young, Rev. Robert (1854), *The Southern World*, London: Hamilton, Adams.

Index